CAVALIER

# *Cavalier*

A TALE OF
CHIVALRY, PASSION,
AND GREAT HOUSES

Lucy Worsley

BLOOMSBURY

Published by Bloomsbury USA, New York
Distributed to the trade by Holtzbrinck Publishers

ISBN-13 978-1-59691-358-5

Printed in the United States of America

# *Contents*

# *Illustrations*

PLATE SECTIONS

TEXT ILLUSTRATIONS

Chapter heads: some of the jobs performed in the household. From Randle Holme, *An Academie or Store of Armory & Blazon* (Book III, Chapter 3), apparently published in 1688. This is a book of ideas for motifs to be used in heraldry.

THE CAVENDISH FAMILY TREE: PART ONE

Sir William Cavendish, d.1557 *m.* Elizabeth ('Bess') Hardwick, later Countess of Shrewsbury, *c.*1527–1608

*Henry Cavendish, 1550–1616*
*m.*
*Grace Talbot*

William Cavendish, Earl of Devonshire, 1551–1626
*m.*1 Anne Keighley
*m.*2 Elizabeth Wortley

William Cavendish,
2nd Earl of
Devonshire,
1590–1628
*m.*
Christian Bruce

William Cavendish,
3rd Earl of
Devonshire

Key: **Cavendish of Welbeck**. Cavendish of Chatsworth. *Other relation*.

# Family Trees

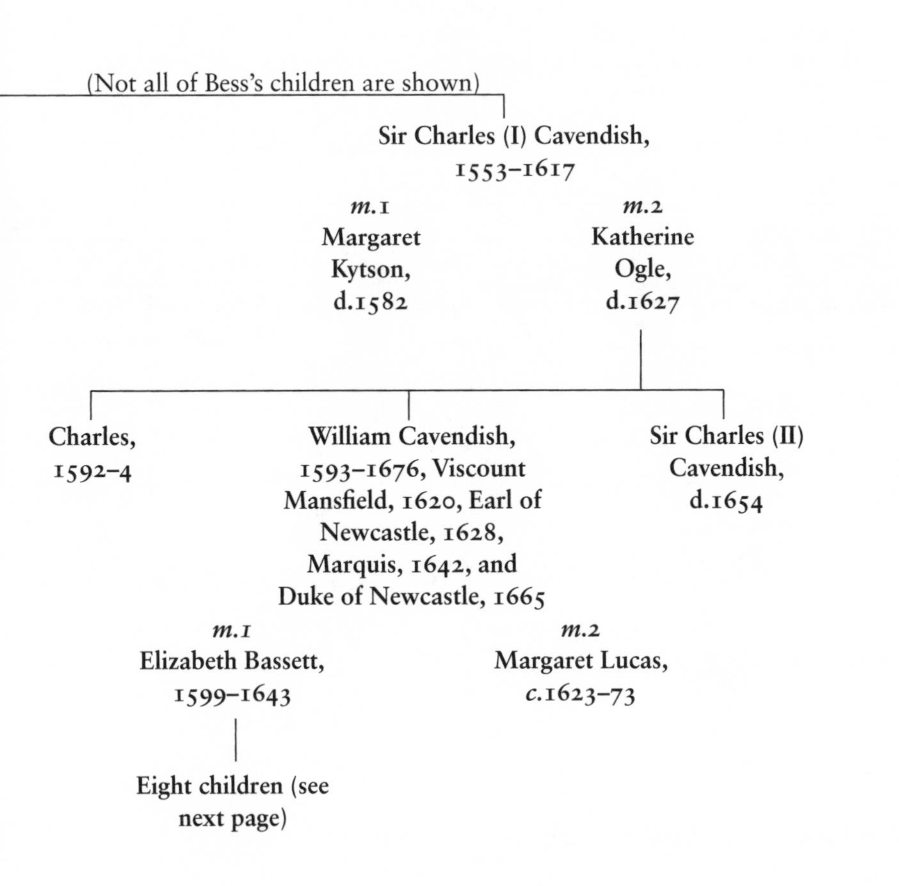

THE CAVENDISH FAMILY TREE: PART TWO

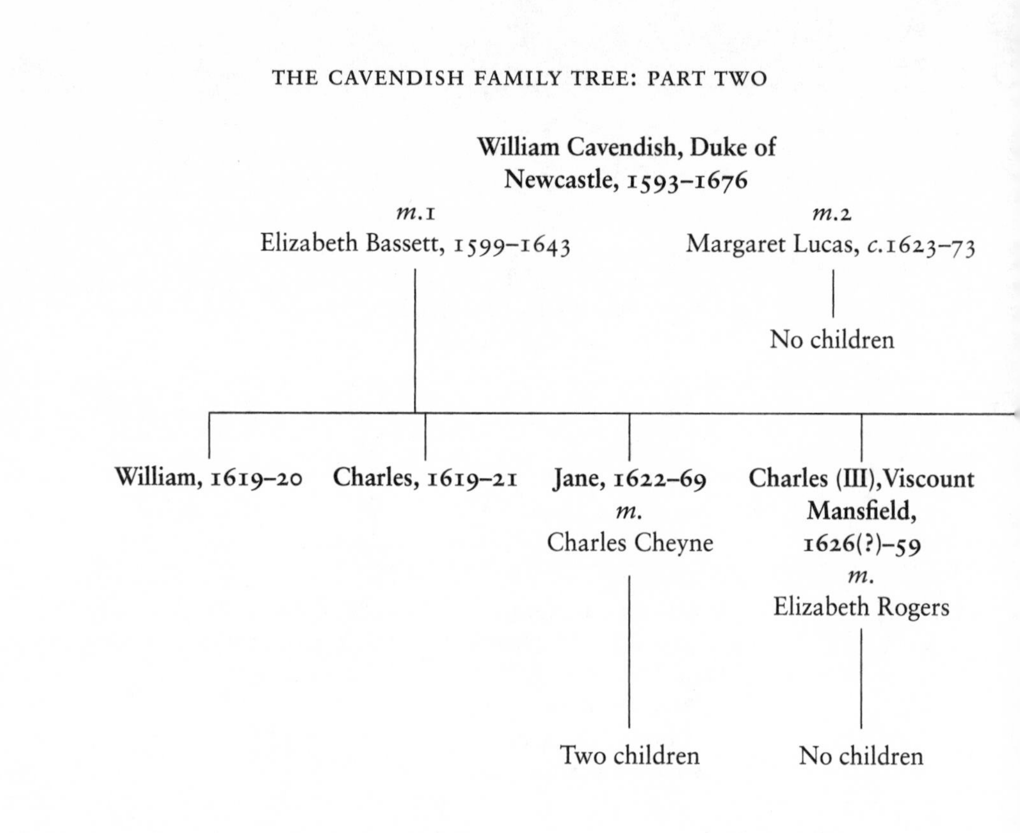


Key: **Cavendish of Welbeck.** Relations by marriage.

| **Elizabeth, 1627–?** | **Henry, 2nd Duke of Newcastle, 1630–91** | **Frances, 1630–78** | **Katherine, died young** |
|---|---|---|---|
| *m.* | *m.* | *m.* | |
| John Egerton, 2nd Earl of Bridgwater | Frances Pierrepont | Oliver St John, Earl of Bolingbroke | |
| | Six children (see next page) | | |

THE CAVENDISH FAMILY TREE: PART THREE

**Henry Cavendish, 1630–91, Viscount Mansfield, 1659–65, Earl of Ogle, 1665–76, 2nd Duke of Newcastle, 1676–91** *m.* Frances Pierrepont, daughter of William Pierrepont, Earl of Kingston, of Thoresby Hall

**Elizabeth, 1664–1734**
*m.*1 Duke of Albemarle
*m.*2 Duke of Montagu

**Frances, 1660–91**
*m.*
John Campbell, Earl of Breadalbane

**Margaret, 1661–1716, Duchess of Newcastle**
*m.*
John Holles, Duke of Newcastle, 2nd creation

**Henrietta Cavendish Holles, 1694–1755**
*m.*
Edward Harley, 2nd Earl of Oxford

**Margaret Cavendish Holles Harley, 1715–85**
***m.***
**William Bentinck, 2nd Duke of Portland**

Key: **Cavendish of Welbeck.** Relations by marriage.

**Katherine, 1665–1712**
*m.*
Thomas Tufton, 6th
Earl of Thanet

**Henry, 1663–80,**
**Viscount Mansfield, Earl**
**of Ogle, 1676–80**
*m.*
Elizabeth Percy, grand-
daughter of the Duke of
Northumberland

**Arabella, 1673–98**
*m.*
Charles Spencer, 3rd
Earl of Sunderland

England, France and the Low Countries, showing places mentioned in the story. The insert shows Derbyshire and Nottinghamshire – Cavendish country

# *Timeline*

| | GREAT EVENTS | CAVENDISH EVENTS |
|---|---|---|
| 1593 | | William born 16th December |
| 1595 | Sir Walter Raleigh travels to South America | |
| 1601 | The Earl of Essex is executed for his unsuccessful rebellion | |
| 1603 | Elizabeth I dies at Richmond Palace; James I becomes king | |
| 1605 | The Gunpowder Plotters seek to blow up the Houses of Parliament | |
| 1608 | | Bess of Hardwick dies |
| 1610 | | William is knighted |
| 1611 | James I's first Parliament is dissolved | |
| 1612 | | William tours Italy |
| 1613 | | Foundations for Little Castle laid |
| 1616 | William Shakespeare dies | |
| 1617 | | Sir Charles, William's father, dies |
| 1618 | | William marries Elizabeth Bassett |
| 1619 | | Two sons are born, neither lives long |
| 1620 | The Pilgrim Fathers board their ship, the *Mayflower*, to sail for America | William becomes Viscount Mansfield |
| 1624 | | James I visits Welbeck |
| 1625 | James I dies, Charles I becomes king | William becomes Lord Lieutenant of Nottinghamshire |

| | | |
|---|---|---|
| 1628 | Charles I reluctantly agrees to 'The Petition of Right', a declaration of his subjects' liberties | William becomes Earl of Newcastle upon Tyne |
| 1629 | Charles I dissolves Parliament and rules without it until 1640 | |
| 1630 | Prince Charles, the future Charles II, born | Henry Cavendish born |
| 1633 | | Charles I visits Welbeck |
| 1634 | | William hosts a masque for Charles I at Bolsover |
| 1638 | | William appointed governor to Prince Charles; goes to live at Richmond Palace |
| 1640 | The 'Short' and then the 'Long' Parliaments are summoned | |
| 1641 | | William leaves his post as governor |
| 1642 | Civil War breaks out | |
| 1643 | | William becomes Marquis of Newcastle |
| 1644 | | William, aged fifty, loses the battle of Marston Moor and goes into exile |
| 1645 | Parliament creates the New Model Army, which defeats the Royalists at Naseby | William marries Margaret Lucas in Paris |
| 1646 | Charles I surrenders to the Scots | |
| 1647 | | William and Margaret move to Antwerp |
| 1649 | Charles I is executed | |
| 1653 | Oliver Cromwell becomes Lord Protector | |
| 1658 | Death of Oliver Cromwell | |
| 1659 | | William, in Antwerp, and his son Henry, at Welbeck, exchange letters |
| 1660 | Charles II returns from exile and is restored to the throne | William returns home and becomes Lord Lieutenant of Nottinghamshire once again |
| 1665 | | William becomes Duke of Newcastle |

| | | |
|---|---|---|
| 1666 | The Great Fire of London | |
| 1667 | | John Evelyn visits William at Newcastle House |
| 1670 | Charles II makes a secret promise to become a Catholic in return for subsidies from France | Servants at Welbeck conspire against Margaret |
| 1673 | The Test Act bans Roman Catholics from political appointments | Margaret Cavendish dies |
| 1674 | | William begins Nottingham Castle |
| 1676 | | William dies |

# 1 – *A Deathbed*

WELBECK ABBEY, 27TH MARCH, 1617

Sir William Cavendish, twenty-three years old, is hurrying through the draughty stone passages of Welbeck Abbey towards the chamber where his father lies ill. A servant opens a low door, and a breath of fresh air accompanies William into a dimly lit bedchamber. His silhouette, seen against the light from the passage, describes a tightly tailored upper body and arms above voluminous breeches. His face and high white ruff show brightly against his dark doublet and his hair is brushed into a fashionable peak over his forehead. Crossing the threshold into the room, William leaves behind one stage of his life and enters another, for his father is suffering from a grievous illness and has summoned his son for one of the most important conversations in a great landowner's lifetime.

Inside Sir Charles Cavendish's room the air is heavy with the scent of fresh blood drained from the patient's veins by his doctors. There is also a tang emanating from his close stool, the upholstered seat that hides his chamber pot. The bedchamber's walls are richly hung with tapestry, and a fringe hangs down from the canopy or sparver of Sir Charles's great curtained bed.[1] Only a murky finger of light enters through the flecked, translucent leaded panes of the stone-mullioned windows. Sir Charles's stout shoehorn, carved with the miniature figures of Adam and Eve and the Cavendish family's symbol of a stag's head, lies near to hand upon a table draped with a rich Turkish carpet, but it is doubtful whether he will ever need it again.[2] In his long nightshirt, a kerchief tied round his head, William's father lies propped up in bed, half-sitting against plump pillows; sixty-five years old, he is accustomed to sleeping semi-upright rather than prone. Sir Charles's nose is lengthy and aquiline. Hair still sprouts thickly over his high forehead and kinks round his ears; his beard is chest-length below clean-shaven cheeks, and his fingers are long and pointed.[3] Until now, he has maintained his health with some success. Despite his advanced years, he has been a hale, active man, keeping himself fit with regular riding and swordplay, an art at which he is a great master. Such martial pursuits have brought him pain as well as pleasure: today he lies uncomfortably upon an old injury to the buttock that he suffered in a pistol fight with a group of his Nottinghamshire neighbours. Sir Charles has been thrusting, successful and well-connected, but also valiant and generous. He still possesses a clear mind and memory, and his household has little idea of how ill he is. But now, crossing the room and seeing his father's face, William realises that this sickness could be fatal.

As William approaches his father's bed, many other people are waiting to hear why Sir Charles has summoned his son with such solemnity and whether the head of their household is going to pass safely through his illness. At this pivotal moment in the quiet bedchamber at Welbeck Abbey, the very epicentre of the vast Cavendish estates, the fears and expectations of the many members of the family and household remain pinned to their patriarch. Elsewhere in the house, Sir Charles's wife and younger son await news of his condition. They are anxious to know whether Sir Charles believes that he will recover or whether he has decided that the time has come to make provision for the future management of the household. Also waiting for news are Sir Charles's confidential upper servants (many of them his relations), his lower servants going about their menial tasks in the kitchens, gardens and stables, the servants out at the farm, the builders at his half-finished new castle at Bolsover, seven miles away, the tenants of his estates across the Midlands, their own maids and servingmen, the labourers in the fields and the paupers who depend on the Cavendishes' charity. The household and estates revolve like a vast wheel around the fixed point of Sir Charles's bed. As William's father's life moves towards crisis, change will ripple through all these lives, and the power bases and allegiances of the household will now begin to shift.

The person most immediately affected by the danger to Sir Charles's health is the young man now sinking to his knees on the matting of plaited rushes by his father's bed. William is a true Cavendish, ambitious and proud. His grandmother was one of her age's greatest builders: the Countess of Shrewsbury (*c.*1527–1608), commonly known as 'Bess of Hardwick', who constructed the famous Hardwick Hall. William was brought up in the landlocked Midlands, where the country houses built by competitive neighbours form a dense clot of England's most impressive architectural achievements. Sir Charles, Bess's youngest son, is one of the courteous and chivalrous Elizabethan knights who will leave a lasting reminder of their pleasant and prosperous lives in the form of their near miraculous houses, and the new stately suite he has added to Welbeck Abbey is only one of his many building projects. The grandson of a Derbyshire sheep farmer, Sir Charles is now the proud possessor of an abbey, a castle and two healthy heirs.

His elder son William is a similarly likeable, warm-hearted young man, but he is also impulsive and addicted to risk-taking and pleasure. He is, and will remain, a lifelong lover of horses, architecture and women. His smile and manner are engaging, but he has yet to grow into the grave, responsible figure who may successfully hold high office at court or govern a household, let alone manage the raucous and competitive Cavendish servants. Physically, he is only moderately tall, but 'his shape is neat, and exactly proportioned'. He is extremely fit and upright in bearing from his daily exercise on horseback or with the sword. He eats like an athlete, keeping himself on a strict diet, and his habitual supper consists only of 'an egg and a draught of small-beer'. Fastidious and careful in dressing, he wears bright silks, lace collars, feathered hats and high boots, following fashion so far as it is appropriate 'for men of Heroick Exercises and Actions'.[4] He rides his beloved dancing stallions every morning, demonstrating the flying leaps of the art of horsemanship or *manège*, while his curls and feathers mirror the horses' luxuriant manes. This moment in his father's bedchamber is one of the rare occasions on which he is to be seen without a whip in his gloved hand.

Despite the carefully calculated image of arrogant perfection that William presents to the world – jaunty beard and high-heeled shoes – he relishes his body's natural functions. He is a fluent and enthusiastic, if as yet unpublished, writer, devoted to his mentor the poet Ben Jonson (1572–1637), and colourfully records his experiences of spitting, removing gum from his eyes, blowing his nose, extracting earwax with an ear-pick, his 'lecherous sweatings', his 'greatest pimple' and his 'buttocks married to his open close stool' during a bout of diarrhoea.[5]

No one can fail to warm to William's attractively voluble enthusiasms; his love for horses and women; his unerring ability to sabotage his own interests. He has attended the court with his father from a young age and already holds the title of a Knight of the Bath. His glamour and his vulnerability are two sides of the same coin: he has all the charming insouciance and panache of a brave young blood ambitious to make his mark at the Stuart court, haunt of the Cavaliers, where success waits for many a well-dressed and well-mounted young man. Yet it may already be guessed that, like his fellow Cavaliers, William suffers from a potentially fatal lack of diligence, sobriety and common sense. He longs to be a serious player at court, but he can ruin a delicate meeting with his 'customary swearing', and one of his friends says that if you tell him a secret 'it might as well be proclaimed at the [market] cross'.[6] His love for the arts in all their guises – and his reputation for chasing women – mean that he is accused of frivolity, of being forever 'fornicating with the Nine Muses, or the Dean of York's daughters'.[7]

Unlike many of his fellow aristocrats, William is a true lover of poetry and music, and is devoted to their craft as well as their art. In different circumstances, he could have lived a pleasantly feckless life in the playhouses and taverns like so many of the writers he admires. He pens poems almost incessantly, processing his daily experiences through verse, and his informal musings, essays and plays all reveal how he sees his world. His love for literature is so great that he is shaping up to be the only aristocrat of his generation who might produce a vast and varied body of work.

It seems that this young man may possess something special: the opportunity to experience a life of power and privilege as he moves between his family's great houses and the heady world of the Stuart court with its masques and music, palaces and stables, coupled with the talent to observe and record it all. But he is young yet, and daunted by the thought of losing his father. This is the day on which he must begin to face up to his responsibilities as the future head of one of England's great families.

William's lifelong passions for horses and weapons were already apparent in his youthful pastimes. He was born in Yorkshire, and is proud of it. His birth in 1593 took place in a manor at Handsworth, near Sheffield, belonging to Gilbert Talbot, seventh Earl of Shrewsbury (1552–1616), his father's stepbrother and greatest friend. William's mother Katherine is Sir Charles's beloved second wife and the daughter of a Northumbrian baron. After William was born, Sir Charles withdrew from his previous involvement in Parliament, because 'being an indulgent Father, he was altogether intent on the Affairs of his Family, and the Education of his Sons'.[8] In particular, his two boys studied horsemanship and swordsmanship, wherein Sir Charles was 'a most ingenious and unparallell'd Master of that Age'.[9] 'I have Practised, and Studyed *Horse-manship* ever since I was Ten years old,' William writes in later life.[10]

The youthful William was sent to live in the household of Gilbert Talbot, Earl of Shrewsbury. The households of social superiors act as a kind of boarding school for well-born children to learn how to command and provide service properly. Honour rather than stigma comes with personal service to a social superior, and in the seventeenth century about half of England's population work as servants at some point in their lives. The most important courtiers are those who attend the monarch in the bedchamber, and William aspires to becoming a Gentleman of the Bedchamber to the king himself one day.

William was knighted in 1610, at the age of sixteen. Two years later, and just before the family began to build their new house, Bolsover Castle in Derbyshire, his father sent him on a grand tour of Italy to acquire an architectural education. This tour gave William a taste for the new classical style of architecture that is just beginning to manifest itself in a handful of English buildings, but he had already inherited from his father and grandmother a passion for building houses.

As a result of their obsession, a Cavendish household is set up like a building company, with specialist designers always on the payroll. Every English aristocrat needs an enormous house to accommodate his enormous household, but William desires houses that will outshine those of his most ambitious contemporaries. Living and working so closely together, loyalty and economics apparently weld the Cavendish household into a tight unit, a little world, a microcosm of society. The seventeenth-century architectural writer Sir Henry Wotton (1568–1639) writes that a man's country house is

> the *Theatre* of his *Hospitality*, the *Seat* of *Selfe-fruition*, the *Comfortablest part* of his own *Life*, the *Noblest* of his Son's *Inheritance*, a kind of private *Princedom* [. . .] an *Epitomie* of the whole *World*.[11]

Yet the Cavendish household is not merely a smooth-running machine focused upon the comfort of its master: conspiracies, sexual intrigue, clandestine marriage and gossip form the unseen side of life in any great seventeenth-century house.

Here lies the nature of William's challenge as he contemplates the possibility of his father's imminent death. As the head of the Cavendish household, he will have great power, but with it the weightiest of responsibilities. It will not be an easy matter for this young man to win the respect of the forty people with whom he shares his home, or to steer a safe course for them through the coming years of peace and war, or to develop a landowner's keen concern for the prosperity of his estates.

In this book, we will watch his progress by entering into the life of his household, walking from room to room and meeting its members as they live through the best and worst of days. The risks and the rewards are high: can this bold young peacock – charming but easily charmed, gallant but reckless, handsome but vain – make a success of his life?

While William strains to hear the low-voiced requests and confessions of his father, many other people beyond the bedchamber door are waiting to hear whether Sir Charles is on the road to recovery. The low hills seen through the abbey's windows are cloaked with the dark and remote Sherwood Forest, which covers many of the Cavendishes' estates in the northern Midlands of England. The abbey itself is a former monastery, converted by William's father into a magnificent – if rambling – mansion. Sir Charles's bedchamber is set within the ancient fabric of the monastery, yet along the twisting passages lies the spacious splendour of the new wing, topped by its round, onion-domed tower that allows access onto a flat, leaded roof for promenading and viewing the water gardens below (Plates 3 and 4).

Monks had once walked along Welbeck's stone cloister and climbed its stone stairs, and Sir Charles has always loved the 'fair vaults' of the Middle Ages.[12] The abbey had belonged to the Premonstratensians, one of the most powerful orders in medieval England. After the Dissolution of the Monasteries, the monks were scattered and their abbey suffered the demolition of its church and two of the ranges around its cloister. The other two ranges survived and passed into the hands of a series of secular owners, and the old abbey was transformed by degrees into an unusual and atmospheric country house surrounded

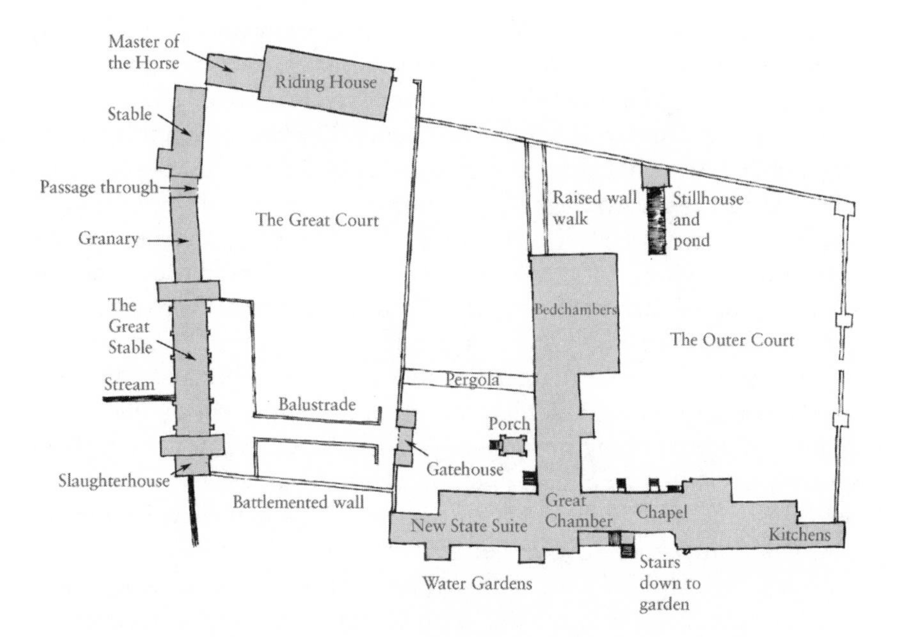


Welbeck Abbey in the early seventeenth century, after the addition of William's Riding House and Great Stable

by oaks, pines and yews, 'seated in a botome in a Park, & invironed with Woods, a noble yet melancholy seate'.[13] Sir Charles has added the suite of stately first-floor chambers in the local silvery-grey limestone, employing the airy and more regular contemporary style with its huge windows. A suite like this is a vital possession for any aspiring courtier who wishes, as Sir Charles does, to offer hospitality to the present king, James I, during one of his annual royal progresses around the countryside. These, the grandest rooms in the house, are intended purely for royal use. A royal visit is the greatest possible compliment that a family can receive; father and son are hoping to be chosen for that honour in the next few years.

While William confers with his father, Sir Charles's wife Katherine and her second son Charles are pacing nervously in the Great Chamber of the house.[14] This lofty and recently completed room overlooks the ornamental canal and banqueting houses to the south. It is the family's main living room and a focus for household life. It is here that Katherine spends her days with her waiting gentlewomen, where guests are received and entertained, and where actors or musicians perform.

The room is splendidly decorated with tapestries, a wide fireplace, vast windows and a plethora of richly upholstered chairs. Some of the textiles may be recycled from the magnificent velvets and old embroideries used in pre-Reformation priests' vestments. The Great Chamber is only the first link in a chain of interconnected first-floor rooms: beyond it lie the best bed chamber, the dining chamber next to it and the gallery, all in the same spacious style. The furniture and hangings for these rooms are usually kept in storage, being brought out for grand occasions just as the scenery is arranged on a stage before a theatrical performance.

Katherine, formidably intelligent and well organised, was brought up in her family's several ancient castles in Northumberland. Her face, as she waits for news, is set into the stern lines that will survive in her tomb sculpture: a long nose; thin, pursed mouth; a pair of tight lines delineating cheeks from nose and lips. Her long visage, alabaster white, emerges from a tight carapace of restrictive clothing: a winged headdress that arches up to give her head the domed profile of an exotic insect, a high and full ruff, and long, tight sleeves to her pleated gown. Katherine is more than capable of understanding business, of managing an estate and buildings, and of writing notes to herself in the assured and beautiful Renaissance-style handwriting that signals her fine education.

Her own family is of far greater antiquity than the Cavendishes, and her austere grandeur flows from its long and proud history. Her father, the Baron of Ogle, has no sons to inherit his title, yet the Ogle barony is so ancient that the king is reluctant to see it extinguished. Most unusually, he will perpetuate the barony by bestowing it on a woman: Katherine herself. The antiquity of this title, in contrast to those that James I is indiscriminately handing out to many of his courtiers, is especially valuable. Only after three generations can a member of a titled family claim to be a 'Gentleman of Blood'.[15] Servants from Katherine's native Northumbrian estates form a close-knit group within Sir Charles's household, their mutually beneficial bond encouraging them to conspire against other household members.

Katherine's younger son, the second Charles Cavendish, lacks his elder brother's athleticism and is a 'little, weak, crooked man' suffering from a twisted spine. His sweet nature and intelligence, however, make him popular with his contemporaries. Despite his lack of brawn, he possesses a magnificent brain, and has devoted 'himself to the Study of Mathematiques' with the hope of becoming 'a great Master'.[16] Although

Charles has an inferior position as a younger son, he hopes to receive generous provision for the future from his father, for he too is afflicted with an expensive mania for architecture and design.

Katherine and her younger son do not keep their vigil alone. With them waits a solemn group of Sir Charles's senior household officers, dignified men of business dressed in dark colours, with brows furrowed by genuine regret for their master's sickness. Katherine takes the place of honour in the room, by the fire, and her companions are disposed in descending order of rank between her and the door. A writer on good conduct decrees that 'in the presence of a well bred company, it is uncomely to turn ones back to the fire, or to approach nigher than others, for the one and the other savoureth of preheminence'; nor is it polite to sit with crossed legs.[17] In fact, the truly refined even refrain from sitting 'with their back towards the picture of any Eminent person'.[18]

None of the household members present look Katherine in the face, for it is contrary to courtesy that 'the inferiour should fixe his eies upon his superiour's countenaunce; and the reason is, because it were presumption for him to attempt the entrance or privie passage into his superiours minde'.[19] Yet these senior household officers are in fact privy to all the gossip and intimacies of family life. Their female equivalents are Katherine's well-born waiting gentlewomen, who are also present in the background, their gowns modestly blending into the room's rich backdrop of tapestries. These senior ladies of the household are served by a species of rather tame manservant – the 'ushers of the great chamber' – whose tasks include conversation, 'making sweet' the Great Chamber and running messages. So light are their duties that boredom compels them to become inveterate gamesters and gamblers.[20]

The highly paid household officers and the waiting gentlewomen together form a small but significant cadre in the household, like the officers of an army, to whom the remainder must show deference and loyalty. This morning the lower servants try to continue their work elsewhere in the house, yet upper and lower servants alike are linked by a palpable sense of community: they will all be deeply affected by any news filtering out from the claustrophobic sick chamber.

The family names of these men and women of the household reflect the world of seventeenth-century Nottinghamshire, as William mused on one occasion in an essay on the origins of the surnames of the people he knows. Some second names are still being acquired during the course of a working life rather than through inheritance, although the latter is now the norm. Some are named for the building skills that they bring to the household, such as Smithson, Carpenter and Tyler. Others take their cue from the house itself: Kitchen, Hall, Garrett, Chambers, Dore. Everyday household objects provide the names of Captain Tubb, Mr Bowls, Mr Trencher, Mr Platter, Mr Tankard, Mr Beaker and Tom Kettle. Some are named for trees and plants, such as Mr Ashe, Mr Plumtree, Mr Birch, Mr Thorne, Mr Brier and Tom Rose. Some take their name from a current or ancestral household office, such as Mr Bailiff or Mr Servant, Tom Fiddler, Mr Harper or Mr Pipes. Some are named for clothes, such as Tom Shorthose, Mr Bande, Mr Cuff, George Stocking and Will Hatter, while the human body itself provides the names of Will Legg, Mr Cheeks and Mr Armstrong. Finally, as William notes, there are further 'scurrilous & bawdy Names, which we will omit'.[21]

Among the long-time retainers who accompanied Katherine on the journey south from her native Northumbria are several minor Ogle relations. By the window on the great stair that leads up to the Great Chamber is Henry or 'Harry' Ogle, straining to watch the horses at exercise in the courtyard below. He has lived with the family for more than ten years and shares the Cavendishes' fondness for horses. Directly beneath him lies a small enclosed garden court, and beyond it lies a vast yard used for training horses. Sir Charles employs specialists, masters of *manège,* to care for and train his great horses. The riding master who gives daily coaching to Sir Charles's sons finds his pupils absent today, but the exercise of the valuable horses must take place as usual.

Although he is their 'most faithful Servant and Cousin', the Cavendishes also consider Harry Ogle to be more than an employee: 'Servant, no, friend thou were & truly so.'[22] A fond favourite of Katherine's, the plans for the future that he reveals in his will show how deeply he is embedded within the Cavendish family, treating the Cavendish children as his own. Should Harry die, he intends his best horse 'Black Richardson' to go to William's younger brother Charles. In addition, he has set aside a cloth suit for his own personal servant, Raphe Wolley.[23] There are plenty of other Ogles in the household in addition to Harry, such as Lancelot ('Launce'), who serves throughout his life, beginning as a page and ending as a senior officer.[24] The Ogles benefit from Cavendish patronage and favours in return for faithful service: William will go so far as to choose a spouse for his servant James Ogle.[25]

William Eagle, also present in the Great Chamber this morning, is another servant of Katherine's and oversees estate management and building work on her behalf.[26] Then there is Sir William Carnabie, or Carnaby of Northumberland.[27] He represents the Cavendishes in London, and relays to his master all the news from court.[28]

One of this group of respectable-looking, middle-aged gentleman officers in the Great Chamber may well have a secret double identity, known only to Katherine and her son but suspected by the rest. Sir Charles takes daily risks with his status and reputation in society, for secretly he is a Catholic, and is likely to have a priest on his staff masquerading as a household officer. He and his stepbrother and great ally Gilbert Talbot, Earl of Shrewsbury, are crypto-Papists, or secret followers of the old religion now outlawed by the state. A state of 'Cold War' exists between Catholics and Protestants, complete with its language of ideological extremism, spies and assassins. Roman Catholics adopt one of two positions: either they must refuse to attend the Protestant service and consequently pay regular and ruinous fines, or else they become crypto-Papists, making a tactical decision to conform in public and follow the old ways in private.

High risks surround those like Sir Charles who continue to practise the Catholic religion in secret, and private chaplains are forbidden to householders beneath the rank of peers under statutes dating back to Henry VIII's reign.[29] Under the more severe Elizabethan legislation of the previous century, the crime of housing Jesuits or seminary priests was punishable by death, while the sentence for attending Mass could be a year's imprisonment.[30] Sir Charles has learnt the hard way that discretion is necessary. Six years ago, in 1611, the government sent its agent Sir John Holles to hunt down crypto-Papists in Sherwood Forest. He found Sir Charles and his friends in collusion over the hiding of dangerous Catholic paraphernalia, such as 'crucifixes, & old papistical books' (in 1606 the very possession of Roman Catholic prayer books had become a punishable offence). Sir John carried out a lurid hunt throughout Sir Charles's stepbrother Gilbert Talbot's house, undertaking 'a long, & curious search in vaults, sellars, chamber & garrets' containing 'dyvers trap-books, to conceal, & issue forth such pernicious vermin, as [he] sought for: many empty old trunks'.[31] The most significant and sinister items had already been sent away, it was noted, to Sir Charles Cavendish at Welbeck Abbey. On this occasion, however, Sir Charles escaped without punishment.

These soberly dressed senior servants normally spend their days in pursuit of rents from tenant farmers or mineral extractors, on legal business, or else with their heads bent over their desks in the chambers that are used both for sleeping and for administrative tasks in the old wing of the abbey. A hum of business normally pervades the house, for as well as being a home it is the headquarters of a major economic enterprise. On a day like this, however, with the master's life hanging in the balance, no documents are being filed in the Evidence House and no money is being counted in the Treasury.

The Evidence House is the chamber that contains the vital deeds of title upon which the Cavendish fortune depends. The increasing sophistication of estate administration means that such documents now require a room of their own. The distinctive scent of the Evidence House remains trapped in the documents created and stored there: a warm, brown aroma of pencil shavings, faded spice, ancient mould. The iron in seventeenth-century ink causes it to age to a pale ochre. When the documents are tilted to the light, fragments of minerals sparkle in every letter.

The contents of an Evidence House are extremely valuable and must be checked quarterly for 'dust or ratts &c'.[32] At Welbeck, a certain 'boundary book' has to be prised out of the grasp of a bailiff who has been accused of embezzlement because, in the words of the senior servant John Booth, it 'contains many secrets of my Lords interest [and] it will (in my opinion) be very requisite that he have no longer custody of it'.[33] When the bailiff Andrew Clayton falls spectacularly from the Cavendishes' favour, he is found to have a mass of important 'books papers writings' in his own chamber where he has been accustomed to 'tell money and paste accompts' all day long.[34] The system cannot work unless the family trusts its officers, and this means accepting an element of sharp practice. In one of the verses about his own life, loves and servants that he is in the habit of jotting down almost daily, William complains about his unscrupulous bailiff:

> In short, the Truth I'll tell, & will not jeer
> You steal in selling cheap, & buying dear.[35]

The Great Chamber and their own chambers are not the only rooms available to the members of the household. Rumours about Sir Charles's health now circulate through further servants clustered in the Long Gallery, a room used communally for exercise and leisure, as well as for listening to the harpsichord and claviorganum (an organ and harpsichord combined) kept there.[36] It is easier of access than the Great Chamber, and members of the household of different ranks may intermingle here. The news that William has gone in to see his father is passed along to other servants with more specialised technical skills, such as the musicians, or to Henry Lukin and his colleagues in the household's surveying department, and to the bailiffs Thomas Atkinson and John Wood.[37] Lukin is talented in the writing of ingenious verses, in mathematics and in the closely related skills of map-making and estate and building surveying. It is his job to oversee building works. He is courting a woman named Katherine Jessopp, and when he marries her, will have to move out of the household to become the tenant of nearby Soukeholme Manor.[38] This is the pattern for household officers: on marriage they leave Welbeck Abbey to set up households of their own. Lukin suffers from 'melancholy' and will eventually commit suicide in the attic of his manor house. For hundreds of years to come, his ghost will occasionally be glimpsed in the room known as 'Lukin's Garret'.[39]

Another servant skilled at surveying is John Smithson (d.1634). While he appears to be just another member of the household, he will become famous to posterity as one of the greatest architectural designers of the early seventeenth century. John has modernised the spelling of his family name, though he too is occasionally referred to as 'Smythson' as his father customarily was. John's father Robert was the great country-house designer whose work includes the vast and innovative Elizabethan palaces of Longleat in Wiltshire and Wollaton Hall in Nottingham. Once he had risen up from the rank of mason, Robert served as an officer in a succession of noble households. His son likewise serves in a variety of capacities, including estate surveying and design, though he is described as merely a 'servant' to the Cavendishes.[40] John is another favourite of Katherine's, and she has become godmother to one of his sons. The occasion of Sir Charles's sickness has brought him to the abbey, although he now lives elsewhere and is engaged in supervising Sir Charles's building work at Bolsover Castle.[41]

These stately semi-public chambers at Welbeck Abbey – the Great Chamber, the Gallery, and in particular, the Chapel (which was once the frater, or refectory, of the monastery) – often ring with music. Today the Gallery is silent, but the players are not far away. Perhaps they are repairing their instruments – viols, theorbos and citterns – instead of conducting their daily rehearsal.

Positions in this music-loving household are highly sought after among professional musicians. A violist and singer called Martin Otto bragged in 1608 that he had 'almost a promise' of becoming organist to Sir Charles, and found his future master 'honest religious and exceeding studious'.[42] Such a luminary of the Elizabethan musical world as the madrigalist John Wilbye described Sir Charles as having 'excellent skill in musicke, and [a] great love and favour of Musicke', and himself lived in the Cavendish household at one time.[43] The six-part harmonies of the old-fashioned Elizabethan madrigals must occasionally sound along the stairs and passages of the house, as do the more up-to-date Italian madrigals collected by Nicholas Yonge in a book dedicated to Sir Charles's stepbrother Gilbert Talbot. Yonge writes that the lyrics to the songs had been translated 'by a Gentleman for his private delight'; the anonymous 'Gentleman' was Sir Charles Cavendish himself. [44] William's great love is the viol, and he possesses many different models of the instrument, including the two known by the household as 'The Lyon' and 'The Foole' because of the carvings that replace the more usual scroll at the head of their fingerboards.[45]

The musicians will not remain silent for long. The Cavendishes are passionate about music, ascribing to it remarkable powers of healing and redemption, and it is closely intertwined for them with love and grief. In another of his poems, William writes that music can melt the hardest heart:

> Your Lady's snow white breasts, though frozen were
> Thaw them, & each eye drop a loving Tear,
> At least soft smothering sighs, we mean to Raise,
> With amorous speeches, & sweet Roundelays,
> For musick hath such power you have no choice
> Moving all passions, with her warbling Voice
> And soft toucht string, Harmoniously a long
> Taking your Hearts all prisoners in a song
> And to your selves shall softly whispering say
> Though Came not lovers, lovers went a way.[46]

The musicians must be hoping that Sir Charles will call upon them to play for him once again.

*

Descending the wide stair from the stately chambers of the first floor, we now sink into the cavernous gloom of the Great Hall and the world of the lower servants. Their voices rise up to the Hall's venerable rafters, hidden in shadow between the shafts of light coming in through the vast windows; once the servants of the medieval abbots ate their meals here. The household's lower servants loll on the long tables and benches in unaccustomed idleness, heads turned towards the great stair, as their daily orders have not been issued. They are not usually allowed to enter the upper, richly decorated parts of the house such as the Great Chamber or Gallery unless specially summoned to a meeting or to bring refreshments. Today, however, the stair – a conduit for news from above – holds a magnetic attraction for them. The Usher of the Hall makes only a perfunctory effort to raise his silver staff of office to maintain order and to keep the lower servants away from the stair's foot, himself aware that a household meeting could be called at a moment's notice.

These household members, male and youthful for the main part, are united in appearance by their livery. All the servants in the household receive an annual wage, lodgings, meals (known as 'diet') and medical treatment: the Cavendish family book of recipes, for example, includes instructions for 'the manner of making that water which Dr. Davison did Prescribe for Sir Charles' footman, where with he was Cured of a great, & strange Coughe'.[47] The servants also receive a coat or cloak in the Cavendish mallard green. In his will, Harry Ogle will dispose of his highly prized livery, 'a green velvet suit laid with silver lace [braid] for my Lady Newcastle's service'.[48] Each noble household has its own peculiar livery colour, and the servants belonging to it wear the family badge on their clothes. Blue is the most common colour for household wear, so much so that gentlemen avoid wearing blue because of its menial associations. During his tour of England in 1611, the traveller Fynes Moryson noticed that the servants of gentlemen are:

> wont to wear blue coats with their Masters *badge* of silver on the left sleeve, but now they most commonly wear cloaks garded [trimmed] with lace, all the servants of one family wearing the same liverie for colour or ornament.[49]

Each of the servants gathered in the Hall today displays the coiled Cavendish reptile – described in heraldic terms as the 'snake noué' or 'knotted snake' – on a metal plate sewn onto their sleeves.

Despite the momentous circumstances, there is still a good deal of

Members of the household of the Duke of Albemarle – specifically his watermen – wearing his badge on their sleeves.

noisy work in progress on the ground floor of the house today. In the great kitchens, brick-built and tacked onto the extremity of the east wing, the cooks are busy preparing for the household's midday meal in the Great Hall. Beer is being brought up from the brewhouse to the buttery adjacent to the Hall, loaves of bread are being stacked in the pantry, and vegetables brought in from the garden. Lambs are being butchered in the slaughterhouse, horses are being watered, fish plucked from the brewhouse pond and fruit from the walls of the sheltered orchard. Other forms of sustenance came from the stillhouse, liquorice yard, rabbit warren, dovecote and deer park at Welbeck. Vast quantities of milk and grain are sent up daily to the house from the Grange, as the home farm is known. Over a period of four months, the household consumes 4,840 eggs, twenty-three lambs, 173 slaughtered 'Muttons', fifty-two pigs, twenty-five carp, twenty dozen 'Larks and small birds', two barrels of herrings and three hogsheads of 'Claret wine'.[50] Even today, the household will still need to eat, although the sick man's wife and sons may shun the household meal in the Great Hall in favour of dining alone in their private parlour.

Appetites sharpen towards midday, for the servants have risen early; five o'clock is not an unusual hour. Breakfast is an informal affair, and there are two set meals: dinner at noon and supper at five or six o'clock. Unlike many other noble families, the Cavendishes themselves still occasionally show themselves at the top table in the Hall and eat with their household. Today, as noon approaches, the preparations are nearly complete. At one end of the two-storey Hall, a raised dais contains Sir Charles's empty table; at the other, a carved wooden screen hides the entrances to the offices, such as the buttery (so called because it houses butts of beer) beyond. While the usher seats the household and guests at tables appropriate to their rank, the pantler brings out bread from the pantry and the butler approaches with the beer.

Catering on the grand scale that the household requires takes up a large proportion of the Cavendish family's considerable annual income from its vast estates, including the profits from mineral extraction, farming and forestry. Thomas Wentworth, who will become the first Earl of Strafford and a powerful political patron of William Cavendish, received useful advice from his father on limiting expenditure on his retinue: 'if you spend but a third part of your revenue in your house you shall do the wiser and better'.[51] The Cavendish estates bring in £22,393 a year, while the very highest-paid servants earn an annual wage of £25.[52] That even a third of the turnover of this large estate and house might be spent on the household is staggering.

What is the point of this expensive, ravenous and sometimes riotous organisation called the household? It is the basic and most important unit of seventeenth-century society. The average size of a household has been shrinking since its medieval heyday, yet the Cavendish household now gathering in the Great Hall at Welbeck has grown in size and status in recent years as the family has progressed up the social ladder.

The word 'family' is used in two senses: both for the master's blood relations and for his constantly changing body of household members. Visitors bring with them their own 'families', and despite the enormous size of great houses such as Welbeck Abbey or Hardwick Hall, accommodating them all is problematic. Beds are placed two or three to a bedchamber and are similarly arranged in the service rooms, lobbies, on landings and even in the stables. It is this rich, complex layer of ever-changing occupation – cacophonous and stinking, as well as ceremonial and splendid – that creates the atmosphere of a great household.

Today, in 1617, there is a growing concern that the status of household service is falling. In medieval times, a lord's closest servants were always well-born; now it is becoming harder to find appropriately genteel staff. The anonymous writer 'R. B.', who compiled a list of putative regulations fit for the household of an Elizabethan earl, recommends that the senior servants be 'not only well born and of good livings, but also grave and experienced, not proud and haughty, neither too affable and easy'.[53] There are few women in an old-fashioned noble household: R. B. suggests that in a household of two hundred only a dozen – including the mistress of the house, her gentlewomen, chambermaids and laundry maids – need be female.

The Cavendishes' Nottinghamshire neighbour Sir Francis Willoughby compiled a similar book of rules to regulate his own establishment. As at Welbeck, his household of forty-five was managed through a strict chain of command extending down from the Usher of the Great Hall to the Usher of the Great Chamber, the butler, the underbutler, the pantler, cook, gentlemen waiters, yeomen waiters, slaughtermen, carter and grooms, the pages and finally the kitchen boys. Their responsibilities were closely defined, from keeping the dogs out of the hall to bearing a lighted torch at the head of the procession of servants carrying the master's dinner from serving place to dining room.[54]

Every household member must know and keep to his allotted place in this slow dance of ceremony that revolves around the head of the household. In general, the lower servants are proud of their master's munificence rather than resentful of their own servitude. According to the writer Sir Thomas Overbury, a household servingman is commonly a fiery fellow, proud but lazy:

> He tells without asking who ownes him, by the superscription of his Livery. His life is, for ease and leisure, much about *Gentleman-like*. He hates or loves the men, as his Master doth the Master. He is commonly proud of his Masters horses, or his Christmas [. . .] He never drinks but double.[55]

Meanwhile, his female equivalent, the maidservant, should be 'careful, faithful, patient, neat and pleasant [. . .] cleanly, quick and handsome, and of few words, honest in her word, deed and attire, diligent in a househould'. Women have a lesser role in household ceremony, and while her tasks include washing, baking, brewing, sewing and spinning, the maid's most important skill in the male-dominated world of the household is said to lie 'chiefly in holding her peace'.[56]

*

Sir Charles, happy-go-lucky by nature, has made no will. It was only earlier this morning that he finally faced up to the fact that he might not recover from this illness, and his purpose in sending for his eldest son was to tell him how he intends to dispose of his worldly goods. Now, in his bedchamber, he begins to whisper his wishes aloud. Also discernible, in the shadows of the room, is the hunched figure of a secretary: Sir Charles's will is to be 'nuncupative', or dictated.[57] His sickness has taken him by surprise and he no longer has the strength to hold a pen.

The great four-poster in which Sir Charles lies is commonly the most expensive item of furniture in a house; the master's bed often costs more than the rest of the furnishings put together. He intends that the bed and its expensive hangings will become the property of his widow. Along with the marital bed, Katherine will receive all the family silver and gold plate that stands upon her cupboard, a piece of furniture that is still literally a construction of boards for 'cups' to stand upon rather than a cabinet with a door. She will also have the use, for her lifetime, of the rich tapestry hangings that have been packed up, transported and unrolled at each of the couple's constant changes of residence as they progress from estate to estate. Sir Charles, perhaps suspecting his son's weakness in matters of money, makes his wife the executrix of his will, and leaves her in charge of the family finances for the time being. But in due course everything else – riches and power, responsibility and expectation – will come to William. The motley group of individuals making up Sir Charles's household have high hopes of their future master, as he begins to prepare himself for the challenge of governing, loving and chastising them.

If Sir Charles dies, the servants will expect a magnificent funeral, possibly organised by the heralds from the College of Arms who travel the country ensuring that families' coats of arms and badges are correctly composed and displayed. The cost will include food, drink, black clothes for the household, black drapes for the house and gifts for the poor; a generous funeral 'dole' will ensure that a large, status-enhancing crowd attends. The upper servants will expect gifts of mourning cloaks. Twenty years before, members of a great household in mourning would have worn tailored three-quarter-length mourning coats with tight wristbands, but now swinging, heavily embroidered cloaks are becoming fashionable; long pointed mourning hoods are likewise dying out in favour of black sashes or scarves.[58] Servants of even the lowest rank will also be hoping for cash legacies in Sir Charles's will. When Sir William Paston of Norfolk died six years ago, eleven servants signed a receipt recording the payment of their promised legacies, eight of them merely making the cross of the illiterate.[59]

The old servants will perhaps fear for their places under the new regime. They will hope to receive their wages at regular intervals, something never to be taken for granted. In his own role as an officer in Gilbert Talbot's household, Sir Charles had to write in 1610 that he was 'laboured by my Lord's servants here to write [. . .] about their wages, and to say truly they need it greatly for they have no clothes nor any money'.[60] Even Sir Charles, as an occasional servant of the earl's, was entitled to 'diet' or a food allowance when he went to London on Talbot business: he and Katherine submitted receipts as part of an expense claim for £20 spent during ten days in London in 1604.[61] The upper, managerial servants will also be anxious about the annuities, farms and tenancies of manor houses that they have been promised on marriage or as the reward for a lifetime's service.

One of the important differences between the lives of the Cavendishes and those of their servants is their age at marriage. The mid-to-late twenties is the average age for a wedding, yet for aristocrats or would-be aristocrats it is much lower: at, or just after, the onset of puberty. The main reason for the servants to delay is that they have to leave the household on marriage. They must either save up their wages or wait until their parents die in order to inherit the wherewithal to set up a small household of their own. The children of aristocrats, on the other hand, are bargaining chips in their parents' hands from a young age, as marriage alliances with other families are negotiated. Excessively young husbands and wives are not expected to cohabit: husbands are sometimes sent on an educational tour of Europe until their brides are old enough to bear children.

The assembled Cavendish servants will also wish to see the household's recent and dramatic rise in status continue. William, as its new head, will be expected to make a name for himself at court but also, equally importantly, to build up his position locally. Passions run high in local politics, and the Cavendishes are allied with the Talbots against other Nottinghamshire magnates.

These local quarrels can be bloody, though complainants often exaggerate the violent nature of a dispute in order to secure a speedier arbitration in the Court of the Star Chamber. In 1593, for example, Sir Charles had taken the Talbots' part in a celebrated quarrel with his neighbours Sir Thomas Stanhope and Sir John Holles. The latter had not taken kindly to the rigging of the Parliamentary election of 1593 in Sir Charles's favour.

A full-blown skirmish between Sir Charles's household and that of the Stanhopes followed in 1599. John Stanhope's keeper, whose job it was to care for the game in his master's forest, was a key witness. On the morning of 18th June, the keeper was about his business in the park, 'being without Boots, or other Weapon but a pyked Staff'. Suddenly Stanhope and a company of about eleven horsemen swept into view and commanded the keeper to follow them to the Nottinghamshire town of Kirkby-in-Ashfield. Not suspecting foul play, he 'knew not whether he was carried, or what to do, until he came to that Hill's Side'.

Meanwhile, at Kirkby, Sir Charles and his servants Harry and Launce Ogle were riding to visit a building site where work was in progress on a new house for Sir Charles. Sir Charles noticed the party of Stanhope horsemen, and initially took them for a merry hunting party. Yet the Stanhopes were in search of human prey. As the keeper in his turn spotted Sir Charles and his two servants, accompanied only by a page and a 'horsekeeper', the mounted Stanhopes bore down on the Cavendish party. 'Suddenly they all galloping apace towards him', Sir Charles 'perceived he was beset'.

Sir Charles then desperately set his spurs into his 'little Nagg', hoping to reach the protection offered by the foundations of his new building, but his horse tripped. With his foot caught in the stirrup, Sir Charles was overtaken by the approaching horsemen, and before 'he could draw his Sword, 2 Pistols were discharged upon him, the one of them, with 2 Round of 2 Bullets, hit him in the Inside of his Thigh, but missed the Bone, and yet lyeth in his Flesh, near the Point of his Buttock'.[62]

Despite his wound, Sir Charles and the Ogles now embarked on a killing spree themselves. They faced eleven horsemen, yet 'unhorsed six of them, and killed two of them in the Place; a 3d fell down in the Forest [. . .] a fourth was left behind them in the same Place, so sore wounded as it is not thought he can recover, and lyeth at the Village adjoining'. This latter was the bootless park keeper, whose quiet morning in the park had ended in a fight to the death. This is the kind of service and sacrifice the head of a household can expect, and indeed the builders from Sir Charles's new house had likewise come running to their master's defence. They, too, were part of the extended Cavendish household and were expected to pay for this privilege with their lives if necessary.

Despite the good progress that had been made on the house at Kirkby-in-Ashfield and the completion of a brick kiln there, this mansion would never be finished. The site was soured by the unexpected violence that darkened that morning in 1599, and was abandoned in favour of Bolsover Castle.

On this occasion the law creaked into action against John Stanhope, and the High Sheriff of Derbyshire demanded 'the Queen's peace to be kept by him, his servants and all other by his procurement, against Sir Charles Cavendish, his servants and people'.[63] Six months later Sir Charles's injury was healing, and it was reported that the gash in his buttock 'was near closing up, but yielded some small moisture by reason of the sudden shutting up of so deep a wound'.[64]

This dizzying disrespect for peace and the law, despite the outward appearance of prosperity, shows how the counties of Derbyshire and Nottinghamshire still teeter upon the brink of casual violence. Despite the fact that the gentry feel safe enough to live in houses rather than in castles, both Bolsover Castle and Welbeck Abbey have turrets and battlements that give at least an impression of martial authority. The household's most fundamental expectation of William Cavendish is that he should provide good, strong and fair governance for its community. Its activities, prosperity and morals will be in his hands one day.

Back in the bedchamber, Sir Charles now pauses to rest, exhausted by the effort of dictating. Having dealt with the matter of his choicest goods, he now speaks to William of his own and his sons' lives. He puts William in mind of the future and the need to have a house and an heir of his own. William must find a wealthy wife 'both to his own very good liking, and his mother's approving'.[65] Unlike his mother, William has a poor head for figures; he 'naturally loves not business, especially those of state (though he understands them as well as anybody)'.[66] Katherine has overseen her husband's building works at Welbeck, and William will be short of money at first, as the builders of Sir Charles's incomplete Little Castle at Bolsover are yet to be paid. And there is another achievement for which William must stop at nothing to attain: it will take skilful networking, sumptuous entertainment and perhaps even blackmail, but Sir Charles desires that his son will enter the peerage and become a baron.

Now Sir Charles describes the monument which he wishes his wife and sons to erect for him in Bolsover Church. It is not to be too grand or too cold, but must convey a vibrant personal message from father to children: Sir Charles wishes his sons to remember his life, not his death. The poet Ben Jonson is to be commissioned to put Sir Charles's last words to his sons into poetry, recording a statement far removed from the dry, dusty, pious convention of the time:

> It will be matter loud enough to tell,
> Not when I died, but how I liv'd, farewell.[67]

In fact, Sir Charles is an irreplaceable father: loving, sincere, honest, worthy of emulation. He has a gift for happiness, and his son William has inherited his buoyant spirits and love of pleasure. Henry Lukin, the household mathematician, considers that Sir Charles is (Plate 2):

A MAN
WHOME

| | |
|---|---|
| KNOWLEDGE ZEALE SINCERITY | RELIGIOUS: |
| EXPERIENCE DISCRETION COURAGE | MADE VALIANT: |
| READING CONFERENCE JUDGMENT | LEARNED: |
| RELIGION, VALOUR, LEARNING | MADE WISE: |
| BIRTH, MERITES, FAVOUR | NOBLE: |
| RESPECT, MEANS, CHARITIE | MADE BOUNTIFULL: |
| EQUITIE, CONSCIENCE OFFICE | JUST. |
| NOBILITIE, BOUNTYE, JUSTICE | MADE HONOURABLE |
| COUNSELL, AYDE, SECRECIE | A TRUSTY FRIEND: |
| LOVE, TRUST, CONSTANCIE | MADE A KIND HUSBAND: |
| AFFECTION, ADVICE, CARE, | A LOVING FATHER: |
| FRENDS, WIFE, SONNES, | MADE CONTENT. |
| WISDOM HONOUR CONTENT | MADE HAPPY. |

This emphasis on happiness is most unusual, as piety and faith are qualities much more frequently dwelt upon in an encomium.[68] But Sir Charles now tells his son to live joyfully.

Yet the finale of Sir Charles's precautions to his son as they remain closeted in the father's bedchamber on 27th March, 1617, concerns the major building project that remains unfinished. The extended Cavendish family lives in a heated atmosphere of architectural endeavour. Sir Charles's latest contribution to the family's growing body of architectural patronage has been his half-complete Little Castle at Bolsover, on the edge of a dramatic cliff beyond the western border of Sherwood Forest. It is intended to be a small house for pleasure and retirement. Like a sophisticated jewel box with many concealed compartments, father and son have planned the castle to provide the perfect setting for a leisured aristocrat interested in art, literature and music. But today it remains disappointingly incomplete.

William now leaves the bedchamber and goes forth to face the household, for the first time in possession of the knowledge that he will soon be its master. He does not have long to prepare himself for his new role. The instinct that led Sir Charles to prepare for death was sound: his end comes only a week later.

Within months William has notable success in carrying out his father's final instructions: he seeks and finds a wealthy bride, he tries to provide good governance for his household, he searches diligently for happiness. Most urgently of all, he makes plans to bring his father's unfinished castle at Bolsover to spectacular completion.

# 2 – *A Building Site*

BOLSOVER CASTLE, 12TH JUNE, 1613

Four years before Sir Charles suffered his final illness, William and his father spent an afternoon clambering through the incomplete cellars of the new house at Bolsover.[1] On 12th June, 1613, William's seduction by the art of architecture is already well under way.

By eight o'clock in the morning of the day of their visit, the Cavendishes' surveyor John Smithson has already reached the outskirts of the town of Bolsover.[2] As he trots on horseback towards the windy hilltop where the Little Castle is slowly emerging from the controlled chaos of a seventeenth-century building site, Smithson's thoughts run anxiously ahead: to his inspection of progress and this afternoon's planned excursion from Welbeck Abbey by the young William Cavendish and his father.

The view that forms the backdrop to Smithson's journey is astounding. Much of William Cavendish's story is set in the Peak District, the remote, landlocked region of England where the tawny peaks of the hills rise up like the frozen waves of an inland sea. This is the land of Sherwood Forest and Robin Hood, of natural wonders such as the great cavern known as the Devil's Arse and the mines where Blue John crystals are harvested. It is also Cavendish country.

These rolling hills are liberally strewn with great houses, as if a giant hand had rolled a pocketful of dice across the land. The adjacent counties of Nottinghamshire, Derbyshire ('the Region of Ale'[3]) and Yorkshire become known as 'the Dukeries' from their density of dukes and ducal mansions. As Smithson looks west across the Doe Lea valley, the foreground is made up of undulating swells of cosy fields, hedgerows and banks of hawthorn, and behind them the purple-blue folds of the Peak District mount up towards the horizon. He can look back down the wide valley to catch a glimpse of two towering houses at Hardwick, the Old Hall and the New Hall, sixteenth-century skyscrapers built between 1587 and 1599 by William's grandmother Bess of Hardwick. To the north, the view leads up to the grey skies of Yorkshire.

Smithson has two contrasting impressions of the landscape spread beneath him. Firstly, he is an experienced estate surveyor, skilled at measuring and nursing the Cavendishes' land, and he sees fields in terms of the wealth they can generate. He is efficient and effective in running the building project at Bolsover. Yet, almost at odds with this picture of a keen man of business, Smithson has made a treasure trove of drawings showing the fruits of his fertile architectural imagination. Ingenuity is the cornerstone of both John's and his famous father Robert's designs: clever plans, dramatic facades and high towers characterise their architecture. John must also see this hilly landscape as full of potential perches for houses.

He passes on the other side of the same valley two further impressive houses built by competing neighbours: Sir Charles's brother William, Earl of Devonshire, owns a house named Oldcotes, while neighbouring Sutton Hall is the pride of the Leake family. Oldcotes is alternatively called 'Owlcotes', and local tradition has it that Bess of Hardwick built the house for her second son William out of chagrin at the size and splendour of Sir Francis Leake's new Sutton Hall. She intended to make her son's house 'as splendid for owls as his was for men', hence its name.[4]

Smithson clatters into the small town of Bolsover at the conclusion of his usual weekday journey from his home on a farm in Kirkby-in-Ashfield.[5] The building site at Bolsover, with its vast views, is ceaselessly buffeted by the wind, and changes in the weather are visible over the distant hills long before they reach the castle. This hilltop chills and numbs the fingers, ears and feet. Yet from here Sir Charles Cavendish will be able to see and be seen.

During the last fortnight, Smithson has already made nine supervisory visits to the castle, and his expense claims include 'provender' for his hard-working horse. Ben Jonson, the Cavendish family poet, describes a surveyor as 'An overseer! One that oversee-eth you. A busy man!'[6] Smithson would probably agree. There are more than sixty-three people on site, making it one of the biggest private building projects in the country.[7] Today is the well-deserved fortnightly payday, and the labourers swarming over the half-built carcass of the castle are looking forward to feeling the weight of coin in their hands. Smithson is hoping to be able to report good progress to William and his father.

This June morning, work has been under way for nearly six months. Sir Charles began the process of acquiring the old medieval castle of Bolsover from his stepbrother Gilbert Talbot several years ago, and it was the ruinous Norman keep at the end of a rocky spur that provided the inspiration for the new house. This ancient site was formerly a key defensive position in the great landholding called the 'Honour of Peveril', which was created for William the Conqueror's illegitimate son William Peverel just after the Norman Conquest. The Conqueror's grandson built the first castle at Bolsover. The building now rising phoenix-like from the old castle site will be a playful, fanciful, delightful rebuilding of the Peverels' keep, and the line of the medieval curtain wall is being reused as the garden wall of the Cavendishes' new house.

This is the busiest season of the year. Construction must be crammed into the warmer months because frost will break up the lime mortar used to secure the masonry. Only about eight vertical feet of wall can be constructed in a single year. To build any higher would distort and weaken the mortar in its lower courses, for it needs several months to set. In the autumn, the unfinished wall tops will be thatched with brushwood and many of the workers laid off. Smithson must make maximum use of the good weather.

As a surveyor, he has a wide spectrum of duties. He has to prepare drawings: the masons must now be more than familiar with his sketch for the semi-complete cellar rooms of the castle – including kitchen, pastry, Great Beer Cellar and storerooms – but many details remain to be settled. Smithson's drawing of the cellars comes complete with an alternative arrangement of the stairs laid out on an ingenious lift-up flap for Sir Charles to choose the option he prefers. Smithson also has to break up the building work into the packages or 'bargains' to be undertaken by different craftsmen. His masons are masters of their art: their carving remains so sharp that visitors to the castle in later centuries will report that they can still hear the chink of chisels or elusive snatches of music seeping from the violins frozen in the stone-carved fireplace of an upper room.

John Smithson also has to attend frequent conferences with William's father, who is both the project's paymaster and a respected amateur

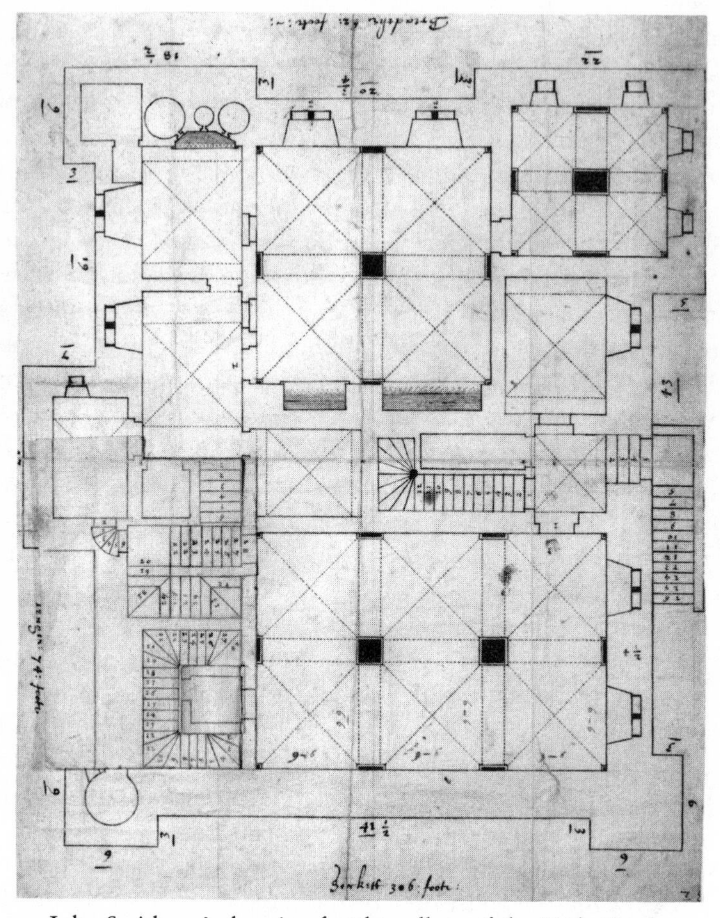

John Smithson's drawing for the cellars of the Little Castle at Bolsover

architect in his own right. During his building of Cranborne Lodge for the Earl of Salisbury in 1610, the chief mason William Arnold would likewise spend 'every day a whole hour in private with' the earl in order to discuss the work.[8] Smithson also has to order the materials needed for the next fortnight, and annotates his drawings with his calculations of the quantities required.[9] Finally, it may even be Smithson himself who keeps the project's account book up to date and dispenses the money, though if so he refers to himself in the third person.

Work on site began at five this morning, as it does throughout the summer. The Statute of Artificers of 1563 still notionally controls labourers' working hours, though the law is not stringently applied in remotest Derbyshire. From the middle of March until September, the official working day runs from five in the morning to between seven and eight in the evening. In winter, hours will be shorter, 'from the spring of the day in the morning until the night of the same day'.[10] There are breaks, including a siesta, spread throughout the day. On a summer's day like this one, each workman is entitled to:

> at every drinking one half hour, for his Dinner one hour, and for his Sleep when he is allowed to sleep, the which is from the middest of May to the middest of August, half an hour at the most, and at every Breakfast one half hour.[11]

Smithson plans to tour the whole site to make sure that everything is in good order before William and his father arrive from Welbeck. He begins down in the quarry of Shuttlewood, at the bottom of the hill below the castle site, where pinkish-gold sandy stone is being hewn out of the ground.[12] The quarry is like the bite mark left by a set of teeth in a giant biscuit: a semi-circular, scarred wall of tawny stone. It is full of dry churned mud from the stone carts, and nettles gather in its untended corners. The bright yellow stone fresh from the ground darkens to a duller, greyer colour on exposure to the air. As Smithson rides into the quarry, the masons are breakfasting in the draughty lodge that provides them with shelter from the weather. Built of timber provided by the carpenters, it has a roof thatched with bronzed bracken fronds. Workaday masons' lodges such as this one are the ancestors of the purely ceremonial Masonic lodges of future centuries, where brotherhoods of 'theoretical' (rather than practical) freemasons will meet for social pleasure and moral improvement. Grainy yellow stone dust fills the air in the lodge, making clothes pale, hands dry and sore, and breathing painful. Smithson dismounts, a deferential murmur of welcome arises, and there is a hasty curtailment of the breakfast half-hour. As the masons rise, they replace their hand protection of rags or leather; sometimes a master gives his masons a gift of gloves at the start of their work, as well as livery in the household's colours. Once again they take up their tools: chisel (icy cold and heavy) in one hand, and mallet (bulky head and wooden handle warm and light to the touch) in the other.[13] The masons are lopsided in appearance: their mallet arms have overdeveloped muscles.

There is a clear hierarchy among the masons. The lowest-ranking workers now return to their sweaty job of 'getting' stone from the ground, or else 'scappling' (roughly shaping) it, using crude, toothed chisels for speed. It is a relatively easy job to remove the soft sandstone from the cliff face: they chisel a crack across an outcrop, force wedges into it, then lever the block free with iron bars. Many such rough lumps lie scattered around the quarry, as only the most suitable are carried into the lodge for further working. Seven men are at work today getting stone from the ground, while two others, whose names are Shore and Roylles, are scappling. These labourers earn much less money than the skilled freemasons who dress the stone or the 'layers' who will hoist and set it into position; best paid of all are the fine 'carvers' who will complete the decorated fireplaces.

The names of the tools used at Shuttlewood echo onomatopoeically the thwacking blows that ring round the quarry as work resumes: the maul (hammer), the gavelocke (crowbar), the kevel (hammer for rough hewing or breaking the stone) and the wedge. Stone is shaped in the quarry so as not to waste effort transporting excess weight, but also because this sandstone is more easily worked fresh, or 'green', from the ground. It will gradually harden on contact with the atmosphere.[14]

Over the past two weeks the masons Goodwin, Baram and 'their fellows' have completed a great stack of dressed stone with their sharp, smooth-ended chisels. The freshly cut stones look like pale creamy-yellow pieces of cheese or butter, an illusion soon dispelled when their cold weight is touched. Each piece is discreetly signed with its mason's individual mark of identification: a letter or some other strange hieroglyphic according to the master mason's list, although the masons' individual styles of working are also apparent to the trained eye. The eye is the mason's most important organ, as brute force is useless without precision. Smithson now needs to check the quantities and quality in order to authorise payment, with Goodwin and Baram drawing attention to any excesses or explaining away any inadequacies. Smithson calculates that they have completed 124 feet of finished ashlar (smooth stone blocks), 57 feet of 'window stuff' (jambs, mullions, cills and lintels) and 66 feet of the axed stone that will be used to create steps for the many twisting staircases running down into the cellars of the Little Castle. Goodwin and Baram have also made 13 feet of 'channell' to drain the kitchen floor and a window head for the room called the pastry, where baking will take place. Finally, they have completed a 'springer', one of the two stones from which a pointed vault rises.

Smithson now commissions the next fortnight's work. He wants bases for the pillars in the Great Beer Cellar and a spout for the kitchen sink, telling the masons exactly what he requires to a response of sage nods. Goodwin and Baram belong to a skilled and honourable profession. In 1599, the Shropshire mason Walter Hancock was commemorated in resonant phrases in the burial records of his parish, for his community was proud of his 'most sumptuous buildings, most stately tombs, most curious pictures'.[15]

These senior masons are usually peripatetic, working for no more than ten years on a particular house before seeking out or being recommended for another building project possibly hundreds of miles away. There are even cases of unscrupulous patrons trying to steal celebrated masons. Sir Edward Hext, when supervising the construction of Wadham College in Oxford, wrote of his pleasure in having secured the services of the fine freemason William Arnold:

> If I had not tied him fast to this business we should hardly keep him; he is so wonderfully sought being in deed the absolutest & honestest workman in England.[16]

Bands of masons are therefore accustomed to leaving their homes and travelling across England from one great house-building project to the next. John Smithson himself has worked as a mason in his youth, as did his own father Robert. When the latter was asked to build Hardwick Hall in Derbyshire for Bess of Hardwick, three principal craftsmen followed him from his previous project, Wollaton Hall in Nottinghamshire: Thomas Accres, carver in marble, and two masons named Rode. Further members of the Rode family – a labourer, a 'boy' and a woman – are now working for Robert's son at Bolsover. During the building of Hardwick Hall, the masons lived in its incomplete shell, and one of the rooms on the roof became semi-officially known as the 'turret where Accres lyeth'.[17] The masons working at Bolsover also sleep and work in the same half-finished rooms.

Living far from home and family, often in squalid conditions, a gang of travelling masons may present a formidable, almost feral, appearance to the locals. Strangers of any sort are unusual in Bolsover, and these men inhabit a tiny world of sweat by day and near-comatose exhaustion at night, taking their pleasures as well as their labour very seriously. Drunkenness is far from unknown, though few reach the levels of depravity reported in a 'lewd company' of travelling French stonemasons at a sixteenth-century building project of Sir John Thynne:

I never saw the like [Thynne wrote of the foreign masons]. They be the worst conditioned people that ever I saw and the dronkenst; for they will drink more in one day than three days wages will come to, and then lie like beasts on the floor not able to stand.[18]

The most experienced masons are the jealous owners of drawings of both ancient and the very newest designs; piles of well-thumbed paper are available for consultation and discussion as Smithson describes what he wants. The Elizabethan designer John Thorpe, like Smithson the son of a mason, inherited part of his father's collection of drawings. All but one of the drawings in Thorpe's possession show the upper floors of buildings, because his brothers inherited the lower floors and elevations.[19] Smithson likewise possesses a collection of drawings given to him by his father, and the presence of some late Gothic drawings among them suggests that Robert had himself inherited material from an earlier generation.

During the masons' rest periods in the lodge at Shuttlewood, books also circulate from hand to hand. They examine, for example, Walter Gedde's discursively entitled *Booke of Sundry Draughtes principally serving for glasiers: and not impertinent for parterres, and gardeners; besides sundry other professions* (1615). At Bolsover, this book will give someone the idea for the design of the intricate paved floor in the Pillar Parlour.[20]

Goodwin and Baram now check that they are using the correct templates to guide them in shaping the stone. Smithson draws the sections he requires for decorative mouldings (for a window jamb, for example) onto paper at a one-to-one scale. He gives these paper templates to the joiners, who then make cut-outs for the masons in oak or beech. Sometimes these paper or wooden patterns are reused at another house. This is how architectural details creep from house to house across the countryside: masons carry old templates with them to new projects, and a regional architecture develops.

There are no definitive plans of the building site for the masons to consult. Many details are agreed in daily discussion, and minds are often changed along the way. When William Cavendish comes to build his Riding House opposite the Little Castle, there is a major switch halfway through the process: the windows are raised by about a metre. The walls show the scars left by their original position. This is a fairly minor mistake by the standards of the day. At Chastleton House in Oxfordshire, for example, the door into the Great Hall itself is squeezed into an odd little corner because the central courtyard of the house had been incorrectly laid out.[21] In the seventeenth century, the foremost designers are beginning to understand that the Italian practice of drawing every single part of a building beforehand minimises these risks, but the process involves a conceptual grasp of three-dimensional space and detail which is not yet common in British building.

Some of those working in the quarry are not up to their jobs, and Smithson is on the lookout for slow or shoddy work. In April, he had to dock the wages of a mason called Arthur Reade 'for bad scappling'.[22] It looks like Reade's work did not improve, for he left the project in May. Meanwhile, at another house-building project taking place this same June at Kyre Park in Worcestershire, an inept mason is paid, reluctantly, 'for 15 days naughty work [. . .] & so discharged for a bungler'.[23]

Once dressed, the stone will be taken up the hill in groaning carts. Towards midday, Smithson becomes anxious to reach the castle site before his masters' visit. He now brushes some of the stone dust from his breeches and mounts his horse to accompany a cartload of stone travelling up to the building site. Transport is in short supply, especially during the harvest season, and those who live locally and have carts in their possession find themselves earning lucrative fees for their use. This hill is dangerously steep. On one occasion Henry Kitchen of Bolsover is killed when his wagon, pulled by six horses and four young bullocks, overturns on Castle Hill; on another, a baby girl named Isabella Bennet is crushed to death by a runaway cart on the 'hilly highway' at Shuttlewood.[24] The Cavendish habit of building their houses on hills inevitably poses transport difficulties: at Hardwick Hall, for example, Bess was forced to use nimble packhorses to bring up stone from her nearby quarry.

The carts ascending from Shuttlewood quarry to the castle site weave their way through a landscape where shallow opencast coal mining is already under way. Today Smithson authorises payment to the colliers of Bolsover for sixteen loads of coal to feed the building site's limekiln.

After climbing the hill, Smithson's horse follows in the wake of the

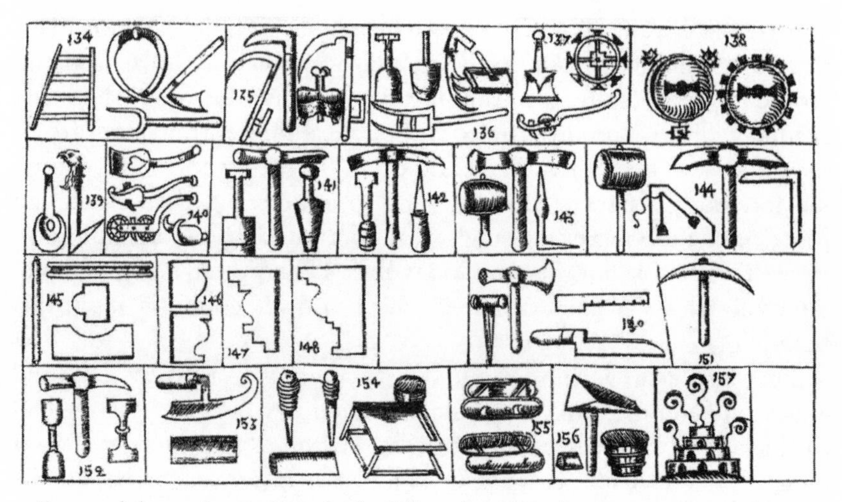


Some of the tools used on the building site, including masons' templates

cart of stones, crossing the causeway through the bank and ditch that provided the medieval castle with its outer ring of defence. As he enters the outer bailey, now a grassy field, Smithson glimpses the bowed figures of labourers creeping across the rough ground of the castle site. Some are lugging heavy buckets of water, sand and lime. Others are breaking or loading limestone, digging foundations, taking down old walls, tempering mortar, sifting lime, sorting and cleaning wall stone and sand, or serving the masons and layers.[25] The building site is relatively quiet: the loudest noises are the rasp of saws, the tap of chisels and the rattle of a load of limestone rubble being tipped out of an up-ended cart.

The figures pausing to observe Smithson's approach include women and boys, and whole families can be found employed in different jobs across the site. William Yeavlee of Bolsover, for example, works as a labourer, as do his wife Bess and his son Thomas. In a field to the north of the castle, the limekiln puffs out its clouds of noxious smoke. It is manned by the lime burner and his group of female assistants, while other women carry out a variety of back-breaking jobs: sieving lime, carrying sand or getting bracken to cover the tops of walls.[26]

Unlike the peripatetic professional masons, these poorly dressed and lowly paid labourers come mainly from Bolsover town. They return home at night to work in their own fields or vegetable patches. Small-scale agriculture is a popular safety net against hard times among craftsmen of all sorts. Of sixty carpenters who lived in rural Lincolnshire in the late sixteenth century, probate inventories show that all of them possessed the necessary tools for farm labour as well as for carpentry.[27] The wages earned by the labourers' wives form a vital part of their home economy: only in the nineteenth century will it become possible for a working man and his wife to live off a single income.[28] Now that Protestantism is the state religion instead of Roman Catholicism, the loss of saints' days as holidays means less rest for the workmen. A few festivals endure, however, and later this year eight labourers will sacrifice their '3 Christmas holidays' to work only because of the urgent necessity of demolishing a dangerous wall.[29] Because of the steep inflation in prices that is taking place throughout the early seventeenth century, the labourers are in the gruelling position of needing to work for an ever-increasing number of hours simply to maintain their purchasing power.[30]

As midday approaches, the men and women of the building site prepare to break for dinner. A labouring man needs 3,000 calories' worth of food daily, which he can buy for tuppence. A day's sustenance usually comes in the form of two pounds of bread, nine ounces of peas, 3½ ounces of cheese, and beer. Beer is an important source of extra energy, as well as being safer to drink than water with its risk of dysentery. Workmen also eat beef with their bread, fish on Fridays, and sometimes eggs; cheese, surprisingly, is often more expensive than beef.[31] During the building of Hardwick Hall, where some of these Bolsover labourers gained experience, cheap bread for the workmen was made out of the inferior materials of 'oats and dredge' and peas.[32]

On any building site, the layers form a caste higher than that of the general labourers. Smithson's horse now passes through the gateway into the inner bailey of the medieval castle and he dismounts near the depression in the ground containing the new cellars and the stubs of the Little Castle's walls. Here the layers are hard at work, hoisting the dressed stones into position and placing them on a bed of mortar mixed with oyster shells; crustaceans contain a chemical which helps the mortar to set. The layers also undertake the responsible work of setting out arches and vaults like those now beginning to rise over the cellar roofs. They will also perform whatever alternative work is to hand.[33] As the building rises, the layers' job will become even more arduous and dangerous. Treadmills are the usual means of lifting stone, and it is only in 1637 that the architect John Webb will devise a pulley for use at St Paul's Cathedral that works by turning a capstan 'to raise great stones with ease'.[34]

The scaffolding sprouting from the rising walls of the castle's semi-subterranean basement is a precarious construction of wooden poles, with wickerwork shields called 'fleakes' slung between them to walk upon. Pulling these poles out will cause a gruesome death during another Cavendish building project, that at Nottingham Castle. As one George Jackson 'was fetching out a short end of wood', the arch it had supported, 'built of brick, & ye lime not well set', fell down upon his head. He was so badly crushed and bruised that he died two hours later. The building site is far from safe, and those injured have only the charity of the Cavendishes to fall back upon.

In the final stages of the project, masonry of an even higher order will be required for the decorative carving both inside and out. Sometimes carvings are imported from the expert workshops of London: the delicate decoration for Sir Charles's tomb, for example, is ordered from Southwark, and the well-known sculptor Nicholas Stone sends whole fireplaces from his London workshop to the provinces.[35] Yet over the next few years at Bolsover, the carving of the Little Castle's fireplaces will be executed locally. They will become uniquely famous for their brilliance, individuality and use of rare Derbyshire marble.

Many other activities are drawing to a halt across the building site for the rest period. James Wilson, in charge of the kiln in Limekiln Field, now releases the labourers breaking up forty cartloads of limestone for him. Lime mortar, which will be used right up until the 1930s, when it is supplanted by Portland cement, is made out of a mixture of lime and sand. To make mortar, quarried limestone is split into small pieces and slowly burned in the kiln. Once the stone is burned into a powder, Wilson's assistants use a rectangular sieve to remove lumps. At this point, it can be used as an agricultural fertilizer, but to create mortar it is 'slaked' or mixed with water, a dangerous process that gives off scalding heat and results in a sludgy paste. Finally, the lime is pummelled with an instrument called a beater and left to mature for several months. Only then is it served up to the layers.

Elsewhere on the building site, perhaps in one of the ramshackle buildings of the old castle, the carpenters Chester and his son are taking a break. They have been making scaffold poles, wheelbarrows, hods and wooden centring for the construction of stone arches. The building will very soon rise high enough to require structural timber.

Then, the Chesters will journey out from Bolsover into the surrounding Cavendish estates to select trees. They will slice up the best trunks on the spot in sawpits dug into the ground, a recent innovation that has made it far easier to make boards. Structural timbers are heaved directly into position, but wood intended for finer work such as panelling or joinery has to be seasoned to avoid future warping. In John Smithson's youth, timber was treated by the simple method of standing it up to 'dry with sticks between it so that it may season', but now there are superior methods, such as soaking the pieces in water to remove the acid sap before drying them in a kiln or oven.[36] No better way of treating timber will be discovered, and much of the fine internal woodwork of the castle will survive intact for four centuries.

Craftsmen and labourers now congregate in the sheltered corners of the old castle ruins, settling down amid clover and dandelions to eat their bread. They are all hoping that John Smithson will find nothing to fault in the work for which they expect payment this evening. Smithson himself expects to be reimbursed for ten meals eaten during the course of his duties in the last fortnight.[37] Unlike other great families, the extended Cavendish household has grown accustomed to its almost continuous programme of building; most noble families realise just one major building project in a generation. Sometimes extra labour is drafted in from as far afield as the family's Northumberland estate, and these men eat meals cooked by Winifred Rambott, the innkeeper at Norton Cuckney near Welbeck.[38] Everyone on this building site is bound to the Cavendishes for his or her livelihood.

Now a stir runs through the prostrate figures. Everybody was expecting the arrival from Welbeck this afternoon of a couple of Cavendish officers with the bag of wage money. The labourers stagger to their feet and exchange comments, however, because the group of horsemen coming up through the outer bailey additionally includes both Sir Charles Cavendish himself and his son William. William, now nineteen years old, has inherited his father's love of architecture and has come to see the castle that will one day be his home.

John Smithson steps forward to welcome the newcomers, and while the masons respectfully stand back, they climb down into the cellar of the Little Castle. After touring and approving the excavations and the half-finished rooms, Sir Charles and his son repair to the lodge close by that Smithson uses as an office.[39] Here he has a table on which to make drawings or tot up quantities. Chairs are provided for the visitors, and Smithson begins to outline plans for the next phase of the work.

William's father is more than usually interested in building. He understands the language of classical architecture, with its secrets of harmony and proportion, and his discussions with his surveyor take the form of a conversation between two experts. So great is Sir Charles's expertise that he is consulted by aristocrats throughout the country. In Elizabethan and Jacobean England the passion for building has spread like an infectious disease. In 1577, the Essex clergyman William Harrison wrote that:

> Every man almost is a builder and he that hath bought any small parcel of ground, be it never so little, will not be quiet till he have pulled down the old house (if any were there standing) and set up a new after his own devise.[40]

Smithson now outlines his preparations for the later stages of the building, and William listens closely, eager to learn. The project requires a plumber to shape soft lead into piping with his 'dresser', or mallet. Lead will also cover the Little Castle's flat roof, which is intended as an airy place for family and guests to walk while admiring the view or huntsmen in the park below.

Basic ironwork is bought from a local smith in Bolsover at piece-work rates, while a superior smith at Norton Cuckney, six miles away, has the more highly skilled task of creating the door hooks, grates and glazing bars. Sir Charles also has his heart set on a profusion of sparkling windows. As Walter Gedde claims in his book for glaziers, 'cunningly wrought' windows are 'the principal beautie, and countenance of Architecture'.[41] Until recently, glass has been a luxury item, and windows were taken down when a great house was shut up, either to travel to another residence or else to be stored out of the rain.[42] In Sir Charles's youth there was an explosion in the demand for glass as the craze for houses with outsize windows undreamed of in medieval times took off. Smithson is something of an expert in glass production. In 1615, he will himself design a glass-production plant for Sir Percival Willoughby of Wollaton Hall, as part of a plan to develop the local glass-making industry to meet every gentleman's wish for windows. The Willoughby family's famous coal pits, which have provided them with great wealth for a century, are now running out. The glassworks is only one of their many madcap schemes for diversification.

Skilled glassmakers were in short supply in England until the enterprising Frenchman Jean Carré brought a group of them to England in 1567. A colony of French craftsmen developed in Sussex, holding their own religious services and annoying the locals by refusing to reveal the secrets of their glass-making methods.[43] Once the supplies of fuel began to run low in the Weald, the glassmakers moved northwards and congregated in Staffordshire. Here they used coal instead of wood faggots as fuel. Two years from today, in 1615, a proclamation will be issued forbidding the manufacture of glass with wood fuel, ostensibly to preserve supplies of timber, but actually to enrich the powerful group of courtiers who hold the patent for making glass with coal.[44] Such are the potential prizes of court life that William too hopes to win.

William now asks John Smithson to explain the process of making glass. Sand is heated in a furnace until a blob of molten glass can be lifted with the end of a long pipe and blown into a balloon by the glassmaker's strong lungs. The glassmaker blows a long cylinder that he then slices lengthways to create a flat rectangular sheet. This method produces characteristically uneven, green-yellow glass seeded with tiny air bubbles.[45] During the construction of Hardwick Hall ('more glass than wall'), Bess set up her own glass-making plant, but for the Little Castle Smithson plans to commission a glazier to travel over from Mansfield.

In due course, the project will also need bricks to finish off the interior walls.[46] The Cavendishes have scoured the eastern counties of England, where stone is scarce and brick common, for a skilled brickmaker, sending a servant named Edmund 'into norffoke for the brickmen' in 1601.[47] Back in January of this year, a 'brickeman' came from Wollaton to Bolsover to discuss technical matters with Sir Charles.[48] The method is simple, yet involves fine judgement. Clay is dug out of the ground and scattered across fields to be broken up by a winter's frost. In the spring, the pebbles are carefully picked out and the clay mashed and trodden underfoot. Then the brickmen press it into shape using wooden moulds and leave the uncooked bricks to stand in stacks for a month or more. Firing takes place either in a kiln or in a temporary construction called a 'clamp'.[49] Coal, with its steadier heat, is better in the kiln than the traditional fuel of wood. The skill of the brickmen lies in selecting the right kind of clay and in supervising the making and firing of the bricks.[50]

*

Having dealt with the matter of materials, Sir Charles and John Smithson turn with enthusiasm to their great shared love, the sketches showing the next stages of the design. Despite their differing social status, Sir Charles and Smithson are linked by something of the convivial and classless freemasonry of designers working together: enlightened patron and dedicated servant united in their obsessive search for the most ingenious, most convenient, perfect house. As they now study the drawing for the fireplace in the Great Hall, perhaps, or the balustrade that will line the steps to the entrance door, William leans forward with interest, for he has already had plenty of opportunities to form his own views on design.[51]

William has learned much from his grandmother Bess, builder of great houses at Chatsworth, the two Hardwick Halls (the old one and the new one) and Oldcotes. She amassed the money that paid for her projects through a series of extraordinarily canny marriages. In the eighteenth century, Horace Walpole will quip waspishly of this 'costly countess' that

> Four times the nuptial bed she warm'd,
> And ev'ry time so well perform'd,
> That when death spoil'd each Husband's billing,
> He left the Widow ev'ry shilling.[52]

William's grandfather was Bess's second husband, the first Sir William Cavendish, who gained his vast wealth through his work as one of the administrators of Henry VIII's Dissolution of the Monasteries and purchased the estate of Chatsworth in Derbyshire for his wife. His son Charles was born in 1553, the first year of Queen Mary I's reign, and the queen herself became his godmother. Four years later, in 1557, Bess's young family suffered a temporary but severe setback: Sir William died, his reputation irrevocably damaged by the whispered charges that he had fraudulently siphoned off royal revenues. 'I most humbly beseech the Lord to have Mercy and Rid me and his poor Children of our great Misery,' wrote his widow.[53]

Bess, always alert to the changing constellations of power at court, accepted that Mary I's Catholicism was the prevailing religion of the day. Nimble-footed as ever, though, she remained on good terms with the Protestant queen-in-waiting, Mary's half-sister Elizabeth. Cancer of the stomach killed Mary in 1558. On 2nd January 1559, Charles and his brothers had their hair cut in preparation for their attendance at Elizabeth's triumphant coronation two days later.[54] And the court of Elizabeth I would prove to be a rich hunting ground for rewards, royal favour and husbands for Bess. Having already outlived two spouses, she would now marry twice more in quick succession: firstly the elderly and doting Sir William St Loe, and then George Talbot, sixth Earl of Shrewsbury (1528?–90).

In her old age beaky-nosed Bess became a formidable legend, and her Cavendish descendants in later centuries will continue to use their memory of 'the old Countess of Shrewsbury' as a yardstick of awesome power. The former jailer of Elizabeth I's dangerous cousin, Mary, Queen of Scots, Bess was said to 'ruin all persons she had to do with'.[55] With her red hair and whitened, skeletal face she closely resembled the aged Queen Elizabeth. Her fierce independence eventually estranged her both from her fourth and final husband and from her own youngest son Charles. After their marriage, Bess and the irascible George embarked upon a great quarrel that appears to have been a clash between two domineering personalities but that in reality revolved around the distribution of the glittering fortunes won by these two victors of a competitive age. Bess's youngest son now found his loyalties divided. While he owed affection to his mother, his step-brother Gilbert (George Talbot's son) had become his best friend.[56]

Bystanders complained endlessly that 'the wars continue betwixt the Earl of Shrewsbury and the Countess', and that a mysterious episode involving money was at the root of their quarrel.[57] On their reaching the age of twenty-one, Bess's second and third sons William and Charles Cavendish were entitled to some substantial sums of money from their stepfather. The earl had difficulty in honouring this and decided instead to sign a deed making over to William and Charles the lands that Bess had brought to the marriage. George would later bitterly regret, and attempt to revoke, his gift. Most unusually, he signed the deed without witnesses, and later claimed that his signature had been forged.[58] He would die still holding onto the belief that Bess had somehow cheated him; Charles also took his stepfather's part against his own mother.

As well as learning about the rich pickings to be gleaned at court and the pain of quarrels between parents and children, William has also discovered the secret of commissioning the architecture of intimidation from his redoubtable grandmother. After her fight with her husband, she retired to Hardwick to build her palatial New Hall (Plate 5). On a sharp April morning in the year 1600, Bess had received a rare visit from six-year-old William and his little brother. The endless flights of stairs climbing up through the vast cold house to the Great Chamber and their ancient grandmother must have left a strong impression on the two boys.

Yet on the morning of their visit, Bess was in a genial mood. Her household accounts show that she gave 'little Will and Charles Cavendyshe' four angels in money on 15th April, with a further gift to their nurse.[59] (The coin called the angel-noble, with its device of the archangel Michael and the dragon, was worth about eight shillings.) William still remembers the lesson he learned at his grandmother's: that height above the ground is proportional to social status. Her new house's ground floor contained the offices and Great Hall. The first floor contained rooms for Bess: her chamber, the neighbouring chamber of her granddaughter Arbella Stuart (who, through her Scottish father, had a claim on James I's throne) and her business room. The wide staircase from the Great Hall, however, led the most important visitors straight up to the second floor, where they entered some of the grandest rooms in Elizabethan England. Here, a Great Chamber was intended for a visiting Elizabeth I to sit under a cloth of state in order to receive homage from all the nobles of Derbyshire. Adjacent to it were the stupendous Long Gallery and bedchamber. These were rooms only to be used on the most splendid occasions; William's cousin the young Arbella Stuart, for example, was warned not to play on the matting in the Long Gallery because it had to be saved for visiting courtiers. Hardwick Hall's design is intended to intimidate: to separate the servants from the masters, the worthy from the unworthy.

Bess's Hardwick Hall may have been an ambitious statement of power by a semi-royal family, but it was also a story in stone about a remarkable sixteenth-century life. William would have been told that the plasterwork over the fireplaces at Hardwick Old Hall, including gargantuan trees modelled around real tree trunks, reveals the narrative of Bess's stormy relationship with her fourth husband. The title to the source engraving used for one scene explains that it depicts 'Desire' beckoning forth 'Patience' on a triumphal cart. It is clear that Bess, depicting herself as a patient wife, desired to triumph over her cruel husband at last.[60]

This hidden message in Bess's Great Chamber was intended for her family, household and the tenants of her estates who kept the quarrel between Bess and her husband alive throughout the countryside. The clash was between two households, as well as between the blood families of Hardwick and Talbot. Buildings such as Hardwick Hall are not the work of individual architects, dreaming up schemes and executing them exactly according to their wishes. They are the work of households, and as such reflect the passions, factions, quarrels and preoccupations of their creators. Bess's son carried on in the same fashion, and her grandson William will maintain the family tradition.

Bess brought together expert craftsmen for her projects through the recommendation of friends around the country, and aristocratic patrons at home and even abroad also exchange architectural ideas in letters and plans. The slavish following of a plan explains how the 1630s house at St Nicholas's Abbey in Barbados will come to contain fireplaces that are completely unnecessary in that island's climate.[61] Yet these well-born would-be architects, following a serious hobby rather than a profession, are not architects in the later sense of the word. In his *Alvearie or Quadruple Dictionary* (1580), James Baret defines an architect as 'the maister mason, the maister carpenter, or the principall overseer and contriver of any work'. The word 'architect' or 'architector' is still used to describe carpenters or craftsmen – or surveyors like John Smithson – without suggesting a professional role that focuses purely on design.[62]

At the very time that the Little Castle is under construction, the birth of the architectural profession is also taking place. Renaissance ideas, with their emphasis on following the precedents of the ancient Greeks and Romans, are arriving in England. The art of design was gradually metamorphosing into something that could be learnt from books or observation rather than from the accumulated years of practical experience that formed the training of a master mason. In due course, architecture will become a 'liberal art', fit to be practised by gentlemen, while masons will have a lesser status as practitioners of a 'mechanical art'. James Cleland writes in 1607 of the 'principles of *Architecture*: which I think necessary also for a Gentleman to be known'.[63] Many craftsmen acquire books and drawings of the new Renaissance motifs, but lack the learning to read and apply the principles of proportion that the new style requires. This will be the preserve of the 'gentleman architect', with the result that by 1624 the word 'architect' comes to be defined as the person 'whose glory doth more consist, in the

Designment and Idea of the whole Work'.[64] However, in 1613, the new state of affairs has not yet crystallised. Sir Charles and his son are slightly ahead of their time in being passionately interested and involved in architecture.

How would Sir Charles describe his perfect house? Fortunately, he wrote a letter outlining his ideas to his sister at a time when she was contemplating a new house of her own. Sir Charles makes rough sketches of his designs, which are then translated into proper drawings by professionals like John Smithson. In his letter, Sir Charles advises his sister to study his designs, for 'there cannot be a sweeter house'.[65] He is somewhat xenophobic in his architectural tastes, speaking with scorn of a house with a draughty hall and a dining room fit only 'for an Italian gentleman [. . .] their diet being but salads and frogs'.[66] William's father holds this very English opinion of foreign cuisine despite having travelled round Europe in his youth. Yet by now, 1613, Italian designers are even at work in chilly England: only two years ago Costantino de' Servi arrived from the lavish court of the Medici in Florence in order to make 'fountains, summerhouses, galleries and other things' for the royal palace at Richmond.[67] William has already developed important connections at court: he used to share riding lessons with de' Servi's patron, the young Prince Henry, who suffered an untimely death last year.

In fact, Sir Charles's ideal home is rather old-fashioned. Behind his description of suites and galleries glimmers the blueprint of another type of building altogether: a monastery. Many of the grand and sprawling mansions of Sir Charles's youth were converted from the former monasteries that lost their original purpose when Henry VIII expelled the monks and confiscated their land in the early sixteenth century.[68] Sir Charles's dream house has, with its two suites of lodgings for king and queen, a central courtyard like the cloister of a monastery. The plans of many great houses – Audley End, Welbeck Abbey, the Cavendishes' London home Newcastle House, and others – are determined by the remains, and the cloistered court, of medieval monastic houses.

The household required to maintain a house big enough to receive both king and queen is immense, noisy and nosy. Yet scholars like Sir Charles are becoming more familiar with the idealised lives of cultured Roman scholars and writers. It is becoming fashionable to spend time alone, accompanied only by books, absorbing ancient wisdom, as Pliny wrote of doing in his Tuscan or seaside villas. At Burghley House near Stamford, Thomas Cecil, first Earl of Exeter (1542–1622), has a lodge with four towers, rather like Bolsover's Little Castle, to 'retire to out of the dust while his great house was a sweeping'.[69] This is the role – a holiday home, a private and personal place for study – that the Little Castle will perform.

Sir Charles's Little Castle is at its heart a Gothic building. This afternoon in 1613, he and John Smithson visualise it as a neo-medieval masterpiece with split levels, four staircases, fantastic vaulting and fireplaces adapted from continental designs but overlaid with northern Gothic influences. Sir Charles chooses the foreboding, ancient Northumbrian castles of his wife's family and their medieval barony of Ogle as his inspiration. This is not least because the archaic style has become fashionable as a chivalric craze sweeps through the court.

Despite a Cavendish nouveau riche fondness for the antique, James I's court has a mania for chivalry that also helps to explain Bolsover's fanciful, impractical turrets, battlements, lodges, twisting staircases and outsize arrow slits, which make it more like a stage set for a whimsical courtly masque than a defensive fortification or a comfortable country residence. Its fountain, gardens, battlemented walkway and balconies, beneath their veneer of continental sophistication in the form of classical door cases and wall paintings, will invite the visitor to imagine that knights are still bold and that their ladies laughingly retreat beyond every turn of the twisting staircases.

A year ago, the Cavendishes' favourite poet, Ben Jonson, wrote a masque – a courtly entertainment combining words, music and fabulous scenery – entitled *Oberon, the Faery Prince* that illustrates this antiquarian attitude towards architecture. In fact, the design for one of its stunning backdrops, showing Oberon's Palace with its turrets, crossbow slits, cupola and battlements, bears a strong resemblance to the Little Castle. In the ancient days of King Arthur, Jonson claimed, houses were novel, fanciful and heroic:

> There porticoes were built, and seats for knights
> That watched for adventures, days and nights.[70]

The Little Castle, then, takes its cue from medieval castles, but also from the designs for masque sets.

Yet chivalry is gradually going out of fashion, and Bolsover Castle

Inigo Jones's design for 'Oberon's Palace', a piece of scenery for the masque *Oberon, the faery Prince* (1611). This design has much in common with the Cavendishes' Little Castle

will be superseded by the ideas of a new generation even before it is completed. As William sits and listens to his father's conversation with John Smithson, he silently chafes at his elders' obsession with the Gothic.

Just a year before beginning his project at Bolsover, Sir Charles sent William abroad with an architectural expert to learn about the latest classical ideas in architecture. Sir Charles carefully considered but rejected the new classical fashion before beginning work at Bolsover. William, however, clings obstinately to the memory of the architectural ideas he encountered in Italy at such an impressionable age. He already understands that classicism will be the coming court fashion, and knows that his tour of Italy and knowledge of classical architecture will stand him in good stead with the most advanced and cultured circles surrounding the king.

William, born in Yorkshire, bred in Nottinghamshire, will always be happiest at home in the Midlands. His childhood was carefree and lively, with 'a great inclination to the Art of Horsemanship and Weapons'.[71] When he was six, William and his brother were described as 'very proud gentlemen of their new coats [probably the Shrewsbury livery], they continue their wonted health & mirth'.[72] William once blew a legacy on 'a singing-boy for £50, a horse for £50 and a dog for £2'.[73] Sir Charles, instead of condemning this prodigality, said he would have disinherited a son who bought something as unimaginative as land. William 'never shew'd a great inclination' to schoolwork, writing that 'the greatest Captains, were not y^e^ greatest scholars, neither have I known book-worms great statesmen'.[74] Nevertheless, at Michaelmas, 1608, aged nearly fifteen, William went to St John's College, Cambridge, of which his aunt Mary Talbot was a great benefactor. He left four years later without a degree, a circumstance not unusual among young men expected to make their careers in the social and political ferment of the court rather than in the library.

The next stage in any young Cavendish's life lies beyond the sea. William's cousin, another Charles Cavendish, was bitten fatally by the travel bug during his tour of Europe. He took the usual route of travel through France and Italy, but afterwards 'he would go to Babylon, and then his Governor [tutor] would not adventure to go any further with him'.[75] William, too, was sent abroad to learn foreign languages, and as one of the family poets addressed him,

> Then did you practice foils, to tilt and dance,
> For Horsemanship, you went beyond all France.[76]

Studying the art of horsemanship or swordsmanship at one of the great continental academies, or learning the steps danced at the courts of Europe, is an important part of an educational tour. When the courtier Endymion Porter's son visited Madrid, his tutor reported with pride that the king of Spain 'hath given him leave to ride his horses'. Young Porter 'hath also a fencing and dancing' master, the tutor self-righteously considering 'his time and monies well spent'.[77]

Today, on 12th June, 1613, William has only recently returned from northern Italy. He travelled there with the ambassador Sir Henry Wotton on a diplomatic mission to Turin to discuss possible marriages between the English princes (sons of James I) and the daughters of the Duke of Savoy.

Wotton was the perfect chaperone. He is familiar with Italy, has secretly entered Catholic Rome (disguised in a blue hat) and will soon write one of the most important English books on building: *The Elements of Architecture; collected by Henry Wotton, Knight, from the best authors and examples* (London, 1624). It was this trip that confirmed for William his lifelong love for horsemanship and swordsmanship. Wotton's party had in its care 'ten ambling horses sumptuously caparisoned' and 'a jewelled sword', gifts from James I to the Duke of Savoy.[78] The records of the trip also hint at picture purchases in Milan, visits to Venice and masques at the court of Savoy. For the rest of his life, William will remember the courtly entertainments of Italy with admiration, recommending that when one prepares 'a maske for twelve tide, – Italians makes ye scenes best'.[79]

The party departed on 18th March, 1612, crossed the English Channel to Boulogne, and took three weeks to reach Lyons in the centre of France.[80] They were briefly delayed at the town of Troyes because William was ill, an indisposition caused 'first by the extre[me of cold] and wind, and then of heats'.[81] At Lyons there was another delay because one of the 'ambling horses' sliced its foot on a vine-keeper's pruning blade. The royal equerry, Sir Peter Saltonstall, whose job it had been to look after the gift horses, was so mortified that he replaced the king's horse with a fine animal of his own. Planning their crossing of the Alps, Wotton wrote that his 'whole troop together, when we shall pass the mountains, will be about fifty horse'.[82]

By May, 1612, William's party had arrived in Turin, and English reporters observed that their 'coming over the mountains hath already filled Italy with discourses of ye marriages of our Princes'.[83] Wotton, William and the princesses of Savoy watched a great jousting match in the city's main square. The rapport between the skilful and diplomatic Wotton and the Duke grew so swiftly that Wotton was treated with a flattering intimacy. 'He is entertained by the Duke at jousts, tourneys, dances, the chase, but all without any pomp of liveries and quite ordinary,' reported one observer. 'Neither his Highness nor the Princes treated him in any way out of the ordinary; indeed I am told in walking down the gallery the Duke took the right hand side of the Ambassador.'[84] The right-hand side is always the more honourable position when two people walk or sit together, and by the rules of formal behaviour it should have been accorded to Wotton as the representative of James I. This was studied informality, the subtle manipulation of social rules that constitutes the continental art of *cortesia*, or graceful behaviour. Wotton noted that the courteous Marquis di Lanz 'be so popular that in the street he will put off his hat to the meanest artisans, and even to beggars (as we thrice noted), yet all men agree that he is otherwise not very cheap of his person'.[85] In later life William, too, will practise this art of *cortesia*: 'to the meanest person he'll put off his Hat, and suffer everyone to speak to him'.[86]

The route home was to be via Germany, to please William and the other 'gentlemen of [Wotton's] suite who have come out solely to see the world'.[87] Soon they were in Milan buying 'the curiosities of that place', and by 14th July they were at Cologne travelling homeward.[88] William returned to England with a supremely well-chosen parting gift from the Duke of Savoy: the aspiring horseman was given 'a Saddle very richly embroidered' and his very first Spanish horse.[89]

What did William learn from his mentor as they rode together through the fields and cities of northern Italy? Sir Henry Wotton is one of the few people in Britain who fully understand classical architecture, and years later a first edition of his architectural treatise will be found in the library at Welbeck.[90] In Italy, from the fifteenth century onwards, houses and churches have been built in the guise of the temples and palaces of the ancient Romans. The northern Italian designer Andrea Palladio (1508–80) did more than anyone else to bring the architecture of antiquity back to life, with his designs for villas scattered across northern Italy and especially in the Veneto. The most famous of all Palladio's houses is the Villa Rotonda, which is perfectly symmetrical, with columned entrances under triangular pediments facing in all four directions across the countryside. It will become one of the most illustrious ancestors of the Palladian movement that dominated country-house design in England for two hundred years, from the late seventeenth century onwards. Those interested in architecture purchase Palladio's celebrated illustrated publications, while those rich enough and keen enough, like William's cousin by marriage Thomas Howard, Earl of Arundel (1585–1646), scour northern Italy to buy genuine drawings in the master's hand.

Palladio's success lay not only in his careful observation and emulation of ancient temples but also in his unravelling of the esoteric mysteries of proportion. Wotton's advice, based both on his reading of modern authors such as Palladio, ancient Roman writers such as

Vitruvius and his observation of Italian architecture, is that well-designed buildings 'ravish the Beholder, (and he knows not how) by a secret Harmony in the Proportions'. This secret could nevertheless be learned by carefully measuring, recording and analysing the dimensions of each part of a classical building and establishing the proportional relationship between the height and width of a window or door, or between the areas assigned to blank wall and an opening within it. Classicism, or the revival of the styles of the ancient world, is far from unknown in England, but buildings display classical columns or pedi-

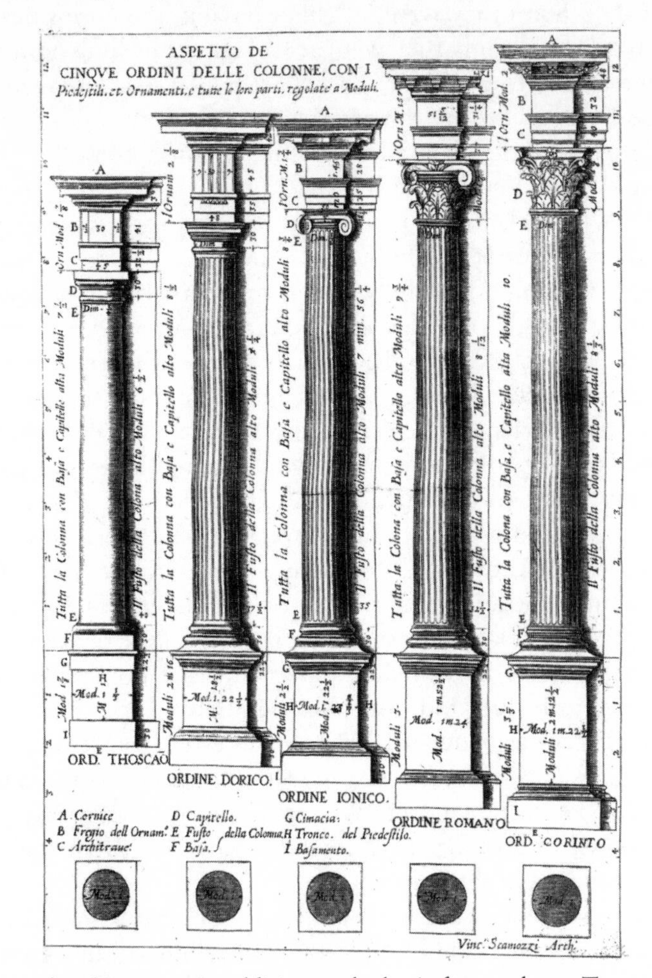


The orders of architecture. In addition to the basic four orders – Tuscan, Doric, Ionic and Corinthian – there is here a fifth, composite order, the 'Roman'

ments as token gestures rather than adopting the overall programme of rhythm and wall-to-window proportion that the architects of the Italian Renaissance understood.

In a classical building, hierarchy is of the utmost importance, and the purpose and status of a building will determine the type of decoration to be applied. A facade requires an appropriate classical pillar or 'order' selected from the standard repertoire. James Cleland considered that well-educated young gentlemen should be able 'to tell what is [. . .] the *Tuscan*, *Doric*, *Ionic*, *Corinthian*, and *composed order*, like a *Surveyer*'.[91] In his book, Wotton explains the ranking, use and personalities of the classical orders: the most basic is the Tuscan order, 'a plain, massy, rural Pillar'; then comes the grave and simple Doric order, followed by the more elegant Ionic order representing 'a kind of Feminine slenderness'. Finally comes the elaborate Corinthian order, 'lasciviously decked like a Courtesan'.

Wotton's most famous and ringing pronouncement is his 'fundamental Maxim, that the Images of all things are latent in Numbers', and measurement determines 'the comeliest Proportion, between breadths and heights, Reducing Symmetry to Symphony'.[92] He hates the pointed arches loved by Sir Charles, considering that they 'ought to be exiled from judicious eyes [. . .] amongst other Reliques of that barbarous Age'.[93] At first sight, Wotton's views appear to have been astonishingly uninfluential at Bolsover. Yet close analysis uncovers an intriguing aspect of the building. Looking at Smithson's plan of the cellars, the 'barbarous' vaulted units themselves can be seen as parts of a modular system of construction, squares being added together to make a larger square.[94] There are hidden harmonies in the Little Castle that are not readily detected behind its facade of British chivalry. In Smithson's basement plan, symmetry does become symphony.

This, however, is too subtle for William. If he had his way, the Little Castle would be more classical, less Gothic. In due course, when he takes control of the project after his father's death, William will send John Smithson to London to find ideas for classical decoration – doorcases, statues, paintings – to veneer the Gothic bones of Sir Charles's building.

In London, Inigo Jones (1573–1652) is the greatest proponent of the new classical style, and he introduces a revolution in English architecture with his work for James I. The Banqueting House, for masques

Inigo Jones's Banqueting House in Whitehall

and for receiving important visitors at the palace of Whitehall, will be his best-known work. This is a building more like those designed by Palladio in northern Italy than anything else to be seen in England.

Yet there are significant obstacles to overcome if William wishes the Cavendish household to reproduce accurately the classicism of Palladio and Inigo Jones. In the later textbooks on architectural history, the Cavendish houses fall within the category of classicism named 'artisan mannerist'. The classical features seen in seventeenth-century England would be described as 'mannerist' – the tortured, over-complicated style of the later High Renaissance – if seen in Italy. The contemporary Italian art historian Vasari claimed that the architects of the later Renaissance wilfully broke 'the rules' of fifteenth-century Renaissance classicism in a 'mannered' or knowing fashion. The English, the argument goes, did not know 'the rules' and therefore broke them through ignorance; this is borne out by the letter-writer John Chamberlain, who referred to a house at Greenwich designed for the queen not as a revolutionary classical building, but simply as yet another in a string of novelties, 'some curious devise of Inigo Jones'.[95] During a visit to London, John Smithson draws a gateway designed by Inigo Jones at Arundel House. Yet, untrained in classical architecture, he fails to measure it or to capture its proportions.[96] Smithson simply makes a

A design for a gateway at Arundel House by Inigo Jones (left), contrasted with John Smithson's drawing of the finished work (right)

crude, unscaled representation of its component parts, as a child might.

The term 'artisan mannerist' recognises that the Cavendish artisans or masons working for William in the Midlands are attempting to recreate the mannerist styles of the High Renaissance. But it also suggests that the household is capable of producing only an inferior, substandard version of Italian originals: intriguing, certainly, but slightly botched, imperfect, flawed. This is unfair.

It is tempting to assume that styles in architecture follow each other in a series of waves, the Gothic being replaced by the early classical, the classical being replaced by the mannerist, with William as the harbinger of a total sea change. This is too simplistic, in fact, for architectural styles do not creep across continents like sharply defined weather fronts: books or travellers, for example, may leapfrog ideas from France to northern Scotland before they reach England, or differing styles may coexist. While classicism is slow in seeping into the consciousness of English designers, their native heritage is still lively in their memories. What Sir Henry Wotton described as '*medley* and *motley* Designs, confined only to the *Ornament* of *Friezes*, and Borders, their properest place', will not be forgotten overnight.[97] Grotesque ornament – strange foliage, faces and figures – continues to appear in seventeenth-century houses, especially around the edges of doors or as borders to classical decoration. Viewers can almost *hear* this decoration coming alive as 'a cat-call from the back': the visual equivalent of the derisive hoots made by illiterate masons who cannot afford to travel and who cannot read the books brought from Italy.[98]

In fact, Gothic, phantasmagorical British architecture continues alongside the new minimalism of the Italian Renaissance, and the designs that John Smithson spreads across the table in June, 1613, skilfully capture elements of both styles. Both Smithson and William can agree that there must be a tension between old and new in all the houses the Cavendishes build. Not one of them is built on a virgin site, and in each case the survival of fabric from a medieval castle, nunnery or abbey makes a vital contribution.

Indeed, Smithson's masterpiece at Bolsover will strike contemporaries as neither purely classical nor purely chivalric. Discovery, wonder and amazement are key words used to praise architecture in the seventeenth century.[99] Although they lie far distant from the court style propagated by Inigo Jones, Bolsover Castle and the other Cavendish houses are born of creativity rather than misunderstanding; they are magical rather than mechanical copies. One visitor to these northern palaces will describe them as 'More extraordinary, than are to be seen in Europe.'[100] An absolutely unique building is taking shape on the Bolsover hilltop in June, 1613.

Sir Charles is more than satisfied with the work. As the afternoon wears away, he arranges for Smithson to receive a present of three shillings in addition to his expenses, which will be dutifully recorded in the household accounts. At the close of the day, the labourers collect their money and go for their beer. William and his father ride home to Welbeck Abbey, having experienced an almost perfect afternoon together, and Smithson returns to Kirkby.

Twenty-one years from today, Charles I and his queen Henrietta Maria will visit Bolsover Castle for the performance of a masque. In the tail end of the same year, 1634, John Smithson's life will draw to a close: he makes his will in November and dies in December. It seems that he has nothing left to live for after the royal visit sets the seal of approbation on the completion of his masterpiece, the Little Castle at Bolsover.

# 3 – *In a Closet*

WELBECK ABBEY, 9TH JULY, 1625

It is 9th July, 1625, and William is now master of the household. While his young wife and baby daughter are in residence at Welbeck Abbey today, William himself is in plague-stricken London. He has spent the years since his father's death in 1617 making a name for himself at court. His marriage to Elizabeth, a great heiress from Staffordshire, took place the year after his father's death. In 1619, he hosted the long-anticipated royal visit to Welbeck, has subsequently spent part of each summer attending the old king, James I, and is today in attendance on the new king of three months, Charles I. Now thirty-one, William feels that the time is ripe for his diligence to be rewarded with a responsible job, but, as yet, the elusive honours and appointments he hopes for have failed to come his way. With William spending the summer seeking his fortune, there are fewer servants in residence at Welbeck and the household revolves in its accustomed lazy pattern around his wife and child.

In a few moments, however, the sleepy, relaxed atmosphere of the household will be shattered. Exciting news is about to arrive, as a messenger bearing a letter from William to Elizabeth is making his way towards the house at the end of his long journey from London.

Only news of the very highest importance warrants a letter delivered door-to-door by a Cavendish servant. 'If there be any matter of moment you shall be sure to hear it speedily,' he warns Elizabeth on one occasion, 'otherwise content your self with carriers & so will I.'[1] The regular carrier service between London and Nottinghamshire takes post only as far as Mansfield, the nearby market town,[2] but today a Cavendish horseman is bringing this letter directly to Welbeck.

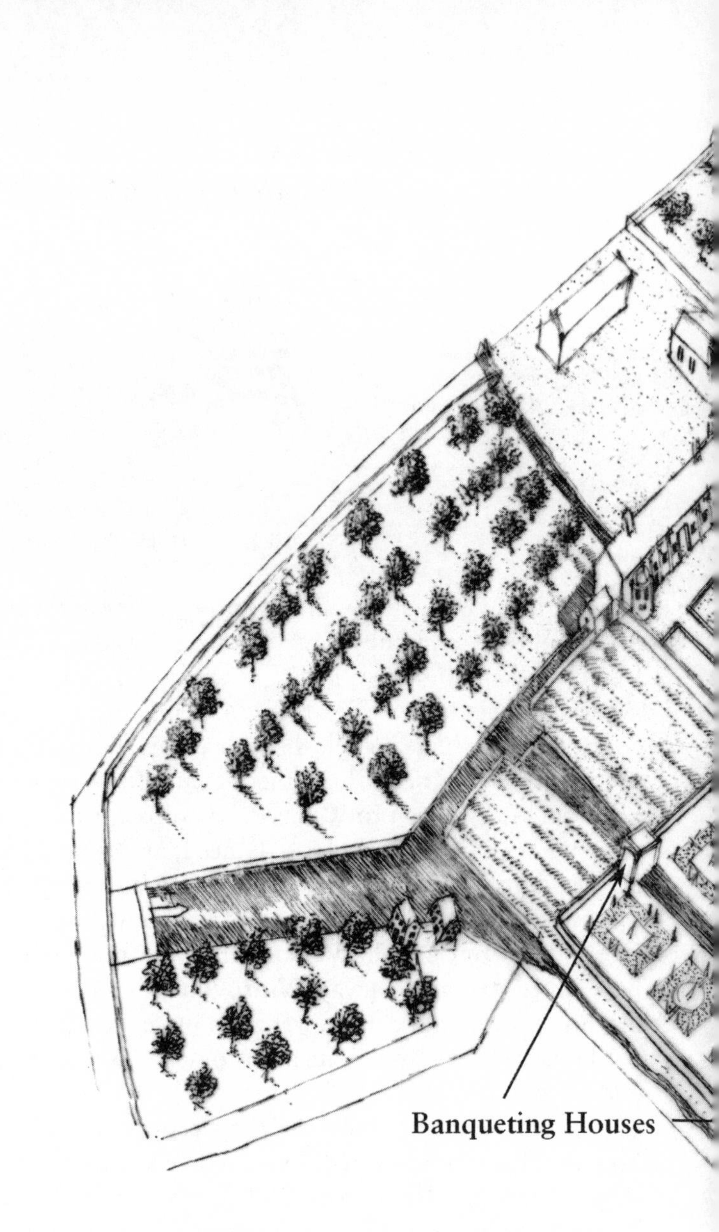


A bird's-eye view of Welbeck as it is in 1625

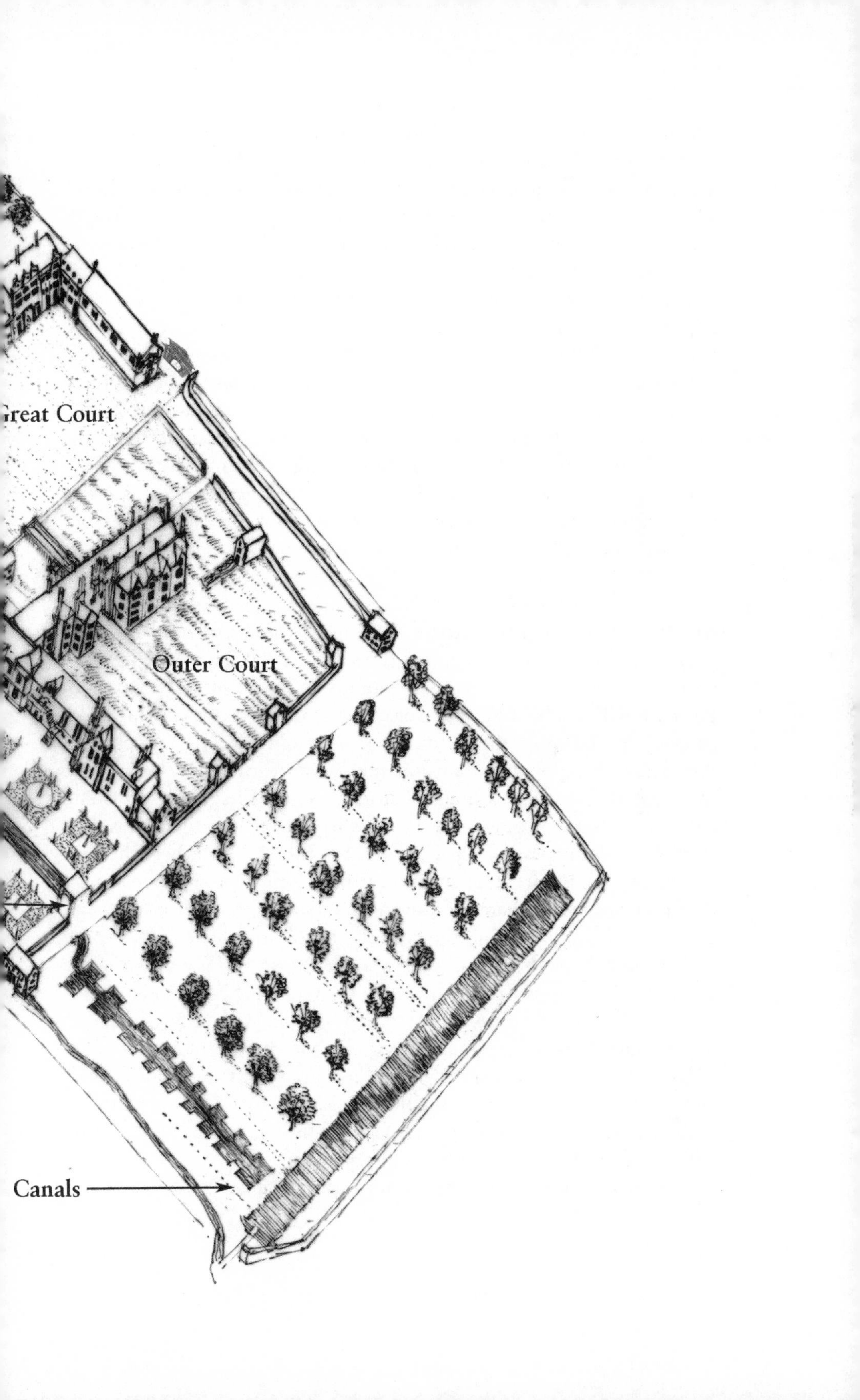

reat Court
Outer Court
Canals

When William sends his precious *manège* horses down from Welbeck to perform in London, they take nine days over the journey, jogging along at a comfortable pace to ensure that they arrive in fine condition. The journey by coach, an increasingly fashionable means of travel for the nobility, is generally completed in four days. But this messenger, on horseback, probably has instructions to do it more quickly.

Towards midday on 9th July, the tired horseman carrying the letter approaches Welbeck Abbey through the low hills of Sherwood Forest, his route winding through woods of oak, birch and hazel. Bracken carpets the forest floor, its strongest stems sometimes shooting eleven feet above the ground. At this time of year, the squealing swifts make the forest their home, as do the golden plovers often seen on the Cavendishes' dinner table. Tonight the woods will ring with the dissonant, two-note call of the nightjar and perhaps the melodious song of a late nightingale.[3] Among the summer bracken underfoot grow bilberries, 'wont to be an extraordinary great profit and pleasure to poor people'.[4]

The word 'forest' does not necessarily mean a piece of impenetrable woodland but rather an area of land under the jurisdiction of forest law, with its restrictions on hunting and cultivation. However, the oaks in this part of the forest are justly famous: in later times, the Dukes of Portland will be able to drive their coaches and horses right through a gateway penetrating the trunk of a vast old oak in the park at Welbeck.[5] The sprawling mansion, now coming into view, looks more like a small town than a house. Before he sights the gabled roofs and glinting mullioned windows of the main house, the horseman must first skirt the outlying parts of the complex: the colt stables, where the spirited young horses are kept separate from the fillies and brood mares; the bowling green, where the Cavendishes entertain other noble families with evening play; and the liquorice yard. Today the colts are out in their field, for in fine weather they are let loose 'to *Play,* and *Rejoyce* themselves' and to eat their fill 'where the Grass is Short, and Sweet'.[6] The roofline of the house is ornate with chimneys, and flags fly from the banqueting houses in the garden. The horseman now passes under a gateway through the stable range and arrives in the house's wide Great Court, or piazza. He wearily swings his leg over the high hard lip at the back of his deep leather saddle, and stationary at last, finds himself surrounded by the smell of hot horse.

The Great Court is bounded to its west by the stable range, which includes the Great Stable for the stallions of *manège*, accommodation for their grooms, attics full of grain and the slaughterhouse. To the north is William's enormous, newly built, barn-like Riding House, with its large windows set high up to prevent the horses being ridden within its walls from being distracted by glimpses of the outside world. To the east is the long main range of the house, and to the south the state suite and the garden wall. The Great Court is a focus for the household's busy outdoor life and many people are employed at tasks in and around the stables; the messenger's arrival causes an anticipatory stir among them. As the horseman dismounts, he may well see the Master of the Horse or grooms leading the stallions back from the Great Court into the Great Stable. This court is a place for coming and going, but it is also used as an outdoor *manège*, a word that is used in continental Europe to describe both the art of horsemanship and the place where it is practised. The English have given it the prosaic name of the 'mannage', or else the 'riding place'. On a summer's day like this, the horses' morning exercise will take place outdoors.

When William Cavendish is at home, he oversees the morning's

The Riding House at Welbeck designed by John Smithson. The smaller building to the left contains the lodging of the Master of the Horse

training personally. He stands, or sometimes even sits in an upholstered chair, in the middle of the floor of the *manège*, whip in hand, with horses and servants circling round him. Today, in his absence, William's Master of the Horse, Captain Mazine, is in charge.[7] John Mazine has been enticed to Nottinghamshire from France, home of Europe's finest horsemen, by the promise of fine horses and excellent training facilities. Here at Welbeck the indoor Riding House, with its soft but firm floor – constructed from John Smithson's designs in 1623 – is one of the best in the country. It measures 40 by 120 feet, and Captain Mazine's own lodging is immediately and conveniently adjacent to it. Horsemen need to cultivate an almost spiritual affinity with their animals: when William is at home, his horses 'rejoice whensoever he [comes] into the Stables, by their trampling action, and the noise they [make]'.[8]

Today Mazine is dressed as usual in thigh-length boots with high wedge-shaped heels and sharp star-shaped spurs buckled onto them. William counsels the use of 'very Sharp *Spurrs*' that a horse 'may Feel them to the Purpose, so that Blood may follow; for otherwise it is not a *Correction*'.[9] Mazine's short and functional jerkin is a dark red, the floppy collar of his shirt beneath it is white, and his trousers dark green: his master insists on clothing which is 'not troublesome and uneasy' for the activities of the *manège*.[10] Mazine lifts his heavily gloved hand to raise his plumed hat to the new arrival, allowing his shoulder-length wavy hair to spill out from beneath it. He is still sweating and breathless after his recent exertions on horseback.

Behind him stand tall posts, each topped by a knob and set deep into the sandy surface of the Great Court. A post is used as a point of reference when training the horse in circles, and in other exercises it is used to prevent the horse from moving forward. A morning's training consists of this basic exercise at the pole followed by the gallop or canter, then the more advanced manoeuvres, such as the *terra a terra* and *curvets*. For a few of the most highly skilled and valuable horses, the session concludes with the great leaps, such as the *balottades* and *caprioles*.[11]

Acknowledging Captain Mazine, the messenger with his valuable packet walks bow-legged up to the gatehouse that guards the inner garden and the flight of steps leading up to the first-floor door to the house's Great Hall. Two stern towers and a stout gate frown down upon him, and now the porter pokes his head out of his lodge with a challenge. The porter spends all his time in his gatehouse and even sleeps there to deal with nocturnal arrivals. Only those whose names are on the approved list are allowed to cross the garden court and ascend to the front door. In another of his frequent verses capturing household life, William sums up the porter's job description and mentions his wish that his porter, a rather unsavoury character, should stay out of the house:

> to clear the Gates make good your tower
> To see your fellows Lodged, keep decent hour
> To Lock out beggars all early or late
> But then your self you may lock out of Gate.[12]

The porters themselves are on the periphery of any household and often dice with the danger of deviating from its rules. A list of regulations for the household of an Elizabethan earl instructs that the chief officer of the household must frequently 'go unto the Porters Lodge, to see it be not the place for the receipt of the unthrifts of the house, nor the harbour of drinking companions'.[13] Today the porter is awake and sober, and recognises a Cavendish servant: his badge and livery cloak, if not his face, are immediately identifiable. He is given leave to cross the inner garden court and to climb the steps.

The horseman's journey is very nearly over. Perhaps he pauses for a moment under the newly built porch to savour the sensation. This is also a recent design of John Smithson's, tacked onto the ancient abbey and topped with an elaborate balustrade. Amazingly, this porch will be dismantled more than a hundred years later and re-erected three miles away against the door of a lesser manor house in the village of Whitwell. It will remain there for future generations to see as a tiny token of the Smithsons' marvellous seventeenth-century designs created for Welbeck.

Stepping into the shadows behind the heavy cream-painted door (decorated with its complicated strapwork pattern in wood and embellished with numerous iron studs), the tired messenger blinks in the sudden darkness of the passage lined in panelled wood that now stretches away before him.[14] He is in the service area known as the screens passage; to his right a carved wooden screen shields his view of the Great Hall itself. Bread, beer and dishes of food make their frequent one-way journeys across this passage, from kitchens to Great Hall; during holiday seasons it also forms the backstage area for dramatic performances taking place in the Hall itself. Three doorways in the screen open into the brighter expanse of the Great Hall with its vast windows. The visitor must now select one of them, turning right to see the long tables and the dais at the Hall's far end, and inhaling the Hall's scent of smoke, stew and dogs.

The Great Hall, the heart of the household, is rarely empty, and now the Usher of the Hall comes forward. Those who have already finished their morning's duties may be sitting on the benches and playing at dice to while away the time until the midday dinner. They call out to the messenger to find out the news from London, but he knows better than to usurp his mistress's prerogative of informing the household of the information he carries. The usher's job is to maintain order in the Great Hall and to keep an eye on the alms tub standing there ready to receive coins from generous members of the household. William claims, in one of his poems, that this provides any usher who is less than honest with frequent opportunity to provide his 'Boye or hoore' with gifts.[15] Behind the usher, preparations are under way for the midday meal, the pantler laying the greasy, well-used tables and his colleague the butler dispensing ale.

The household orders of Sir Francis Willoughby, master of nearby Wollaton Hall, note that the butler's role has already expanded beyond simply serving the beer: he must additionally see that 'no filching of bread or beer be suffer'd', and that 'no breakfast, afternoon meats, nor hancks [snacks?] after supper be had or made'.[16] In due course, the butler in future households will become an all-round factotum. Now, however, he is setting out tankards on the tables. John Hyberson, the butler at Welbeck, has the virtue of generosity – a quality much admired in a butler by the other servants – and is a kind benefactor to local paupers; his tight-handed successor, Ranndulph Alexander, will not be remembered in the same favourable light.[17] While beer is safer to drink than water, excessive consumption of alcohol is an occupational hazard for butlers. The Tudor writer on health Andrew Boorde lists a few straightforward solutions to drunkenness: 'if anye man do perceyve that he is dronke, let hym take a vomite with water and oyle, or with a fether, or a rosemary braunche, or els with his finger, or els let hym go to his bed to slepe'.[18] According to William Cavendish, 'All Butlers Grumble', and the reason is their tendency to over-indulge: 'They're seldom dry, yet still they make them drink.'[19] The beer drunk at Welbeck is unique to the household, as each brewhouse has its own special methods. Every year sees some forty brewings at Welbeck and the production of different grades of beer that range from the 'strong beer' drunk by William himself to the 'small beer' drunk by lower servants and children; most alcoholic of all is the 'October ale' brewed with the new season's malt that is saved for celebrations.[20] William considers that his brewer habitually cheats him ('sure you're a knave') by purloining the ingredients intended for use in the brewhouse; its products are 'so thin, & naughty [. . .] you steal the malt, and we the water drink'.[21]

Meanwhile, the pantler, in charge of the bread supply, fetches loaves from the pantry. He places fine white 'manchet' bread (sometimes made richer with eggs or butter) on the upper table, and 'cheat' or brown bread on the lower tables. A fifteenth-century book of manners has some words of advice for a pantler: 'look that your napery be sweet and clean, and that your table-cloth, towel and napkin be folded exactly, your table-knives brightly polished, and your spoon fair washed'.[22] William insists upon a neat and well-dressed dinner table, and praises his pantler's precision:

The Pantler Is neat
To set his fine cheat
In Napkins that is nipped so finely
His spoons, knife, & fork
wine Bottles with Cork
Cooled in Snow that drinks so divinely.[23]

Another of William's poems captures the smoky, noisy, hearty atmosphere of the Great Hall when, as now, the household gathers for dinner. There are loud complaints if the meat is burned:

The Smoking Boiled Beef,
Is a Cosening [fraudulent] Thief
For it steals the best stomach away
And leaves better meat
For others to eat
In the Hall the very same day.

On most occasions, though, the household happily devours an old-fashioned side or 'chine' of beef – upon 'The Bold Lustie Chine, A dosen may Dine' – and there is even food left over at the end of the lavish meal. The generosity of the servings at Welbeck means that the servant clearing the tables staggers under the weight of the 'voider dish'.

This is the vessel used to 'void' the table, or in other words, to gather from discarded trenchers the leftovers intended for animals or paupers.

The serving men and scullions have prior warning of the arrival of the kitchen's best offerings and use their inside knowledge to grab hot venison pasties as they come out of the kitchen or else to treat their friends to excessive, and illicit, beer:

> The Scullions are nasty
> Not the Venison pasty!
> That's neat & Comes up Piping Hot
> Then Eat It In Haste
> with Crust of pufte Paste
> And ply thy friends still with the Pot.[24]

Like the porter, the Usher of the Hall now recognises the messenger who has carried William's letter from London to Welbeck, relieves him of his burden and calls for a footman or page. We don't know the footmen's names at Welbeck, but in the establishment of William's aunt Mary Talbot messages are run either by the two well-born pageboys (Mr ffoxe and Mr Urney) or by the three footmen (William Heast, Wylliam Pringle and 'Richard', so low-born that his second name has been forgotten). The Cavendish footmen have silver-topped staffs for clearing their master's way through a crowd when passing along the city streets.[25] There's an important social distinction between the well-born pages, placed in a grand household to learn how to emulate their betters, and footmen, whose position is merely menial. William's son Henry will one day offer a place in his household to a Northumbrian relative, 'if Mr Ogle is willing to have his son bred up to my Butler and to go of messages here in ye Town (not to be foot boy God forbid)'.[26]

In many great households, there is a further, more specialised breed of manservant: the running footman whose job it is to deliver urgent messages or to run before his master's coach on journeys. He helps out if the coach becomes stuck in mud, but more importantly, his presence lets the world know that a personage of significance is approaching. A running footman does not wear a coat but only a doublet, breeches and stockings, made in white material for high visibility on the roads. As a physical specimen, he will always be superior to 'any cross gartered gentleman-usher'. He 'lives more by his owne heat than the warmth of cloathes: and the waiting-woman hath the greatest fancy to him when he is in his close trouses'.[27]

Whether a page or a footman does the job, the valuable packet containing the letter passes from hand to hand, and is now taken up the great stone staircase of the house and along further passages. We are still in the old part of the building that was once an abbey, with its smaller rooms and gabled roofs. It was formerly the abbot's lodging, and now contains the family bedchambers. The servant scrapes his fingernails across the panel of a low door; it is rude to knock at the door of a bedchamber and footmen are trained 'only to scratch'.[28] One of Elizabeth's waiting gentlewomen opens it. This is her favourite, Bess Moken, the female servant to whom Elizabeth will leave the biggest legacy in her will. Behind her the footman now glimpses a rich bedchamber, similar to the one where William's father lay dying in 1617. Elizabeth is nowhere to be seen. The footman hands over the letter and takes his leave of the world of the women, while Bess rustles across the rush matting to another door partially concealed behind a looped-back tapestry. This leads to the most private and exclusive room of the house: my lady's closet.

Here, at last, we find tiny, black-haired Elizabeth, almost as small as a doll, seated in her red, richly upholstered chair with its crossed legs, drawn up to a table covered with a rich Turkish carpet.[29] Prayer books, writing paper and Dutch quills are scattered about her. Jewels on her long white fingers flash as she seizes the letter, checks the seal and cracks through the wax imprinted with her husband's ring (Plate 6).

Daniel Mytens, the king's favoured painter, completed his great portrait of Elizabeth a year before this day.[30] She is twenty-five or twenty-six years old, slight, pale-skinned and pretty, and has profuse dark hair that she wears brushed straight back from her narrow white forehead. For her portrait she dressed in her best, and many of these same items of finery must be stored in the trunks and cupboards around her in the bedchamber and closet. Her ostrich-feather fan, the pendant pearl that hung from her ear, the jewelled heart with a crown of pearls that fastened her long lovelock, the jewelled chain that encircled her shoulders, the plain gold ring worn on her left hand and her double bracelet of pearls will all be somewhere near to hand, perhaps in a barrel-lidded jewel box. Elizabeth considers her string of pearls to be distressingly short: when her mother-in-law dies, she will inherit two hundred pounds 'to be bestowed in Pearl to enlarge her chain'.[31] On a quiet day like today, she is unlikely to be weighed down with jewels but may instead be wearing a pair of delicate gauze bracelets embroidered with flowers and scrolls. Instead of thread, the embroiderer used soft brown hair plucked from the head of Elizabeth's mother.[32] Elizabeth also possesses a red-enamel heart-shaped earring, from which swings a tassel of her husband's hair (Plates 7 and 8).[33]

Despite the affectionate relationship that has developed between William and his wife over the last seven years, this was initially no love match but the calculated merger of the interests of two great landed families. Elizabeth's father William Bassett was a soldier and administrator, and sheriff of the counties of both Staffordshire and Derbyshire, and Elizabeth was his only child. While she has always been richly dressed and housed, her life has long been controlled and directed by powerful figures outside her family who seek to make money from her. When her father died only two years after her birth, Elizabeth became a ward of court. The job of looking after a great heiress in the seventeenth century could be bought and sold, and she was treated as a flesh-and-blood form of investment.

The Court of Wards, by 1625 staffed by corrupt courtiers, had its origins in medieval times, when each landowner in the country had to provide the king with knights in times of war. If a squire died leaving only a baby heir, the job of raising fighting men still had to be completed. An underage landowner would become a ward of the court, and the Office of Wards would administer his estate until he reached his majority. Even though the days of mounted knights are long past, the Court of Wards still retains its privileges; Henry VIII had even strengthened them as a profitable source of income for the Crown.[34] The court also takes over an estate in the case of its owner's lunacy.[35]

By the seventeenth century, it is common for those appointed by the court to administer an estate under the laws of wardship to bleed it dry, and the privilege can be bought and sold. Elizabeth's problems were caused by one John Baxter, formerly her father's solicitor. Baxter had discovered that historically the Bassetts held their land 'of the crown', with the accompanying obligation to provide knights, although this had long been forgotten. Baxter took this explosive piece of information to Robert Cecil, Master of the Court of Wards, who was therefore entitled to sell the young Elizabeth's wardship.[36]

Cecil required money for his extravagant building project at Hatfield House, and rarely passed up an opportunity for embezzlement. He made plans for the newly discovered wardship of Elizabeth Bassett to fall into his own possession, via a circuitous and supposedly untraceable route involving his friend Lord Cobham and then Sir Walter Raleigh. Elizabeth's mother Judith protested at this turn of events. She was granted 'custody of the body' of her daughter, but in return she had to compensate Raleigh with an annual payment of £40 until Elizabeth was ten years old, when the yearly figure would rise to 100 marks (£66. 3s. 4d.).[37]

Raleigh intended to arrange a marriage between Elizabeth, a notably wealthy heiress, and his son. But the younger Raleigh was killed fighting the Spanish, and Raleigh himself was imprisoned in the Tower of London on a charge of treason. Yet for Elizabeth things went from bad to worse. In 1613, she was married off instead to Henry Howard, the drunken and violent third son of the corrupt Earl of Suffolk. She was aged only thirteen or fourteen, and gave birth to a stillborn child a year later.

Fortunately, after only a couple of years, Howard died while indulging himself – 'suddainly at table'.[38] Young and beautiful, with an infant daughter and a huge estate in the Midlands, Elizabeth became one of the most desirable prizes in the Jacobean marriage market. She was as lucky in her second marriage as she had been unlucky in her first, for she found a man who would grow to love her. In October 1618, after months of negotiation, William Cavendish won the hand of his 'Sweete Harte' and installed her in Welbeck Abbey as his wife.

What is this curiously ornate little room in which we find ourselves with Elizabeth? Closets are the smallest, yet the richest, rooms in a seventeenth-century great house. Once noble and significant spaces, closets will all but die out in Britain. However, they will survive on the other side of the Atlantic, and American clothes and belongings are stored in closets into modern times. The closet is the ancestor of the study, and is perhaps the only place where Elizabeth can expect to find solitude.[39] Our visit to Elizabeth on 9th July, 1625, is for the purpose of seeing her closet, but also for the rare chance of catching her alone.

The walls of the room itself are richly decorated. At Bolsover Castle, one of the three closets is panelled with green-painted wood. Another is decorated with lacquered panels showing Chinese scenes; both have ceilings and friezes painted with a riotous profusion of classical and Christian figures, and elaborate marble corner fireplaces. The third, floored and vaulted in black and white Italian marble, contains semi-

John Smithson's design for a marble closet at Bolsover Castle. Note the little fireplace decorated with coloured marbles, and the taffeta hangings

circular pictures showing the Virtues personified as women, and its walls are generously hung with red cloth against green panels.

Elizabeth's closet at Welbeck, similarly colourful, contains a table, chair and writing equipment, and she will have a book or two to hand, with the Cavendish stag's head glinting in gold from its finely tooled bindings and the musty scents of leather and paper contributing to the closet's unique smell. Although there is a library elsewhere at Welbeck, highly valued and personal books remain in the closets, which are places favoured for reading.

A young lady shown in one of the wall paintings at Bolsover Castle sits at a table something like the one at which Elizabeth sits in her closet: it is spread with a green velvet cloth, with an astrological globe showing the heavens standing on one side and several books, their pages tied together with ribbons, lying near by (Plate 10). Rather than facing outwards, Elizabeth's books are shelved with their spines to the wall in order to protect their bindings.[40] Some closets contain special cupboards or presses for papers: Robert Smythson, full of good practical ideas as usual, designed an ingenious closet with a wall completely fitted out with shelves and compartments ranged from floor to ceiling.[41] William's brother Charles is a notable collector of books, especially on the subject of mathematics, but his collection comes to a sorry end: he 'collected in Italy, France, &c, with no small charge, as many Manuscript Mathematical books as filled a Hogshead, which he intended to have printed'; yet the collection is sold, by mistake, 'to the past-board makers for Waste-paper'.[42]

As well as her jewels and books, and a musical instrument described as a 'double Sagbutt in a case', Elizabeth is surrounded by a plethora of other rich and rare objects.[43] Closets had originally been identical to oratories, places used for prayer as much as writing. Their character as private chapels has been eroded with the passage of time and replaced with the idea of a room for solitary study and the assembly of precious objects. In the seventeenth century, closets begin to become mini-museums, crammed with rarities and art objects as well as books. When Samuel Pepys visits the king's closet at the Palace of Whitehall, he writes that he found it full of 'such variety of pictures and other things of value and rarity that I was properly confounded and enjoyed no pleasure in the sight of them'.[44] The king's closet, also now known by the French name of 'cabinet', develops into something more than a room: it also becomes the name for his closest group of advisers.

Their closets are also Elizabeth's and William's favoured places for meditation. At Bolsover Castle, William's main bedchamber has two closets – 'Heaven' and 'Elysium' – one with a Christian and the other a more pagan character. In keeping with the house's purpose of pleasure, the former shows Christ dancing on its ceiling and the latter shows the gods and goddesses of Mount Olympus disporting themselves amorously. Here William writes, prays, reads, experiments, thinks.

The Elysium closet at Bolsover Castle lies at the far end of the ceremonial route through the Little Castle, which itself is guarded by lodges and two battlemented courtyards, and set at a distance from the main house. Its walls are decorated with sumptuous green panelling overlaid with gold paint, and the closet's painted ceiling includes gods, lascivious satyrs and the figure of Hercules flirting with a nymph. The window looks down onto the fountain below, with its statues celebrating lust. The Elysium closet is the most intimate and private place that its owner, William Cavendish, can create. Over the window is a painted banner saying 'All is but vanitie', as if in this room he can step out of his ceremonial role as head of the household for a while. William is accustomed to sitting here writing poems, while his wife, forty-five servants, endless petitioners from his estates, heralds, officials of local government and messengers from the Privy Council wait for him outside the closed door.

The idea that an aristocrat, or his wife, would benefit from time spent in solitary study is something rather novel in 1625: only the innovative consider, as Montaigne does, that solitude is the 'store-house for our selves', a place in which 'to discourse, to meditate and laugh, without wife, without children, and goods, without train or servants'.[45] Now, as Elizabeth unfolds her husband's letter in her own closet, something happens that is invisible in her straight-faced portraits. No one else is present to witness this baroness and mistress of her household surrendering her dignity for a moment, and it is highly likely that in Elizabeth's closet, on 9th July, 1625, we witness a smile.

Elizabeth bends over her husband's closely written letter with its idiosyncratic spelling. William often addresses her as 'Derest Harte' and signs off as 'your moste faythfull lovinge Husband'. In their correspondence, he sometimes scolds her gently: she has sent a messenger to him, but has forgotten to enclose a message; he thanks her for her letters, 'but they seem to be of an ancient date'.[46]

Do William and Elizabeth really love each other? Despite her inferior position in law and their lack of knowledge of each other when they married (at William's mother's suggestion), William is intimate with Elizabeth and shares his fears, his exhaustion, his bruised pride, his low, and indeed his high, spirits with her. He is glad when her illness provides him with an excuse to miss the jousting at court and return to Welbeck, where he suggests an alternative form of physical exercise. 'Sweete Harte', he writes,

> now listen to the Joyful news:
> Your cruel sickness, this year, did excuse –
> Me from the Tilting: therefore (do you hear?)
> Fail not I pray of Sickness Every year
> And as I am a knight, with spurs all Gilt,
> When I Come home, I'll run with you at Tilt.[47]

Yet Elizabeth's status in the relationship and in the household is far from equal to his. Cherished by her husband, she is also completely in his power. Throughout her life Elizabeth has lacked status in society, firstly as a ward and then as a wife. 'Women in *England*', wrote Edward Chamberlayne in a commentary on seventeenth-century society, 'so soon as they are Married are wholly [. . .] at the will and disposition of the Husband.'[48] Unable to enter into a contract as they are not legally recognised as individuals, Elizabeth and other wives can own nothing, not even their clothes. Only as a widow can a woman like Elizabeth gain control over her family's wealth, which is split into three, with one third given to her for life before reverting to her children after her death. Nevertheless, the situation of women is thought to be worse elsewhere. 'Such is the good nature of Englishmen towards their Wives', wrote Chamberlayne, rehearsing a well-known proverb, 'that if there were a Bridge over into *England* [. . .] it is thought all the Women in *Europe* would run hither.'

Despite this vaunted 'tenderness and respect' towards women, Elizabeth is not even able to move freely round her husband's house.[49] She may not enter the service areas, offices or outbuildings, and her choice of activities is severely restricted. Throughout their sheltered – and occasionally sterile – lives, aristocratic women move about the house in groups of two or three, meeting only a narrow range of people.[50]

Elizabeth comes into contact with men in a limited number of situations. She may have to deal one-to-one with senior household servants, or others providing professional or spiritual services, such as her doctor, poets or priest. She was accompanied into the Cavendish household by old Thomas Bamford, a servant of her father's from her childhood home of Blore.[51] Elizabeth often has occasion to meet, talk and play cards with male family members, but is only likely to meet those outside the family at the set-piece occasions of the household's hospitality: dinners or masques in the Great Chamber, banquets in the gardens, plays in the Great Hall, or musical performances. She and her gentlewomen spend their days in the Great Chamber or bedchamber, eating together in private, though sometimes the gentlewomen dine with the maids or the children and nurses at their own table in the Great Hall.[52]

Elizabeth looks up from the letter, having digested its contents, and decides that she needs to dress. With her husband away, she often

An English lady's bedchamber, *c.*1640. This engraving was owned by Samuel Pepys and is one of the earliest known depictions of an English bedchamber

passes the day in her loose jacket or gown, but now she must make an appearance as mistress of the house to give an urgent announcement to the household officers. She hurries into her adjacent bedchamber in order to replace the embroidered jacket that she wears over her cambric chemise with a tight bodice and motions to her waiting gentlewomen to tie her elaborate jewelled pendant round her neck.

The word 'bedchamber' only came into use in the middle of the sixteenth century, because before that all chambers had multi-purpose use as sitting rooms, working rooms and sleeping rooms.[53] Now a withdrawing chamber placed adjacent to the bedchamber, and a closet off it, take on some of the functions of entertainment and writing respectively. Dressing, sleeping and recovering from sickness remain concentrated here in the bedchamber.[54]

Another of the wall paintings at Bolsover shows a half-dressed young lady, whom Elizabeth now resembles as she completes her toilette. The woman sits in an ornate chair, her feet on a red cushion, a red-curtained bed behind her, and peers at her face in an oval hand-held glass. Elizabeth wears no drawers beneath her skirts, and they will not form part of women's costume until late in the eighteenth century.[55] Each morning she rubs her teeth with a paste made of salt and cuttlebone,[56] and daily anoints herself with the treasures of the perfumer's shop, as experienced by William on visits in her company:

> Here is muske & Amber-Greese
> That Is worth the Golden Fleece
> Civet, Benjamin, Excelling
> And all sweets, that are for smelling.

In this particular poem, he goes on to enumerate the other requirements of his wife's toilette: Spanish pockets (pockets are still tied on round the waist rather than forming an integral part of a dress or gown), fans, gloves, Spanish red to paint a blush onto the cheeks, face washes, frangipani, 'Bolognia balls' to make the hands smooth, Balsam of Peru, hair powder 'such as Venus used'. In her bedchamber, Elizabeth now reaches out a hand for her

> Orange flowers, to Anoint-you
> With sweet Jessamin appoint-you
> Then lemon dew, & Rose-water
> All your Bodys, sprinkle After.[57]

Elizabeth also remains in her bedchamber for a variety of activities related to her health. It is possible that this very morning she has had an enema or 'glister' to purge her bowels, or else a consultation with her midwife about the colour of her urine. In fact, William and Elizabeth spend an inordinate amount of time in their bedchambers being ill. This is because their lives are so much like a performance: they are constantly on show before their household, servants and family, and only in the bedchamber and closet can they find relaxation. It is 'indecent', when in company, 'to pull off your Cloak, to pull off your Periwig, or Doublet, to pair your nails [. . .] to mend your Garter or Shoo-string, or to call for your Gown or your Slippers to put yourself at ease'.[58] To withdraw to a bedchamber and to take medicine is therefore a regular feature of their lives, whether they are sick or not.

Purges, bloodletting through the use of leeches, and vomiting all remain standard medical practice: Dr Matthew Boucherett, for example, will recommend that Elizabeth's grandchildren should use a weekly stomach-purging pill, to be taken 'in a spoonefull of syrup of

Violotes'; Elizabeth's son Henry's wife, who suffers from 'blemishes on her face', is given the unattractive option to 'take a Vomitt or else one of the doses of purging powder I sent in May'.[59] The Cavendish family's book of 'mineral receipts' (recipes for medicines) shows exactly how such purging powders or syrups are to be made. [60] Some recipes come recommended by Sir Theodore de Mayerne, the king's own doctor, their length and complexity explaining the necessity for a still room and specialised maids to run it in a house of any size. Bloodletting is at least forbidden during Elizabeth's pregnancies, but she must keep her belly 'loose, not retaining her excrements [. . .] if it be not done naturally, it must bee helpt, taking every morning some broth of Damaske-Prunes; Also Apples stewed with Sugar and a little Butter, is very fit and good.'[61]

Bathing – which also takes place in the bedchamber – is something to be enjoyed with circumspection, as Elizabeth thinks that water could soak into and destroy the body during prolonged immersion. However, taking mineral waters in the town of Bath, for example, is already popular, and it is possible that the Cavendishes' fountain at Bolsover Castle is intended for use as a bathing pool in a similar manner, with seats provided in niches in its sides for naked bathers to rest between bouts of splashing.[62] Hair washing is an annual ritual for the seventeenth-century diarist John Evelyn: he embarks upon a 'yearly course of washing my hair with warm water, mingled with a decoction of sweet herbs, and immediately, with cold spring water, which much refreshed me'. The Cavendish family doctor, on the other hand, 'mislikes ye bathing of your head in cold water especially in winter'.[63]

The process of being 'physicked' is a mixture of discomfort and the kind of pleasurable relaxation techniques to be found in a health spa. During bathing, the inside of the bath is draped with linen cloths before the water is poured in, and the bather uses more thin linen cloths to dry him- or herself afterwards. The tub might still remain in Elizabeth's bedchamber from her earlier enjoyment of a sweet-smelling mineral bath, such as that prescribed for her son Charles:

> let the liquor bee as warme as you can suffer it when you first goe into the bath & have hot ready to poure in as yt first cools continue in the bath neer an houre & while you are there chafe in well with your hands or a sponge ye liquor into both sides especially the left. When you have sate out your full time let some cotton wool well soaked & quilted with ye ointment be applied to each side & then get with all speed into your bed & sweat there the space of

an houre, after which rub your body well with warme cloaths & dry it & remove the ointment if troublesome, & drinke a draught of warme broath or caudle, keeping your self from cold for some times after.[64]

In this bedchamber Elizabeth also lies isolated from the household for months at a time by the arduous and dangerous duty of childbirth. 'Children come on apace,' writes William in 1633, and Elizabeth will give birth to eight of his children. She had already had three children by the age of nineteen, with her first husband Henry Howard, of whom only one, Catherine ('Cate'), survived infancy. Only six of Elizabeth's eleven children will reach adulthood. The birth and death of children in the seventeenth-century mortality lottery will cruelly leave her husband with only one male heir at the time of his death. Rates of infant mortality are actually higher in Stuart England than in the previous century: new diseases such as smallpox, and new strains of old diseases such as flu, carry off a grim proportion of babies.[65]

The family's London physician often sends his wife north to be with Elizabeth 'at the time of [her] travail', her labour made all the more arduous when William is at court and she is left lonely without him. At these times the company of women becomes even more important, and indeed, life-saving. William describes the women of the family taking over the household and creating feminine chaos when Elizabeth comes to term:

> My wife did waken in a fearful fright
> Falling in Labour in the dead of Night
> Wives, widows, maids, disorderly did rise
> Shoes off & stockings, rubbing off their eyes,
> Mistaking things, & Every Things was said
> Being half wakened from their drowsy Bed.[66]

Today, in July, 1625, Elizabeth's daughter Jane is nearly three and is upstairs in the nursery with her nurses. Who are these servants to whom Elizabeth entrusts the care of her daughter while she dresses in her bedchamber?

Some of these peculiar but important household characters appear in a dramatic entertainment written by Ben Jonson to celebrate the birth of a little Cavendish boy named Charles. This was possibly Elizabeth's son Charles, who died aged three in 1621. Jonson introduces the characters and duties of the wet nurse, dry nurse and midwife with whom Elizabeth is intimately acquainted.[67] He jokingly names the dry nurse

'Kecks' (the word means 'dry stick') and the wet nurse 'Dugs' (breasts). A childbirth manual recommends of a nurse that 'her brests be full and have sufficient plentie of milke, and that they be neither too great, soft, hanging and flagging, neither too little, hard or contract'. Nor should the nurse's character be 'too fearfull or timorous: for these affections and qualities be pernitious and hurtfull to the milke, corrupting it, and passes forth through the milke into the child, making the child of like condition'.[68] Jonson also introduces Mistress Holdback, the midwife, whose job is to hold the back of a woman in labour. The position favoured for seventeenth-century childbirth is squatting rather than lying down so that gravity can aid the process; a straw mattress is used to soak up the blood. Elizabeth may well have had a consultation with her midwife this morning, for the latter's prowess in discerning the presence and course of a longed-for pregnancy are highly valued. The techniques used are rather crude, and a boy baby is usually predicted with great gusto. One simple test is whether a woman experiences an orgasm during intercourse: if her husband 'finde[s] an extraordinarie contentment in the company of his Wife; and if he feele at the same time a kind of sucking or drawing at the end of his yard [. . .] a woman may have conceived'.[69] However, the Cavendish midwife caricatured as Mistress Holdback is well acquainted with the more advanced techniques for diagnosing pregnancy outlined in Guillemeau's contemporary book on *Child-Birth*: 'When upon ye first view of my Ladyes breasts, and an inspection, of what passed from her [. . .] I told her Ladyship at first she was sped'.

After receiving the good news, Mistress Holdback's master was anxious to know whether the baby would be the hoped-for son. Mistress Holdback had grounds for optimism, having considered her lady's complexion, the shape of her belly and the fact that her right breast grew harder than the left:

> ye Nipple red, rising like a strawberry, ye milke white and thick, and standing in pearls upon my nail [. . .] a boy for my money; nor when ye milk dissolv'd not in water, nor scattered, but sank; a boy still; no, upon ye very day of my Lady's Labour, when ye wives came in [. . .] her Ladyship set her right foot, foremost, ye right pulse beat quicker, and stronger, and her right eye grown, and sparkling, I assure your Lordship, I offered to hold Mr Doctor a discretion, it was a boy.[70]

This and every morning Elizabeth hopes to hear good news of this nature, for she is under pressure to replace her lost son Charles with another male heir. Elizabeth is not expected to be present at her children's christenings, for they generally take place only three days after the birth. She remains in her darkened and sealed chamber, removed from the household and the world, for a further month of 'lying in'. Only after two or three weeks is a new mother washed, her soiled straw mattress removed and she herself allowed to sit up: the 'upsitting' and in due course the 'footing' a fortnight later are events often celebrated by the women of the household with a party.[71] So keen was Thomas Salmon, a servant at Great Tew in Oxfordshire, to join in the 'good cheer' at the house of one Eleanor Rymel, who had just been 'brought a-bed', that he put on women's clothing to join in the drinking and gossiping undetected.[72] However, the christening entertainment written by Jonson incorporates the raucous celebrations of the household that will take place downstairs while Elizabeth lies in her bloodied bed. In his words, the midwife Holdback triumphantly shouts out:

> This is my day! my Lords and my Ladye howe like you my boy? Ist not a goodlye boy? [. . .] I ha' given measure, i'faith; hee'l prove a pricker (and god will) by one privie marke y$^{t}$ I founde about him.[73]

When a seventeenth-century midwife says she has given a baby boy a full measure, she means she has left a good long piece of his umbilical cord attached. Midwives allow 'more measure to the males: because this length doth make their tongue, and privie members longer: whereby they may both speake the plainer, and be more serviceable to Ladies'.[74]

Given the small chance their babies have of surviving to adulthood, how do William and Elizabeth equip themselves emotionally? It is tempting to suggest that seventeenth-century parents must harden themselves, holding back affection from their children as too great a risk for their peace of mind. Yet on the death of his baby boy, William's friends and relations write to him with their heartfelt condolences, and he does indeed seem to be a truly affectionate father.[75] He is playful and teasing with his children, his letters creating a little window into a nursery world where, unexpectedly, even girls are encouraged to become writers. On another occasion he writes from court to little Jane:

> Sweet Jane, I knowe you are a rare Inditer –
> Ande hath the pen off a moste redye writer.

She replies shyly:

> My Lord, I know you doo but Jest with mee
> & so in obdence I right this nothing. Jane Cavendysshe.

William also tries to tempt his son Charles to reply:

> Sweet Charles, This letter iff you like itt nott, then race-Itt [erase it?]
> Butt Answer itt for Usus promtus facitt.

But Charles, a boy of few words, replies succinctly:

> My Lord. I can not tel what to wright. Charles Mansfeild.[76]

Elizabeth does not doubt her husband's affection for his children: 'now my Lord', she writes, 'for your Childer I am confident that you Love them'.[77] Yet despite William's liberal views on the possibility of his daughters becoming writers, he takes a domineering, high-handed line with his children, and this will cause a good deal of unhappiness.

Dressed at last, Elizabeth now leaves her bedchamber and calls for her servants in order to spread the news contained in her husband's letter from court around the household. There are stores to be obtained, clothes to be brushed and beds aired for an influx of people, for the household must begin the preparations necessary for William's triumphant return home. Three days ago, according to the letter, William received momentous tidings: his appointment as Lord Lieutenant of Nottinghamshire, an important job that will now bring him back from court in London to the countryside with some urgency in order to take up his new administrative responsibilities. To be chosen as the leading figure in a county is a great responsibility and privilege, and he will have a role in raising the militia, in supervising justice and tax collecting. To Elizabeth, however, her husband's return means something more personal: relief from her loneliness and the resumption of her efforts to conceive.

# 4 – *A Masque*

BOLSOVER CASTLE, 30TH JULY, 1634

Nine years later, at around six o'clock on a summer's morning, William Cavendish opens his eyes in the bedchamber of his father's Little Castle at Bolsover.[1] The creak of the studded door on its massive hinges has woken him as Gertrude, a maid, slips into the room. His personal servants enter William's line of vision from the left, provided the position of the bed's curtains admits enough of a view; his bed's head stands against the room's panelled southern wall. The delicately hinged shutters of the windows to the right of the bed are imperfectly closed and early fingers of sunlight are falling across the foot of the bed from their east-facing panes. On a special occasion like today, the servants are well advanced in their preparations, but ordinarily William is accustomed to shout out for Gertrude to bring his morning drink if he wakes before her arrival:

> When I did wake from my perturbed dreams,
> And saw forerunning Light of the Sun Beams,
> I said 'twas day, chid Gertrude for the jar,
> She swore 'twas moon-light but she was a Liar.[2]

Lying in bed, William can admire the shutters themselves and the panelling of the windowed wall of the room, intricately decorated with stencilled designs of flowers and foliage in black and gold. Much of the rest of the panelling is concealed behind tapestries of the 'verdure' or leafy variety commonly hung in bedchambers, apart from the areas where shelves set into the panelling contain books, jars and items of clothing.[3] Between the windows bulges one of the Little Castle's distinctive ornate fireplaces, jewelled with touchstone and fossil-filled

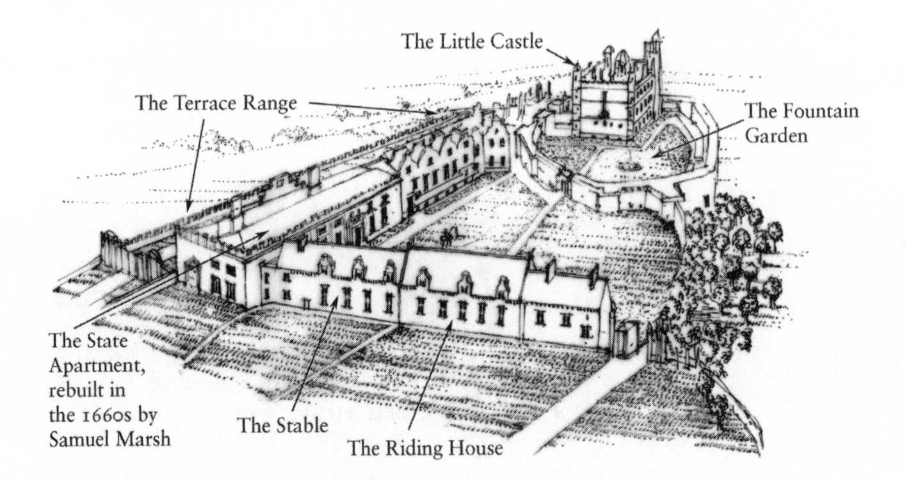


A bird's-eye view of Bolsover Castle. This shows the castle as it was towards the end of William's life when all his works were complete

marble; translucent white alabaster lions' heads wink and growl at William from its hood.

Gertrude steps carefully through the doorway. The thresholds into this room are slightly elevated so that the rushes scattered across its floor are not trodden beyond its confines. Beneath the rushes the floor is made of lime ash, the ashy dregs from the bottom of a limekiln formed into an exceptionally durable grey plaster. She is carrying the tray containing the 'Morsel of Bread' that William is accustomed to eat for his breakfast.[4] Setting down her burden on a side table, she pours out a glass of sack, the sweet wine that William always drinks at this time of day. He sits up and takes from her a conical glass with a circular base. He and his contemporaries are accustomed to take the delicate disc at the base of the glass between a thumb and forefinger rather than wrapping fingers and palm around the vessel.[5] The liquid sugar scent of William's wine must fight for attention with the fading freshness of herbs scattered among the rushes on the floor and the whiff of the night soil.

Should William wish to relieve himself on rising from his bed, he needs only to turn right and push open the door to the tiniest of closets set into the turret of the castle, with its tawny limewashed walls and its own little latticed window overlooking his beloved Riding House. Here William's close stool stands, its padded velvet seat surmounting a

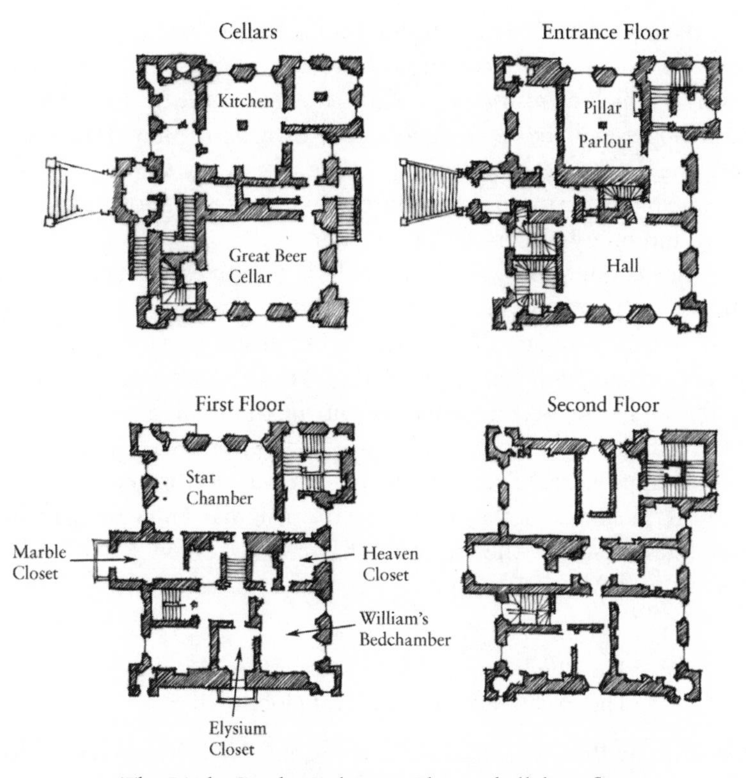


The Little Castle, Bolsover. Plans of all four floors

wooden box concealing a chamber pot within. A convenient niche in the wall holds a candlestick during nocturnal visits. After setting down the breakfast tray, Gertrude removes the chamber pot from the close stool and sets it down outside the door for an inferior colleague – the 'necessary woman' – to hump away.

Normally when William wakes up for a day at Bolsover Castle his mind is on pleasure: on horses, on poetry and on retirement from the cares of business and household. Yet this will be a uniquely stressful day. Early in the morning of 30th July, 1634, William's household is already busy preparing for the most exciting event it has ever known: the entertainment of the king and queen at Bolsover with a feast and a masque.

William has enjoyed nine years as Lord Lieutenant of Nottinghamshire, and six years ago he received the significant promotion to an earldom. He is now the first Earl of Newcastle, Elizabeth is his countess, and for the rest of his life he will sign his letters 'W. Newcastle'. His title was chosen because he does indeed have a 'new castle', the building at Bolsover in which he now lies.[6] Today's masque is the next step in what William hopes will be a swift journey towards the highest of court offices. The day's entertainment will bring together architecture, music, food, dancing and garden design into a worthy setting for the peacock preening and finery of Charles I's courtiers.

A masque is not a play, nor is it a ball. It combines speeches, musical interludes, costume and marvellous special effects into a form of early opera in which members of a household themselves, as well as professional performers, will sometimes take part. The audience often stands up at the end of a performance to join in the final grand masquing dance. There is a particularly haunting description of a masque in William Shakespeare's *The Tempest*, which was performed for the first time in 1611. Some of the magician and ringmaster Prospero's best-known lines describe the masque that he stages on his island for Ferdinand and Miranda and the sense of evanescent wonder that it arouses.

> The cloud-capp'd towers, the gorgeous palaces,
> The solemn temples, the great globe itself

conjured up by Prospero are in fact the scenic backdrops created for a masque, magnificent yet quick to fade away when the performance is over. For a masque's magic to work, many hands must labour behind the scenes, and at Bolsover the preparations have been in progress for weeks. But at this point, early in the morning of 30th July, this masque's Prospero – William Cavendish – rises from his bed.

Excited but anxious about the day ahead, William now goes through to the Heaven closet off his bedchamber to run through his lists of provisions, instructions and copies of letters sent. Beyond the Heaven closet's dark green door painted in gold with Chinese scenes lies a cornucopia of colour. On the ceiling of this closet a crowd of painted cherubs with triangle, harp, pipes, recorders, tambourine and viol play the country-dance tune (a song about Robin Hood and Little John) to which the central figure of Jesus is dancing (Plate 11). Into the green-lacquered panelling are set a number of lockable cupboards, which, along with William's desk, contain books, bundles of letters and other treasures. A great many people both inside and outside the immediate household are involved in the masque's production, and William now flicks through the relevant papers to refresh his memory. As he settles to his work at the desk placed beneath the window, he hums to himself another song about Robin Hood, composed by himself: earlier this year his secretary John Rolleston carefully wrote down the words to his master's 'proper new Ballad, to be sung or whistled to the tune of Bessy Bell'.[7]

William needed someone to provide a script for today's performance. Fortunately, he has a cordial relationship with one of the country's leading poets. Ben Jonson has long received financial, and sometimes emotional, support from the Midlands aristocrat to whom he refers as 'My best patron'.[8] Contemporaries consider Jonson to be at least equal, if not superior, to William Shakespeare. His riotous, raucous plays echo the man himself, 'passionately kind and angry', and most lively 'after drink, which is one of the Elements in which he liveth'.[9] Jonson has killed one man during military service in the Low Countries, a second in a duel in London in 1598, and still has on his thumb the brand of a convicted felon; he will automatically hang if convicted of a further offence.[10] But now, by the 1630s, his work for the court and the London theatres has dried up, and Jonson suffers from melancholy, a dependence on alcohol and a physical disability affecting his back. A poem by the doctor Richard Andrews, included in William's bound collection of his favourite poems, mocks Jonson's fondness for sack and the paralysis that has affected him since he was 'strucken with the Palsey in the Year 1628':[11]

> Big Benjamin hath had a Cup of sack
> so often at his mouth, that now his back
> is almost broke.[12]

The Cavendish household often receives visits from the various scholars and artists to whose work William is attracted: these include players, writers, artists and scientists. As well as Jonson, William employs the royal organist Mr Tomkins, the Florentine sculptor Francesco Fanelli and Anthony van Dyck, the king's favourite painter: all the finest artists of the cosmopolitan royal court. Poets visiting the household write on subjects calculated to please, such as the Cavendishes' magnificent building projects, and the philosopher Thomas Hobbes dedicates his great work *The Elements of Law Naturall and Politique* to William.[13] Hobbes, pernickety and anxious about his health, is an occasional visitor to Welbeck when he is free from the demands of his other patrons or from the dangers of the road.[14]

William and his brother Charles are enthusiastic purchasers of lenses for making telescopes as well as mathematics books from the continent. Although the apparatus of their multifarious experiments lies abandoned in their chambers today, William's chaplain Robert Payne will often be called upon to perform scientific experiments as part of his duties. Jonson captures the atmosphere of such a coterie of would-be scientists, 'poring through a multiplying glass,/ Upon a captiv'd crab-louse, or a cheese-mite/ To be dissected.'[15] These experiments took place behind locked doors because of their possible association, to the uninformed, with witchcraft or the conjuring of devils.

In sketching out the characters that might appear in another dramatic entertainment at a household feast, William introduces a cast of specialists not usually found in a great household, yet one quite familiar within his own scientifically and academically inclined family: the alchemist, the mathematician, the physician with his 'rare secrets', and the engineer.[16] Dr Payne the chaplain, whom William values because of his 'very witty, searching brain', occasionally locks himself up with his master in a chamber to create substances such as 'Lapis Prunellae, which is saltpetre and brimstone', in order to speculate on the composition of the sun.[17] Yet Hobbes, like many of these visiting scholars, is suspiciously overeager to reassure William that their discourse is between intellectual equals: 'my love to you is just of the same nature that it is to Mr Payne, bred out of private talk, without respect to your purse'.[18]

The moody and touchy Ben Jonson has become part of the extended circle of Cavendish patronage by writing for William, and William has been good to the old poet, sending Dr Payne on mercy missions to Jonson's London lodgings when he himself was in the country. In 1631, Jonson had tempestuously complained in a letter to William at Welbeck about the slow progress of his work: 'It is the Lewd Printers fault [. . .] with his delays and vexation [. . .] I may bid the world good Night.'[19] Soon after this, Jonson reached the end of his financial tether, writing from London to Welbeck 'a most humble petition to your Lordship's bounty, to succour my present necessities'.[20] William's action was decisive and generous: he sent Jonson money (which to the poet 'fell like the dew of heaven') and a commission to write two entertainments to be performed at Welbeck and Bolsover. Jonson wrote that he thanked God for William's commission and prayed that his work deserved the honour: 'I meant it should in the working of it and I have hope the performance will conclude it.'[21] In the Heaven closet on the morning of 30th July, 1634, William now riffles through the sheets of dialogue upon which Jonson has expended so much effort, hoping, too, that the performance will bring a conclusion to many hopes as yet unfulfilled.

Now, with the early sun coming through his east-facing window, William runs a finger down the list of those of his neighbours who have accepted his invitations to the feast, for he has 'sent for all the Gentry of the Countries of *Darby* and *Nottingham* to come and wait upon their Majesties'.[22] Well-born men and women for miles around will also be rising and preparing a splendid toilette before entering their lumbering carriages; if, that is, their carriages can negotiate the rough roads to Bolsover.

There is much at stake for William today. His purpose in staging this costly entertainment is to win one of the high and lucrative court offices that Charles I has it in his power to bestow. William would particularly like to be Master of the Horse, for which he feels his equestrian skills equip him uniquely. Yet he entertained the king at Welbeck Abbey only a year ago, and on that occasion was left empty-handed. At the time, William complained to his chief political patron the Earl of Strafford, writing, 'I have hurt my estate much with the hopes' of office. After his splurge on the 1633 entertainment, William was 'sick in mind, body and purse', and found it 'too late to repent'. 'I am so much plunged in debt,' he wrote, that more expense 'would help very well to undo me'.[23] He has ignored his own better judgement: today he once more risks his financial solvency in a high-stakes gamble for royal favour. Later it will be reported that 'nothing was spared which might add Splendour to the Feast', and it will be bandied about that William has spent £10,000 on this single day.[24]

As William sits in his closet checking his lists and scripts, the busy household rotates as usual around him. Outside his bedchamber, the small dark lobby in the centre of the building is crossed and recrossed by servants entering their own closet and bringing out whatever is needed to complete the furnishing of the adjacent Great Chamber. William's wife Elizabeth remains at Welbeck rather than sleeping in the secondary bedchamber next to her husband's or in her former mother-in-law's chamber on the floor above. The reason is that the entire Little Castle, although planned by William's father as a romantic retreat for his wife and himself, has gradually been made into a more masculine place by William, for use either by himself alone or in the company of other men. This is more than clear from its saucy wall paintings. Elizabeth may well feel out of place here, in a house decorated not for a wife but a mistress.

Shut in his closet with his papers, William is oblivious to the lowly necessary woman who now picks up William's night soil and plods down the backstairs. The Little Castle's staircases are more than ingenious. The main stair connects the ground floor with the roof in a stately ascent that winds up inside a spacious square turret. Four short service staircases link the cellar offices with the main spaces of the castle. And, from the bedchamber floor down to the cellar kitchen, a long secondary back staircase twists tightly in a shaft in the southwest corner of the house. This is the stair that William's night soil now descends, going down into the very bowels of the building.

The backstairs sink past the level of the Little Castle's mock-medieval Hall. From them we can catch a glimpse into this room, where shafts of light slant down from the high, mullioned windows, bleaching stripes on the stone floor and grey panelled walls. Here various household members are hurriedly breaking bread and lifting horn cups full of 'small' or household beer at long tables. Far above them, tall pillars washed with a golden colour support the lofty vaulted ceiling. The wall paintings in here show the mythical hero Hercules performing several of his twelve labours by vanquishing various vicious beasts. The images are designed to encourage the household to think of William Cavendish himself in this heroic role. In one particularly apposite painting near the staircase, a muscular Hercules tames a wild and dangerous man-eating mare, just as William himself subdues his powerful horses in the Riding House. The household, however, may well find the hour too early for iconographic discussion. They do not eat breakfast en masse; individuals gather informally in the Hall or else wait until dinner time. Fynes Moryson, touring England in 1617, noted that 'some sickly men staying at home, may perhaps take a small breakfast, yet in generall the English eat but two meales (of dinner and supper) each day'.[25] The necessary woman now continues down the twisting backstairs to the level of the kitchen and other

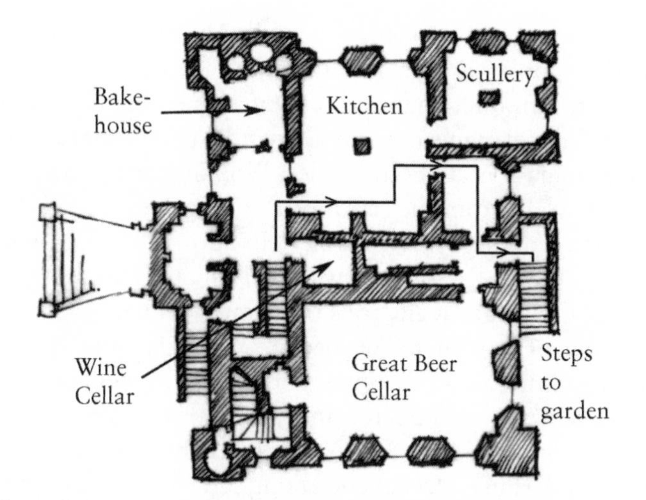


The cellars of the Little Castle. This plan shows the necessary woman's passage through the offices and out into the garden

offices below ground, where a grim-faced chaos must surely reign.

She is planning to empty her vessel onto the rough slopes of the hill below the castle, but the route to her destination is tortuous. It would be unseemly for her to leave through the main front door of the castle and across the elaborate turreted forecourt. She aims instead to traverse the kitchens to reach the back or service door. From here a flight of steps leads up to the garden, and from the garden a variety of discreet exits will take her out from the castle enclosure onto the hillside.

Leaving the bottom step of the backstairs, she passes to her right the door of the windowless room known as the 'wine cellar'.[26] Beneath its arched roof, great wooden barrels of wine are stored on brick or stone platforms to allow easy pouring. When wine is required, the butler comes down here to fill a bulbous stoneware bottle, placing a cork in its neck and then carrying it up to the dining room, where it will stand nestled in ice in a wine cooler on the floor or sideboard. Wine will not be stored in bottles for many years to come, and glass bottles will not appear until 1658. As she passes, the necessary woman glimpses William's butler working in the darkness by the gleam of a rushlight (a rush dipped in melted fat or grease, a much cheaper form of lighting than wax candles), drawing off the best wine and sampling what he pours.

The wine in this cellar is less commonly from France or Germany than from Portugal and the Canary Islands. The excise duties placed on the formerly popular French products have had their effect, as have occasional prohibitions against the Dutch merchants who used to bring much French wine over to England. While 'claret wine' and 'white wine' remain household staples, William's preference is for the sweet dessert wines from the south of Europe (like the sack he drinks for breakfast), imported via Bristol.[27] In future years it will be the responsibility of Francis Topp, steward of William's lands in Somerset, to send pipes of Canary wine, rolls of Spanish 'Tobacckoe' and cheese from the port of Bristol to Welbeck.[28] Smoking and drinking are among William's favourite pastimes, and while he recognises that some people (including his own doctor and James I) think the former habit foul, he does not care. 'Come fill us the Pipe,' begins one of William's poems entitled 'Drunked Debauched Song', for although smoking is an invention of the devils of Hell,

their Clouds do choke
But ours Is sweet Smoke
And wish I could suck thus Eternal.[29]

As the necessary woman passes the wine cellar, the pastry and bakehouse now lie before her. Through the door, she can see the fiery mouths of ovens opening into the wall and servants using paddles to heave loaves into them. The fine white 'manchet' bread eaten by William himself will be much in evidence today. According to Gervase Markham, writing in 1615, dough for manchet bread has to be kneaded either by hand or else wrapped in a cloth and trodden underfoot. After an hour's rising, the baker forms 'manchets round and flat'. 'Prick it with your knife in the Top', Markham advises, 'and so put it into the Oven, and bake it with a gentle heat.'[30] The household as a whole generally eats inferior dark brown 'cheat' bread, and this too is being produced for the great crowd of servants who will attend the visiting courtiers today. Markham prescribes 'for your brown bread, or bread for your hinde-servants [. . .] you shall take of Barley two bushels, of Pease two pecks, of Wheat or Rye a peck, a peck of Malt: these you shall grind all together, and dress it through a Meal-Sive'.[31] Indeed, those even further down the social scale, such as the builders who worked at the Little Castle in 1613, eat the lowest form of bread, made entirely from beans or peas. William Harrison describes how the price of corn is sometimes so great that 'the artificer and poor labouring man is not able to reach unto it but is driven to content himself with horse corn, I mean, beans, peason, oats, tares and lentils'.[32]

Instead of entering the bakehouse, the necessary woman now takes the squat doorway to the right into the kitchen proper, where fire licks the two vast hearths. She is now entering the kingdom of the cooks.

Preparations are well under way for banqueting and feasting on an unprecedented scale. On normal days the household is fairly self-sufficient, with only luxuries such as wine and fish being brought from market. Today is very different. The kitchens are almost certainly under the control of a member of the dynasty of Cavendish cooks named Yates. Last year, in 1633, William and Elizabeth's cook William Yates signed a lease on a farm in return for his 'good and faithful service' to the family. There was, however, a condition in the contract: that he must be ready to return and 'do his best personal service' in the event that it be required.[33] He has probably returned to the kitchen for today's feast to counsel his younger relation, John Yeates, who has followed on as 'cook at Welbeck'.[34]

The cook has a clearly defined place in the household hierarchy, reporting upwards to Nedd Watson, the caterer or officer responsible for making food purchases (or '*acates*' in Latin).[35] Watson is one of the members of the household also able to turn his hand to the role of musician, and has in his room at Welbeck a flute, a flute recorder and a broken bass violin.[36]

The caterer usually has an administrative assistant to keep a record of the supplies needed; in later years his name is 'Mr Bayly the Clerke of the kichen'.[37] Additional noise and action in the kitchens is also provided by 'the Kitchining Boyes' and 'the Sculleriemaid', and during great feasts they are further supplemented by other temporary members of staff, such as 'Goodwife Lemon' brought in to clean the sculleries.[38] In addition, professional cooks have almost certainly been drafted in for today. French cooks, the aristocrats' choice for special occasions, have a bad reputation among stolid English servants because a Frenchman 'doth not feed the belly but the palate [. . .] the Servingmen call him the last relique of Popery, that makes men fast against their Conscience'. A French cook 'dare not for his life come among the Butchers; for sure they would quarter and bake him after the English fashion; hee's such an enemy to Beefe and Mutton'.[39]

John Smithson's commissions from the masons in Shuttlewood Quarry in April 1613 included twenty-two 'arch stones for the kitchen ranges', and pots or kettles are suspended over their fires by the pot-sways or chimney cranes raised or lowered by notched bars.[40] The two hearths at Bolsover feature some particularly advanced technology, for Smithson has designed a unique chimney crane that suspends a huge cauldron of boiling water above a fire. The crane swings along a horizontal plane for ease of filling and emptying the cauldron, and is adjustable vertically so that the water can be lowered towards the flames.[41] Last night the fire's embers will have been banked up and covered with a domed brass curfew (or *couvre-feu*) so that they could be puffed back into flame with bellows first thing this morning.[42]

Around its massive central pillar with its primitive capital, the kitchen's floor is paved and laid around its perimeter with 'channell' for drainage. The windows are small, high and prison-like; the stone room rings with sound like an empty cistern. Two 'great stones' form the kitchen sink, which is fed by a 'spoute stone' in the north wall.[43] Water reaches this spout along a pipe passing through the castle's outermost wall. This pipe slopes down from a tank at the top of the water tower standing just north of the castle on a hillside into which water is

A seventeenth-century sketch of Bolsover Castle from the north. To the right are the lodges of the forecourt, to the centre is the Little Castle, and to the left is the battlemented wall walk that encircles the Fountain Garden. The freestanding building on the hillside just before the keep is the water tower

pumped from the spring at the bottom of the hill. This is only one among many ingenious routes by which water is brought to the Cavendishes' castle.

A second pipeline approaches from the south, leading from a spring about half a mile away. Along this pipeline stands a series of little 'conduit houses', built in 1622, containing tapping points for the use of the townspeople.[44] A third comes from the north, its source another spring on an adjacent hill. From here, a lead pipe crosses the valley and climbs to the lowest level of the three-storey 'Cistern House' set into the thickness of the castle's garden wall.[45] The uppermost floor of the 'Cistern House' contains the cistern itself, while the middle floor, with its large windows, is used as a shady banqueting room for pleasant meals on hot summer days. The lowest chamber contains the engine, perhaps operated by a donkey treading a wheel, which pumps water up to the cistern. From here, the water descends through a series of valves to power the fountain in the Little Castle's garden.[46] Amazing ingenuity has gone into these networks of lead pipes supplying kitchen, fountain and stables, but this is a Cavendish speciality. At Hardwick Old Hall, another house on a hill without ready access to water, William's grandmother Bess had her own 'well house' built, from which lead conduit pipes carry water into the kitchen. Here water was likewise raised to the tank by a 'water horse' in the well house.[47]

Back in the kitchen of the Little Castle, a vast range of dishes is being prepared. A list of the 'dyet' or rations issued to nine servants at Welbeck for thirteen weeks in the 1650s shows the sort of food the household is accustomed to: a phenomenal consumption of eggs (very nearly ten per person per week), and staples of beef, mutton and veal flavoured with salt. Mead and an allowance of hops for brewing ale are also on the list, along with cheeses, corn for bread, oatmeal and mustard seeds.[48] A household member's chance of a tasty and varied diet rises dramatically with status. Dining records for the Great Hall at Welbeck – entitled 'A note of what Beef, Mutton, Veal, Lamb, Pig etc is spent daily in my Lords family' – show that the Cavendish children and nurses, for example, commonly share a dinner of a savoury porridge (cooked with meat stock), boiled beef and a joint both of mutton and veal. Their supper consists of porridge, more joints of mutton and veal, and two chickens, while the supper of 'those that wait on the masters' is limited to mutton alone. Those at 'my lords table', on the other hand, feast upon four joints of mutton, two joints of veal, one joint of lamb, a capon (a domestic cockerel, castrated and fattened for eating) and other small boiled meats 'to furnish the table' each supper time.[49]

On Fridays, salt fish replaces the ubiquitous joints of meat. Over three months the household consumes three salmon, twenty trout, twenty-five carp, one hundred soles, one hundred and twenty smelts, ten lobsters and crabs, five cod's heads and eight eels and lampreys.[50] William, his wife and eight guests of their choice benefit from a special dispensation from the Archbishop of Canterbury allowing them to eat flesh on Fridays in return for donations to the poor, although William does enjoy a 'fine Codds heade Jelly'.[51]

Today, with the feast and masque for the king and queen only hours away, the countryside has been scoured for provisions and the cellar kitchens at Bolsover are in turmoil. When William's uncle, the Earl of Shrewsbury, was preparing to entertain the king in 1603, he was forced to ask for help. 'Let all my good friends in Derbyshire and Staffordshire know', he commanded, 'that I may have their company against such time as his Majesty shall come thither.' He added that he would not refuse 'any fat capons and hens, partridges, or the like' to serve to his royal guests.[52] For once, this choleric earl craved courtesy from his neighbours. Local support is vital for drumming up the provisions and persons required to create a magnificent impression.

Nedd Watson has drawn up an epic list of provisions for today.[53] The cooks in their blood-stained aprons are disembowelling fowl including thirty swans, thirty peacocks, thirty turkeys, ten dozen geese, ten dozen capons, twenty dozen pullets, five dozen hens and five dozen fat chickens. The Yateses are preparing to roast pigeons, pheasants, gulls, larks, redshanks, herons and bitterns in an orgy of the ornithological cuisine so loved in the seventeenth and earlier centuries. 'I have no delight', wrote a medieval schoolboy,

> in beef and mutton and such daily meats.
> I would only have a partridge set before us, or some other such,
> And in especial little small birds that I love passingly well.[54]

He was expressing a general preference, which lasts well into William's lifetime, for eating small birds above any other form of flesh. Another list of provisions shows that in three months the Cavendish household consumes thirty partridges, four pheasants, thirty quails, five gulls, three dozen peewits, five dozen plovers and twenty dozen larks and small birds, many of these ending up as the 'small boiled meat to furnish' William's own table.[55] The comparison is striking: today a greater number of birds than the household generally eats in a quarter of a year are being prepared. Temporary kitchens somewhere out of sight, as well as those in the adjacent, half-finished new range, must also be in use, with perhaps just the dishes for the royal table being prepared here in the Little Castle.

The fowl are being stuffed, boiled or roasted, and a recipe book from the fifteenth century explains how to kill and cook birds. Cooks are instructed to take a swan or any other bird and to 'cut him in the roof of the mouth toward the brain of the head and let him bleed to death. Then keep the blood to colour with the cauldron and knit the neck and let him die. Then scald him, roast him and serve him.'[56] William himself is doubtful whether the swan or the turkey takes pride of place among the roast fowl, joking that:

> The swan she did boast
> The best of the Roast
> 'Nay soft', said the Turkey, ''tis I,
> So Plump & so fat
> What say you to that
> When In sauce of onions I lie?'[57]

The sheer diversity of the birds being cooked in the kitchen today indicates another of the secret ingredients of a successful royal entertainment: conspicuous consumption. Nothing, in fact, will be thrown away, because the leftovers from the feast will work their way down the scale to the very lowest ranks of society. The funeral sermon preached in 1687 for Sir John Norton of Rotherfield, Hampshire, explains how his table was 'always found loaded with such substantial Provisions, as having serv'd the Parlour, afterwards feasted the Hall, and plentifully reliev'd the Poor at his Gates'.[58]

Beyond the busy kitchen is the scullery, the damp workplace of the chapped-handed scullery maids. This is another chilly, stone-vaulted room, with stone sinks for washing plates and for salting meat for the winter. Now the necessary woman makes her way between the cursing cooks across the kitchen to the back door. On her way, she passes by a final door leading to a huge subterranean room lit in a murky manner by sloping-silled windows high in its walls. This is the 'great beer cellar' whose vaults appeared in the builders' accounts in November, 1613.[59] Stone channels in its floor allow spillages to be slopped out of its door. Now, however, William's chamber pot passes through the door, up the seventeen stone stairs and out into the garden.

The heavily laden necessary woman emerges blinking into the light and air. The hidden garden at Bolsover is set within the curving wall of the medieval castle's inner bailey, long since demolished and rebuilt by William's father (Plate 13). Along the top of the thick stone wall runs an open-air walk – 'ye stone Walk' – capped by battlements.[60] Occasional obelisks break up its length, contributing to the castle's dramatic silhouette when viewed from the neighbouring hills. The garden's thick wall once protected the castle, and it is not unusual for Renaissance gardens to be designed as fortifications in order to ensure the seclusion and privacy of their owners. When Elizabeth I visited Hampton Court Palace as queen, she ordered that all the windows overlooking her Privy Garden be blocked up so that she could walk in private. Here, on cold mornings, she would march about vigorously in the heraldic gardens laid out by her father 'to catch her a heate'; only if onlookers approached would she adopt a slower, more queenly pace.[61] Her chief minister, William Cecil, famously sought rest from the cares of state in his fine and extensive gardens at Theobalds. He was happiest while riding his little mule across his estate, jogging along so that no one could talk to him.[62] Sir Henry Fanshawe in 1606 had more than forty labourers at work in his Hertfordshire garden at Ware Park making 'a fort in perfect proportion, with his ramparts, bulwarks, counterscarps and all other appurtenances, so that when it is finished it is like to prove an invincible piece of work'.[63] An enclosed, circular garden also has a religious meaning: it can stand for the complete, intact Virgin Mary, mother of Christ. Many a secluded medieval garden – the *hortus conclusus* – was dedicated to her. Perhaps there is an echo of William's father's Catholicism here as well.

The garden is laid out with paths and grass in one of the simpler designs now replacing the complicated heraldic and knot gardens of the previous century. Elizabethan parterres with their complex beds have given way to smooth green lawns, gravel paths and statues. At Bolsover, a sandy path encircles the central lawn, while between path and wall lie beds with flowers and climbing plants that creep up trellises nailed into the glowing sandstone. There are three shady alcoves containing love seats and two banqueting houses set into the thickness of the garden wall. In the centre of the lawn stands the showpiece of the garden – and in fact, one of the highlights of the whole castle – the fountain of Venus.[64]

The formal, enclosed gardens of the Stuart age are like extra rooms of the house for showing off wealth and culture and for intimate entertaining. Those at Bolsover and at Welbeck provide the Cavendish family and their guests with a variety of delightful outdoor activities. During the previous week at Welbeck Abbey, labourers have been hard at work prinking to perfection the camomile walk and the jasmine planted against the walls for the royal visit.[65] Suspended over the canal at Welbeck, two little buildings with arched openings in their walls are banqueting houses, outdoor dining rooms where William entertains his highest-ranking guests to a dessert course of ginger, marzipan and fennel sweetmeats after dinner. Banqueting houses are always in secluded or scenic locations: for example, they stand upon the high roofs of Lacock Abbey or Longleat House.[66] Here at Bolsover, the garden also contains a hidden meaning for those in the know: its almost perfect circular form symbolises the perfect circle of love that links a husband and wife in the fashionable philosophy of Neoplatonism that Charles I's court has adopted. The king and queen's love is to be the theme of the masque to be performed here this very afternoon.

The fountain of Venus in the centre of William's circular garden must have been created after 1628, the year in which he became Earl of Newcastle, because its heraldry contains an earl's coronet. However, only now, with the imminent approach of the royal masque, is the fountain reaching final completion. Its white marble statue of a curvaceous Venus, rising from a bath and demurely clutching a towel to her chest, looks northwards, her broad, placid face turned modestly away from the windows and balcony of the master's Elysium closet not far above her. A local carver has depicted this Venus as a meaty Derbyshire lass rather than closely copying the original statue that provided the idea for her pose: an etiolated and graceful figure produced in Italy by the famous sculptor Giambologna, whose work is known in England through little bronze miniature versions. Below Venus, her madly decorative column rises from a square basin with the earl's coronet carved upon it. Stone birds peck at luscious fruit, their stone wings beating gracefully each side of heraldic devices belonging to William and his wife. Lions' faces below Venus's feet are intended to spit water into the basin, and below its corners her four little boys, carved in a dark marble, are designed to squirt water (as if urinating)

Detail of John Smithson's design for the fountain at Bolsover Castle. The ladies sitting in the niches may be statues squirting water or perhaps real swimmers using the fountain as a toilet

down into the deep octagonal basin below. This basin has niches set into its eight walls. In these recesses, the white, bulbous visages of a set of busts of the Roman emperors peek up lasciviously at the naked Venus. Between the niches, a series of circular platforms contain other spurting figures: four priapic beasts (a kind of heraldic dragon with enlarged genitals) spit water, while horned satyrs and griffins riding swans complete the whole crazy ensemble. These niches may originally have been intended for swimmers. There is even a drawing by John Smithson showing a gaggle of nymphs or ladies seated in them, engaged in the rather unusual activity of squirting breast milk, urinating and even defecating into the water.[67] Its extraordinarily lewd design suggests that the fountain was at some level intended for a playboy's pool parties.

This fountain is one of the most bizarre agglomerations of water and sculpture to be found anywhere in seventeenth-century England, and its meaning seems dense but elusive. Is it a fountain of Love, with the semi-naked Venus providing a piquant view from the Elysium closet for her master, William Cavendish? Or is it a fountain of Lust, with

Venus assaulted on all sides by the lascivious gaze of the engorged priapic beasts, satyrs and those lecherous old men, the Roman emperors? We cannot know for certain, but we can say for sure that the fountain has never worked smoothly. The stone seats for the statues are unworn by the play of water over long periods, and the fountain's plumbing will always cause difficulties. In any case, it can only play for a short period after the tank in the Cistern House has been filled to its brim by the efforts of the donkey in the water engine. Once the tank is empty, there must be a lengthy pause while it is refilled.

Today, on 30th July, 1634, a tense knot of workmen and plumbers, conscious of the imminent arrival of the royal visitors, are gathered around the basin, vainly scratching their heads and willing water to come gushing out of the lions' mouths, the lips of the beasts and the flanks of the swans. The most quirky and inventive fountain in England has stumped the ingenuity of its designers by refusing to play.[68]

This morning, there's a great deal of other activity in the garden, for a key scene in the masque will take place here, out of doors. After their feast, the king and queen will walk out into the garden and take their seats for an entertainment of speeches and dancing. A character called Colonel Vitruvius, a comic architect, will introduce his troupe of dancing builders. In preparation for this, a band of musicians is tuning up, taking their seats near the royal cloth of estate rigged up over the chairs intended for the king and queen. The grizzled actor who will play old Colonel Vitruvius is vainly trying to get the attention of his 'Mechanicks' away from the cluster of men viewing the fountain in order to make a final rehearsal. On the lawn, the real plumbers working on the fountain rub shoulders with the dancers in their costumes, who carry outsize tools of the building trades as props.

A remarkable 'special effect' is planned to follow the dance of the builders. The king and queen will have 'a second banquet set down before them from the clouds, by two Loves'.[69] This means that boy actors playing a pair of cupids will serve the king and queen with another meal of delicate sweetmeats, after making a spectacular entrance in a mechanical cloud (Plate 12). There is, therefore, a third focus of activity in the garden this morning: as well as the head scratching of the plumbers round the fountain and the limbering up of the dancing builders, there is a group of carpenters finalising the mechanics of this device.

When masques are staged at court, up to a hundred workmen are employed to make the scenery and the 'degrees' (stacked seating for spectators).[70] Today, William Cavendish's carpenters are putting the finishing touches to the seating for the courtiers, but their most important work will be the checking of the cupids' mechanical cloud. The cloud will descend from the battlements of the high Stone Walk itself. The equipment is being set up and tested, with many cries of instruction and warning. Billows of silk, representing the ether, are intended to disguise the ropes and pulleys.

The mechanical cloud, remarkable though it sounds, is actually something of a staple among masque effects. Nicolà Sabbatini will include a diagram showing how to construct one in his *Pratica di fabricar scene e machine* (1638). When the room or garden where a masque is to be performed lacks a balcony or high place, a series of pulleys controlled by a capstan beneath a temporarily built-up stage can be used to lift and lower a cloud, and such devices have often been seen in court circles. In John Marston's 'Huntingdon Masque', performed in 1607 at Ashby de la Zouch Castle, 'a cloud was seen to move up and down almost to the top of the great chamber'. During the 'Entertainment at Theobalds', written by Ben Jonson and staged the same year, a 'boy figuring Good *Event*' was suspended in a cloud, with 'nothing seen to sustain him by all the time the Shew lasted'.[71]

Tension is running high in the garden as the final preparations take place. Those involved in staging masques at court curse the frequent last-minute disruption caused by guests who insist upon making behind-the-scenes visits to see how the special effects will be achieved. The necessary woman with the chamber pot is certainly de trop; perhaps someone questions her presence, or even more forcefully, suggests that she remove herself. Yet, as she hastens past, she is lucky enough to hear a loud and jubilant shout go up from the Cistern House, where someone is tweaking the valves. Everyone now turns towards the fountain. Hats are pulled off the heads of the more observant, for the cheering has drawn William Cavendish himself out of his closet and through the hinged, full-height windowed doors onto his balcony overlooking the whole panorama of plumbers, actors, workmen and dancers. Beneath the balcony, a stone Hercules delivers a blow to a lion and a cherub smiles out from between feathered wings. Directly above them, William places two hands on the chunky stone balustrade and leans forward to see into the fountain's basin.

A silence follows the shout: pulleys stop still as those holding the ropes turn towards the fountain, the musicians' twanging ceases and Colonel Vitruvius's groans and curses fall away. Now water slowly begins to drip from the flanks of the satyrs and the mouths of the priapic beasts. The Caesars begin to spit, and water starts to trickle down the beards of the lions on the central pillar. Only when the upper basin is full will the urinating putti begin to work, but the process is now in motion and the fountain has burst into life. The stage is set, the actors are ready, and very soon the audience will arrive.

On the morning of 30th July, 1634, the thirty-three-year-old Charles I and his wife Henrietta Maria open their eyes at Welbeck Abbey. Charles is doubtless occupying the grandest rooms of the state suite in the new wing overlooking the water garden to the south, set up for his temporary residence with the household's richest furnishings and textiles.

Charles has now been king for nearly a decade, and his courtiers have had a good chance to assess his personality. William will always overlook Charles's weaknesses in favour of his strengths, which include great personal charm and a love of art and culture. Yet the king's intransigence and his insistence on monarchical Divine Right – the belief that kings are answerable to God rather than their people – are making him increasingly unpopular. Six years ago, he was presented with, and reluctantly agreed to, the Petition of Right, a declaration by his subjects of their liberties, but the next year Charles dissolved Parliament and since then has ruled without its advice.

Shy and full of self-doubt, Charles can nevertheless appear obstinate and demanding, and his French wife Henrietta Maria is equally fond of having her own way despite her sweet and mild appearance. The Earl of Holland, negotiating the treaty of marriage between Charles and Henrietta Maria, informed the king that the French princess was 'the loveliest thing in nature [. . .] she dances – the which I am witness of – as well as I ever saw. They say she sings most sweetly; I am sure she looks as if she did.'[72] However, during the early years of their marriage, Charles remained in emotional thrall to his deceased father's favourite, George Villiers, first Duke of Buckingham. He relied upon 'Steenie', as he called Buckingham, for admiration and devotion. There were rows between Charles and Henrietta Maria over matters such as her failure to learn the English language and her insistence on maintaining her own French household, complete with

Catholic priests. It was only in 1628, with the Duke of Buckingham's shocking assassination by a fanatic, that Charles was left free to fall in love with his wife.

This is not the king's first visit to Welbeck. He stopped off here a year ago on his way north to his coronation in Scotland. His intense enjoyment of his brief but luxurious stay with the Cavendishes explains his decision to return this summer, accompanied by his queen, and the court has already spent a whole week at the abbey. Today will be the high point of their stay, a day-long outing to Bolsover Castle five miles away.

By late morning, the king and queen are in their coach and bowling out of the courtyard at Welbeck on the drive to Bolsover. Their route takes them through the villages of Cuckney and Langwith, where they scatter coins to the gathered crowds, and out of the county of Nottinghamshire into Derbyshire. Welbeck is set in a wooded bowl, and the road to Bolsover leads gradually upwards from the loamy, bracken-floored forests of Nottinghamshire towards the open fields and moors of the plateau where Derbyshire begins. This airy plateau appears limitless as the royal coach approaches Bolsover from the east through deep-cut lanes fringed with stone walls and wind-blown hawthorn. There is

William on horseback before the western front of Bolsover Castle

no warning of the sudden and dramatic falling away of the ground, or of the astounding view that opens up to the west, as the king and queen pass through the small town and out onto the edge of the escarpment on which the castle sits.

Their coach edges through the gates onto the long drive leading to the Little Castle; great care is needed in negotiating the steeply sloping corner. Now the long, incomplete hulk of William's new Terrace Range lies to their right, a barracks-like building punctuated by its strange cannon devices, its gutters jutting out proudly and its whole facade sprouting excresences of vermiculation and carved stone.[73] The wind whistles through the unglazed windows, and cheering workmen gather at the incomplete doorways and as-yet unguarded balcony.

To the king and queen's left, a low battlemented wall guards them from infinity. Below it, the hillside drops away and elder, early rosehips and beech carpet the steep slopes down to the park. Further distant, fold upon fold of fields rise up to Sutton Hall, with the darker folds of the Peaks as a backdrop. The royal couple's goal is the Little Castle at the very tip of the promontory, and its brave, chivalric appearance must intrigue and enchant as they approach between stone on the one hand and sky on the other.

Now the royal coach draws up at the double staircase, where William is waiting in the lowest of bows, his hat in his hand. The king and queen alight, and William accompanies them up the steps to the Little Castle's forecourt. Pausing with a hand on the balustrade, they admire the outsize crossbow slits, the obelisks and the battlements. Passing between the tiny lodges and through a heavy gate, they find themselves in a courtyard. All around them is stone: tawny, yellow, rose-coloured, even a pale violet in its shading. The battlemented walls now protect them from the wind. Directly ahead, gold knobs sparkle on the lime-green railings of the first-floor balcony. In this forecourt, the king and queen sense that they are being transported back into a romantic medieval world. The weight of the balcony is supported by the shoulders of a red sandstone statue of Hercules, who holds it up just as he held the world on his back when, according to ancient mythology, he temporarily took over Atlas's job. Now the king and queen climb a staircase to the front door, noting that the decreasing width of the steps creates an optical illusion of even greater height and grandeur. Yet the effect aimed for is intricacy rather than scale: this is a tiny, toy-like jewel of a building.

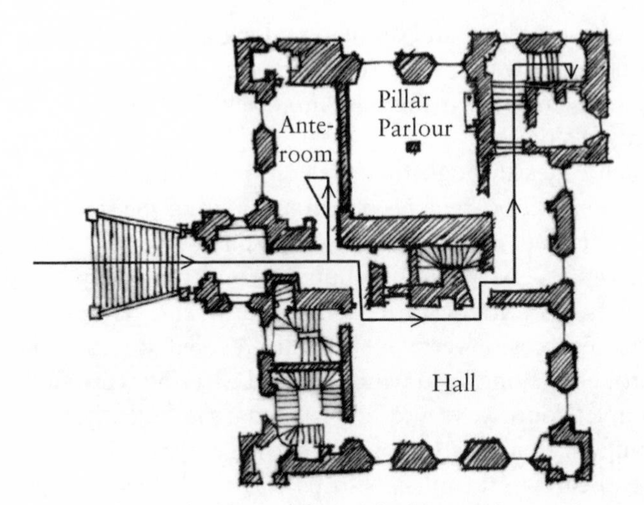


Plan of the Little Castle, ground floor. The king and queen's route is marked

Passing now through the red door, the king and queen are ushered into the ante-room and look with interest at the strange chamber they find themselves in. Small, with a vaulted ceiling, its most remarkable features are the semi-circular paintings positioned above the stencilled panelling of the walls.

William now introduces Charles and Henrietta Maria to the first in a series of abstruse but ingenious secret messages hidden throughout the decoration of his Little Castle. He explains that by choosing to stand, as he now does, before a backdrop of a painting showing a strange and desolate landscape including a temple, sea and flame, his own body completes a sequence begun in the other wall paintings. The other scenes in this room depict three of the four 'humours', the substances of which it is thought in the seventeenth century that the human body is composed. The preponderant humour in a person's body determines his character, whether phlegmatic or choleric, melancholy or sanguine. In these paintings, a fisherman and his wife represent the phlegmatic humour, a red-faced, debonair soldier and his mistress the choleric, and the titillating view of an old man seducing a beautiful and bare-breasted young lady the melancholic humour.[74] The fourth lunette, with its strange composition of sea and temple, has been left without figures. William has taken his position before it in order to complete the sequence by representing the 'sanguine' humour himself. This is quite in keeping with his character: in the seventeenth century, those of a sanguine disposition are red-blooded and passionate. This, then, is the position from which William greets the king and queen: he is introducing himself as well as his castle.[75]

Since his father's death, William has had his house for retirement and pleasure sumptuously decorated.[76] Each room contains a hidden message as the figures of gods, goddesses, humorous characters, heroes and family devices are combined with secret significance. In William's lifetime there lingers on a Renaissance love of the obscure, meaning-laden picture that contains a story to be unravelled only by the erudite. Geoffrey Whitney wrote in 1586 of the use of 'emblems' to stand for a whole train of thought or didactic message, a shorthand to be appreciated by the learned who have studied emblem books. William's father and William himself belong to the last generations to appreciate art containing 'some witty devise expressed with cunning workmanship, something obscure to be perceived at the first, whereby, when with further consideration it is understood, it may the greater delight the beholder'.[77] Now William and his guests embark upon their tour of the castle. Their next destination is the Great Hall, where the mystery deepens.

The statue of Hercules positioned over the very front door of the Little Castle has already announced to the guests that they are entering the house of someone who models himself upon the ancient hero. Here, in the Great Hall, the wall paintings show Hercules himself, performing his labours in scenes of such deceptive verisimilitude that the painted background blends into the real stone masonry of the walls around (Plate 17). He will appear once more in the Elysium closet upstairs, and the myth of Hercules is the key that unlocks the secret meaning of the Little Castle. In legend, a jealous goddess curses Hercules with divine madness, and under its influence he murders his wife and children. In order to redeem himself, he carries out his twelve labours. The message is that bad behaviour, or self-indulgence, can be redeemed by the special qualities and abilities of a hero. At one point in his mythical journey, Hercules has to make a choice between the rough path of virtue and the easy path of pleasure. Because of his arduous labours, he is justified in choosing pleasure for a while. At Bolsover the message is clear: this is the house of a man like Hercules, capable of great industry, strength and virtue – a man who also therefore deserves to pursue pleasure.

The question of whether pleasure or virtue is the more important is highly topical. A great row broke out during the reign of Charles I's father about whether it was acceptable or not for villagers to play games on the green on a Sunday after church; William himself is strongly in favour not only of the games but also of cakes and ale and dancing round the maypole.[78] The increasingly strong Puritan movement was dead set against such cavorting, but James I eventually pronounced himself to be in its favour. He issued a 'Book of Sports', a set of laws making it admissible, among other things, to play games on Sundays, pleasure being permitted in the context of a legitimate holiday from the hard grind of virtue. The question was so hotly debated that in 1618 Ben Jonson devoted a whole masque to the issue. It was this masque, 'Pleasure Reconcil'd to Virtue', showing the hero Hercules setting out on his laborious journey and ending up in a garden of pleasure, which inspired the decoration of the Little Castle.

Now the king and queen leave the Great Hall to make a stately ascent of the stairs. Passing through the great Star Chamber already set up for the feast, the king and queen accompany William into his bedchamber. Of course, access to this, the most intimate room of the house, is a compliment to the guests, not an invasion of William's privacy; the king is master of the house for the afternoon and must make use of all its facilities. So far their processional progress through anteroom, Great Hall, stair, Star Chamber and bedchamber has been easy

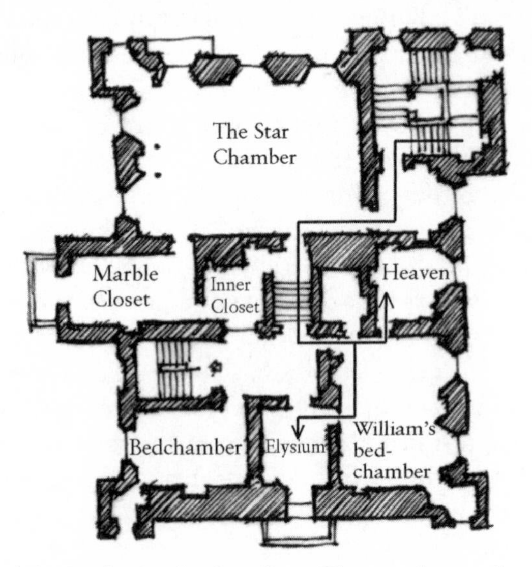


Plan of the Little Castle, first floor. The royal route is marked

to follow. Now the king and queen have to make a choice – just like Hercules in legend – between William's two closets, decorated respectively with scenes of pleasure and virtue. There is no question about William's own preference. He has chosen to show Hercules, on whom he models himself, dallying with a naked nymph in the frieze of the Elysium closet. Around them other gods and goddesses of Mount Olympus fondle each other, flirt or are caught in adultery (Plate 20). William's own opinion is clear: pleasure is more important than virtue. Amused debate between king and queen surely follows.

Throughout the 1620s, William's programme of fabulous paintings at his palace of pleasure began to include an increasingly explicit celebration of sexual pleasure, and the Little Castle has become a monument to his lifelong love of women. He has put so much effort into making the point that pleasure can be more important than virtue because he has to counter the popular perception of himself as a great pleasure-seeker. In his wall paintings, he takes pride in his image as a womaniser. In the ante-room an old man seduces a young woman, the Pillar Parlour pictures celebrate sensuality, and in the Marble closet pairs of naked ladies (symbolising virtue) caress each other. William's Elysium closet shows scenes of debauchery among the inhabitants of Mount Olympus, and the room looks down onto the goddess of love below, surrounded by her lascivious beasts. There is much in William's private life to support this view of him as someone comfortable with his image as a great lover.

Despite William's close relationship with his 'Derest Harte' Elizabeth, no seventeenth-century aristocrat expects to receive sexual fulfilment from his wife. Wives (for bearing children) and mistresses (for pleasure) have complementary roles, and an earl will frequently have both without scandal. His 'Whoore', for example, is more sexually gratifying: unlike his wife, she 'kisseth open mouth'd, and spits in the palmes of her hands to make them moist'.[79] The existence of an earl's mistress should not upset or embarrass his spouse: William is known to be 'a great lover and admirer of the Female Sex', but 'whether it be so great a crime to condemn him for it, I'll leave to the judgment of young Gallants and beautiful Ladies'.[80]

Even William's daughters appear to accept and take pride in their father's prowess with the ladies. They scoff, in their poems, at the women who make a pretence of bracing themselves for the onslaught of their father's attentions:

Me thinks now I see them, how they do profess
Preparing for Siege, yet means nothing less . . .

. . . Thus ends their resolves with this total sum
Oh, tell me, where is he, why doth he not come?[81]

Yet others are less understanding. William is probably more deeply addicted to pleasure than most, and criticism for his *affaires*, his foppishness and his indolence dogs his career as the Puritans grow in strength. He is accused of being overly fond of 'witty society (to be modest in the expression of it)' and his 'softer pleasures', and of having a weakness for 'delightful company'.[82] William's son Henry warns him that some 'presumptuously and extravagantly ambitious' young women of the household are filling the town and country with stories 'to dishonour your Grace'.[83] William's own poems about the young women of the household indicate that he does indeed prey upon them in a seigneurial manner. One couplet about the 'starcher' who works in the laundry is full of double entendres: 'you're nimble in your trade, at any hand/ you love to starch to make It stiff to stand.' And the 'young lusty wenches' who sweep the floors at Welbeck find an unusual use for the tool of their trade:

You sweep all clean, but sin, your flesh is wild,
But dares not dare lest you be with child –
What shift do you make, since flesh you refuse?
Your Broom-staff for a Dildoe then you use.[84]

Yet William does not confine his *amours* to those socially beneath him. He writes a long series of love poems to a noblewoman addressed simply as 'Madam'. Only the clues hidden within the poems – references to the High Peak area of Derbyshire and its town of Bakewell, and to his beloved's fine 'manners' – reveal the secret of her identity: she is Cecily Manners, Countess of Rutland, whose family home is Haddon Hall near Bakewell.[85]

Today, then, William is undertaking a high-risk strategy. He knows that he has a reputation as a pleasure-seeking lover of women, but he remains unabashed. The king and queen will either be charmed by his nerve in justifying himself as a lover of pleasure, or else they will be slightly disgusted. William will not have to wait much longer to find out their reaction.

It is time for the king and queen to dine, so they return to the Great

Chamber.[86] In the Little Castle this room is called the Star Chamber (Plate 14) because its plaster ceiling is divided by ornate ridges into elaborate compartments painted duck-egg blue and set with roses and lead stars painted gold. Beneath this cerulean ceiling, the outer two walls of the room (with their window alcoves) are covered with elaborate panelling, decorated in green, brown and gold and set with paintings on religious themes. Despite all this colourful splendour, the most magnificent feature of the room is the marble fireplace. On its front stands the coat of arms of the Earls of Shrewsbury – the relations by marriage to whom the Cavendishes owe the greatest debt in terms of honour and status – flanked by their proud hounds. Today, rich tapestries from Welbeck have been hung against the bare grey inner walls of the room; the Elizabethan writer William Harrison extols the English love of tapestries, featuring 'diverse histories, or herbs, beasts, knots and suchlike'.[87] This room seems particularly alive with the household's presence even when empty, for which there is a curious reason. The paintings in the panelling show a sequence of saints and the figures of David, Solomon and Moses, indicating that having ascended to the Star Chamber we are in the celestial world of the heavens rather than in the more mundane world of humans on the floor below. But there are two unknown gentlemen in contemporary clothes in the northwest corner of the room, and they have no obvious link to the rest of the room's iconography. Maybe these are images of William's household officers, laughingly watching what goes on in their Great Chamber.

In any seventeenth-century house, the Great Chamber is used for receiving important visitors and for entertaining them with food, conversation, music or sometimes a masque. The family may eat here too, if they wish to avoid the hubbub of the household, although they will also use a cosier private dining parlour in chilly weather. Today only a single dining table has been laid. William's royal guests are of too high a rank to share a table with the Cavendishes or anybody else in Derbyshire. The king and queen now take their seats while the most important of William's visitors file in and remain standing in an attentive circle to watch the royal pair dining.

The royal dining table set before the fire is decorated with ingeniously folded super-fine napkins; William has spent £160 on a new set of 'Table-Cloths, Sideboard-cloths, Napkins, *&c*'.[88] When his uncle the Earl of Shrewsbury entertained Queen Anne at his house in June

Napkins being folded (top) and made into strange shapes (bottom)

1603, he employed two 'ffrench men' at a cost of eight pounds solely for the purpose of folding the napkins and linen.[89] Damask napkins, roughly a generous 104 by 76 cm in size, are folded to form bizarre and intricate exotic beasts after the Italian practice.[90] The art of folding napkins, called 'nipping off' or else 'pinching', is a special skill akin to that of origami. Possibly a pair of specialists has been drafted in to shape William's napkins into birds and monsters, or maybe the household servant named Thomas, who possesses the knack, has been given the honour of showing off his skills.[91] The fashion will remain popular into the 1660s, when Samuel Pepys will pay forty shillings for his wife to be taught the art of pinching napkins. The fabulous price of the linen purchased for today's entertainment must mean a special commission – probably incorporating the Newcastle arms into its design – from the

Low Countries, the centre of the damask-making industry being in Flanders and at Haarlem in Holland.[92]

The spectators now clear a passage along the centre of the room to allow a solemn procession of ewer bearers (with towels over their shoulders) and servitors to make their way to the royal table. The former carry upon their shoulders basins of water for the washing of the royal hands, and the latter heavy chargers full of food (Plate 18). Once set down, the dishes will cover the entire royal table, overlapping each other at the edges. A book giving instructions to the waiters describes how they should mix the dishes up: a server must not

> set them down as he received them, but setting the Sallats [salads] extravagantly about the Table, mix the Fricases about them, then the boyl'd meats amongst the Fricases, rost meats among the boyl'd, bak'd meats amongst the rost, and the Carbonados amongst the bak'd, so that before every Trencher may find a Sallet, a Fricase, a boyl'd meat, a rost meat, a bak'd meat, and a Carbonado, which will both give a most comely beauty to the Table, and very great contentment to the Guests.[93]

Wine is poured from bottles standing in a cooler and presented with further aplomb; even menial jobs such as wine-pouring or towel-holding are highly sought after among members of the household.

After dining, the king and queen rise and go through to the small chamber that lies immediately to their right. The Marble closet takes its name, obviously, from its striking vaulted ceiling in black and white marble, its black and white marble fireplace, and its black and white diamond-checked marble floor, all made with fine stone shipped from Italy. This room, another small closet, is richly hung with red silk ('Cremsson taffetie hangings' are described in a later inventory) against green-painted panelling.[94] Semi-circular pictures, ornately framed with fruit and cherubs, hang on the upper parts of the walls (Plate 19). They show three pairs of naked ladies against pastoral backgrounds in which an occasional house or castle is scattered across rolling green hills very similar to those surrounding the castle. The ladies represent the virtues and have been copied from a series of engravings called *The United Virtues* by Hendrik Goltzius (1558–1617).[95] This is the room set aside for the king and queen to straighten themselves up in preparation for the afternoon's entertainment. Its furniture is appropriate for an interval of rest: a later inventory will mention '2 backed Chairs; 2 couches with taffeta quilts; 1 picture; 2 stands & 1 table' and '1 looking Glass'.[96]

There's a most ingenious explanation for William's choice of decoration in here, and he now accompanies the king and queen into the room in order to explain another elaborate and long-planned compliment. The erudite and observant guest will notice that there are two virtues missing from the series. The fourth wall of the room has no painting, but instead John Smithson has designed tall 'Frenche wyndows' opening onto a balcony from which the vast panorama of the Doe Lea valley can be seen.[97] By inviting Henrietta Maria and Charles to step out onto the balcony and position themselves against this view, William will have the privilege of seeing the sequence complete for a few brief moments, the king and queen representing the missing virtues of 'Concord' and 'Peace' set against the pastoral background of their own realm of England.[98]

Now, with great ceremony, Charles and Henrietta Maria emerge from the Marble closet and are led down the main stair, its walls plastered yet lined out and washed with a golden colour to give the impression of further fortress-like masonry. In the lobby at the bottom of the stairs, panelled and painted in black, they detect the sound of musicians tuning their instruments. The inventory of William's musical instruments records 'Att boulsouer 1 harpsicall',[99] and now 'two Tenors and A Base' are making themselves ready to sing. Beyond the heavily studded black door to the Pillar Parlour that opens off this lobby at the foot of the stairs the masque will now begin.

William sometimes eats alone, or with intimate friends, in his private dining rooms or parlours, and the most sumptuous of these is the Pillar Parlour in the Little Castle at Bolsover (Plate 15). Dim and north-facing, candlelight plays across the gilding of its walnut and black panelling, with its carved curlicues, flourishes, bosses, studs and stems. Winged horses decorate the ceiling, and William and Elizabeth's arms take pride of place on the alabaster fireplace of strange Gothic proportions and gleaming jewels. It is in this room – so richly redolent of the seventeenth-century court – that Charles and Henrietta Maria now seat themselves for a 'banquet of the senses'.

A world away from the mutton and porridge that the household customarily consume in the Great Hall, William's royal guests are now surrounded by music, food, delicious smells and fine fabrics, as well as the visual delights of the room, in an all-round sensory experience of private pleasure. What's more, the Pillar Parlour is itself decorated with panel paintings showing the five senses. The masque's first song explains that the king and queen are experiencing a banquet of the senses, and as the song begins a real banquet (pronounced 'banket') of sweet desserts is brought in. 'When were the senses in such order placed?' sings the first tenor, and the second tenor echoes:

> The sight, the hearing, smelling, touching, taste,
> All at one banquet?[100]

The room is set up with table, seats and perfume burners; later inventories will mention twelve cloth-of-silver chairs.[101] The seats for the king and queen are richly upholstered and the table richly dressed. A banqueting table is covered with a silk carpet before two layers of linen tablecloth are spread upon it.

Perhaps the table is laid with some of the newfangled implements called forks. Thomas Coryat, the Jacobean traveller, brought back news of the table fork from Italy, and wrote about it in a book entitled *Coryat's Crudities hastily gobbled up in five months travels in France, Savoy, Italy [. . .] and the Netherlands* (1611). He reported that 'the Italians do always at their meals use a little fork when they cut their meat [. . .] their forks being for the most part made of iron and steel and some of silver, but those are only used by gentlemen. The reason of their curious custom is because the Italian cannot by any means endure to have his dish touched with fingers, seeing all men's fingers are not alike clean.'[102] (Coryat also brought back news of another novelty called the umbrella.)

William has likewise toured Italy, and like Coryat, may have seen the sense in this new way of eating, which is so much more hygienic than the knife and fingers. In the sixteenth century, napkins would have been conveniently draped over the shoulder of the diner for wiping greasy fingers. With the seventeenth-century invention of the fork and a less messy passage of food to mouth, napkins have descended to diners' laps to protect their clothes instead. The earliest English silver table fork dates from 1632, just two years prior to today's masque. It was made for a marriage feast and hidden under the floorboards of Haddon Hall, some twenty miles west of Bolsover Castle.[103] With the introduction of forks, seventeenth-century knives will begin to change their shape: before now they have been pointed, used for skewering pieces of food as well as for cutting. In the next few years, knives with round blades, designed for use in conjunction with forks, will creep into fashion. Yet forks will not be in common use, even among aristocrats, until the very last decade of William Cavendish's life.

A later list of the family silverware indicates that the Cavendishes possess all the necessary equipment for dining and banqueting: they have '47 dyshes of severall sizes' for serving the dinner, '5 Basons and Vres [ewers] Silver' for washing hands, '1 Voyder knife' for clearing or voiding a table, and '12 ffruit dishes for crame [cream]'.[104]

The king and queen's olfactory passages are tickled by the burning of perfumed orange or lavender water rather than by fresh flowers on the table. Vases of flowers on a dining table will be an innovation of later centuries, though edible petals may well be on the table today as part of the menu. For the food that is now being served to the king and queen is the delicate banquet course, which is something quite distinct from the main feast of heavy dishes of flesh and fowl.

In medieval times the table was cleared after the main course to make room for the sweet course to be brought to the board. Clearing the table is called 'voiding' or 'deserting' it, hence the term 'dessert'. The job description of a medieval servitor indicates that the practice is by now centuries old: 'when men have well eaten and do begin to wax weary of eating, you shall take up the meat and void the table, and then set down cheese or fruits. Notice if your master is used to wash at the table or standing and cast a clean towel upon your table-cloth and set down your ewer and basin before him.'[105] By the seventeenth century, the serving of this sweet or dessert course often takes place in another room, so that the table itself can be dismantled to allow dancing or the performance of an entertainment.

The food served as this afternoon's banquet in the Pillar Parlour will be a feast for the eye and mind as well as the belly. Often banqueting food consists of both rare and everyday objects remade in spun sugar, and the king and queen will be drinking spiced or sweet wines such as hypocras or muscadine.[106] The writer Gervase Markham in 1615 recommends that for a banquet:

> You shall first send forth a dish made for show only, as Beast, Bird, Fish or Fowl, according to invention; then your March-pane [marzipan], then Preserved Fruit, then a Paste, then a wet Sucket, then a dry Sucket, Marmalade, Comfets, Apples, Pears, Wardens, Oranges and Lemons sliced [. . .] no two dishes of one kind going or standing together, and this will not only appear delicate to the eye, but invite the appetite with the much variety thereof.[107]

There are instructions in the Cavendish family's recipe book for making almond butter, barley cream, white sugar candy, metheglin, essence of honey and other sweets to tempt the cloyed appetites of surfeited guests.[108]

One of the strangest parts of the banquet is its conclusion. Having eaten their fill of the sugar world set before them, the guests take great delight in throwing, crushing or smashing the remaining items, in something of the same spirit that the glasses drained for a toast are tossed over the shoulder. John Partridge, in his *Good Huswives Closet* (1584), outlines the fashions of the rich for those who wish to emulate their betters: 'At the ende of the Banquet they may eate all, and breake the Platters, Dishes, Glasses, Cups, and all things.'[109] We do not know for certain that the king and queen today participate in one of these aristocratic food fights in the Pillar Parlour. It is a type of behaviour associated more with Charles's father, the riotous James I, who liked to drink and carouse. Yet it is possible, now, in the Pillar Parlour, that England's king and queen throw cakes into the air.[110]

'Would it ever last!' sings the bass, but the banquet of the senses draws to a close.

The king and queen leave the Pillar Parlour and climb the stairs once again to reach the russet-red door leading out onto the Stone Walk encircling the Fountain Garden. Ben Jonson's stage directions reveal that after the banquet, the king and queen must retire into the garden for the masque's magnificent climax.[111]

Once upon the Stone Walk, Charles and Henrietta Maria make a circuit of the garden, admiring the views over the hills before descending to the chairs set up beneath a cloth of estate rigged up on the lawn. Now they are ready to be entertained by Colonel Vitruvius and 'his Oration to the Mechanicks'.[112]

Colonel Vitruvius, a pastiche of a pernickety and pretentious architect, with his confused talk of the classical principles and his rather desperate encouragements to his troupe of dancing builders, makes his entrance to laughter. Everyone recognises that he is a parody of the court favourite Inigo Jones. 'Use holiday legs,' he cries to his dancers, 'tune the tickle-foot' in order to spring, leap and jingle.[113]

Now 'Dresser', the plumber in Colonel Vitruvius's troupe, capers onto the stage, bearing his clumsy 'dresser', the tool used for softly shaping lead.[114] 'Captain Smith' beats out the time of the dance on his

Inigo Jones's design for 'two lackeys', comic dancers who would have appeared (like the dancing builders) in the earlier part of a masque

anvil, unable to take part because of his club foot. 'Chisel', the 'curious carver', brandishes his chisel and mallet, while his colleague 'Master Maul' the freemason carries his maul or stone hammer. 'Squire Sumner' the carpenter and his man 'Twybil' carry a carpenter's square (sumner) and axe (twybil) respectively. 'Quarrel' the glazier takes his name from the term for a small pane of glass, and 'Fret' the plasterer takes his from fretwork, the kind of repetitive detail that covers ornate plaster ceilings. Finally, 'Beater' the mortar-man gestures with the beater or paddle that he uses to stir the sludgy lime. The sketches by Inigo Jones showing similar dance troupes of 'fiery spirits', animals, fairies, mountebanks, druids, Scots, Indians and magicians indicate the kind of motley ingenuity that will have gone into their costumes.

The richly dressed spectators also contribute to the glowing splendour of this, the garden's finest moment, and the strange and colourful costumes of the courtiers clustered along the battlemented wall's walk are not dissimilar to those of the performers. At a time when even a simple black suit of a quality fit for court wear costs as much as the rent of a London house for a year, clothes are vital signifiers of rank and wealth.[115] Everyday court dress itself is costly, bizarre and ornate, but even more splendid costumes are worn for masques. When one was planned at Hampton Court for Christmas, 1603, Charles I's mother Queen Anne gave permission for the late Queen Elizabeth's wardrobe at the Tower of London to be raided for costumes.[116] Anne had a great weakness for dressing up, and in 'The Masque of Blackness' (1605) she even appeared in person as a negro nymph. One contemporary thought this 'a very loathsome sight', and found the dresses of the queen and her company 'too light and curtizan-like for such great ones'. For ease of dancing masque costumes do customarily reveal more of the feet and ankles than is common.[117]

Ben Jonson's entertainment is intended to celebrate the perfect love that exists between the king and queen. Inside this circular garden, then, the next scene is a debate on the nature of love, to take place between two cupids, Eros and Anteros. To gasps of surprise, Eros and Anteros now make their descent in the mechanical cloud, bearing with them yet another course of banqueting food. The king's cupid is garlanded with white and red roses, while the queen's wears a circlet 'of lilies interweau'd, Gold, Silver, Purple &c'. The rest of their costumes are identical: 'arm'd and wing'd: with Bowes, and Quivers, Cassocks, Breeches, Buskins, gloves, and perukes alike'.[118] Between them they snatch a frond of victory palm leaves as they squabble. Finally, they come to an agreement that the king's and queen's loves, which they represent, are in perfect harmony. Anteros exclaims that the royal court 'is circular, And perfect!', neatly aligning the Neoplatonic view of the universe as an ascending series of perfectly circular layers with the circular fountain court in which the masque is taking place.[119]

The masque draws to a close with a final declaration on the subject of love by an old philosopher. He draws out a last link between this magical circular garden of William Cavendish's and the love between the king and queen:

> The Place I confesse, wherein (by the providence of your mother Venus) you are now planted, is the divine Schoole of Love. An Academie, or Court, where all the true Lessons of Love are throughlie read, and taught.[120]

The whole of Derbyshire accompanies the philosopher, he says, in wishing the king and queen a long and happy life, 'joined by holy marriage', 'To wch two words bee added, a zealous Amen, and ever rounded with a Crowne of welcome.'[121]

The philosopher's name is Philalethes, or 'truth lover'. His moving personal address to the king and queen praises them, flatters them, inspires them and seduces them with its promises of future success and fecundity. But will it be effective in encouraging them to reward their host?

The sun has travelled over the castle, and Venus's plump shadow now falls onto the lawn to the east of the fountain. The day has worn itself out, and the king and queen have departed in a cloud of dust and elation on their journey back to Welbeck Abbey for the night. William Cavendish himself appeared in this afternoon's masque, albeit in an oblique manner. In the speech that closed the show, Philalethes wished the king and queen's love for each other to be immeasurable, 'their felicity perfect'. William shared in these hopes, Philalethes declaimed: 'So wisheth the glad, and gratefull Client seated here; the over-joy'd Master of this House; and praieth that the whole Region about him, could speake but his language.'[122]

No doubt the love and honour that William feels so deeply for the king and queen do indeed make him feel 'glad and grateful' for their presence, and perhaps this is enough for his satisfaction. Yet one of the perpetual risks run in staging a masque is the sense of melancholy deflation when its magic is over. The aged magician Prospero in *The Tempest* captures the evanescence of a masque's charms, which leave behind nothing but a glorious memory tinged with regret for what has been and a sense of brevity and mortality. Perhaps, despite his proud pleasure in the success of his day, William likewise feels that:

> Our revels now are ended. These our actors,
> As I foretold you, were all spirits and
> Are melted into air, into thin air:
>
> [. . .] We are such stuff
> As dreams are made on, and our little life
> Is rounded with a sleep.[123]

It must be a melancholy sight to see the Star Chamber, Pillar Parlour and Fountain Garden now being returned to their bare, everyday appearance as the trappings and scenery of the day's entertainment are dismantled. The Elizabethan writer George Whetstone also gave an evocative description of how miserable a house's Great Chamber appears after a fabulous masque, and perhaps William turns back towards his castle with similar thoughts in mind. Whetstone's narrator describes how, the morning after a masque, he found the Great Chamber

> in the space of one slumbering sleep, to be left like a desert wilderness, without any creature, save sundry savage Beasts, portrayed in the Tapestry hangings [. . .] In the end, to recomfort my throbbing heart, I took my Cittern, and to a solemn Note, sung this following Sonnet . . . [124]

Is William Cavendish still buoyed and jubilant, still the 'overjoyed master of the house', or does he too feel the need to comfort his 'throbbing heart' with music? And will this day of extravagance achieve the magnificent results for which he hopes?

His political mentor, the Earl of Strafford, has advised William to delay speaking to the king directly about his hopes for court advancement until after the royal party have left Welbeck to continue their journey to the north. William is planning to ride with the king's train for a few days, at which point he will carry out Strafford's instructions. 'You should yourself gently renew the motion to the King,' Strafford has advised, and 'if his Majesty should be induced to grant that you desire [. . .] you should receive it and value it, as the highest honour you can have in this world to be always near him.' Yet William's friend has also counselled him not to raise his hopes too high: 'On the other side,' Strafford wrote, 'if in his wisdom he should not conceive it fit, you should wholly acquiesce in his good pleasure, and beseech him to reckon you as a servant of his, ready to lay down your life, wherever he should be pleased to require it of you.'[125]

In fact, this day's masque at Bolsover Castle has in some ways been poorly calculated to win William the king's beneficence. Ben Jonson, for example, is out of favour at court. By now ensconced as the favourite court designer, Inigo Jones has supplanted Jonson as the chief deviser of court entertainments, and in fact Jonson has exploited William's masque to settle a private score with his former collaborator. The buffoon Jonson created for today's performance, Colonel Vitruvius, was a dangerous insult to the architect Jones.[126] Also, the concept of the dancing builders was perhaps hit upon to make the best of a bad job, the building work on the Terrace Range not having been completed in time.

It's likewise hard to be sure what Charles I has made of the extraordinary decoration of William's Little Castle, with its celebration of pleasure and sexual love. While the lewd designs may well have intrigued and titillated Charles's bawdy father James I, the new king is much more restrained and refined in his attitudes. As the Puritan Lucy Hutchinson approvingly noted, at Charles I's accession 'the face of the Court was much chang'd [. . .] for King Charles was temperate and chast and serious; so that the fooles and bawds, mimicks and Catamites of the former Court grew out of fashion, and the nobillity and courtiers, who did not quite abandon their debosheries, had yet that reverence to the King to retire into corners to practise them'.[127] Perhaps Charles, with his colder and more cerebral character, has even been shocked. In the world at large, the rise of Puritanism has created a climate in which debauchery is less acceptable than it used to be. Puritan writers are commanding their readers to 'shun all occasions of luxurie; Turn away thine eyes from alluring beauties, and look not after women'.[128] Attitudes to adultery and to the type of life that William takes for granted are beginning to harden.

Yet as William watches the dust of the royal party's departure settling over the terrace drive, there must still be a spring of hope in his mind and a glowing anticipation of the quiet word he will have with the king after his departure from Welbeck Abbey. It is fortunate that William has no inkling that the last and best-known pronouncement on his masque will come to be the judgemental comment of his waspish contemporary the Earl of Clarendon, who thought the day's magnificence almost too much to bear. In Clarendon's disparaging words, the masque was a 'stupendous entertainment', to be sure, yet it was also an event 'which (God be thanked) though possibly it might too much whet the appetites of others to excess, no man ever in those days imitated'.[129]

# 5 – A Royal Palace

THE PALACE OF RICHMOND, A DAY IN JULY, 1638

It is July, 1638. At last, four long years after the staging of his masque at Bolsover, William has received the court appointment which he had angled for on that occasion. Triumphantly transplanted from his own houses and gardens in the Midlands to the hothouse world of a royal household, he has recently been appointed 'governor', or tutor, to Prince Charles, Charles I's eldest son. William now accompanies his princely pupil through an age-old daily round of riding, study, eating and recreation.

This should be a time of tranquil satisfaction, yet there are already a few hints that something is awry with William's new palace life. He finds himself being challenged as never before by his post, and his detractors consider that he is not up to his job. William now faces another great question: whether or not he can retain the king's confidence that he can keep the prince safe.

At this moment, however, early in the morning, William is perfectly engrossed in his favourite activity: giving a riding lesson.[1] The prince and his governor customarily begin their day in a barn that serves as a royal riding house, one of the many outbuildings surrounding the former monastery of Sheen on the banks of the River Thames. Although somewhat makeshift compared to William's own purpose-built riding houses, the five-bay barn 'used for riding of the King's great horses' is the classroom where no fewer than three Stuart princes have learned to ride.[2]

The diminutive eight-year-old prince is too young to perform the twirls and leaps of the *manège*, but he is vigorous and courageous, well suited to the antics of the riding house and with more than a passing familiarity with its soft sandy floor. By the age of ten he will be able to 'ride leaping horses, and such as would overthrow others, and manage them with the greatest skill and dexterity'.[3] William has a blind adulation for his pupil, a boy thought by others to be exceptionally ill-favoured in looks. Shortly after the prince's birth on 29th May, 1630, his mother Henrietta Maria told a French friend that 'He is so ugly I am ashamed of him; but his size and fatness atone for his want of beauty.'[4] Yet William thinks his pupil 'the handsomest, and most comely horseman in the world'.[5]

William's new position brings with it responsibility for the prince's 135-strong household at Richmond, in addition to his own household back in the Midlands. When the pressure of the problems of security, precedence and petty theft among the royal household's members threatens to overwhelm him, William still turns to horsemanship for escape, and this morning he runs along beside the prince's mount with pleasure. In years to come, he will boast of having had this privilege of teaching the prince to ride, laying claim to 'the Honour to set Him first on a Horse of Mannage'.[6] There is no doubt that Prince Charles also enjoys his lessons. During one of William's periodic absences, the prince writes to him fondly: 'I ride every day, and am ready to follow any other directions from you. Make haste back to him that loves you.'[7]

William's new job as governor is the reward that he had hoped for on the day of his costly masque in 1634. During the subsequent four years, no court appointment came William's way, and the tone of his private letters grew increasingly desperate as he saw others promoted ahead of him. In 1636, he wrote from court to Elizabeth that 'they did cry me up, & since cry me down', and a month later: 'I am very weary [. . .] I find it is a lost business.'[8] He exasperated his political patron, the Earl of Strafford, with his constant requests for news, and the earl tetchily bid William to 'talk of an other matter, & says he knows nothing'.[9] Still, it was Strafford to whom William wrote when he finally received from the king's secretary the longed-for letter appointing him as governor to the king's eldest son. Prince Charles would henceforth have his own separate establishment. 'I have now the Great Trust in my hands,' William wrote in May, full of jubilant relief. 'God Bless me with it.'[10]

As William runs attentively beside the prince's horse, the nuances of his relationship with his charge are legible in his body language. He is performing the same role as Monsieur de St Antoine, the great French horseman and former riding teacher of Charles I. Both teacher and pupil are shown in Sir Anthony van Dyck's portrait of 1633 (Plate 21). Van Dyck constructed an image of almost godlike nobility, majesty and splendour, yet he also recorded an everyday scene: the horseman coming in from his daily training in the *manège* yard. The king's teacher glances up with an expression combining exquisite deference to his sovereign with half an eye for the way his pupil holds the reins.

Both the young Charles I and his elder brother Henry were taught in this very barn at Sheen.[11] A good deal of money has been invested in improving the outbuildings of the old monastic complex so that they can be used as a royal stable, as there is little room at the palace proper.[12]

Although they are lost in concentration upon their task, William and the prince are not alone in the barn. The tiny prince has a considerable staff to manage his stable. Thomas Dalmahoy, one of the two presiding equerries, has been temporarily promoted to serve as the prince's Master of the Horse until the post can be permanently filled. This important household role involves oversight of all the horses required for transport, ceremonial purposes or pleasure. Dalmahoy observes today's lesson with mixed feelings. This summer has seen growing discontent with the rule of Charles I. Dissatisfied with Parliament's failure to vote him the money he believes that he is entitled to, the king dissolved the institution and has now governed without it for nearly a decade. There is unrest in the country over food shortages, unemployment, taxes to pay for ships and the pressing of troops.

Dalmahoy faces a dilemma that will confront many over the next few years. Exasperated by Charles's failure to respond to the pressure exerted upon him to relax his style of rule, some of the king's subjects are reaching the point of considering an alternative form of government. No one reaches this position without a struggle against their natural loyalty to crown and state, but Dalmahoy secretly holds increasingly strong views that do not bode well for the royal family. Unbeknown to William, his Master of the Horse is ripe to be drawn into – and in fact, may already be being drawn into – a conspiracy to assassinate the prince.

Dalmahoy's increasing ambivalence to his master may or may not have communicated itself to his staff. The other 'Servants belonging to the Stable' and coach house include the purveyor, Henry Medlerott, who is in charge of feed and straw, the two coachmen, the two farriers, the 'Yeoman of the Close Carriage', the saddler, the three grooms, the sumpter (who arranges the meals of the others) and the bit-maker.[13]

These men are all close at hand, the diligent working at their tasks in the warm and pungent stables, and the idle constantly sidling past the barn door to observe the prince at his lesson. The rest of the horses are tethered in the Great Stable across the court from the Riding House. Seventeenth-century stables are entered through the arches of a carved arcade, each stall separated from the next not by a fixed partition but by swinging poles or 'bales'. According to the seventeenth-century architectural writer Roger North, 'horses do not love to be recluse, but hanker after the enjoyment of their company, which is by the eye, and so have pleasing converse'. At the horses' heads, a long manger stuffed with hay runs along the stable's inner wall. Here, however, even the most sociable and good-natured horses must be physically separated. North recommends that 'a post and partition at the manger is good, because it prevents snapping, and unequal feeding, as will be, if they can come at each other's meat'.[14]

Each horse is washed and groomed according to William's instructions: '*Dress* his *Mane* Clean every day, and Pleat it up again, which will make it Grow very much: You must Wash his *Tayl* very *Clean*, up to the very *Dock*, Dock and all; and often *Wett* his *Dock* with a *Spunge*, not only to make his *Hair* lie *Close*, but to make it *Grow*; and also it doth Refresh him very much.'[15] The horse urine that soaks into the timber planks of the stable floor is a valuable commodity. Despite complaints about the unpleasantness – 'the evil savour of horse-piss will be evermore in their nose' – official proclamations are issued against the paving or gravelling of stable floors.[16] The reason is that deposits of animal excrement, a vital ingredient of gunpowder, form beneath the boards. 'Salt-petre men' perform the job of travelling around the countryside from stable to stable, lifting the boards and scraping up the deposits beneath. They search out and collect animal excrement of all sorts which, combined with lime and ashes, makes saltpetre. This, added to a mixture of sulphur and charcoal, becomes highly explosive. The salt-petre men's visits, allowed by law yet most injurious to a stable, are dreaded, and in 1635 the Countess of Leicester gave the salt-petre men a generous bribe to go away.[17]

As the prince's governor, William must strive to enforce the orders regulating the behaviour of the household, orders that give stern warnings against the kind of disorder and abuses that are all too commonly found in the lavish royal households. Dalmahoy should be keeping a lookout for congregations of the curious who have no place in the royal stable. The 'Orders of the Stable' insist that he must 'suffer no Lackeys Boys Women or other Idle People to be about the Stables But the Prince's ordinary Grooms'.[18] When the prince's household rides out, the sequence in which horses are mounted must be observed: 'the Princes horses being placed first', followed by 'those of the chief Officers, the Privy Chamber and other nearest his Person'.[19] The Privy Chamber, a room in the palace, also gives its name to the exclusive body of household officers important enough to gain admittance and serve the prince in one of the most private areas of the building. These officious injunctions to obey the social hierarchy suggest a lack of obedience in the past.

The prince's governor knows that members of the royal household are all too eager for part of the prince's seemingly bountiful allowance to find its way into their own pockets. As Viscount Wimbledon wrote, 'what should I trouble myself to husband his Majesty's money? [. . .] more men prosper with spending and getting the King's money than by saving it. For, I see all will away, and he is the wisest that getteth his part.'[20] In the stables, Dalmahoy has the authority to chastise those who either wilfully waste or purloin hay, oats, provender or litter. Those who take another man's 'furniture' (harness and saddle) are to be dismissed from the stables, as, with firm emphasis, are any 'Women or other loose Persons'.[21]

Horses and stabling consume much of the royal revenue, which is hard-won through the imposition of unpopular taxes. To William and the Stuart royal family, horsemanship is much more than a sport: it is of great political significance and symbolism. Charles I's courtiers will first be labelled as 'the Cavaliers' by the parliamentary faction that despises them.[22] Invented as a weapon in a propaganda war, the term is intended to sum up the courtiers' arrogance, lavish clothes, languid behaviour and air of superiority. In future centuries, the expression 'the Cavaliers' will come to have much more positive and romantic connotations. The historian Thomas Babington Macaulay, for example, finds much to admire in the 'courtesy, generosity, veracity, tenderness and respect for women' shared by 'the Cavaliers', and their shimmering silken plumage as depicted by Sir Anthony van Dyck will

A broadsheet lampooning fashionable young 'hot-spur Cavaliers', each 'spending all either upon his belly or his backe, following the proud, apish, anticke and disguised fashions of the times, to present himselfe a painted Puppet on the stage of vanity'

arouse admiration rather than condemnation.[23] Eventually it will be almost forgotten that the term originated as an insult and reflects what the Parliamentarians saw as the courtiers' most basic shared characteristic: an obsession with horsemanship.

While mastery of the art of *manège* prepares riders for the hunt and the battlefield, it also has another, less obvious, purpose. The graceful figures performed in the riding house are seen as a metaphor for the self-control of passion necessary for a courtier to make a graceful appearance in a life where an audience is never absent. For no one is this lesson more important than for a prince, and no one could be more suitable as Prince Charles's teacher than William Cavendish.

William is aware that his unusual dedication to the perfection of his horsemanship causes curious comment. People 'think it a disgrace for a gentleman to do anything well', he complains. 'What! Be a *Rider*. Why not? He that will take pains for nothing shall never do any thing well.'[24] Persuading the great horses to perform their astounding balletic moves, especially the 'airs above the ground', sometimes involves physical pain too. Horsemanship requires strength, mental agility and the ability to combat the dangerous dizziness that can seize a rider as the horse spins round. William was involved in a dangerous accident on Good Friday, 1624, when his horse 'tumbled over and over, and brake his own neck in the place'.[25]

William is now the foremost English exponent of *manège*, even in this age of Cavaliers. Two influences combine in his horsemanship. Firstly, there is the long tradition of jousting, which survived, or was periodically revived, throughout the sixteenth and seventeenth centuries. Courtly jousts, where champions charged with lances poised on either side of a central barrier, had continued throughout the reigns of both Elizabeth I and James I. William in his youth competed on horseback at 'Running at the Ring' with the other young bloods of the court.[26] The skills of the *manège* are, of course, also useful in war. A horse can rear up into a *levade* to avoid foot soldiers, while the *capriole* (or leap) lifts the horse and rider out of danger.

The second influence on the development of English horsemanship comes from the new Italian school, a style of riding that has reached England via France. Young English gentlemen often go to Paris to train at the famous school at the Palace of the Louvre run by Antoine de Pluvinel, who had himself trained in Naples. France's equine supremacy throughout the early seventeenth century remains so great that it is only in 1649 that Sir Balthazar Gerbier will attempt to open a similar academy in Bethnal Green, offering a syllabus of 'riding the great Horse, together with the new manner of fighting on Horsebacke'.[27] This is a project that keenly interests William too, and a similar scheme for forming an English academy of horsemanship is taking shape at the back of his mind.

This morning, William once again stresses to Prince Charles that horsemanship forms a vital part of his princely training. William considers no sight more pleasing than that of a *manège* horse, 'so Excellent a Creature, with so much Spirit, and Strength', obedient to his rider. He is anxious to impress upon his pupil that an ideal sovereign controls a great horse just as he exerts discipline over his own passions. Horsemanship, like kingship, is a performance.

The prince's stables and riding house are a microcosm of a well-ordered, hierarchical society with an equestrian prince in the saddle. Yet, as the equivocal Thomas Delmahoy could tell us, there are growing political tensions in the world at large that require rather more of a prince or king than mastery of the saddle. There are growing groans of protest at Charles I's apparently insatiable demands for money and his lack of flexibility and empathy in dealing with his subjects. His Puritan subjects fear that the king favours the hated Catholic religion, while his blithely arrogant favourite courtiers, high taxes and dismissal of Parliament rankle equally. Unbeknown to William, various conspiracies centred upon a threat to the king's eldest son will shortly take shape. One involves Thomas Dalmahoy of the prince's stables; another will be led by shadowy senior figures in the king's army. This latter 'Army Plot' will be by far the more dangerous, for its leaders seek to implicate William himself.

When the lesson is over, the prince and his governor reluctantly return to the palace. William must hand the prince over to his academic tutor, Brian Duppa, Bishop of Chichester, for the remainder of the morning's lessons. William and Prince Charles ride slowly from the low huddle of medieval buildings, passing into the hunting park across open grass between fine mature trees. Deer and hares are the prey sought here; only after 1660 will fox-hunting begin to emerge as an alternative.[28]

Between the park and the small town of Richmond, a line of stout palings prevents the deer from escaping, and beyond the fence can be seen the roofs of the houses. This little town, formerly known as Sheen, was given its new name in 1501 after a disastrous fire destroyed the old royal palace in 1497. King Henry VII, who had, before his accession, been Earl of the Richmond in Yorkshire, decided to rebuild Sheen palace and give it his own titular name.[29]

To the right of the prince's party, a lane leads down to the river's edge and the crane for loading and unloading boats. The Palace of Richmond sits close to the river's edge, and boats, whether sailing or hauled by gangs of men tugging at ropes, are a constant sight.[30] William and the prince, however, press straight ahead onto Richmond Green. Before them stands the building known to the town's inhabitants as 'ye palace of our hopeful prince CHARLES, p. of Wales'.[31]

The imposing sight of Richmond Palace must surely capture their attention. The map made just a couple of years previously by the surveyor Moses Glover exaggerates the palace's Gothic, picturesque character, and in his elongation of its towers and turrets, its pinnacles and vanes, and its ranks of glittering windows, he emphasises the building's

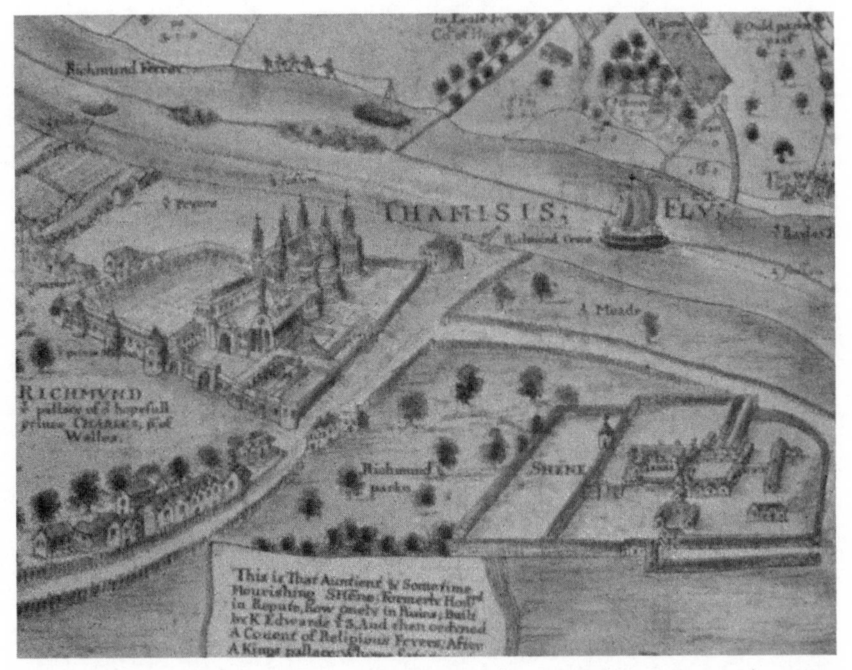


Detail showing the 'ye palace of our hopeful prince', from Moses Glover's map of Richmond (1635)

fairy-tale qualities. This is a castle truly fit for a prince, and no one can approach its gates without experiencing a frisson of anticipation for what lies within.

Through the brick gatehouse lies the palace's wide Great Court. Beyond this, in the direction of the river, rise the cliff-like walls of two great buildings that flank the Middle Court: the battlemented Chapel to the left and the gabled Great Hall to the right. Behind these two hulks rises an even taller and more lavishly constructed block, the private accommodation of the successive queens and princes who have made their residences here since Henry VII's death. Its three storeys of mullioned windows break forward and back with the twists and turns of its walls. There was once a moat separating the Middle Court from these Privy Lodgings, which have a roofline of ornamental chimneys and no fewer than fourteen turrets, each capped with a little lead cupola and wind vane. A herald, describing the palace in 1501, recorded that on top of every tower was a weathervane 'of the King's arms (painted, and gilded, with rich gold and azure) [. . .] the pleasant

Antonis van Wyngaerde's view of Richmond Palace looks over the Great Court and Middle Court (flanked by Chapel and Great Hall) in the direction of the Privy Lodgings. Their onion-domed turrets can be seen in the background. The conical roof shown to the right is that of the Livery Kitchen

sight of them, as the hearing in a windy day, was right marvellous to know and understand'.[32]

William and Prince Charles must now pass through the formidable great gates 'of double timber and heart of oak, striked full of nails right thick, and crossed with bars of iron'.[33] Porters scramble to swing them open. The tasks performed by the Richmond porters Richard Addams and James Bogg are similar to those of William's porter at Welbeck in sleepy Nottinghamshire, but the scale of their activity is far greater, for they oversee the comings and goings of a very much larger household. The written description of their responsibilities throws light onto the seamy underside of the royal household and some of the difficulties that arise for William in managing it.

The household rules reveal that the great gates must remain closed to the outside world except 'upon some urgent occasions, or for bringing of necessary Provisions for the house'. Addams and Bogg must heave the gates closed again, leaving 'only the Wicket door open to pass in and out at'.[34] Security is a particular concern in a royal household, and there must be 'continually one or more of them diligently attending the Gate', suffering 'none to enter it, but such as be enrolled in a List [. . .] Unless they be Servants following their Masters'. Unknown visitors, whose names are not on the list, must be asked 'from whence they came', and 'having informed themselves with whom they would speak', the porters must 'send for the party and give him notice thereof, that he may confer with him without the gate'. The well-dressed will be

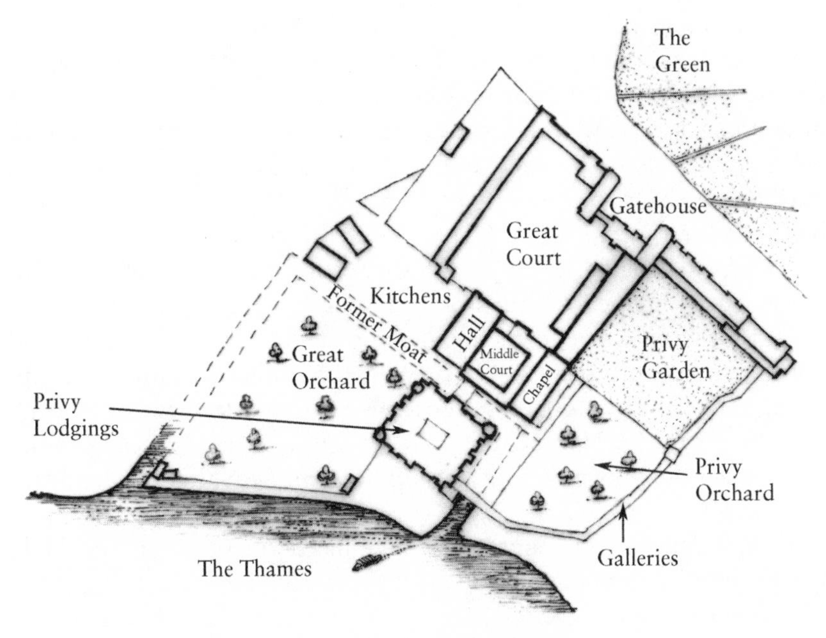


Plan of Richmond Palace

able to obtain entrance to the courtyards of the palace without too much difficulty, but if strangers 'that are not of good note' are found inside the palace, the porters must 'examine them what is their occasion of Stay, and finding them without employment or other good occasions They shall warn them to depart the house immediately'.

The porters have particular instructions to keep out the riff-raff of laundresses, artificers, masterless men, vagabonds and other undesirable 'persons that usually follow the court'. If any of these people manage to gain admittance to the inner courtyards, the porters must apprehend them and call for the marshals to throw them out. The porters must also be on the lookout for rowdy behaviour outside the gates, having 'a care that Artificers and such as follow the Court doe not pitch their Tents' on Richmond Green because the 'nearness of them [. . .] may be offensive to the household', or else 'their unseemly or surly behaviour' may 'annoy the court'.[35] The porters must also keep dogs out of the palace ('other than the Prince[']s') because the keeping of them 'will disquiet, and make the house unsweet', as well as consuming the waste food which would otherwise be given as charity to paupers.[36]

Addams and Bogg also control the early-morning entries and late-night exits of those members of the royal household forced to lodge in the town because of the shortage of rooms in the palace, 'letting them in and out according to their necessary occasions'. They must check, however, that these servants 'do not purloin and carry forth Provisions at those unseasonable hours Nor suffer any silver or pewter dishes to be carried out of the Great Gates'.[37] Finally, the porters must report upon 'any that ought Lodge within the Court' if they 'lie abroad without Licence obtained'.[38] Addams and Bogg, bowing as the prince and his tutor sweep through their gates, must know many of the royal household's untold secrets. Yet they, like the other servants, are kept sweet and silent by William's courteous acknowledgement as he rides past. 'Sometimes a Hat or smile in the right place will advantage you,' he counsels the prince. 'Civility cannot unprince you, but much advantage you.'[39]

Now, in the Great Court, the magnificent prospect of the Hall, Chapel and Privy Lodgings beyond comes into view. Out of sight but within earshot are the cries and groans of frenzied activity as provisions are unloaded and carried into the kitchen complex. To the far right-hand corner of the Great Court lies the service yard, now choked with men and carts. The octagonal roof of the vast Livery Kitchen towers up above the surrounding buildings. Smoke rises from its chimneys signalling the preparation of the household's dinner; the prince's meal will be prepared in the smaller Privy Kitchen. These kitchens and offices form a bewildering complex on an altogether greater scale than William's equivalent arrangements at Welbeck Abbey or Bolsover Castle.

Embezzlement is an ever-present concern in the great warren of rooms that make up the service court tucked away to the north of the palace. As the prince dismounts in the Great Court, the beef and mutton from the Slaughterhouse is being 'very carefully' weighed by the Clerk of the Acatery, as it is each day, and the figures entered into a book in the Office of the Comptinghouse to be 'tallied up monthly'.[40] The Comptroller and Clerk of the Kitchen must 'keep Larder' at nine o'clock every morning and at two o'clock in the afternoon in order 'to see that the meat be good and of the best' for the prince's diet, 'and afterwards for ye household, and severally to keep Records of the Same'. The diet, or daily ration, must not cost more than the set daily rate for the season, and the book must be signed to prove it. Only after it has been inspected may the yeomen and grooms of the kitchen 'carry away the meat & take charge of the same'.[41]

Many other buildings and offices nestle round the high tower of the Livery Kitchen, each with its own staff: the bake-house (run by two yeomen, Ephraim Arkham and Nicholas Annsell), the pantry, the cellar, the buttery, the spicery (whose clerk Robert Hope issues spices and fruit), the chandlery (where candles are counted by Guilame Langley), the confit and sweetmeat room, the ewery and the laundry.[42] In the kitchen itself, the chief clerk, the second clerk, 'Mr Cooke', two yeomen of the kitchen, a groom of the kitchen, two 'children', the skewers and a doorkeeper are hard at work. The storeroom has its own yeoman and the boiling house (where a huge cauldron of stock bubbles all day long) another. More staff work in the other offices: the poultry, the scalding-house, the pastry, the scullery and the wood-yard.[43]

This rambling service courtyard also contains the royal household's communal 'house of office' or toilet. Originally the moat ensured that sewage was carried into the river; now brick conduits are in use. A noxious smell nevertheless clings to the palace, and in a couple of months the Commissioners of Sewers will be called upon to remove 'the annoyance given to the Prince's house at Richmond' by the inefficient drainage that extends across the Green and into the town.[44]

This annoyance is also a hazard to health, and despite the constant attendance of a physician, apothecary and two surgeons, the crowded royal household is always vulnerable to sickness and plague. The risk is recognised in the ever-present household regulations. After a servant has suffered just one night of illness, arrangements are made to expel him or her from the palace. The 'harbinger', the officer responsible for allocating accommodation, must find alternative rooms for the patient in the town.[45] When plague is found in Richmond, 'in two houses near to the pond at the entrance into the town', the seriousness of the situation is revealed in a letter from Cornelius Holland, paymaster to the prince's household. A gentleman usher is immediately sent to the queen to advise her of the news, and a request is submitted for the prince's household to 'remove to some of his Majesty's houses already stored with provisions of beer, etc'. Given the nature of the prince's household and its large number of women and children, a draconian order limiting the size of the party that will be allowed to travel to safety is required. A skeleton staff may go with the prince but the rest will be forced to take their chances in plague-stricken Richmond, 'to help the prevention of a further spreading of this infection by shutting up and restraining all dangerous places'.[46]

Nor are the great officers of the royal household immune from danger in the palace where the prince's uncle Prince Henry, who died of typhoid at the age of eighteen, had lived. When William himself falls sick, Prince Charles writes with a charming scepticism of the efficacy of purgative medicines: 'I would not have you take too much Phisick: for it doth always make me worse, & I think it will do the like with you.'[47] William is cloyingly grateful for this royal attention during his illness, writing:

> Sir, I was sick, and you were with me; since
> I thought to thank You, Not as you are Prince
> Or my lov'd Master, but as You enrol
> Good Nature's Subjects to your Monarch Soul.[48]

Today, the clamorous servants will have gone, as usual, to collect their 'bouches of court'. These are the daily supplies of staple food and fuel issued to all members of the prince's household, who are remunerated according to their status. William's own bouches (collected on his behalf by his 'chamber-keeper') include three loaves of bread and three gallons of beer each day. From the last day in October to the last day in March, he is also entitled to half a pound of 'white lights' (wax rushlights) every night, three torches every week and four faggots every day for a fire in his chambers.[49] This generous custom is open to abuse, and the household regulations forbid the practice to which senior household members have previously succumbed of allowing their chamber-keepers to sell their bouches in the town. The porters at the gates are now on the lookout for the candles and firewood being smuggled out of the palace, and anyone caught selling his bouches has his allowance docked for a month.[50] In addition to the bouches, the household regulations allow twenty-five loaves of bread and forty gallons of beer as 'waste' or gifts to strangers visiting the court.[51] Once again the regulations contain an injunction against greed. Those partaking of the custom of waste must take their fill at the appointed bar, and 'none be admitted to drink at the bottom of the Cellor'.[52]

As tutor and prince pass on foot from the Great Court, away from the cries and crush of the menial servants, and into the more exclusive Middle Court, William Cavendish perhaps still feels a tingle of satisfaction at his ready access to the more important parts of the palace. He has finally made the stratospheric leap to high court office to which he has long aspired. Yet his complicated new life in the royal household is not without its irritations.

It was only two months ago that William received notice of the king's intention 'to settle the government of the person and family of the Prince answerable to his state and years'. William was chosen as 'chief director in the business' of this new royal household for Prince Charles, and became 'the only gentleman of his Bedchamber at this time'. The 'bedchamber' is both a room and a body of senior courtiers even more exclusive than the gentlemen of the Privy Chamber.[53] William's acceptance of the offer conveyed to him by the king's secretary was passionate: 'Truly, the infinite favour, honour and trust his Majesty is pleased to heap upon me in this princely employment, is beyond anything I can express.'[54]

Stuart princes are traditionally kept away from the hectic court to be brought up in the quieter atmosphere of the old palace by the Thames. Here Prince Charles has the company of his younger brother James, Duke of York, and his little sisters Mary and Elizabeth. As the state apartments in Richmond's Privy Lodgings are raised three rather than the usual two storeys above the ground and sit beneath a roofline topped with turrets, they have something in common with the high houses of Derbyshire where William has grown up. He must have found his first ascent to the elevated Great Chamber, with its antique air, like coming home.

Charles I, a loving but strict father, shares few characteristics with his son, who will grow up to become the easy-going, amorous and approachable Charles II. William, as the prince's tutor, with all his pragmatism and *joie de vivre* will be a vital, character-forming influence upon the future 'Merry Monarch'.[55] Charles I wishes his children to be nurtured in an atmosphere of 'virtuous education', kept safe 'from the too frequent vices of the times by a diversion of their minds from idleness and vanity at noble and better employment'.[56] William, a frequent indulger in the 'vices of the times', exercises a greater influence over his pupil than the prince's distant father knows of or would wish for.

Of particular importance is the question of Prince Charles's relationships with women, especially as he now 'hastens apace out of his childhood, and is likely to be a man betimes'.[57] The diarist and public servant John Evelyn's prim judgement on the future Charles II is that he would have been 'an excellent prince doubtlesse had he been less addicted to Women'.[58] This is a verdict that could equally be applied to the prince's governor, William Cavendish. Yet, as one of Charles II's biographers will ask, why should it be 'considered reprehensible for a ruler to enjoy female company or even to discuss important matters of state with people he trusted simply because they were not men?'[59] William, likewise, does not consider intelligence to be impaired by femininity, and encourages his literary daughters in their activities as poets and authors. It may be that Prince Charles, as well as learning from his tutor an atavistic, predatory sexual technique, will also be ahead of his times in learning to value a woman's intellect.

A small part of William is probably glad to be living in rural Richmond rather than at the urban palaces of St James's or Whitehall because he has proved himself to be less than comfortable at negotiating the sharp end of court politics. When he first arrived at St James's, he found 'a little spite at the first' at his appointment as governor to the prince,[60] and a couple of days later he sadly reported: 'I have made few friendships at Court.'[61] According to one of his detractors, it was a 'foolish ambition of glorious slavery' that enticed William to court, and he found nothing there but the 'neglects of the King and Queene and scornes of the proud Courtiers'.[62] William is unable to disguise his feelings and lacks the subtleties and guile of the seasoned courtier. However, this matters little as he accompanies the prince through the inner gate into Richmond Palace's Middle Court.

To their right, as they cross the courtyard, rises the Great Hall, where the majority of the royal household will shortly be sitting down to eat together. The Hall, one hundred feet long and forty feet wide, is hung with 'rich clothes of Arras'. The room is ornamented with educational statues. Here stand the kings of England, with 'swords in their hands, visaged and appearing like bold and valiant knights, and so their deeds and acts in the chronicles right evidently to be shown and declared' to their descendants.[63] The household's upper officers prefer to dine in private, but their occasional attendance in the Hall reinforces the household's communal bonds. The king himself has insisted that his 'white staves' (as those members of his household who carry white batons of office are called) dine every Sunday and feast day in the Great Hall of whichever palace he is then occupying.[64]

William must find the small Middle Court of particular interest because of its occasional use for the staging of masques. While entertainments will be held at Richmond during William's residence in the prince's household, the changing times mean that lavish performances are attracting more and more controversy. The masque itself as an entertainment – heart-stoppingly beautiful, yet foolishly extravagant – will not long survive, and within a few years it will have its swansong. In 1633, the energetic and vociferous writer William Prynne published a book, *Historiomatrix*, which condemned the stage and other 'lewd' practices such as May Day celebrations, bowing in church and drinking toasts. It was published at a moment when it was well known that Henrietta Maria was about to take part in another masque at court, and *Historiomatrix* contained in its index the famously abusive entry 'women actors notorious whores'. Prynne's reward for his unsubtle inference was to be condemned to the pillory, have part of his ears cut off and be imprisoned for life. This cruel treatment simply made him a popular martyr.[65] Stubbornly refusing to bow to the pressure of the people, Charles I and Henrietta Maria resolve to continue taking part in masques as and when it should please them. At Shrovetide it is now customary for the royal couple and 'their royal children' to 'dance again their mask' at Richmond Palace.[66]

Crossing the courtyard, William now passes into the cool shadow cast by the high wall of the Chapel, which sits above the palace's vaulted wine cellar.[67] Inside, the Chapel is decorated with further images of English kings and furnished with handsome seats, 'a fair case of carved work for a pair of organs' and a removable pulpit.[68] As they continue across the little courtyard, William perhaps delays his parting from the prince with conversation. Religion, for example, is one of the many subjects on which he has plenty to say.

William often counsels his pupil to 'Beware of too much devotion for a King, for one may be a good man but a bad King.' Yet he also candidly outlines the importance of religion in maintaining the social structure of the age: 'were there no Heaven or Hell you shall see the disadvantage, for your Government', and 'if you have no Reverence at prayers [. . .] then they have no obedience to God, then they will easily have none to your Highness'.

Prince Charles was baptised by William's friend William Laud (Archbishop of Canterbury since 1633), whose name is synonymous with the conservative faction of the church anxious to repress the Puritan movement.[69] Laud, though not one of the hated species of Catholics, is considered by the Puritans to exhibit dangerously popish tendencies with his fondness for surplices, altar rails, crucifixes and statues. His authoritarian version of religion has begun to squeeze people out of the broad Anglican consensus created by Elizabeth I that has survived for so many years. As the prince's French mother remains a devout Catholic, the prince's own religion is the subject of much debate and speculation. His academic tutor Brian Duppa is one of Laud's protégés, yet William, his governor, is known to be blissfully free from the taint of dogma of any type. A papal ambassador sending dispatches to Rome reports that William 'hates the Puritans, he laughs at the Protestants, and he has little confidence in the Catholics'.[70]

As William and the prince enter the gallery bridging the dry moat, so reaching the Privy Lodgings, Bishop Duppa will be waiting impatiently for his pupil. William, jealous of Duppa's influence, constantly warns the prince not to 'take heed of too much book', believing that actions are more important than words. But Duppa has a fine group of scholars in the Privy Lodgings at Richmond to instruct the young prince: Patrick Young the 'Library keeper', Henry Gregory as 'Teacher to write' and Enlamme de Pierrie as 'Teacher to Dance'.[71] William and Dr Duppa are considering engaging a further member of staff 'to instruct the Prince in the French tongue'.[72]

William's most important piece of advice, and he makes the prince a written reminder of it, 'is to be courteous and civil to every body'. He, unlike Charles I, understands the power of the popular touch. In the claustrophobic, communal life of the royal household and court, the prince must learn to keep a careful check on his tongue. 'Speak well of every body,' William commands, 'and when you hear people speak ill of others reprehend them and seem to dislike it.'[73]

At the same time, William also counsels the prince against informality and seeks to protect his princely dignity through ceremony. In a graphic description of the pomp that builds the charisma of a royal personage, he exclaims:

> what preserved you kings more than Ceremony? The Cloth of Estates, the distance people are with you, Great Officers, Heralds, Drums, Trumpeters, Rich Coaches, rich furniture for horses, Guards, Marshals men making room, disorders to be laboured by their Staff of Office, and Cry 'now the King comes'.

Prince Charles, however, will come to regard William's ideas about ceremony and etiquette as slightly old-fashioned. His habit as king will be to be casual and easy of access to the whole court, from the most senior officers to the 'number of little spaniels' that would 'follow him, & lie in his bed-Chamber'.[74] But William's description of a royal entry gives an impression of the commotion that now starts up as Prince Charles strides into the Privy Lodgings, as the ushers and grooms of the chambers sense his approach along the gallery and up the stairs, and as the cry goes up, 'Now the Prince comes.'

William and the prince must part: the prince to climb the stairs to the first-floor 'school chamber', and William to return to his own suite of three rooms, 'all well floored lighted and seeled' on the ground floor of the Privy Lodgings.[75] Adjacent to his suite are the 'waiter's chamber', three rooms for robes, four rooms for the Master of the Horse, and the servants' dining room. In his chambers, William will change out of the rougher clothes suitable for the riding house. His habit is to be 'neat and cleanly; which makes him to be somewhat long in dressing, though not so long as many effeminate persons are. He shifts [changes his clothes] ordinarily once a day, and every time when he uses Exercise, or his temper [temperature] is more hot than ordinary.'[76] This is now the moment for William to 'shift': after riding, and before his formal attendance at midday dinner.

William takes care over dressing, and indeed the fashions are so foppish that a great effort is needed to wear clothes elegantly. The fondness for jackets with slashes in their sleeves and shirts with lace collars can easily be seen in the portraits of William and his contemporaries, but, in the privacy of the bedchamber, less visible aspects of seventeenth-century costume are revealed. As he strips, William's odour is sharp and noticeable, a combination of sweat, stable and stale perfume; cleanliness plays little part in the general view of physical attractiveness. Rather than being frequently washed, underclothes are sometimes drenched in perfume, faith being put in its ability

> to repel
> When scent of Gusset does rebel
> Though powder'd Allom be as good,
> Well stew'd on, and well understood.[77]

William will not generally wear woollen underwear as silk and linen are less likely to harbour lice, but he now removes drawers made from the tough worsted suitable for the saddle. Because it is July, he replaces them with cool silk drawers in the new fashion. Only a few years ago his drawers would have been tied on like a loincloth, but today the well-dressed wear full, square-cut shorts tied with ribbons, with a small slit behind. In winter, William will wear longer linen drawers with stirrups passing beneath his feet.[78]

Next he puts on his finely worked linen, lace or Holland shirt. Male underwear is an important indicator of rank, and in addition it has now become the fashion to display it as a bold indicator of a man's sexuality. The slashes in the outer garment or doublet, front and back and down the sleeves (which are themselves rolled back), are intended to reveal more of the shirt beneath. Doublets are becoming increasingly short, so the shirt shows above the breeches. As William puts on his shirt, his attendant will tie the strings at the neck and the ribbons round the wrist and possibly the elbows too, creating a puffed effect in the sleeves, with limp lace ruffles hanging down over hands never used for manual work. At night William sleeps in a shirt quite as elaborate as his day shirt, but with even fuller sleeves, a deeper neck opening and a flat collar. His nightcap of linen will be equally ornate, and may be of the type with an opening in the top so that 'the vapour may go out'.[79]

After donning his shirt, William's cravat is tied around his neck, and his doublet and breeches are put on over his underclothes. One of the perquisites of his position is that William can equip himself with fine suits at the king's expense: the prince's two tailors are charged with making 'the apparel of all the servants to his Majesty' the prince, which 'shall be bestowed as gifts'.[80] On one occasion, William is called upon to solve a dispute between the prince's tailor and the women 'rockers' employed to rock the royal children's cradles. The disagreement is about which of them should receive the prince's own discarded clothing. One of William's officers reports that 'Mrs Hopton and another rocker tells me that your Lordship promised [. . .] they should be remembered with clothes of the princes', but on the other hand, the tailor claims 'your Lordship promised him a suit every year'.[81] The prince may call upon the resources of the Great Wardrobe, the department of the king's household in charge of soft furnishings and robes, but Charles I growls that his orders have 'not been observed' for the wardrobe's regulation. A written warrant from the king himself or Lord Chamberlain is now required before the clerk will make an issue.[82]

William's hair is in the current fashion: long, curled, natural, and parted in the middle. The length of courtiers' hair rouses the Puritans to indignant but impotent fury: Thomas Hall rants that 'long hair is one of the sinful customs and fashions of the wicked men of the world', while William Prynne considers long hair (and in particular lovelocks) to be no less than sinful, unlawful, effeminate, vainglorious, evil, odious, immodest, indecent, lascivious, wanton, dissolute, incendiary, ruffianly, graceless, whorish, ungodly, horrid, strange, outlandish, impudent, pernicious, offensive, ridiculous, foolish, childish, unchristian, hateful, exorbitant, contemptible, slothful, unmanly, depraving, vain and unseemly.[83] Yet William Cavendish will faithfully retain his long Cavalier hairstyle until his death.

Once he is dressed, William has business to transact. Firstly, he sits down at his desk and takes up his pen to write a progress report to his old friend and mentor, the Earl of Strafford. Addressing his letter from 'Ritchmonde', William wishes to let the earl know how deeply satisfied he is with his new position. 'I like very well both of my place & my young master,' he writes, 'which I thank God & my old master [the king] for whose favour makes me happy, God Bless him I pray, And send him Contentment throughout all his kingdoms.'[84] Having thus fortified himself with a remembrance of his good fortune, William now has many worrying administrative matters to turn to.

Frequent letters pass between the prince, his tutor and the prince's beautiful mother, the queen. There is no question, despite some misunderstandings in the early years of their marriage, that the king and queen love each other, and that both of them love Prince Charles. 'You are the son of our love,' Charles I will tell his eldest son in one of the last letters of his life (Plate 22).[85] Henrietta Maria's earliest surviving letter to her son was written at William's behest when the prince was, as so often, refusing to take the physick prescribed for him:

> Charles I am sore that I must begin my first letter with chiding you because I hear that you will not take physick I hope it was only for this day [. . .] I have given order to my lord Newcastle to send me word tonight whither you will or not [. . .] so I rest your affectionate mother Henriette Marie R.[86]

As well as keeping the queen up to date, William still has to discharge his responsibilities as Lord Lieutenant for both Nottinghamshire and Derbyshire. He must implement orders from the Privy Council concerning taxes and the 'trained bands', raised and drilled at a local level, that make up the country's army.[87]

He must also receive petitions and resolve disputes between members of the prince's household. He has, for example, to oversee the 'Order for the avoiding of Superfluous persons from the Court'. All the noblemen, knights and officers of the household are required to 'set down in writing the names of those Servants which of necessities they are to keep to attend them'. Perhaps this is William's day to 'view and examine' the lists in order to check that everyone has an appropriate number of servants.[88] He must also make sure that the household consists only of bachelors: 'no Child or Page or any Officer of the Prince his house nor Skewerer [. . .] in the kitchens do from henceforth presume to Marry upon pain of the loss of their several Places'.[89] And there are arguments to settle, such as who should receive 'the fees that belong to the buttery', and discontent that some of the pages of the prince's bedchamber are better rewarded than others.[90] There are appointments to make if a vacancy arises: William will himself recommend the prince's gun maker for promotion to 'under-keeper of the small guns' in the king's household. The younger royal children's governess at Richmond likewise seeks a place for a youth who has 'served in the buttery these four or five years at least'.[91]

William relies heavily on his secretary, the dependable John Rolleston, who has accompanied him from the Cavendish household. Back in Nottinghamshire, William's servant James Whitehead budgets for buildings and repairs, for William's travelling expenses and parting gifts to the servants at Welbeck, and for wages for those left behind in the country.[92] He sends accounts down to Richmond for William to check, but its master's preoccupation with the prince means that the household in Nottinghamshire finds itself increasingly free to spend William's money; Whitehead's accounts are not fully itemised and William must take them on trust. The office of governor comes to William 'not without considerable Charges, and vast Expenses of his own'; it will soon be mooted about the court that he is forty thousand pounds in debt.[93] This is a constant danger of court office, where crippling expense may outweigh the gain. The rise and fall of a courtier whose ambitions outstrip his income is summed up in the memorable description of the Elizabethan Sir Christopher Hatton as 'a mere vegetable of the court that sprung up at night and sank again in his noon'.[94]

After a couple of hours at his desk, and with the work far from done, it is time for William to attend the prince's dinner. He climbs the one hundred and twenty steps of the staircase within the so-called 'Canted

1 *A copy of the painting of William by his friend Anthony van Dyck. Like so many of the other Cavaliers painted in their silken suits by van Dyck, William adopts a conventionally pompous pose. His candid letters, poems and plays, however, reveal the extrovert behind this courtly mask.*

2 *William's parents on their magnificent marble monument in Bolsover Church. The plaque behind Sir Charles is decorated with the Cavendish knotted snake and the sunburst of his wife's family. The epitaph tells us that Sir Charles died happy: full of wisdom, honour and contentment with his family.*

3 *One of William's horses and a groom before the west front of Welbeck Abbey. The artist, working off-site from sketches, has actually missed out a whole wing of the house.*

4 *The east front of Welbeck Abbey, with members of the household going about their business. The nurses walk the children, a keeper sets off with his dog, the master of the horse exercises a mount, housemaids peep out of the windows, and a servant relieves himself in a corner.*

5 *William's grandmother's house: Hardwick New Hall, Derbyshire.*

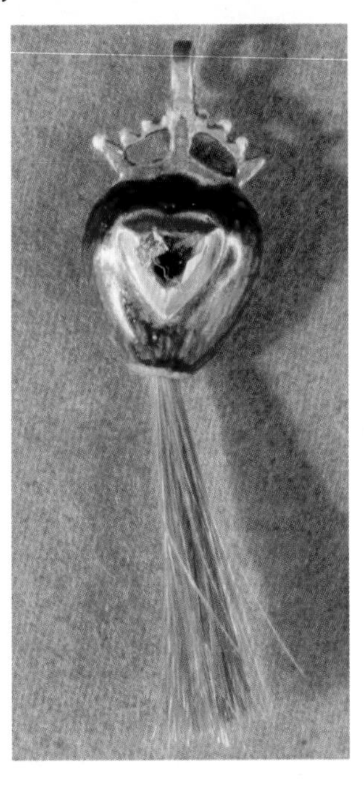

6 *A detail of William's 'Sweet Harte', his first wife Elizabeth, from the portrait by Daniel Mytens, painted in 1624.*

7 *A lock of William's hair swings from the actual earring that Elizabeth wears in her portrait (above).*

8 *A bracelet made from the hair of Elizabeth's mother.*

9 *The Cavendish family's masterpiece: Bolsover Castle in Derbyshire. The Little Castle is to the left, the Terrace Range to the right, and the Riding House Range lies behind them. The Little Castle is a self-contained house full of twisting staircases and hidden chambers. This house, intended as an escapist's paradise, was begun by William's father, and William himself completed its rich and mysterious decoration. Room after room contains an intriguing hidden message in its painted walls.*

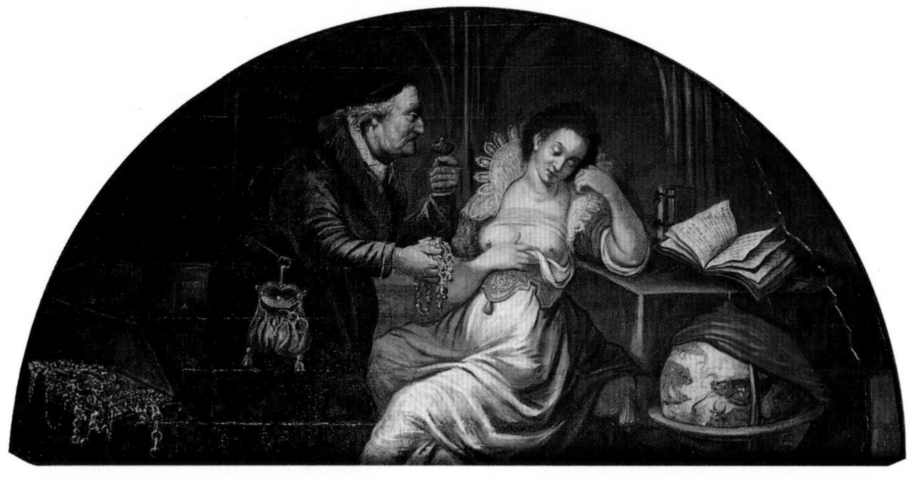

10 *An old man trying to woo a young lady, one in a series of seductive wall paintings in the Little Castle. This one, in the anteroom near the entrance, symbolises melancholy, but is also one of many lascivious images in this house of pleasure. The lady's books are shown shelved with their spines towards the wall in order to protect the bindings from the light.*

11 *The ceiling of the Heaven closet in the Little Castle at Bolsover. The band of cherubs round the edge are playing the country dance tune to which those in the centre (and Jesus) are merrily gyrating.*

12 *This picture, showing a masque in progress, gives an impression of the atmosphere at the entertainment that William staged for the king and queen at Bolsover Castle in 1634. Charles I and Henrietta Maria in the top left are playing the parts of Apollo and Diana. Painted in 1628 by Gerrit van Honthorst.*

13 *The Fountain Garden at Bolsover, looking towards the Little Castle and the balcony of the Elysium closet. The fountain was perhaps used for pool parties after William completed the Little Castle as a playboy's pleasure palace.*

14 *The Star Chamber, the Little Castle's great chamber. The two laughing gentlemen painted on the panels in the corner look like members of the Cavendish household, watching over events taking place in their master's most important room.*

15 *The Pillar Parlour in the Little Castle at Bolsover. It was in this room, so richly redolent of the Stuart court, that William entertained Charles I and Henrietta Maria with a banquet on 30th July, 1634.*

16 *The interior of William's Riding House at Bolsover Castle. Riding houses were not used simply for learning to ride, but for training stallions in the art of* manège *or horse ballet.*

17 *Hercules struggles with the man-eating mare of Diomedes in the hall of the Little Castle. Hercules represents William, struggling with (and vanquishing) the bestial side of his character. The painter has used images by Antonio Tempesta as inspiration.*

18 *Charles I and Henrietta Maria dining with their eldest son Charles, by Gerrit Houckgeest, 1635. Their courtiers are not allowed to join the royal family at the table, but look on respectfully. To the right servants carry in the food and drink. This is an imaginary scene, but gives a good idea of how a great household worked at mealtimes.*

19 *Painted lunette in the Marble closet of the Little Castle at Bolsover. The figure on the right representing Patience is squeezing her heart in a device like a flower- or linen-press to show that she can endure heartache patiently. After engravings of 'The United Virtues' by Hendrik Goltzius.*

20 *Hercules, having relinquished his club for a while, dallies with the nymph in the frieze of William's Elysium closet in the Little Castle at Bolsover. This is the room in which William reminded himself to relax and enjoy life.*

21 *Charles I with his riding teacher, Monsieur de St Antoine, painted by Anthony van Dyck, 1633. St Antoine also trained William in the art of* manège *during lessons at the Royal Mews.*

22 *William adored the young royal family: Charles I, Henrietta Maria and Prince Charles, c.1632. For them he risked and lost everything in the Civil War.*

23 The Garden of Love, *by Peter Paul Rubens, who used the architecture of his house in Antwerp as a backdrop. This became the house that William rented during his exile after his disastrous defeat at the battle of Marston Moor.*

24 *The painting studio in Rubens's House, Antwerp, where William may have later trained his horses.*

25 *William in later middle age. This miniature shows that grief and exile have taken their toll on his appearance.*

26 *The reconstructed dining room in Rubens's house: William's stay in Antwerp was passed in dark, rich interiors like this. William's own houses in England were captured by his Parliamentarian enemies, and the daughters he left behind there were forced to accept a garrison in their homes.*

27 *A printing press at the Plantin-Moretus House, Antwerp, home of one of Europe's liveliest printing businesses. Antwerp was a city that attracted artists and writers, and was a suitable home for the aspirant author, William Cavendish.*

28 *William's polymath friend, John Evelyn, painted by Robert Walker in 1648.*

29 *Henry Cavendish, William's slightly unsatisfactory son, painted by Mary Beale.*

30 *Margaret Cavendish or 'Peg', as William called his second wife. Painted here by Sir Peter Lely (1663–4), she was known as 'Mad Madge' by her contemporaries. Samuel Pepys claimed that 'the whole story of this lady is a romance and all she doth is romantic'.*

Tower', itself 'a chief ornament unto the whole fabric of Richmond Court'.[95] As he reaches the state apartments of the first floor, William is entering a set of rooms laid out identically to those in all royal palaces: as a sequence of increasingly exclusive chambers whose doors act as ever-finer filters. Only the most important courtiers are permitted to pass through every one of the guarded doors to reach the innermost chambers.

These Privy Lodgings at Richmond have become a famous repository for ancient and rare royal treasures. Years later, when Prince Charles has become king, he will send for the furnishings and sculpture familiar from his childhood: 'several boats, laden with rich and curious effigies [. . .] were brought from Richmond to Whitehall'.[96] The Privy Lodgings are open for interested visitors to inspect when the royal household is elsewhere, and some of their chattels have become subject to the mythology so loved by tourists and their guides. In 1614, a credulous visitor reported seeing a book on 'magic or the black art' from Henry VII's library and 'a large mirror in which Henry VII was able to see what he wished; but this mirror broke in pieces when the King died'.[97]

The outermost room of the Privy Lodgings on the first floor is the Guard Chamber. Here the yeoman ushers keep watch over the entrance to the prince's chambers, sleeping on pallets on the floor at night. Their room is occasionally pressed into service for performances, as it will be later this year for plays celebrating the birthdays of Charles's sisters, the princesses Mary and Elizabeth. A new stage and banked seating (or 'degrees') have recently been installed.[98] The regulations for the queen's household record the responsibilities of the ushers of the Guard Chamber: they must keep their workplace 'clean and sweet', and they must not suffer 'any lackeys, footmen, or any other unfit persons to enter'. If 'any of the servants of the gentlemen that attend the Queen come to speak with their masters', the yeomen ushers are not to let them pass but must instead send a page with a message into the inner rooms.[99]

Beyond the Guard Chamber lie the Presence Chamber, Privy Closet, Privy Chamber, passage, bedchamber and Withdrawing Chamber, with other rooms near by for the prince's brother James, for the pages of the bedchamber and for use as a schoolroom. Many of these rooms look down onto the famous gardens of Richmond, which are surrounded by a galleried walk. As these principal rooms are common to all royal palaces, the regulations to which they are subject apply uniformly to whichever palace the court happens to be occupying. The herald who visited Richmond in 1501 described the king's main chambers in generic terms: 'the first, the second, the third, enhanged all three with rich and costly cloths of Arras, ceiled, white-limed, and chequered [. . .] with their goodly bay windows glazed'; his words might equally well describe the rooms of a number of other royal palaces. Beyond the three main rooms were 'pleasant dancing chambers, and secret closets, most richly enhanged, decked and beseen'.[100]

In July 1638, the prince's activities are tightly circumscribed by the oppressive household ceremony constantly unfolding around him. He and his siblings have nurses, for example, like most well-born babies, but they also have official 'watchers' and 'rockers' for their cradles. His meals are eaten in public. The prince is now preparing to dine in his Presence Chamber, and those well dressed enough may seek admittance through the Guard Chamber to witness the ceremony. William, however, as the most senior officer of the household, has the greatest privilege of all: he is allowed to circumvent the guarded doorways of the main state apartment, using a back passage to slip into the Privy Chamber via the bedchamber. He now takes his place in the ranks of those standing to watch at a respectful distance from the prince's table.

Prince Charles is served with much the same ceremony that his parents had experienced at Bolsover Castle four years previously. The procession of the serving staff forms itself in the waiters' chamber on the floor below before ceremoniously snaking its way up the stairs and through the Guard Chamber into the Privy Chamber. The prince has two sewers (or ewer-bearers) who come forward with water for hand washing, and two carvers to cut his meat. The prince's gentleman usher is called John Acton and his waiter Henry Jay.[101] No one, apart from these servants, may approach or step upon the carpet laid beneath the prince's table. In the king's household, the usher who carries the towel that has dried the king's hands will even respectfully raise it above his head as he backs away from the royal table.[102] Charles I intends his well-ordered, dependable court to act as a model for the nation's households. In practice, the ceremonies surrounding this most formal, ritualistic court distance and insulate the king from the knowledge that there is growing discontent with his seemingly isolated and impregnable household. Traditionally kings had shown themselves to their people in regular processions and progresses, and Robert Burton, author of *The Anatomy of Melancholy* (1621), even includes a glimpse of the monarch in his list of cures for this modish malady. But now the sovereign is rarely seen, except by a few courtiers.[103]

After the prince's meal, the procession of carvers and sewers returns to the waiters' chamber, carrying the 'Napkins silver plates and silver dishes and Pieplates thence'.[104] In the past they had been accustomed to reuse Prince Charles's napkins 'at their own Meals after his repast', but as a result the napkins had 'been made unfit for his service'. The king has given new instructions that the waiters should use only coarse table linen, and that none of the servants should 'presume from henceforth to carry away, or make use of any of the said fine Napkins'.[105]

Once the prince has played his part in the theatre of procession, hand washing, carving and serving, and once he has eaten his tepid food, he will rise and go through to his Withdrawing Chamber. Only now may his officers eat their own dinner. William, because of his high position in the household, is entitled to graze from a spread of twelve different dishes. Besides his bouches of manchet and cheat bread, beer, ale and Gascoigne wine, these dishes ordinarily consist of two types of mutton, beef and mutton cooked together, veal and bacon, veal on its own, a capon, goose, chicken, lamb, pigeons, another lamb dish and a tart.[106] William relishes his food and frequently describes it in his poems. He lovingly recollects a memorable roasted pig in a buff coat like a soldier's ('how valiantly he bears up his snout'), a pie of veal sweetbreads formed into the shape of a fortification, with custard lapping against its outworks, and a whole pike in fine sauce 'Like a Whale/ In the ocean doth sail.'[107]

After dinner, William, as the prince's most senior servant and Groom of the Stool, now has the privilege of attending the prince while he relieves himself.[108] At the Palace of Richmond there is no need for a close stool because its Privy Lodgings contain one of the country's earliest water closets. Sir John Harington, godson to Elizabeth I, is credited with the invention (or at least with the importation of the idea) of Britain's first flushing toilet. A cistern full of water is released by the turning of a screw, thereby washing the contents of the toilet bowl into a vault below, so that 'your worst privie may be as sweet as your best chamber'. In his book *The Metamorphosis of Ajax*, Harington joked that the installation of one of his water closets 'in the palace of Richmond' would be a deed worthy of his being made one of Elizabeth I's gentlemen of the Privy Chamber. The title of Harington's book was

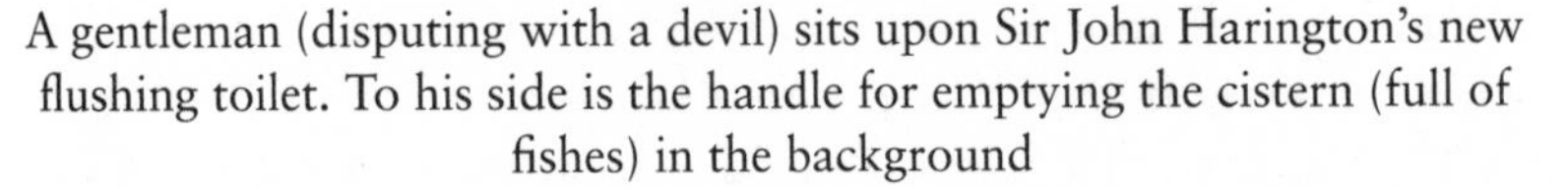

A gentleman (disputing with a devil) sits upon Sir John Harington's new flushing toilet. To his side is the handle for emptying the cistern (full of fishes) in the background

also a joke, for the word 'Ajax' is pronounced identically to 'a jakes', the popular euphemism for a toilet. Despite his frivolous tone, one of Harington's water closets was duly installed at Richmond. He later wrote a poem entitled 'To the Ladies of the Queens Privy Chamber, at the making of their perfumed privy'. Writing about himself in the third person, he angled for further reward for his invention:

> Deem the deed to him no derogation
> But deign to this device new commendation
> Sith here you see, feel, smell that his conveyance
> Hath freed this noisome place from all annoyance.[109]

William, then, as Groom of the Stool to the prince at Richmond, is among the first to perform his tasks with the aid of running water, in the water closet installed for Queen Elizabeth.

Once everyone has dined, a small party leaves the palace. Prince Charles, his four-year-old brother James, Duke of York, William him-

William invites his pupil Prince Charles (wearing hat) to walk in the mead opposite the Palace of Richmond. The little boy behind them with his governess is the younger prince, the future James II

self and a few other attendants make their way down to the river for an afternoon's excursion.[110]

As they leave the palace through a riverside door and stroll through the gardens, the prince and his attendants pass through the vestiges of what was once intended to be one of the greatest gardens of northern Europe. For a few years in the century's second decade, the court of the prince's uncle, the short-lived Prince Henry, had been a hothouse for designers working in the newly fashionable classical style. William, remembering his own water gardens in Nottinghamshire, must be intrigued by the relics of the grandiose scheme that Prince Henry commissioned but never completed. To reach the edge of the water, they pass over ground reclaimed from the river by Henry's celebrated surveyor Inigo Jones.[111]

William's journey to Italy in 1612 was made as part of a mission charged with discussing Prince Henry's possible marriage to one of the daughters of the Duke of Savoy, and the prince decided to improve the old-fashioned Richmond Palace for this putative Italian spouse. While his household included Inigo Jones as well as a host of other talented designers, Henry had no one who was able to design water gardens that were the equal of the fabulous creations of Cardinal Hippolyto d'Este at the Villa d'Este in Tivoli, near Rome. The most exotic protégé that he could muster was the Frenchman Salomon de Caus. Henry now sought a designer with an Italian training, and at his request Grand Duke Cosimo II de' Medici sent him the polymath Costantino de' Servi from Florence. This new arrival elbowed aside de Caus and drew up his own schemes for the new gardens on an even grander scale.

As Prince Charles and William reach the edge of the water, they pass to their right the half-finished ruin called 'The Rockhouse'. This strange building was one of de Caus's proposals, which included among their number a rectangular artificial mountain, a giant reclining river god and cascades.[112] De Caus's ideas, however, had been trounced by the even grander ambitions of de' Servi. For the area now beneath William's feet, between the Privy Lodgings and the river, de' Servi had proposed a great oval court for jousting.[113] To the south, he planned a vast garden, a ball court and a 'Mount Parnassus' from which strollers would be able to look down upon flower beds ornamented with heraldic devices. A copy of Trajan's column would also decorate this garden, which was to be dominated by a vast fishpond decorated with sea monsters and a giant Neptune on an even grander scale than that proposed by de Caus. This sculpture was to be huge enough to contain a whole sequence of rooms, including a dovecot inside Neptune's head.[114] Perhaps these drawings remain at the palace, and perhaps William has pored over them. He may well now discuss with the prince the relative merits of the rival French and Italian schemes. William may even nurse a vain hope that this little prince may one day breathe life into the horticultural pipe dreams that died with Prince Henry.

At the water's edge, they step into a boat painted with the three feathers of the Prince of Wales and duck down beneath its canopy while the rowers push off from the bank into the wide green river. Prince Henry had kept his little ship *The Disdain* moored at this wharf.[115] He had loved to swim at Richmond, and at night after dinner used to take 'a great delight in walking by the side of the Thames in moonlight, to hear the sound and echo of the trumpets'; perhaps his nephew does the same.[116]

Now, Prince Charles, his younger brother, his governor and servants, disembark together to walk on the grassy banks of the 'Great Mead' opposite the palace. Occasionally a troupe of morris men can be found dancing on the river's south bank (to the sounds of a pipe, drum and the bells on their stockings), and this is the attraction today.[117]

Morris men perform on the banks of the Thames in this view of Richmond Palace (*c.*1630) by an unknown artist

If William looks back across the river, he cannot fail to be impressed by the palace's most magnificent turreted facade. Tiny figures, household members, stroll in the gardens by the water and a three-masted ship is drawn up at the wharf. To the left of the onion domes capping the main Privy Lodgings rises the octagonal kitchen, while to the right are the long, low roofs of the galleries surrounding the gardens; light clouds cross the sky and birds wheel overhead.

Now William bows and gestures Prince Charles forward towards a stile, the prince in his yellow suit crossed by the blue ribbon of a Knight of the Garter.[118] The prince was made a Knight of the Garter in the spring of 1638, at the same time as he was given his own household and William was appointed as his governor. Perhaps he is also wearing the medal showing 'the Royal Oak' that was struck for the occasion.[119] A young attendant hovers at the prince's left elbow and an older one behind him; both are hatless, as is fitting. Another courtier reaches out his hand to a tiny figure still wearing a baby boy's dress rather than breeches: this is Charles's younger brother James, Duke of York, the future King James II, with his governess standing behind him. This peaceful moment, as the royal children pick their way through the grass towards the stile, is captured and celebrated in a popular contemporary engraving (see p. 145).

And so, with the pipes of the morris dancers sounding in the next field, we leave the governor and the 'hopeful prince' on the banks of the peaceful river at Richmond, illuminated by the slanting summer afternoon light and guarded only by a small group of attendants with a casual attitude towards security that will become unimaginable in the next few months. Despite his clumsy grasp of politics within the royal household, William can be proud of his work thus far. The prince's tutor Dr Duppa considers that the prince will be 'an excellent man if my presage deceives me not, and flattery and humouring him, the bane of princes, do not spoil him'.[120]

William will be forced to relinquish his position in the royal household as Prince Charles's governor less than three years from now, in June, 1641. The prince's childhood comes to an abrupt end in 1640, the year that William uncovers the 'plot about surprising the Prince'.[121] Thomas Dalmahoy of the stables is arrested, along with his co-conspirator John Arnott, 'who said he would kill the prince'.[122] These plots and security scares become more frequent as the political climate chills, and little Charles is removed from Richmond to be confined within the close security of London's Whitehall Palace.

William manages to cling onto his post as governor in spite of Dalmahoy's attempt on the prince's life, but will finally lose his much-prized job when he is himself implicated – wittingly or not – in the ultra-conservative 'Army Plot', whereby he is intended to kidnap the prince and join a conspiracy against Parliament.[123] As a result, William either resigns (according to a partial observer) or (according to another account) is permanently 'removed from the Prince'.[124] His royal adventure finished, he returns to Nottinghamshire and obscurity.

# 6 – *A Battle*

THE KING'S MANOR, YORK, 2ND JULY, 1644

Six years have passed, and it is shortly before four o'clock in the morning of 2nd July, 1644. William is in his chambers at the King's Manor in the city of York, contemplating a difficult day ahead. He is fifty years old; he has not slept and is deeply weary as he allows his body servants to strap on his armour in preparation for battle. Events have taken a turn unimaginable when William was with the prince at Richmond, and the country is now plunged deeply into civil war.

William wears his finely wrought suit of armour over a white linen shirt; only its outsize collar protrudes from a jointed iron carapace reaching his knees. His fringed cloak goes over the armour, pinned at the shoulder with a brooch, and he pulls on long gloves, tall, high-heeled boots and spurs, and picks up his pistol and sword. Behind him, his lockable writing desk is cluttered by the letters and notes needed to organise an army; John Rolleston is still in service as William's trusted secretary and scribe. Among the papers lies William's secret correspondence with the Hotham family, the turncoats thought by the Parliamentarian party to be among their staunchest supporters.[1] The capture of this cabinet containing their treacherous letters to William could cost them their lives.

This chamber is more than familiar to William, for it is some time since he has slept anywhere other than at the King's Manor. The city of York has been under a 'great and close' siege for two months, one that only ended yesterday, and the Parliamentarian armies who have kept William prisoner for so long are finally on the run. While his servants make the final preparations to his costume, William broods over his most immediate problem: his troops are refusing to march into battle

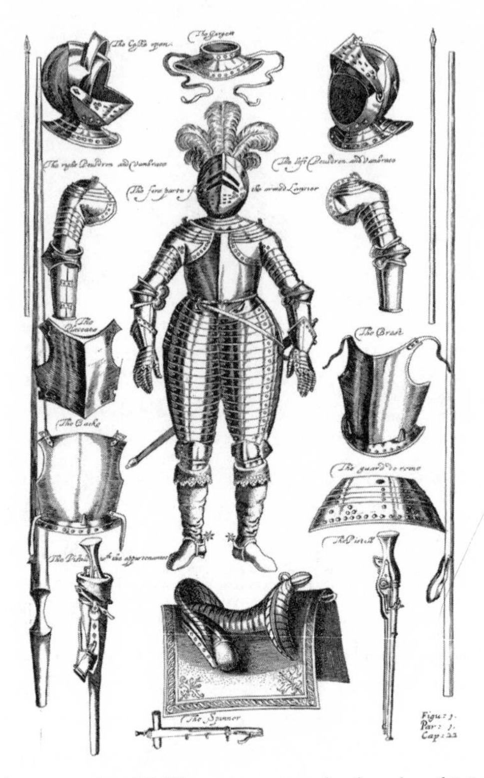


Armour of the type that William wore at the battle of Marston Moor

until the arrears in their pay have been made up, and in fact two hours ago he lost control of them entirely when 'they all quit their colours and dispersed'.[2] At this moment they are looting the encampments of the Parliamentarians, abandoned yesterday in the face of the approach of a relieving Royalist army under the command of Charles I's nephew, the dashing Prince Rupert.

The King's Manor is a spacious and commodious house, yet after two years of fighting William is 'utterly tired with a condition and employment so contrary to his humour, nature and education'.[3] During his campaigning life, William has endeavoured to provide himself with the luxuries that he loves so much: a comfortable bed, poetry, musicians, female companionship. Court gossip has it that he is 'a sweet General' who lies in bed until eleven o'clock and combs till twelve, and that his work is done by his experienced and dependable second-in-command, General King.[4] When a Royalist regiment is

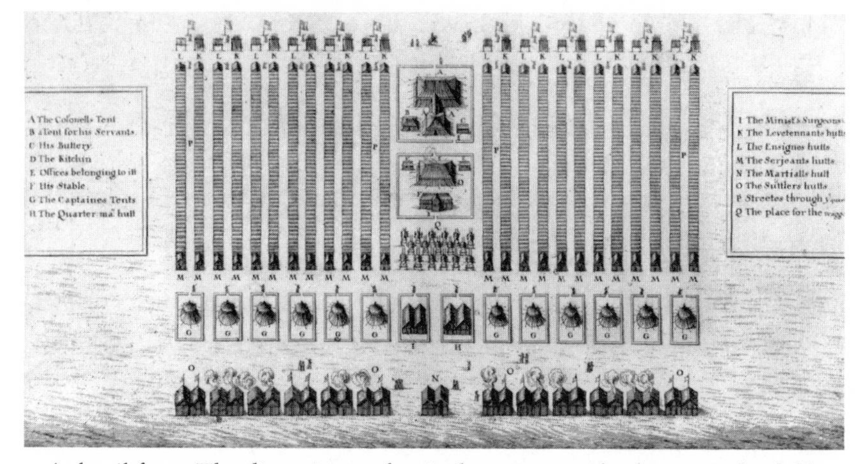


A detail from *The disposition of a single regiment of infantry in the fields (according to the present discipline of His Majesty King Charles)*, an etching by Wenceslaus Hollar. In the centre are the commander's quarters with tents for buttery and kitchens

camping in the field, its commander's tents are arranged along the lines of a great house: at the heart of the encampment the colonel has a large tent (great chamber) connected by a passage to a smaller one (bedchamber). Nearby are tents for buttery, kitchen, kitchen offices and stable. The more professional soldiers of the Royalist army such as Prince Rupert pour scorn upon the habit of bringing 'scullions and beefeaters' into the field, yet William cannot give up his creature comforts.[5]

The King's Manor is the finest house in York, a city dominated by the spire of its ancient Minster and standing in the fertile plain of the Yorkshire Ridings. To the east lies the North Sea, and to the north and west rise the moors. Like Welbeck Abbey, the King's Manor began life as the abbot's house before becoming the official residence of the President of the Council of the North, the administrative body with jurisdiction over the whole of northern England. William's friend the Earl of Strafford (now executed by Parliament for high treason) added various contemporary architectural flourishes to bring it up to date during his tenure of the office in the 1630s. William now strides along the building's gallery to the courtyard where his coach awaits. In his wake scurries his page, carrying William's helmet with its white plume.

Seven miles outside the city, the sun is also rising over Marston

Moor. The day now breaking will be a pivotal point in William Cavendish's long life.

As the political skirmishes between an authoritarian king and his rebellious Parliament escalated out of control in the early 1640s, full-blown military action became inevitable. Charles I had been forced to resume the custom of calling Parliaments to vote him the money he needed for a war against the Scots. In May, 1641, however, Parliament bullied him into allowing the trial and execution of his unpopular chief minister, William's friend the Earl of Strafford, on the grounds of treason. In January, 1642, Charles tried but failed to arrest five of his most vociferous critics in Parliament, lost his nerve and fled the capital. William had waited impatiently for the ensuing call to arms, anxious to demonstrate his horsemanship and gallantry.

After Charles raised his standard against the Parliamentarians at Nottingham in August, 1642, William's responsibilities as general of the king's army in the north took him all over northern England. With him went his great company of eight thousand Cavaliers and white-coated foot soldiers, raised on the strength of the honour and respect owed to the Cavendishes; after all, William is now a marquis, the second highest rank of the English peerage, and senior to everybody but a duke. Yet now, by 1644, it has become clear that his personal bravery and riding and swordsmanship skills are not the only qualifications needed to command an army, and he struggles with his task. In the early days of the Civil War, William's 'courtesy, affability, bounty and generosity' pleased everyone, but it was thought that 'the substantial part, and fatigue of a General, he did not in any degree understand'.[6] According to his colleague Sir Philip Warwick, William's fondness for women or 'witty society (to be modest in the expressions of it) diverted many counsels, and lost many opportunities'.[7] His failings as a commander demonstrate the sense in his opponent Oliver Cromwell's firm preference for 'a plain russet-coated captain that knows what he fights for, and loves what he knows' rather than a so-called gentleman.[8]

The letters from this period of William's campaigns, written in code or on scraps of sarsenet (a fine silk fabric that could be hidden easily about a messenger's person), are redolent of the smoke-filled tents, the rumours, the near-panic and the conflicting orders of the Royalist army. As William campaigned from the town of Hull to Newcastle and to York, Charles I had to stiffen his resolve against 'impertinent or malitious tonges and pennes of those that ar or professe to be your frends'.[9] The spirited queen, Henrietta Maria, commanded William to ignore any insults, but her letters also show the weakness of the Royalist chain of command. She told William in 1643 that the king had sent her 'a letter to command you absolutely to march to him, but I do not send it to you, since I have taken a resolution with you that you remain'.[10] Her wry letters must have kept his spirits up: in the same year, she hoped he had not again '*mangé des rats. Pourveu que les Escossois ne mangent point des* Yorkshier Oatecakes *tour ira fort bien*'[11] ('I hope you have not eaten rats again. As long as the Scots don't eat any Yorkshire Oatcakes everything will be fine'). Despite their flirtatious relationship, even Henrietta Maria had private doubts about William's efficiency, describing him as '*fantasque et inconstant*'.[12] Yet William was chosen to escort the courageous queen on her return to England after raising money on the continent, and she missed him when he returned temporarily to Derbyshire to bury his 'Sweete harte' Elizabeth after her death in April, 1643.

Elizabeth had been ill for some months. Making her will in November, 1642, she had asked for her body to be taken to her childhood home, Blore, to lie with her father, but William chose instead to bury her at Bolsover Church, alongside their dead babies. In her will, Elizabeth left £10 apiece to the long-time household servants Mr Butler, James Whitehead, John Rolleston and Thomas Bamford, although William's absence in London and then on campaign meant that the household was sadly depleted and had lost cohesion. Towards the end of her life, Elizabeth suffered numerous sadnesses: her husband's departure to the wars, the death of her daughter Katherine (the fifth of her children to die young) and the loss of two others, Elizabeth and Cate, to uncongenial marriages. In her will, she begs for the giving of 'five hundred pound a piece to my 4 daughters which will come to thousand to remember me by, not for their husbands but to them, and to my son-in-laws rings 20 a piece with a diamond on it'. The sons-in-law deserve such small bequests for, pitifully, 'they care not for mother in laws'.[13]

William quickly returned to the front line after Elizabeth's death, and by the summer of 1644, the struggle had reached stalemate. His army was trapped inside the besieged city of York for three months by no fewer than three Parliamentarian armies: the Scots under the Earl of Leven, the local forces of Lancashire and Yorkshire under Lord

Fairfax, and an army from eastern England under the Earl of Manchester (with Oliver Cromwell as his Lieutenant General of Horse). At one point, the Parliamentarians even breached the wall of the King's Manor, and fighting took place in its very garden, among the trees of the orchard planted up against the city wall, the vegetable plots of the kitchen garden and the bowling green.[14] Hundreds of William's Whitecoats died in fending off the attack, and scars made by shot will remain in its garden walls for hundreds of years.

On 5th May, the Cavendish household back at Welbeck had heard that William was holding fast. His eldest daughter Jane had received a message that in York 'the markets are kept still' and there was a 'good store of provision'.[15] Over the last few weeks, though, the daily ration for each soldier has dwindled down to one pint of beans, an ounce of butter and a penny loaf.[16] William's two young sons are also with him in the besieged city. When one of William's officers suggests that this is no place for children, he declares that 'His sons should show their Loyalty and Duty to His Majesty' in venturing their lives just as he does himself.[17] A month ago, William asked leave for ladies to pass safely through the lines, but the leaders of the besieging Parliamentarian armies refused. On 15th June, William rejected their terms after a week of negotiation.

The impasse was broken only yesterday, 1st July. The charismatic but arrogant Prince Rupert of the Rhine has been sent by Charles I to save the city of York, and last night he made a rapid and victorious strike on the northern gate.

Despite his relief at the lifting of the siege, indecision is in the air as William twists his commander's baton in his hands. Prince Rupert is the king's nephew, son of Charles I's sister Elizabeth, the romantic 'Winter Queen' who married Frederick, Elector Palatine of the Rhine. She and her family were driven out of their principality to live in exile in The Hague. From there, Rupert and his brother paid visits to England. They even stayed at Welbeck Abbey in 1636, an occasion on which William staged an entertainment for them among the oaks of his park.[18] Rupert plied his trade as a soldier of fortune all over Europe throughout the 1630s, and when he came to command his uncle Charles I's cavalry in the Civil War in England, his shock tactics had an electrifying effect.

Rupert now holds a unique high command in the Royalist army, yet has a soldier's supreme disregard for manners. According to one observer, it was after dark last night when Rupert entered York, but he did not 'linger there a moment; not long enough, I believe, even to see Lord Newcastle, who was so much hurt at this want of ceremony that he did not proceed to seek the Prince'.[19] William wrote Rupert a letter of thanks and welcome, but the prince responded only with a curt order to be ready to march out of the city to battle at four this very morning.[20] His intention was to capitalise on his advantage and to chase the retreating Parliamentarians. Meanwhile, William considers that some respite is due to himself and his army after the rigours of the siege. There is also a clear personality clash between the two men. Outsiders hold the opinion that William is reluctant to serve under the prince, intending 'himself to be the man that should turn the scale'.[21] Indeed, several of his friends have 'advised him not to engage in Battel' today 'because the Command, (as they said) was taken from Him'.[22]

As William passes under the archway of the King's Manor and calls for reports from his officers, he is bound to concede that there is a strong argument in favour of Prince Rupert's eagerness for action at any cost. The Parliamentarian armies are in full retreat, hastening towards Tadcaster. Because of Rupert's speed in going after them, the Parliamentarians will be forced to turn around in their tracks and meet him rather than exposing themselves to attack from behind.

As William frets, the prince's own troops are already moving out of York. But William's officers have little chance of rallying the four thousand Whitecoats who should also be forming up for departure. Their efforts are hindered because Micklegate Bar, York's western gate just by the King's Manor, has been stopped with earth as protection against siege.[23] After a long, confused interval in which orders go unexecuted, William despairs of gathering his men. He leaves his second-in-command, General King, to round up the troops and bring them along as speedily as may be. King, a Scot, has served for more than ten years in the vigorous and successful Swedish army, learning many useful tactics, and his experience has proved more than useful to William.[24] William now sets off in the prince's wake, at the head of a small band of gentlemen including his brother Sir Charles Cavendish and Captain Mazine, the Master of the Horse from the household at Welbeck.

By nine o'clock, as William finally leaves York, Prince Rupert's army has already begun to arrive at a moor outside the village of Long Marston, and the Parliamentarian armies are wheeling round and hastening back to meet it. William and the prince encounter each other at last upon the moor, in the full daylight of a damp and showery summer morning, as the prince rides here and there to draw up his troops. Blocks of men, pikemen with their weapons held vertically and mounted dragoons are slowly moving into line at his signal. 'My Lord,' Prince Rupert cries to William, 'I wish you had come sooner with your forces, but I hope we shall yet have a glorious day.'[25] William's chagrin, as he explains that his forces have not yet arrived, must be almost unbearable.

Prince Rupert, over six feet tall, has a brusque side to his character that the courtly William cannot admire. According to the Earl of Clarendon, he is 'rough and passionate, and love[s] not debate'.[26] In a portrait by Gerrit van Honthorst, a painter at his family's exiled court at The Hague, the prince has a long, narrow and aristocratic nose, a prominent and slightly cleft chin and fine wavy hair. His refined appearance has always disguised a difficult character that earned him his family nickname of 'Robert le diable'.[27] On the battlefield his armour is covered by a scarf and cloak; he looks proud, detached, self-contained. He has recently been awarded the rank of Duke of Cumber-

A woodcut of Prince Rupert and his dog Boye. Rupert had just sacked the town of Birmingham

land in the English peerage, and has quickly become known by the pamphleteers of Parliamentarian London as the 'Duke of Plunderland' for his violent actions.[28] They show him on horseback, waving his pistol in one hand and his axe in the other. By sharp contrast, in his leisure hours Rupert is interested in art, and in particular in the skill of making mezzotints.[29] As he and William move off across Marston Moor, Rupert's famous white poodle Boye (from a breed trained as hunting dogs) runs at his horse's feet. The prince's Parliamentarian enemies consider that Boye has supernatural powers, being a 'strange breed of this Shagg'd Cavalier, whelp'd of a Malignant Water-witch, With all her Tricks, and Feats'.[30]

Rupert believes that today he is under an obligation to fight to the death. He has received a letter from his uncle Charles I containing a stark warning: 'If York be lost, I shall esteem my crown a little less [. . .] But if York be relieved and you beat the rebels of both Kingdoms which are before it, then, but not otherwise, I may possibly make a shift.'[31] William, who knows nothing of this, simply thinks Prince Rupert rude and dismissive. Rupert, relying upon this letter as justification for the aggressive tactics he has determined upon, will keep it about his person for the rest of his life.[32]

William now has to explain that he has lost control of his foot soldiers and that it 'was impossible to have got them together at the time prefixed'.[33] It is only now, while he and Prince Rupert talk on the moor, that General King finally persuades William's Whitecoats to begin marching out from the city.

Earlier this morning Prince Rupert seized Marston Moor's most advantageous ground before the Parliamentarians had time to draw themselves up. Yet he senses that his advantage of timing is beginning to slip away. 'Now the prince bestirs himself, putting his men as such order as he intend'd to fight, & sending away to my Ld of Newcastle to march with all speed,' reports one of the Royalist officers, Sir Henry Slingsby.[34] The morning passes in busy preparations on both sides. By two or three in the afternoon, the Parliamentarians are at a state of full readiness, but the Royalists are still lacking William's troops.

As William waits anxiously for his infantry, a glance southwards allows him to assess the enemy's strength. The Royalists occupy an open boggy moor, generally used as rough pasture by the local villagers and covered with gorse and heather.[35] Before the Royalist lines the open moor gives way to the arable fields of the Parliamentarian position.

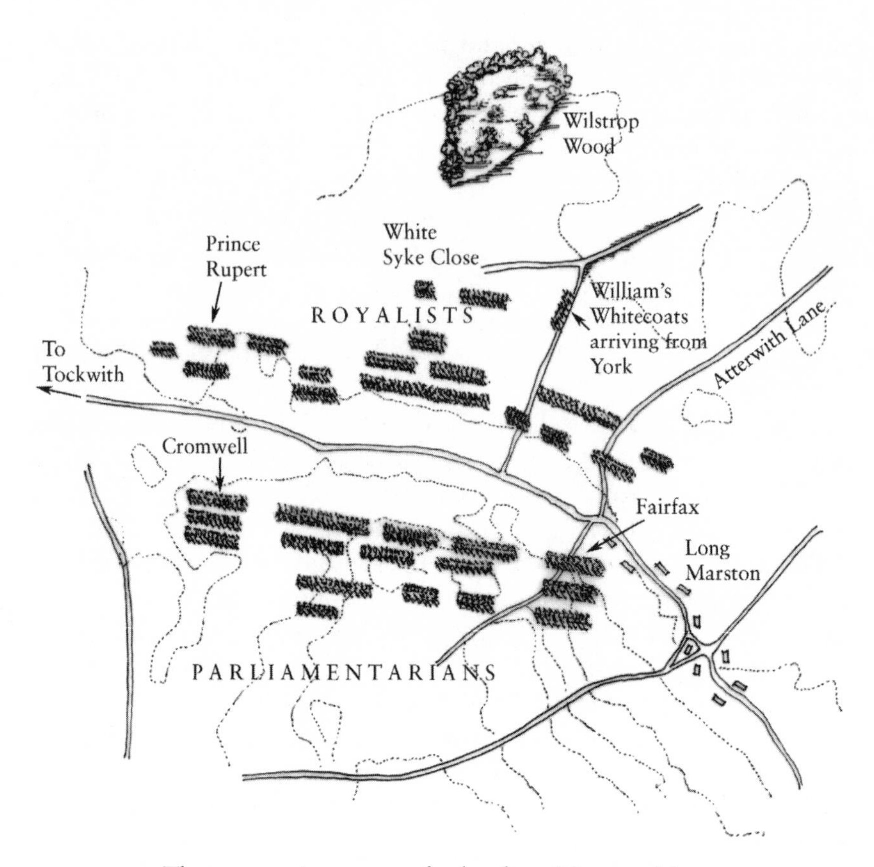


The two armies prepare for battle at Marston Moor

They are drawn up on Marston Hill, beyond the road and ditch running east–west between the villages of Long Marston and Tockwith. To the left of William's field of vision, a road called Atterwith Lane runs north–south, linking the moor with the fields. The Parliamentarians are standing 'in battalia in a large field of Rye, where the height of the corn, together with the showers of rain which then fell, prov'd no small inconvenience' to the damp soldiers.[36] As the afternoon passes, they edge forwards down the hill, facing north, into the wet wind and looking across the ditch that separates them from the Royalists.[37] The vast Parliamentarian army – twenty-eight thousand men in all – now 'in Marston corn fields falls to singing psalms', a sight and sound that strikes fear into the hearts of Prince Rupert's fourteen thousand men.[38] Gathered here on Marston Moor is the largest number of men ever to take part in a battle on British soil. And William's four thousand infantrymen, who could make all the difference to the outnumbered Royalists, have yet to arrive from York.

Both armies have adopted a conventional deployment: cavalry at each wing, pikes and musketeers in the middle. Oliver Cromwell, heading the Parliamentarian left, or western, wing, is not yet marked out as the future leader of his party, yet he is in the process of proving his strategic genius. In 1628, he sought treatment from the doctor Theodore de Mayerne (who will also treat William Cavendish) for *valde melancolicus*, or depression. The same year marked his spiritual rebirth as a radical Puritan. By July, 1644, Cromwell has risen through the ranks on merit and has an important cavalry command. On the other, eastern, wing of the Parliamentarian lines stands Lord Fairfax's son Sir Thomas Fairfax's cavalry. His plan is to advance northwards into the moor along Atterwith Lane. During the afternoon, those at the eastern and western extremities of both armies edge so far forward that the two sides are 'within Musket shot' of each other.[39]

The sight of the Royalist and Parliamentarian armies inching towards each other will never be forgotten by those who witness it. Simeon Ashe, a chaplain with the Earl of Manchester's army, will afterwards describe the mixture of terror and exhilaration he feels: 'How goodly a sight was this to behold, when 2 mighty Armies, each of which consisted of above 20,000, horse and foot, did with flying colours prepared for the battle look each other in the face.'[40]

Both sides are similarly equipped and outfitted, though some battalions have a uniform: William's infantry, for example, will be wearing their distinctive white coats; Prince Rupert's foot soldiers are the Bluecoats, while others in the Royalist army wear green. Both sides wear the rounded iron helmets known as 'pots'; they can be turned upside down and used to boil water over an evening fire. A superior version has a flexible neck cover, giving it the name of a 'lobster-tailed pot', and the troops who wear them are known as 'lobsters'. The basic unit of both armies is the 'troop', sixty men led by a captain, lieutenant, cornet and quartermaster.[41] They are grouped into regiments of about five hundred men, each with its own flags or colours and drums for conveying commands. The officers stand at the back, to make strategic decisions and to deter deserters. Their colours incorporate arcane pictorial references to the individual regiment's prowess or to current events; those carried by Royalists today include a willow green banner 'with the portraiture of a man, holding in one hand a sword, and in the other a knot, with the motto – This shall untie it', and a black banner with 'a sword reached from a cloud, with this motto – Terribilis acies ordinata'. A yellow banner has 'several little beagles' by whose mouths it is written 'Pym, Pym, Pym'. These beagles, chanting the name of a prominent Parliamentarian, are confronted by a royal 'stooping Lion' speaking the words '*Quosque tandem abutere patientia nostra?* That is – How long will you abuse our patience?'[42]

In the middle of the lines, the pikemen clutch the stout weapons, twice as tall as a man, that remain effective even against a cavalry charge. They wear little armour, and their strength lies in the hedgehog formation that is impenetrable to horsemen. The muskets of the sharpshooters are similarly impressive, being nearly a man's height in length. Most of these gunmen carry the type of musket called a 'matchlock', with a length of smouldering rope to spark the gunpowder. Many of these matchlocks refuse to fire in damp conditions like today's; the flintlock, a more advanced and reliable weapon, is carried by few on the battlefield. A dozen little jars containing powder and shot – 'the Twelve Apostles' – hang from a heavy leather belt slung across a musketeer's chest. The musketeers will take turns to fire, arranging themselves into six ranks. After taking their shot, the front rank will run to the back and begin to reload, a process that takes thirty to forty-five seconds, by which time they will have reached the front again; the rate of fire, therefore, seems almost continuous, although sometimes a 'salvo' of three ranks at once is let off. While a soldier wounded by a sword slash may reasonably expect to recover, a musket ball has a much greater deadliness. Passing through dirty clothing and then flesh, it can cause sepsis and a lingering death, as well as the trauma of broken bones.[43] The musketeers may also turn their weapons upside down and brandish them by the barrel, using them like clubs in hand-to-hand combat. Further back behind the lines are the great guns on their heavy carriages and the coaches and wagons containing gunpowder and supplies.

It will not be easy to tell the two sides apart in the struggle to come, so the Parliamentarians signal their allegiance with 'a white Paper, or handkerchief in our hats'. The Royalist commanders often wear bright sashes over their armour or a cluster of oak leaves in their helmets, but today their signal will be to be 'without bands and scarves'. The capture of the regimental flags or colours will signal the end of the fight. The two sides will also compete for the approbation of the Almighty, for the Parliamentarian watchword is 'God with us', while William's troops will know each other by their cries of 'God and the King'.[44]

Scoutmaster-General Lionel Watson, serving in the Earl of Manchester's army, describes the high tension of this afternoon spent in expectation of death. At about two o'clock, the 'great Ordnance of both sides' begins to play.[45] These big guns have a range of 2,650 yards, and at least one cannonball fired by the Parliamentarians, weighing 15 pounds, will remain on the battlefield to be discovered three centuries later. The guns also fire wooden boxes filled with nails and musket balls; these fly up with the effect of shrapnel when the box hits the ground. Thomas Danby, a Roman Catholic Royalist gentleman, is among those who fall victim to a 'cannon bullet' of this kind, being 'cut off by the midst of his body'.[46] But the guns bring small success to either side, and 'about five of the clock we had a general silence on both sides, each expecting who should begin the charge'.[47]

Five o'clock, and this eerie silence, brings with it the welcome and long-awaited sight of General King, arriving at last with about three quarters of William's infantry from York. The Whitecoats begin to take their places in the second rank, behind the centre of the Royalist lines, but Prince Rupert notices that they are 'all drunk'.[48] They can see before them the backs of the rest of Prince Rupert's army, spread out in a formation extending about a mile and a half from east to west. To their right, the Royalist horse are led by Lord Byron (facing Oliver Cromwell), while to the left, the wild and hard-drinking Lord Goring and William's own Northern horse face Sir Thomas Fairfax on the Parliamentarian side. The Northern horse are battle-hardened and experienced, and have a bad reputation among the godly, for 'they carried along with them many Strumpets [. . .] these they made use of in places where they lay; in a very uncivil and unbecoming way'.[49] Among their officers is the terrifying female captain Frances Dalyell, the illegitimate daughter of an earl, who rides under the ominous standard of a hanged man.[50]

The cavalry's formation, if seen from above, would appear like the squares on a chequerboard. William, in his full armour and on his heavy charger, is far better equipped than the bulk of the Royalist riders. Most of them make do with a pot helmet, back and breast plates, a sword, a pair of pistols and sometimes a short musket. They tie themselves into their saddles, the better to keep their seats, and their swords are firmly attached by ribands to prevent them being lost.

The day is drawing in when Prince Rupert and William meet up once again, behind the lines where the officers' coaches are drawn up. They dismount to greet each other, and as they climb back onto their horses a terse exchange takes place. William asks the prince whether he still really means to take on the Parliamentarian army, for the odds in terms of numbers are heavily stacked against the tired Royalists and they have lost their advantage of surprise. Negotiation is not an entirely ignoble option. 'Nothing venture, nothing have,' the prince replies, and gestures William closer. He hands over a paper with the full order of battle drawn up upon it and asks for an opinion.

'By God, sir,' says William's experienced assistant, General King, who is also present, 'it is very fine in the paper, but there is no such thing in the fields.'[51] King disapproves of Rupert's plan, considering the Royalist army to be 'too near the enemy, and in a place of disadvantage'. He warns the prince against impetuousness, reminding him: 'Sir, your forwardness lost us the day in Germany, where yourself was taken prisoner.'[52]

Yet any hope the siege-weary commanders have of diverting Rupert's bloody purpose is futile. 'Not so,' says the proud and prickly prince.[53]

Now William questions Rupert about the timing of his plans. 'We will charge them to-morrow morning,' Rupert says with fatal confidence, brushing aside William's suggestion that the enemy might themselves attack this very evening. The prince turns away and is very soon 'set upon the earth at meat a pretty distance from his troops, and many of the horsemen [are] dismounted and laid on the ground with their horses in their hands'.[54] It is now between seven and half past. William, far from reassured, returns 'to his coach hard by' and is heard 'calling for a pipe of tobacco'.[55]

At this, the very first moment of relaxation in a very long day, disaster strikes.

Now, with theatrical timing, a clap of thunder rings out, and against all the expectations of the Royalist commanders, the Parliamentarian soldiers begin to advance. With horror, the Royalists see the whole Parliamentarian line swing into motion, moving northwards towards them, slowly at first, but quickly speeding up into 'a running march'.[56]

The Parliamentarians had been watching closely for any sign of relaxation and were also aware that about a thousand of William's infantry were still on the road from York.[57] There are even rumours that a

Scottish officer from the Parliamentarian army had slipped in among Prince Rupert's horse and fled back with secret intelligence of the Royalist intention to wait for morning.[58] The Parliamentarians have nothing to lose by attacking this evening, and much to gain. Their forces are complete, while the Royalists are still expecting reinforcements.[59] They are fired with enthusiasm for their business and charge 'with such admirable vigour, as it was to the astonishment of all the old Souldiers of the Army'. Those present saw an unforgettable scene: 'the bravest sight in the world; Two such disciplin'd Armies marching to a charge'.[60]

One of the Parliamentarian chaplains describes the sight of his army moving to the attack with awe – 'like unto so many thick clouds'[61] – and also notes the consternation of the Royalists, who are 'amazed and daunted at our approach'. With this advantage of surprise, the Parliamentarians cause the Royalists 'to quit the hedge in a disorderly manner'.[62]

William is as shocked as his men. As he was making for his coach, the first indication he had of the enemy's charge was 'a great noise and thunder of shooting'.[63] Tobacco forgotten, he rearmed himself as quickly as possible and struggled to mount his horse. But even then the rout of the Royalist right wing had begun.

The foot soldiers in the centre of the lines are quickly locked in combat, the pikemen groaning in the heaving scrum known as a 'push of pike'. To the left of William's vantage point behind the lines, matters are going well for the Royalists. Sir Thomas Fairfax's horsemen are advancing up Atterwith Lane, but the way is so narrow that they can 'not march above 3 or 4 in front'. Both sides of the lane are lined with musketeers, for the well-prepared Lord Goring has adopted the Swedish tactic of interspersing the Royalist cavalry with small groups of gunmen.[64] As Fairfax's horsemen come up the lane they are picked off one by one and slaughtered. Those in the rear struggle to turn and bolt. Galloping back southwards, 'hotly pursued by the enemy', they ride down their own foot soldiers, breaking 'them wholly, and [treading] the most part of them under foot'.[65] As is usual in the battles of the Civil War, the local civilians, villagers from Long Marston, had gathered on nearby hills to watch progress. On this occasion they panic, running in fear for their own lives, and their contagious fear communicates itself to the fleeing Parliamentarian troops.[66]

Many of Fairfax's troopers now ride right off the battlefield, pursued by the Royalist horse. The Royalists chase them as far as the carriages drawn up at the rear of the Parliamentarian lines.[67] The success is so complete that Lord Goring and Sir Charles Lucas, the Royalist commanders, instruct the drums to sound for victory, and Sir Thomas Fairfax's men leave the field, thinking the battle lost.[68] Lord Fairfax, Lord Leven and the Earl of Manchester, the three Parliamentarian commanders, actually flee the field.

Yet, at the same time, Oliver Cromwell has made deep inroads into the Royalist right wing, and Prince Rupert himself is forced to take action against him. Like all cavalry, Cromwell's troops the Ironsides make their charge at a relatively slow speed, in close order, with 'every left hand mans right knee [. . .] close locked under his right hand mans left ham'. As they move 'toward the Enemy with an easie pace', they fire their carbines, always aiming at the breastplate or lower as the 'powder is of an elevating nature', changing to pistols as they draw nearer. One pistol must always be kept in reserve, 'charged, spann'd and primed in your holsters in case of a retreat'.[69]

Once Prince Rupert is 'to horse and galloping up to the right wing',[70] he meets the sorry sight of his own troops turning their backs on the enemy and running towards him, 'so many, so breathless, so speechless, and so full of fears, that I should not have taken them for men'.[71] Now this great, if impetuous, soldier shows his extraordinary powers of leadership. 'Swounds, do you run, follow me,' he calls out, and his troops, more afraid of their commander than of Cromwell, wheel about and make a stand.[72] William, too, hastens in this direction to stiffen the resolve of these troops, though some 'immediately be[take] themselves to their heels again, and [kill] even of their own party that endeavoured to stop them'.[73] Those who remain are now confronting Cromwell's own bodyguard and struggle 'at the swords point a pretty while, hacking one another'. At last, despite Rupert's imprecations, Cromwell breaks through, scattering the Royalists 'before him like a little dust'.[74] Cromwell himself will later describe his scything down of the Royalists with a metaphor appropriate to a battle begun in a field of tall corn: 'God made them as stubble to our swords.'[75]

Cromwell now shows his greatest strength as a commander, which is to keep his men together in order to follow through after a success. Although many men on both sides are now either dead or fleeing, he and his cavalry swing round the back of the Royalist lines. 'Neither wearied by their former hot service, nor discouraged by the sight of that strength' which yet the Royalists have, Cromwell and his Ironsides systematically charge 'every party remaining left in the field'.[76] The very last remaining pocket of Royalist soldiers consists of William's infantry, the famous Whitecoats.

After the rout of the Royalist right wing, William made his way back across the battlefield towards his infantry. He had with him only a small group, consisting of his brother, Sir Charles Cavendish, Captain Mazine, a major and a page. This little band was joined by other volunteer cavalrymen as they recognised William, and they rode right through the 'Two Bodies of Foot, engaged with each other not at forty yards' distance'.[77] The air is full of smoke, the cracking of musketry and cannon, the clash of steel, shouted orders and watchwords, and the screams of the wounded.

During this passage through the mayhem of the infantry lines, William somehow manages to lose his sword. Now survival takes precedence over strategy, and the senses are of little use. There is 'such a noise with shot and clamour of shouting that we lost our ears, and the smoke of powder was so thick that we saw no light but what proceeded from the mouth of guns'.[78] William seizes his page's blade, and after a few desperate moments finds that he has slaughtered three Scotsmen. A single courageous pikeman now bars the way. William charges at him, but cannot break through the man's guard without harming his horse. The others in his party help to cut the man down.[79]

By about half past eight, the very last men standing are William's Whitecoats, and the small party from the Cavendish household finally manages to rejoin them. For another hour William and the Whitecoats defend themselves against Cromwell, their position solidly fringed with pikes in a field called White Syke Close, and the indomitable strength of 'this gallant battalion' wins the hearty respect of the Parliamentarians. Even the fallen thrust their pikes or swords upwards at the Parliamentarian troopers who step over them.[80] Darkness falls, and the killing of the Whitecoats continues by the light of a full harvest moon.

Finally, it is nine o'clock, and all the Whitecoats' ammunition is spent. Having refused to surrender, 'every man fell in the same order and rank where in he had fought'.[81] Despite their tardy arrival at the battlefield, most of William's Whitecoats, 'as good men as were in the world', are slain.[82] Now, at last, it is clear that defeat is inevitable. At the end William's troops did not let him down, but they paid for their gallantry with their lives.

*

It is 'late at night' when William and about thirty Whitecoat survivors leave the battlefield. Accompanied by 'his brother and one or two of his servants', William rides back towards York.[83] The enemy gives chase to the Royalist survivors to 'within a mile of York, cutting them down so that their dead bodies lay three miles in length'.[84] Meanwhile, the city is choked with refugees, and the authorities are only allowing residents to pass through the gate at Micklegate Bar; the whole street is 'throng'd up to the bar with wound'd and lame people, which made a pitiful cry among them'.[85]

On the battlefield William has left behind him all the Royalist ordnance, gunpowder and baggage train, one hundred Royalist regimental colours, over four thousand dead Royalist soldiers and the corpse of Prince Rupert's white dog Boye. Rupert's sumpter horse has been captured, along with all his possessions; soon Parliamentarian pamphlets will be circulating lists of the crucifixes and other notorious items indicative of papistry that were supposedly found among them.[86] When the Parliamentarians seize William's private papers, his correspondence with the treacherous Hotham family is revealed, and both Sir John Hotham and his son will be executed.[87]

A Parliamentarian soldier shoots Boye, and Rupert, dressed as a Catholic priest with donkey's ears, performs the last rites. In the background are the beanfield where Rupert is said to have hidden after the battle and the walls of the city of York

Drawing near to the city, William and his party accidentally come upon Prince Rupert himself, who fled the field after Cromwell's successful onslaught upon the Royalist cavalry. Rupert has managed to survive only by lying down and hiding himself in a field of beans. He and many other commanders of both sides who left the field before the battle was finished have no knowledge of the final outcome, and the prince asks William for news. 'All is lost and gone on our side,' is William's dismal answer.[88]

Next comes one of the defining moments of William's life. He is filled with despair. This final, makeshift council of the Royalist leaders sees him make a hasty decision:

Says General King, 'What will you do?'
Says ye Prince, 'I will rally my men.'
Says General King, 'Now Lord Newcastle what will you do?'
Says Lord Newcastle, 'I will go into Holland', looking upon all as lost. The Prince would have him endeavour to recruit his forces, 'No,' says he, 'I will not endure ye laughter of ye Court,' and King said he would go with him; and so they did.[89]

William is as good as his word. The next day he, his sons, his closest servants and General King are on their way to Scarborough, where they find a ship to take them to Hamburg.

The swiftness of this decision, taken so soon after the battle and apparently without much consideration of the consequences, is completely characteristic of William. The reason he gives – if the record of the conversation is indeed accurate – is also characteristically and childishly egocentric: it is not the welfare of his men that he has in mind, nor the rightness of the Royalist cause; it is the prospect of being laughed at by his colleagues at court.

Yet William's decision to run away is in some ways sensible and pragmatic. He has suffered terribly over the last few years, let alone hours, and as a general has been forced to perform duties out of step with his talents and inclinations. The Earl of Clarendon was not surprised about William's choice to step down. 'It was a greater wonder', he wrote of William's military role, 'that he sustained the vexation and fatigue of it so long, than that he broke from it with so little circumspection.'[90] And nothing could appear blacker at that moment than the military future of the defeated Royalists: to flee was a reasonable choice of action.

Still, it remains surprising that William, the most noble, generous and gallant of the Cavaliers, can be so disloyal as to abandon the king's cause. His fear of the laughter of the court stems surely not from injured pride but a sense of shame at the defeat and the hopeless feeling that he lacks the ability to fight on. Our judgement must be finely balanced between condemnation and pity.

After losing the battle of Marston Moor, William sails for the continent, taking with him only his sons and a skeletal household. He immediately finds himself in want of friends and money. 'After the great misfortunes & miseries I have suffered', he writes in despair to his former pupil Prince Charles, 'I cared not how soon death closed my eyes.'[91] He has also abandoned his houses, his family and his money. The Cavendish household is now divided: while a few servants accompany William and his sons into exile, others are left behind at the family homes. William's daughters and servants will be forced to reach an independent accommodation with their Parliamentarian enemies.

Before the battle, Charles I had sent to Prince Rupert the fateful message that 'if York be lost, I shall esteem my Crown a little less'. Overconfident after the triumph of lifting the siege, Rupert has lost York and much more besides. Back in England, six counties of the north now fall to the Parliamentary forces, and nothing remains of the Royalist army but Rupert's cavalry. This is the war's turning point. The Parliamentarians are now set upon the path leading to their ultimate victory under Oliver Cromwell. Charles I's prophecy will come true: he will indeed lose his crown.

Despite his bravery in the field, William has deserted his household, his country and his king. Worst of all, both enemies and former friends now think him a coward. The public perception is that the man previously defined by his courage and loyalty has been found wanting: he is now know as the 'silken *Generall*, that ran away *beyond Sea*'.[92] The common view is that Prince Rupert should be 'mightily condemned for his rashness, but the Marquis of Newcastle [William] more for coming away [. . .] his going lost his army and all those that depended on him'.[93] Parliamentarian pamphleteers will tease William for his love of theatricals as well as his cowardice, calling him 'the brave Marquess of *Newcastle*, which made the fine plays, he danced so quaintly, played his part a while in the North, was soundly beaten, shew'd a pair of heels, and exit *Newcastle*'.[94] It remains to be seen whether William can ever recover from this blow to his reputation.

# 7 – *A Household Divided*

THE HOUSE OF RUBENS, ANTWERP, 15TH NOVEMBER, 1659

It is mid-morning on 15th November, 1659, fifteen years later. William is settling himself into the saddle of a horse of extraordinary ability and arrogance, whose supreme quality is matched only by his name. 'Le Superbe' is a beautiful beast, a bright light bay in colour, although tempestuous by nature: 'hard to be rid, yet when he was hit right [. . .] the readiest horse in the world'.[1] At a subtle nudge from William's leg, Le Superbe now begins his routine. His performances are legendary and frequently recollected in glowing terms: 'he went in corvets forward, backward, sideways, on both hands; made the cross perfectly on his voltoes; and did change upon his voltoes so just, without breaking time, that a musician could not keep better: and went terra a terra perfectly'. A corvet is a prancing movement, achieved by holding back a horse when his energy is raised; a 'volto' is a circle ridden to supple and limber the horse up; and 'terra a terra' (ground to ground) means a backwards and forwards rocking-horse motion performed on the spot or else pivoting round a central point. A rider's experience of these manoeuvres is truly exhilarating, as man works in partnership with a creature that could easily kill him but instead accepts his leadership.[2]

There is silence in the riding house, except for the regular muffled thuds of Le Superbe's landings on the soft floor and his snorted exhalations of concentrated effort. It is not the silence of solitude but the rapt attentive hush of a crowd of fascinated spectators. They are crammed into the first-floor balcony that overlooks the double-height riding house, and some of them even squeeze dangerously into the corners of the floor itself. A heavy film of the yellow dust kicked up by the horses stains the whitewashed walls. This riding house is a makeshift

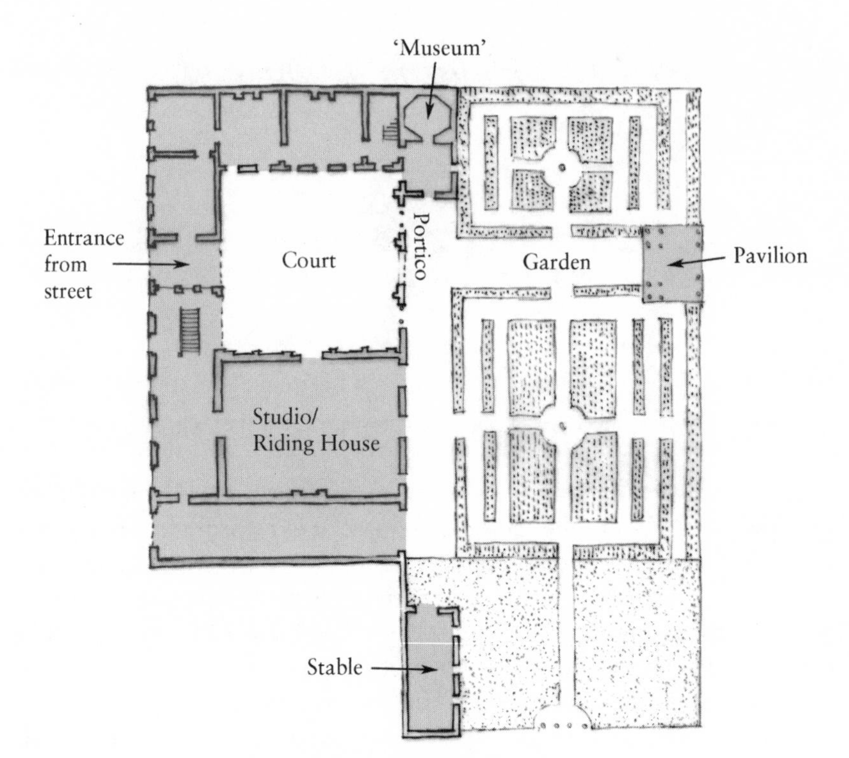


Plan of Rubens's house

space, adapted from another very unusual room. William is now renting the Antwerp townhouse formerly lived in by the painter Peter Paul Rubens, and the riding house has been fashioned out of the vast studio where the artist created his masterpieces (Plate 23). The clear northern light from its windows is perfect for riding but was designed with painting in mind. The huge canvases commissioned by Charles I from Rubens for the ceiling of the famous Banqueting House in the Palace of Whitehall were painted here. Yet William can hardly remember what they look like, for he has been in exile from England for fifteen years.

Back in London, there have been great political changes afoot throughout October and early November, and news of them will delight the exiled Royalists and rekindle hopes that have almost died. This news, however, has yet to trickle through to Antwerp, and on 15th November, William's challenge is to keep the habitual melancholy of an exile at bay for one more day.

At the end of the display, William dismounts to applause. With a bow, he deflects the praise of the bystanders to his mount. Le Superbe is a Spanish horse and therefore superior, in William's opinion, even to the highly sought-after Barbary horses. A Spanish horse is 'the most *Beautiful* that can be', William considers, and 'the Lovingest and Gentlest *Horse* [. . .] in the World'.[3] 'Barbs are the gentlemen of horse-kind', he calls out to the audience, 'and Spanish horses the princes.'[4]

This remark induces an ecstasy of delight in his largely Spanish audience. The city of Antwerp is now under the control of the occupying Spanish Hapsburg family, and many of these bystanders are visitors from the court of the Marquis of Caracena, ruler of the province. William has long been accustomed to staging riding displays for high-ranking visitors. In the old days he would bring his horses of *manège* down from his Nottinghamshire home to perform for the Stuart court. 'I have rid my Horses before the king & he liked them Extreme Well, they are the best horses in the town,' he wrote, with his characteristic

William in a characteristically insouciant pose. A preparatory study by Abraham van Diepenbeeck for one of the plates illustrating William's book of horsemanship

insouciance, to his first wife Elizabeth in 1636.[5] Now his visitors are from the Spanish rather than the English court.

William moved to Antwerp in 1648, scrabbling together the money for the lease of this house from Rubens's widow. The house was Rubens's artistic manifesto, demonstrating his talents as a designer and painter, and William's new home is a stimulating architectural experience. The rooms inside are darkly and richly furnished, with heavy hooded fireplaces and high windows.

Now a shaft of cold air enters the riding house as servants open the door to the courtyard, and William rides out to change horses. Outside is a small square piazza, so intricate and perfect in design that it seems almost like a stage set created for an opera, and William's gaze passes in a full circle around it as Le Superbe impatiently dances beneath him. The riding house stands to the south of the courtyard. Almost every available piece of its wall left free of doors and windows is decorated

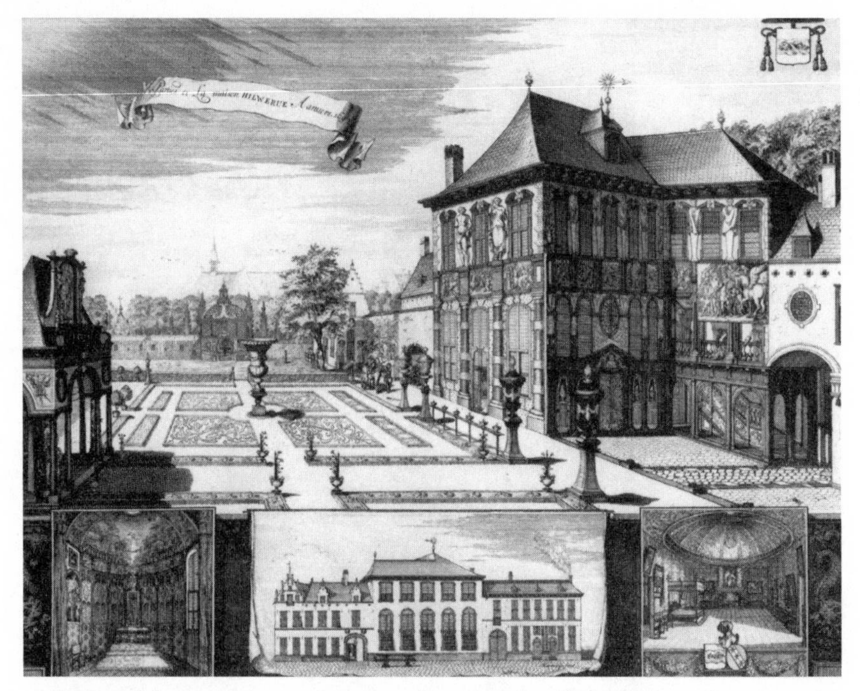

Rubens's house as it was in 1692, the most detailed seventeenth-century views of the building. The portico has been magically removed to show the *trompe l'oeil* balcony and painting left out to dry. To the far left is the little pavilion in the garden

with busts of ancient philosophers set in niches, with urns, wreaths, stern ladies and rugged men whose lower halves are pilasters. The most intricate part of this wallscape is the wide frieze band, which tells classical stories: the slandering of Apelles; the triumph of Alexander the Great; the sacrifice of Iphigenia.[6] They appear to be three-dimensional sculpted panels like those on ancient Greek temples, but this is a trick of their grisaille paintwork. Rubens, like his artist predecessors Andrea Mantegna, Giulio Romano and Giorgio Vasari, frescoed his house in homage to the great masters from the past. He had visited and drawn many palaces in Italy, but here at home, in his own version of an Italian palace in the Low Countries, he copied their exuberant decoration in paint rather than stone.

The virtuosity of Rubens's painted decoration is even more striking to the western side of the courtyard, where great gates give onto the Wapper canal outside. To the left of them, painted birds perch, a painted hound plays upon a *trompe l'oeil* painted balcony and one of Rubens's canvases, showing Perseus rescuing Andromeda, hangs out to dry: all of this a virtuoso trick on the eyes executed with the brush. Hans Holbein was likewise a master of this kind of game, painting deceptively three-dimensional staircases on the walls of houses in Germany.[7]

A quaint brick accommodation block forms the north side of the courtyard, and to the east, a wonderfully baroque portico frames a view of the little summer house in the garden. This portico speaks with bravura of the south and Italy. The screen is topped by the brooding figures of Mercury and Minerva, their feet firmly planted on the balustrade and their weapons pointed high into the sky. Beneath them, eagles flap their wings around a helmeted bust in the confines of a strange triangular pediment, and further busts, bulls' heads and writhing satyrs hover above the two side arches.

Another horse's whinny sounds out. A second rider – none other than Captain Mazine – is coming through the garden from the stable towards the arch of the portico, his breath misting the air and steam rising from his horse's heaving flanks. This garden in summer is an earthly paradise and provided Rubens with endless inspiration. Here, using the portico of his own house (constructed to his own design) as part of the backdrop, Rubens imagined the twilit scenes of flattery and dalliance that he painted time and time again. This garden and portico appear in the background of his painting of *The Garden of Love*, for example, where secrets are whispered, a stone nymph squeezes the water of a fountain from her breasts, ostrich-feather fans gently waft through the air, a lute is plucked and pearls dangle from every lady's ear (Plate 24). Today, however, the statue of Hercules in the ornate little pavilion that Rubens also painted so often appears to loiter forlornly in the frosty garden, its tulip beds dank and empty, the squared hedges surrounding them bare, the wooden trellises without plants, the peacocks silent and shivering.[8]

'Le Genty', this second horse now coming through the portico, is a wonderful sight as he skitters to a halt in the courtyard. William considers Le Genty to be 'the finest-shaped horse that ever I saw, and the neatest; a brown bay with a white star on his forehead: no horse ever went terra a terra like him, so just, and so easy'. William leaves a groom to return Le Superbe to the stables and signals that Captain Mazine should take Le Genty into the riding house. William now mounts and demonstrates Le Genty's speciality, 'the piroyte in his length, so just and so swift that the standers-by could hardly see the rider's face when he went'. 'Truly,' William has been heard to say after one such performance, 'when he had done, I was so dizzy, that I could hardly sit in the saddle.'[9]

After Le Genty, there is a third horse ready and waiting to perform: a Barb 'that went a metz-ayre very high, both forward and upon his voltoes, and terra a terra'. William now has his audience in raptures, reporting that the Spaniards cross themselves and call out: '*Miraculo!*'

William must be flushed with pride and pleasure. During his time in Antwerp, he has become Europe's greatest living horseman. Over the last few years he has written and published a seminal manual on the subject: *La Méthode et Invention nouvelle de dresser les Chevaux [A New Method, and Extraordinary Invention, to Dress Horses]* (1657–8).[10] In the English edition of this book, he praised the hospitality of the city of Antwerp, being especially grateful to the many '*Noble great Persons, who did me the favour to see my* Mannage'.[11] As well as Spanish courtiers, he receives visits from '*worthy Gentlemen, of all Nations*, High *and* Low-Dutch, Italians, English, French, Spaniards, Polacks *and* Swedes'. So many people wish to see the English Marquis ride (on horses that he has not paid for) that the riding house itself is sometimes so full that there is hardly room to perform.[12]

William now has eight horses.[13] When he arrived in Antwerp, after a penniless residence in Paris and weary months spent trailing from town to town across the Low Countries, he had only two, and their ensuing deaths were a low point in the early years of his stay in the city. Despite a lack of ready money, William has built up a stable on his almost limitless credit. He is offended if anyone offers him money for his horses, for he will not part with his favourites at any price.[14]

Yet William cannot enjoy his life in Antwerp unconditionally, for the remembrance of his exile and what he has lost is never far from his mind. The Cavendish household remaining back in England is now headed by William's younger son Henry. While the Civil War has disrupted trade, religion and politics, the greatest price the Cavendishes have paid is in family unity, as father and son have not seen each other for nearly fourteen years. Henry's letters to Antwerp report on family affairs: the recent death of his elder brother, the false pregnancy of his sister-in-law, the condition of the family houses and furniture. William in Antwerp has a more pressing concern: the long-awaited arrival of the money promised by Henry for living expenses.

William was lucky enough to wheedle a loan from the Duke of Buckingham at the beginning of his residence in Antwerp, and the ready money impressed the shopkeepers of Antwerp into giving his household credit for further purchases. Rather than the fabulous dessert courses of the old days at Bolsover and Welbeck, William jokes that he can now afford only '3 preserved cherries and 5 drops of syrup by them for the banquet' after a celebratory dinner.[15] When the debts press in too closely, he charms his way out of the situation: he is accustomed to sending for his creditors and telling them his story, his recitation making 'such an impression in them, that they had all a deep sense of my Lord's Misfortunes: and instead of urging the payment of his Debts, promised him, That he should not want any thing'.[16] So impressive is William's manner and his candid account of his fall from wealth that his household live in some 'Splendor and Grandure'.[17] Yet cash has on occasion been so short that one devoted servant, Elizabeth, sold her own jewellery so that the household could eat.

Once the morning's performance is over and the coaches of the Spaniards and other visitors have creaked away from the queue along the canal outside the house, William goes to change his clothes in one of the first-floor chambers. A recent portrait shows that William – now aged sixty-five – has put on weight. His jowls are fuller and his eyes deeper-set and ringed with baggy flesh. While his hair is still plentiful, it has a flyaway, unkempt quality and is thin at the temples.[18] This house is decorated in dark, warm colours: leather hangings embossed with gold patterns, rich carpets on the tables, black and white marble on the floors (Plate 26).[19] William ascends to the best room in the house, the bedchamber where Rubens died, with its light tinted by the faintly reddish panes in the windows (heavily leaded in a square- and lozenge-shaped pattern) that overlook the gardens. The quality of the light in all of William's houses is coloured by the seventeenth-century cylinder glass in their windows: it always possesses a submarine tinge, rich, dramatic and subtly shaded. As William changes, he stands upon a red-and-grey tiled floor before a fine fireplace in which flames burn against an iron fireback surrounded by blue and white tiles, with black and white marble pillars to each side and a fringed velvet cloth above the flames and below the weighty chimney breast.

This bedchamber is situated directly above one of the oddest rooms in the house, the gallery where Rubens kept his museum of art and sculpture. At one end is a semi-circular, domed sculpture gallery in white, black, yellow and other veined marbles. Here niches are designed to set off sculpture, and perhaps William has had time to fill them with new treasures bought on credit. Antwerp, like other Dutch cities, is becoming filled with the wondrous artefacts and spices brought from the East by her merchants. According to John Evelyn, visiting as a tourist from England, the Dutch were such enthusiastic investors in art because the shortage of land in their country made its price unaffordable.[20]

After dressing, William is ready to go out to seek further diversion. Along with all the most prominent citizens of the city, he takes great pleasure in a frequent promenade through the streets in his coach, 'which we call here a Tour, where all the chief of the town go to see and be seen, likewise all strangers'.[21] There are sometimes a hundred of these preening non-pedestrians clogging the streets.[22] The Cavendish coach pulls off northwards, along the road hugging the Wapper canal, which is itself jostled on both sides by narrow houses with their stepped gables. At the junction the coachman turns left, heading towards the Grote Markt, cathedral and the centre of town, and passing skaters on the frozen waterways. Yapping dogs, pairs of sober matrons in white collars, well-dressed burghers and a party of strolling comedians crowd the streets. Yet rather than admiring the sights of the

A crowded square in seventeenth-century Antwerp, with coaches and street performers

city, William is deep in conversation with the young woman now seated next to him, for she has a limitless fascination for him.

After his flight from England, William had travelled to the court of the exiled queen Henrietta Maria in Paris and had lived there in dispirited poverty. His rash decision to go into exile had drawn heated criticism. Yet here in Paris William would also find consolation in this dark hour. He was about to meet the great love of his life.

Elizabeth, William's first wife, died in 1643. In 1645, while in Paris, William met Margaret Lucas, a young girl without prospects who was the same age as his eldest daughter and came from a respectable but not exalted family from Colchester. Margaret was a waiting woman to the queen, and in marrying her William displeased Henrietta Maria. 'I fear she will tak it ell if she be not mad acquanted with our intenshoins,' wrote Margaret, with her idiosyncratic spelling, and 'she may doe us harme'.[23] The feverish atmosphere of the exiled court at St Germain and royal disapproval created a hothouse for their romance. 'I hop the qeene and I shall be very good frindes againe, and may be the beter for the deffarances we haue had,' she fretted.[24]

Margaret Cavendish, standing in a niche, wearing a little crown

Flying in the face of the pragmatism of aristocratic marriages, this was a match based on compatible interests and emotional needs. William urgently needed a companion rather than a shrewd, financially advantageous match like his first, in which he had been lucky that love followed. William and Margaret, two amateur writers, exchanged witty, passionate and truly romantic love letters.[25] William, already over fifty, was conscious of his disadvantages:

> I know I'm old, it is too true,
> Yet love, nay, am in love with you
> Do not dispise me, or be Cruell
> For thus I am loues best of fuell
> No man can love more, or loves higher
> Old, and dry wood, makes the best fier.[26]

He also joked in the same vein about his financial plight. When the

English princess Mary married, William made light of his destitution to his fiancée:

> The Princess Mary, Marrys Kinge of Poland
> And you my Deer, do marry Prince of Noland.[27]

William and Margaret married at the house of friends in Paris in December, 1645, and departed from the exiled queen's court soon after. In 1649 came the dreadful news that the defeated Charles I had been executed by extremists among his many enemies. William and Margaret remain part of the continental circle of exiled Royalists who still hope that Charles I's son may one day sit on the English throne. William occasionally attends upon the uncrowned king Charles II as he moves ceaselessly around the cities of Europe, living on meagre handouts from his fellow monarchs. Last year, William entertained his former pupil and many of the exiled Royalists with a glittering ball at Rubens's house. He is proud of recently having received special permission from Sir Edward Walker, Garter King of Arms, to use the title of 'Prince' in addition to that of Marquis.[28]

William and Margaret came to Antwerp in 1648. The first sight to greet them would have been the steep spires of the city's churches spiking a winter sky. Well-constructed bastions protect the city from assault by land or, to the west, from the river Scheldt; windmills are scattered across the low pastures beyond the gates. The fine sights of the city include the triumphal portico constructed for the emperor of Austria, the merchants scurrying across the courtyard and through the arcades of the bustling Exchange (now over a century old), and the church of the Society of Jesus with its baroque facade, described by John Evelyn during his visit of 1641 as 'that sumptuous and most magnificent church of the Jesuits, being a very glorious fabrique without; and within encrusted with marble'. In the Jesuit school near by, Evelyn saw the 'eagles, foxes, monkeys, etc.' kept to divert the pupils during their leisure hours. Overall, he considered that he had never seen a 'more quiet, clean, elegantly built, and civil place, than this magnificent and famous City of Antwerp'.[29]

Antwerp has been heavily shaped by the conservative, baroque forces of the Catholic Counter-Reformation. Despite the Exchange, the city is indeed quieter than it would have been a hundred and fifty years ago, when German bankers headed the influx of foreign traders who made it the greatest seaport in northern Europe. In 1576, however,

Spanish troops plundered Antwerp after religious strife, a bloody event known as the 'Spanish Fury', and the city's population and prosperity subsequently plummeted. A visitor in 1619 described Antwerp as 'a disconsolate widow, or rather some super-annuated Virgin, that hath lost her Lover, being almost quite bereft of that flourishing commerce with which she had previously abounded'.[30] Becalmed in the strict Catholic torpor of the Spanish, Antwerp has lost out to Amsterdam in the United Provinces, where the Protestant religious authorities are too disputatious to have imposed censorship.

Despite the city's loss of much of its trade, it entered the seventeenth century upon a golden wave of art and artists. Rubens had mourned his city's decline, but he was leading the way for other masters of painting, such as van Dyck and Jordaens. This cosmopolitan city of artists and collectors is still highly impressive to the English and provides a setting of suitable size for William, who likes to dominate a social scene. Today, he and Margaret, accompanied in their coach by Margaret's maid Elizabeth Topp, are heading for the square named Vrijdagmarkt (Friday market) and the best bookshop in the city.

Their vehicle now draws up outside the House of the Golden Compasses, home of the Moretus family, whose ancestor Christopher Plantin had founded Europe's first 'industrial' printing press in this building (Plate 27). Around the side of their imposing townhouse is the entrance to the bookshop. William has experienced the pains and pleasures of writing a book at first hand. It had been a labour of love. 'I am so tormented about my book of horsemanship', he wrote in 1656, 'as you cannot believe,'[31] and the printing cost him over £1,300. William and Margaret now send their waiting woman Elizabeth into the shop to pick up a spare copy, or perhaps some other work has taken their fancy. With her goes a manservant: the Cavendishes themselves never carry money, depending instead on a 'purse bearer' among the servants, whose accounts mysteriously never quite seem to tally with their own recollection of what has been spent.[32]

Elizabeth Chaplain, as she then was, had served Margaret as a waiting woman in Paris. It was only on reaching Antwerp that she met and married her husband Francis Topp, an English merchant who has attached himself to the household. Margaret survives with a mere four maids.[33] Other members of the small remnant of the Cavendish household in Antwerp include a local maid called Jane (known as 'dutch Jane'[34]), and of course, the faithful Captain Mazine. Sir Hubert Cartwright serves as a senior man of business, as does Mr Loving. William's brother Sir Charles Cavendish had also been part of the household until his death in 1654 and had proved wonderfully useful in returning to Commonwealth England and negotiating for the family estates. William had brought a larger train into exile but 'finding his Company and Charge very great [. . .] sent several of his Servants back again into *England*'.[35]

Elizabeth now climbs down and enters the low door to the shop. Immediately inside the entrance hangs a poster containing the Index of Prohibited Books. Three columns of text are set out: authors whose work is completely banned by the government of the Hapsburg family, authors with only certain of their works under prohibition, and finally, the titles of forbidden books by anonymous authors. The previous few decades have seen the Counter-Reformation sweep across Europe, as the forces of reaction attempt to stamp out radical Protestantism. The Plantins themselves have been forced to print this list of the books that they are now forbidden to sell on the very same presses used to publish many of the books in the first place. The banned authors include Erasmus, whose works the Plantins had brought into print.

The works that the Cavendishes (both of them, for Margaret is a voracious consumer of books) require are ready. At his long wooden counter, the clerk is packing up several parcels of loose leaves for Elizabeth. She must take the printed pages to a bookbinder to have leather bindings made; on William's books these will typically incorporate the Cavendish stags' heads. The clerk now weighs the proffered money on the delicate scales he keeps for checking the value of coins. Behind him, an internal sash window with leaded lights opens into the office, where another employee is making up the accounts for the (mainly wholesale) customers of the press. Deeper in the building beyond lies the correctors' room, where the proof-readers are seated at a large built-in reading desk below the window, peering shortsightedly at pages of completed text in a bewildering profusion of languages. Beyond further leather-lined offices lies the printing workshop itself, where the compositors are at work making up words from type and the printers are flicking the leather balls spread with ink across the trays of text completed in metal. Even in the bookshop there is a faint background thudding sound as the printers slam down the heavy flap that presses the paper down onto the inked type. Each printer typically makes this movement 2,500 times a day during the course of the fourteen hours from six in the morning, when work begins, until eight in the evening, when it ends.

Antwerp, this city of artists and printers, is as exciting a place as any for two aspirant writers like the Cavendishes to live. Elizabeth and the manservant return to the carriage with their parcels, and the party continue their tour with some satisfaction until it is time for dinner.

After dinner, William climbs to his closet to write a letter to his son. It is dangerous to send letters into the Commonwealth of England. William and his family are constantly trying to outwit the authorities, who will seize a family's estates at a hint of treason. William's sons Charles and Henry long ago took the decision to 'compound', or to make a ceremonial apology for the crime of fighting on the Royalist side in the Civil War; indeed, they were young enough at the time to argue that they had no choice but to follow their father's orders. Having compounded, former 'delinquents' become eligible to buy back the property their family had owned. For William, however, this option does not exist. His name is on the list of proscribed 'malignants' who are forbidden from compounding and for whom a return to England would mean death. If William's sons were known to be in correspondence with their father, their precarious place in the new order would be untenable. William uses a pseudonym in his letters to his sons, signing himself 'John Forest' in letters to Charles and 'Robert Deane' when he writes to Henry. He completes letters with a chilling instruction that was nevertheless ignored: 'As you love me, After you & my Lady hath read this letter burn it.'[36]

Apart from the visits of continental grandees or members of the exiled royal family, letters are the high points of William and Margaret's rather lonely lives. Since Charles has recently died, it is to his only surviving son Henry that William prepares to send a barrage of orders and criticism. Despite the transitory pleasures of the riding house that have always consoled William in times of trouble, his now habitual frame of mind is downcast and anxious. His health is poor: his doctor describes William's condition as 'Melancholyk, Hippocondriack, troubled with vapours.'[37] In one letter to his son, William writes (referring to himself in the third person) that 'he cares not how soon he dies, for he is not very much In love with this world, nor hath he any great reason to be Enamoured with it'.[38] William is not taken seriously by the other Royalist exiles and they do not include him in their intrigues. In 1658, he let slip that the Earl of Ormonde was making a dangerous secret journey into England; other members of the circle were aghast 'that anyone who knows Newcastle would trust him with so important a secret'.[39] He could also be foul-mouthed: there were reports in 1650 that a supposedly diplomatic visit to Breda had ended with his being 'rebuked [. . .] for his customary swearing, & sent home'.[40] His usual good spirits deserted him when he wrote: 'I am so astonished dizzy & amazed with misfortune, as I know not whether I am a wake or no.'[41]

William sits down at his desk and searches for his penknife to trim his quill, calling for candles and a pipe of tobacco to warm the dim winter afternoon. He is still an inveterate smoker, even against his doctor's advice. Sir Theodore de Mayerne begs William not to be 'bewitched by such a stinking commodity' and suggests that 'it would be better to find out some other recreation to divert your troubles, then to fill your head & lungs with wind', but his advice is ignored.[42] While William prepares his pipe and his pen, Margaret is almost certainly at work in her own closet near by, being an indefatigable writer. Despite her youth and the professional help she has sought, she has been unable to have any children. William called in De Mayerne, who counselled: 'Touching conception, I know not if in the estate she's in, you ought earnestly to desire it. It is hard to get children with good courage when one is melancholy, and after they are got and come into the world, they bring a great deal of pain with them; and after that very often one loses them as I have tried to my great grief and am sorry to have had them.'[43]

Now William dips his nib and spreads his paper, preparing to cover every inch with his slanting, spidery handwriting and unusual spelling, with the letter 't' doubled wherever possible ('but', 'it' and 'not' become 'butt', 'Itt' and 'nott'). The recipient of his letter, twenty-nine-year-old Henry, has just moved back into the family home at Welbeck. Since Henry's brother's death a few months ago, it has been slow work getting his widow to vacate the family's houses. Unfortunately, Henry is temperamentally unsuited to the job of heading the family. He had been living quietly and happily at Thorpe Salvin Castle near by, more than content to let his siblings take on the responsibilities of Welbeck Abbey and Bolsover Castle.

William pens a page of terse instructions to Henry, sick with worry about his beloved houses, wondering if he will ever see them again, and

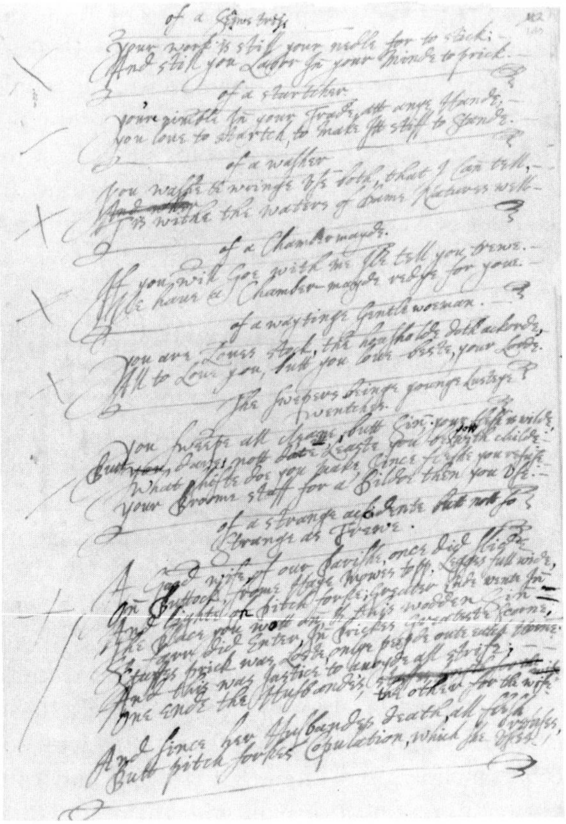

A sample of William's handwriting. Here he is composing a series of jokey couplets about members of his household

anxious about his goods and valuable furniture. The health and morale of Henry himself, his wife or the 'little ladies', their daughters, is secondary; material goods are William's concern today.

He begins with the complaint that the ports have been closed and that letters from Henry have only just reached Antwerp after a three-week delay.[44] He is glad of the news that Henry has been busy finding out what remains of the family's furniture at Bolsover. William is irate, however, that some things appear to be missing from Henry's report. Servants of the errant widowed daughter-in-law, Charles's wife Elizabeth, must have made off with many items, William calculates, including some cases of crimson velvet for the chairs in the parlour at Bolsover. 'The Gold Lace, & Embroidery on the purple Velvet bed', now absent, 'was worth at least £300,' he complains, and its sparver – the wooden frame for its canopy – had cost a good deal of money. Elizabeth also appears to have taken some 'very fine hangings'.

'But let it go,' William counsels. He has a pragmatic and cold-hearted attitude towards his daughter-in-law: he baldly stated shortly after his son's death that her 'not being with child makes us know that we can pretend but little interest in her'.[45] William is more concerned about the fine pictures at Bolsover Castle, which had included works by Sir Anthony van Dyck and the Dutch painter of luminous interior scenes, Hendrick van Steenwijck.[46] He has received reports on the condition of the castle and its contents from a painter whom he has previously sent over from Antwerp to repair the works of art, and he offers the services of this man to Henry. He is 'a very Honest Man, and Careful, and cannot but deserve his wages in preserving the paintings,' William advises. This painter was perhaps Abraham van Diepenbeeck, one of the finest artists in Antwerp, whom William has commissioned many times and who has illustrated William's book on horsemanship.

William also has some instructions for Henry regarding Charles Eagle, a servant who wishes to re-enter the household. Charles, the son of the William Eagle who had served William's mother and father, was born at Welbeck in 1634. His movements in the last few years have been a mystery, but he is now anxious to join William in Antwerp. William's need, however, is for a servant to act as an agent in London, 'for buying of many parcels of little Commodities which we daily want & can not have them here', and he offers to pay Charles £20 a year for this service.[47]

William also begs Henry to put his name to further bills of credit to support the household in Antwerp, and suggests that Henry refrain from making a few proposed alterations to the houses of which he has now taken possession. 'I should be very willing to any thing you desire but only entreat you to let it alone for a while, and then to do what you please,' William says, revealing his reluctance to have his son stray into the architectural province that he considers his own. 'Truly if it please God I ever see you I will make Welbeck a very fine place for you,' William says longingly, 'and I am not in despair of it.' 'I believe you and I not so good architectors as your worthy Grand Father,' he concludes, 'nor never shall be yet we will do our best.'[48] For William, though, Henry's best never seems to be quite good enough.

*

Back in Nottinghamshire, Henry is in disconsolate possession of the semi-derelict Welbeck Abbey, with repairs impossible for want of means. The abbey, bereft of its lord, his hospitality and its magnificent contents, is a dark, lonely place:

> But then sad Welbeck will stand desolate
> And think the Country Love is turn'd to hate
> No more the Neater wine turn the house round
> And Strangers' Cares in the Arch'd cellars drowned;
> Or dainty Fare best dressed, Apollo's Beer,
> And softer Musique ravishing the Ear,
> Or sumptuous hangings, heavy Antique Plate,
> Carpets of Persia, Cloth of Gold the State,
> Pictures, Rome's pride would emulate to see
> The entertainments made Men Statues be
> And all the Pleasures, Arts that man desires,
> Welbeck could warm you at her better Fires
> Therefore farewell, since now thou'rt left alone,
> Nothing to brag on, but old wood and stone.[49]

Henry lacks the spirit expected in a marquis's son, and is vacillating and jealous (Plate 29). Where his elder brother was dark, Henry is fair. In a double portrait of the two brothers, Charles exhibits something of his father's confident swagger, while Henry looks over his shoulder with an air of mild surprise.[50] On 15th November, 1659, while his father is riding expensive horses and buying books on credit in Antwerp, Henry is heartily regretting the trouble and expense that Welbeck Abbey has put him to. He is teetering on the edge of debt and owes £500 for clothes for himself, his wife and their servants. He also has a list of ancient promises unfulfilled: as well as furniture bills from his last house, he has 'Apothecary's bills in my sickness, from 17 years of age till I was 19 years old', expenses from 'My wife's miscarriage & my sickness six years since, & at that time a Journey to London cost me £500'.[51] He is in poor health, suffering intermittently from 'convulsive tremblings' caused by 'huge malignant vapours, rising from the low region of the Stomach' and making 'the knees knock one against another.'[52] His wife and daughters concern him more than the finances of his father and his stepmother. On one occasion he reminisces that 'he never lived so well & contentedly as he did' in the days before he had to bear the burden of his father's expectations.[53] Henry, this reluctant saviour of the family fortunes, is a less impressive character than his clever and confident older sister Jane. It is thanks to her that there is anything left at all of Welbeck Abbey.

The abbey has witnessed many dramatic changes in fortune since William last rode away from it on campaign early in 1644. He left it garrisoned under a succession of colonels of the Royalist army.[54] Leaving the country directly after the battle of Marston Moor, William took with him his two sons, but abandoned his daughters and servants to their fate. They were forced to negotiate with the new regime.

In July, 1644, as the bad news about the defeat at Marston Moor seeped southwards, William's loyal servants James Whitehead and old Thomas Bamford could have been seen excavating a hole in the earthen floor beneath one of the vast vats in the brewhouse in order to bury the family's silver: candlesticks, salt containers, knives and dishes.[55] After the catastrophes at Marston Moor and the fall of York, the Parliamentarian army was daily expected at Welbeck. Royalist soldiers were stationed in the abbey for the household's protection, and the household's members helped the soldiers to dig a 'fortification ditch' in the field called Cow Crofts; its construction was overseen by a foreign engineer.[56] Yet Welbeck and Bolsover Castle (the latter likewise garrisoned by the Royalists) had little hope of holding out.

By default, William's spirited twenty-two-year-old daughter Jane was now head of the household, and 'What *Courage* and *Loyalty*, as the right Daughter of a *General* [. . .] did she show, in keeping the Garrison'd House of her Father'.[57] Although these dangerous days made heroes and heroines out of the most unlikely of materials, the Cavendish daughters were truly extraordinary seventeenth-century women.

Hand-to-hand fighting had already taken place in many of the houses and gardens of Derbyshire, and Jane and her sisters Elizabeth and Frances gradually became accustomed to the frightening but liberating conditions in which they found themselves during the Civil War years.[58] Enemy and friend were sometimes hard to tell apart. Despite the bloody battles, there was a certain generosity and gallantry about the behaviour of the upper classes of both sides. William himself, for example, was widely praised on one occasion for capturing the wife of Lord Fairfax, his deadly enemy, yet sending her home safely in her carriage.[59] Now his daughters would receive similarly courteous treatment.

Their home fell to the Parliamentarians under the Earl of Manchester a month after Marston Moor. Although its battlemented walks and the castellated towers of the garden wing gave Welbeck a spirited military air, there was little resistance from the Cavendish servants and the Royalist garrison, and the Earl of Manchester allowed the Royalist soldiers to march out with 'all their arms and colours flying' after a gentlemanly parley. The money in the Cavendish treasury was seized, although William's 'several Curiosities of Cabinets, Cups, and other things' were pillaged by the Royalists, not the Parliamentarians.[60] The Earl of Manchester left the house intact and placed a garrison of Nottinghamshire men to guard it. The earl informed Parliament that William's daughters and family still remained at Welbeck and that he had 'engaged [him]self for their quiet abode there'.[61] The sight of this hostile but chivalrous earl walking in their own water garden as if he possessed it inspired a scene in a play written by the Cavendish daughters in which a captive, frustrated and powerless Royalist soldier observes a similar sight.[62] His ability to express his rage and hatred is limited to a refusal to take off his hat to his jailers. The Royalists consider the omission of this ceremony to be a grave insult, but the Royalist soldier's silent act of defiance would actually have made little impression upon the Roundhead troops. The Puritans among them have introduced the handshake as a more egalitarian form of greeting, and they consider it a mark of integrity not to doff their hats.

The Parliamentarians held Welbeck for a year. 'Come, prithee, let's talk no more of our captivity,' says one of the heroines of Jane Cavendish's play. 'I wish I could not think, that I might not remember, I had been once happy.'[63] Like Jane herself, the female leads in the play are the Royalist daughters of an absent general, kept prisoner in their own garrisoned house. The Cavendish household was rescued in a desperate action on 16th July, 1645, by Cavaliers from Newark, the last centre of Royalist resistance remaining after their defeat at the battle of Naseby. A soldier present recorded how the Royalist horses lay in ambush in the woods near the gate. When the Parliamentarians let down the bridge over the canal in the water gardens for their scouts, the Royalists 'rid hard, and though they pulled up the bridge a foot high yet they got in and took it'.[64] The Cavendish sisters watched in high hope as the Parliamentarians 'disputed every yard' of their garden, but the Royalists leapt down from their horses, pistols in their hands, and stormed in. The Riding House gate was demolished and windows were shattered.[65] Yet, as the Royalists regained Welbeck, Jane had humanity enough to plead with her rescuers for the lives of the Parliamentarian jailers who had kept her sister and herself captive.[66]

Despite the change of regime in the household, life went on: the births of children to soldiers of the garrison and local girls were also recorded in the parish records.[67] The sisters remained sane through writing the poems and plays that their father had always loved, and Jane in particular spent 'the time that best pleased Her with her *Pen*'.[68] Their longest play, based on their own lives, describes how the daughters of an exiled father live in longing for his return, while enemy soldiers occupy their family homes; the girls break into their father's locked study and taste the lozenges and comforts stored there in order to remind themselves of him. Elsewhere, Jane describes peering into her looking glass and seeing only a 'lean ghost' of herself, with a face of 'pale despair'.[69]

Plays such as those written by the Cavendish daughters were not necessarily intended for publication or performance, but were circulated in manuscript form among family and friends, earning the genre the name of 'closet' or 'coterie' drama. Jane addressed poems to these friends and neighbours, such as the Mr Richard Pypes who weekly sent her plums and flowers from his fine garden.[70] Many of the defeated Royalists, maintaining old networks of friendship in the face of crushing defeat, quietly kept up their spirits in such a manner. Some, including members of the secret Royalist organisation the Sealed Knot, went further, taking rebellion from the page into action. Meanwhile, Jane recorded the highs and lows and ambivalence of 'the Horrid Circumstances of War':[71]

> The Devil take me if I can tell what
> I am, or can be, so my wavering lot
> Yet thoughts tell me, I'm chance's weather glass
> For now I'm low, & high, I'm sure I was.[72]

High points were the arrival of infrequent letters from her father in Antwerp, always an occasion of great drama in the household. One poem describes Jane's excitement at hearing that a messenger had arrived:

> But when your Letter I did take
> My Joy did truly make me quake
> And when I read, & read, & read again
> Then thought I read not, then read over ye same.[73]

As well as letters, William would send his daughters presents from the markets of Antwerp to adorn their closets, chambers and persons: a 'curious Fan', a sweet-toothed comb 'to comb bad thoughts away', bracelets, silks, masks, china cloths.[74] Jane often relieved her feelings by writing inept love letters in verse back to her father:

> I am indeed a congealed piece of grief
> And without sight of you have not relief
> In every place, where I have seen you in
> Now's horrid to me as a deadly sin.[75]

Her plays and poems reveal an ocean of longing for stability, her father and her family, and her subjects include panegyrics to her many relations, as well as other topics as diverse as 'On the 30th June to God' and 'The Discursive Ghost'.

Jane had the responsibilities of a head of a household thrust upon her, and she reluctantly rose to the challenge. She was diligent in protecting other pieces of family property beyond the silver hidden 'in two hogsheads' beneath the brewhouse.[76] She even had the jewels and plate left to her by her grandmother turned into cash and sent for the support of her father's small household in exile.[77] She politely requested permission to inspect Bolsover Castle, then in the hands of the Parliamentarians.[78] With 'care and industry', she managed to salvage 'some few Hangings and Pictures' from the remains of its once-lavish decorations.[79] Yet the castle itself had been rendered indefensible through the demolition of key walls and gates, and was left in a desperately sorry state.

As well as assessing the damage, Jane had also to manage the servants and to try (not always successfully) to encourage them to continue their work under the difficult conditions. She and her sister drew a series of vivid pen portraits of the wayward Cavendish servants with whom they spent their days trapped in the garrisoned house. The dreary old Thomas Bamford, who lacks the charisma to get the other servants to carry out his orders, 'doth give a Humm/ And always looks according to hum drum.' Of 'modest Daniel', a shy footboy, 'his looks daily say/ I do no hurt pray therefore let me stay.'

Many of the servants who appear in Jane's poem about the household are female, and households of the gentry and aristocracy after the Civil War contain a higher proportion of women than had been the case twenty years before. The sort of well-born young men who would previously have become stewards or gentlemen ushers are now beginning to go into business or a profession, and their old duties are being taken over by those of lesser social status or by women. The usher's role becomes the preserve of the footman, and the male clerk of the kitchen is replaced by the female housekeeper.[80]

Jane and her sisters spend most of their time with the female members of the household. The Cavendish daughters sit at the top of a hierarchy, with their waiting gentlewomen immediately beneath them and the chambermaids one more step down but superior to the maids of the laundry, scullery and kitchen. Sir Thomas Overbury describes how a chambermaid

> is her Mistresses shee Secretarie, and keeps the box of her teeth, her haire and her painting [make-up], very private.[81]

In her advice to aspirant chambermaids, the author Hannah Woolley recommends that:

> you must also learn to wash fine linen well, and to starch Tiffanies, Lawns, Points and Laces, you must likewise learn to mend them neatly, and wash white Sarsenets with such like things. Then you must learn to make your Ladies bed, well, soft, and easie, to lay up her Night-clothes, and see that her Chamber be kept neat and clean, and that nothing requires to be done. Then you must learn to be modest in your deportment or behaviour, to be ready at her call, and to be always diligent.[82]

Waiting women of gentle birth seem to have been absent from Welbeck in the garrison years, driven away either through fear, sickness or the general disruption of the times. In these circumstances a chambermaid could be promoted to a waiting gentlewoman's place. Woolley advises an ambitious chambermaid to 'dress well, that you may be able to supply the place of the Waiting-Woman, should she chance to fall sick'.[83] In Jane Cavendish's play, the chambermaid named Pert has hopes 'of a gentlewomanship' but fears that an accidental slip-up in her duties might 'pull [her] down to a washermaid'.[84]

In the Cavendish household at Welbeck, shy Daniel has no chance of holding his own against Pert's model in real life, the self-confident Judith, who 'doth boldly say this flat/ I have my Ladies' love, so I care not.' The maid Nan Woolley scarcely speaks, while Nan Bouketter, full of flattery for everyone, is never silent.

Bess Burden, however, is a chambermaid after Jane's own heart: she likes poetry, and unlike the others, can be trusted to keep her mistresses' secrets. Jane and her sister use Bess as a judge of their work.[85] Literacy is not uncommon among chambermaids: William himself was taught to read and to 'learn the horn-book, by his mother's chambermaid'.[86] The lovely Bess, 'so plump & young', is the soul of discretion and always 'looks most secret sure'.[87] In fact, one of her secrets may have been an unauthorised lover, if she was anything like the chambermaid that William himself addresses in one of his amorous poems:

> If you will go with me, I'll tell you true
> I'll have a Chambermaid ready for you.[88]

There is only a blurred boundary between the duties of the chambermaid and the slightly inferior housemaid, but the latter can expect to do more cleaning. Hannah Woolley in *The Compleat Servant-Maid* (1677) lists a housemaid's weekly duties:

1. Your principal Office is to make clean the greatest part of the House, and see that you suffer no Room to lye foul.
2. That you look well to all the stuff, as Hangings, Chairs, Stools, *&c.* And see that they be often brushed and the Beds frequently turn'd.
3. That you do not misplace any thing by carrying it out of one Room to another, for that is the way to have them lost, or you soundly chid for not keeping them in their proper places.
4. That you be careful and diligent to all strangers, and see that they lack nothing in their Chambers, which your Mistress or Lady will allow, and that your close stools and Chamber pots be duely emptied, and kept clean and sweet.
5. That you help the Laundry-Maid in the morning on the washing day.
6. That in the afternoon you be ready to help the Waiting-woman or Housekeeper in their preserving and distilling.[89]

Prominent among the junior maids are the laundry maids or washers, who perform their great feat of washing all the household linen only at monthly, or even longer, intervals, for it is a matter of pride that a household's stock of sheets and napkins should be able to last a considerable length of time. The laundry, as the architectural writer Roger North puts it, is 'an office wholly of women; and the men, however officious to aid their sweethearts, should not be allowed to frequent there' as their 'impertinent conversation hinders the business of the family'.[90]

When the laundry maids go into the Welbeck washhouse, their first task is to push the sheets and underclothes into a barrel and to pour in the 'lye', a liquid made from a mixture of urine and wood ash. The lye is left to soak the stains out of the linen for some hours before being drained out of the bottom of the barrel with a spigot.[91] Then the laborious task of rinsing commences. More delicate items are cleaned with soap made of ingredients (combined in different ways in different households) such as ashes, lime, tallow, Barbary wax and salt. Sir Hugh Platt, author of *Delightes for Ladies*, recommends a delicate 'washing ball' scented with rose leaves, lavender, orris root, cypress and scrapings of Castille soap as a more attractive alternative,[92] and indeed to perfume a pair of gloves the instructions are even more complicated:

> Take four Grains of Musk and grind it with Rosewater, and also eight grains of Civet, then take two spoonfuls of Gum dragon steeped all night in Rosewater, beat these to a thin Jelly, putting in a half a spoonful of Oil of Cloves, Cinnamon and Jessamine mixed together, then take a Spunge and dip it therein, and rub the Gloves all over thin, lay them in a dry clean place eight and forty hours, then rub them with your hand till they become limber.[93]

The next stage in the laundry maids' routine is the drying of the linen in the garden, ideally spread across scented bushes such as rosemary (privet is also recommended by Roger North). Then comes the ironing, with flat irons simply heated in the fire, box irons that contain hot coals or goffering irons for frills. The ironed sheets go into the linen press, and its screw-down lid is tightened to squeeze them even flatter. The laundry maids in William's own household were often the subject of his lewd fantasies. He penned bawdy verses to a washer, and to the chambermaid responsible for the starching he wrote:

> Your'e nimble in your Trade, att anye Hande,
> You love to starch, to make Itt stiff to Stand.

Not even the well-born waiting women of his household escaped his lascivious attentions, which, whether out of duty or inclination, appear on occasion to have been returned.[94]

Like their master, the menservants of the household appear to be incorrigible and predatory in their behaviour towards the maids. Margaret Cavendish claims that her own mother would never let the 'vulgar serving men be in the nursery among the nursery-maids, lest their rude love-making might do unseemly actions, or speak unhandsome words in the presence of her children'.[95] Hannah Woolley counsels the lowly Under-Cook-Maid to keep herself neat and clean and observant, but if she should 'think none will meddle with such as you, it is a mistake, for sometimes brave Gallants will fall foul upon the Wench in the Scullery'.[96]

One of William's poems about household life describes a scene of playful seduction underlain by menace when a party of maids leaves the house to go into the meadows to cut rushes for the floor. William creates with great gusto many such scenes in his plays, in which low-born household characters jest, argue or soliloquise. At first the open air and unaccustomed freedom from the house leads to an atmosphere of relaxed flirtation, yet the young women have to defend themselves against the advances of the men. They are anxious to remain untouched:

> Presumptuous men had not,
> Our maidenheads yet Got
> We'll keep them safe till marriage.

This time, the battle of the sexes is fairly and squarely won by the triumphant maids:

> Sweet Girles, lets goe Agen
> To Laff at foolish Men
> Ande Love's Rushing try once-more.[97]

The lower-ranking maids in the Cavendish household, like the other servants, have to share their beds. The senior laundress has a bed and a room to herself, while the wash maids share two beds; the scullery maid sleeps alone but that is because of her extreme inferiority.[98] Sharing a bed, even with a stranger, is not a hardship. The gossipy camaraderie between the maids in a seventeenth-century household comes over in a letter written by Jane Greethurst, a servant at Woking House, to her former colleague and friend Mary Stotcher, who has recently left the household. Jane was left in a dilemma by her friend's absence:

> . . . for my part I am not satisfied in my mind whether I were best to go or stay. I have been so much alone since I lost your good company which have troubled me very much; I have never laughed when I was in Bed since you went away for I have no body to speak to, neither was I warm in my Bed till I put on my Stockings. I am not troubled now to provide a Chair for I do not think my Bedfellow which I have now good enough to sit in my Chair.[99]

To own a chair or a new pair of stockings was the highest level of material ambition that the maids could hope to achieve: at Welbeck the wash maid called Margaret earns £3 a year, her junior colleague Mary Maden earns £1 and 10 shillings, and Elizabeth Glasper the kitchen maid only £1; meanwhile, Captain Mazine, as Master of the Horse, is paid £25.[100] Entrapped in their country community, shops and shopping are unknown to them, and they taste the pleasures of consumerism only through the wares of travelling pedlars. The arrival of a pedlar and the unrolling of his pack was an occasion of drama and excitement, captured once again by William Cavendish in a poem. He describes with relish the knick-knacks that make up a maid's idea of paradise: brushes, combs of tortoise shell, cambric cloth, lawn 'as white as milk', taffeta 'as soft as silk', Spanish needles, garters with silver roses, rings, thimbles, rainbow ribbons, silver bodkins, hair-bobs, amber bracelets, coral, jet, picktooth cases, Flanders laces, tobacco boxes, crystal Cupids, looking glasses, night caps, gilt prayer books, and that enduring token of affordable luxury, 'fine silk stockings'.[101] For maids who do not marry, a lifetime of service will be repaid only with a measure of uncertain charity in their old age. Yet a monotonous life in the household with its comradeship, regular gifts of clothing and reliable meals could often be better than a hand-to-mouth existence outside.

At the heart of the busy community of women at Welbeck Abbey, Jane Cavendish sought, but could not find, solitude in which to write. Like their father, she and her sisters much prefer writing poems to checking the kitchen accounts. In their play, Jane and Elizabeth depict a scene in which an old household servant named Gravity (modelled perhaps upon old Thomas Bamford) cannot interest his young mistresses in his bill of fare for dinner:

GRAVITY: Jack, what o'clock? Is not the bill for dinner gone to my lady? Speak, have you lost your tongue? Speak I say!
JACK: Yes sir, the bill was carried to the ladies.
GRAVITY : Know how they like dinner! Now, there's no tart!
JACK: Mistress Sage told me they were not up.
GRAVITY : Fie, fie, as I am an honest man those wits will never be housewives, and nothing angers me, but they'll neither chide nor commend.
JACK: Yes, under favour sir, I remember they chid you for not making a quince tart sweet enough.[102]

The finale of Jane and her sister's play is the miraculous appearance of two gods 'coming down out of the sky' (as Eros and Anteros had done at Bolsover Castle in the masque of 1634) and triumphantly bringing the girls' exiled father back to the household. If Jane and her sister ever managed actually to stage this wistful scene at Welbeck during this time, the figures of the gods were probably dressed in the melancholy remnants of the bright costumes created in 1634.[103] In 1645, a final echo of the royal masques of the 1630s sounded. Charles I, vainly trying to outrun his pursuers by travelling through the now almost completely hostile country, arrived at Royalist Welbeck for two days. He signed a warrant, heard a church service and left in haste.[104] In 1649, he was beheaded on a scaffold like a stage erected immediately outside his father's Banqueting House, playing his part in enacting a scene that was not dissimilar to the many fantastical masques that had taken place inside it. This was no accident: the building's sophisticated classical architecture symbolised everything that was superior, 'foreign' and hated about the Stuart court, and it provided a fitting background to the end of the king's life.

Thrust into a position of harrowing responsibility by her father's absence, the war and her role as head of the household, Jane did not finally acquire a suitor until the advanced age of thirty-eight. Welbeck Abbey had been de-garrisoned by mutual agreement between the combatants in 1645, and Jane had been able to abdicate from her role as head of the household when her brothers returned from Paris.[105] Yet her father, possessive even in exile, failed to approve the match, considering that Jane's suitor was socially inferior and made love to her marriage portion rather than to her person, '& all the ill sonnets & romantical love discourses was to that'. He wrote sharply to Jane and others on the subject, stating that although 'she was in love with him I would never give my consent to a man that I knew nothing of, either of his person, parts or estate'.[106]

Jane tried to win her father over by asking his senior servants in Antwerp, Sir Hubert Cartwright and Captain Mazine, to intervene on her behalf, but William remained unimpressed. Jane's hope that Captain Mazine could persuade him to change his mind was fruitless. 'I thank God servants could never yet do any thing with me but what I pleased my self,' William boasted, '& for truth sake I must tell you the Captain knew me too well to say any thing' at all.[107]

Yet Charles Cheyne, who gave his name to Cheyne Walk in London, finally succeeded in carrying off the marquis's daughter. Jane found great happiness in her new life in London, although she preferred 'the salutary walks of Welbeck, than the crowd, & dust, of Hyde Park'. Despite her passage through so many dangers in the Civil War, she took her brother's advice to stay away from crowds and throngs.[108] Going out into public places in the city, however innocent the motive, was ill-advised for ladies of gentle birth. You 'intend no harm', reads one book of advice, 'in your *Promenades* or *Walks*; but by so doing, you give too often *occasion* for *licentious Amorists* to meet with you'.[109] But the real reason for Jane's bashfulness was her forthcoming baby. Her sister Elizabeth was pregnant at the same time, and had a far harder time of it, complaining that Jane was not yet 'near so big as I am: she breeds the best that ever I knew for she makes nothing of a great Belly'.[110] To her loving husband's pleasure, Jane was successfully 'brought to Bed of a Daughter' in Chelsea in May, 1656.[111]

By November, 1659, Jane is still in London, while her father is in Antwerp and her brother Henry in Nottinghamshire. To Henry and William, the political situation looks bleak, and father and son are equally dissatisfied on the day that William writes to Henry from Antwerp.

Yet, within months, the family's fortunes will be completely recast. Oliver Cromwell has now been dead for over a year. Despite the wish for democracy that had motivated his troops in the Civil War, Cromwell had latterly ruled the Commonwealth of England as a virtual dictator. Taking the title of 'Lord Protector' in 1653, he took to spending weekends at Hampton Court Palace, enjoying the art collection of Charles I and even revelling in the nude statues to an extent that scandalised some of his more puritanical supporters.[112] His death was little mourned, and the diarist John Evelyn reported that his funeral in London was 'the joyfullest that I ever saw, for there were none that cried, but dogs, which the soldiers hooted away with a barbarous noise; drinking, and taking *Tobacco* in the streets as they went'.[113] Cromwell's few surviving supporters recognised the reality that in life he had been at some pains to deny: they buried him wearing a crown.

After his death in 1658, the state he had held together began to fall apart. His incompetent son Richard, also known as 'Tumbledown Dick', has made a miserable business of picking up the reins of power. There are deep divisions in the Commonwealth, and a month ago its senior army officers locked the current members of Parliament out of the Palace of Westminster as the result of a quarrel over whether there should continue to be a Protectorate led by a figure rather like a king or a more democratic form of government instead. Indeed, many Englishmen favour neither option. Exhausted by the constant upheavals that have followed the Civil War, more and more people are beginning to look back nostalgically to the days of the Stuarts.

England is in turmoil, and by an extraordinary twist the thirty-year-old Charles Stuart will shortly be invited to return to his father's throne. Among those in Antwerp who will rejoice at the news, not least in the expectation that his loyalty and sacrifices will at long last be rewarded, is the prince's old tutor, William Cavendish. Best of all is the prospect of coming home.

# 8 – *A Bedchamber Conversation*

NEWCASTLE HOUSE, LONDON, 11TH MAY, 1667

It is six years later, 11th May, 1667, and John Evelyn is on his way to Clerkenwell in Middlesex, just north of London. Evelyn is a Royalist, a courtier and a public servant, and will become famous to posterity for his extraordinary diary. He is on his way to Newcastle House in Clerkenwell, the residence of his old friend William Cavendish.[1] William has recently been made Duke of Newcastle, the very highest rank of the peerage. As well as visiting the newly minted duke, Evelyn is also hoping for an encounter today with the elusive and exotic person who has made a great impact on London society: the woman, some thirty years younger than William, with whom he shares his home.

Evelyn leaves his house near Deptford and travels towards London Bridge, heading for Clerkenwell through the heart of a city of three hundred thousand people. London is once again under the rule of the Stuarts, as the Commonwealth has ended and William's former pupil, Charles II, has been restored to his father's throne. After the long, dull years of the kingless Commonwealth, Restoration London has an atmosphere of jovial, careless extravagance. The buildings and streets are still inconvenient, old and unspeakably dirty, however, at least in the areas where they survive unaffected by last year's catastrophic Great Fire. Evelyn himself is vociferous on the subject of London's air pollution, deploring the fact that 'this glorious and antient city [. . .] should wrap her stately head in clowds of smoake and sulphur, so full of stink and darknesse'. He complains 'that the buildings should be compos'd of such a congestion of misshapen and extravagant houses; that the streets should be so narrow and incommodious in the very center and busiest places of intercourse'.[2] London is plagued not only by the smoke of cooking fires but also by the fumes from bones being boiled for glue or animal fat for soap. Evelyn also fulminates against dyers, brewers, lime-burners, sugar-boilers, chandlers and slaughter-houses for their noxious practices. He considers that Londoners, as a result, breathe nothing but 'an impure and thick mist, accompanied with a fuliginous and filthy vapour, which renders them obnoxious to a thousand inconveniences, corrupting the lungs [. . .] so that cathars, phthisicks, coughs and consumptions rage more in this one City than in the whole earth besides'.[3]

Yet the problem of London's poor planning has been partially solved by the cleansing catastrophe of the fire. Evelyn's route takes him through the blackened and twisted heart of the city, where fire has destroyed the houses from London Bridge to St Paul's Cathedral. The way lies through a wasteland of burnt-out buildings, out of which signs of renewed life and habitation are now springing daily. Landowners have been obliged to clear their holdings of debris, and the Rebuilding Act is now in force, with its requirement for two- or three-storey houses to line the newly laid-out streets.[4] A new tax on coal is allowing the City to fund replacement prisons and churches and to pay for the reconstruction of the Guildhall.

After his passage through the burnt-out area, Evelyn enters once more into the narrow crooked streets that survive on the northern side of the town past Smithfield. Now his coach's passage might be hin-

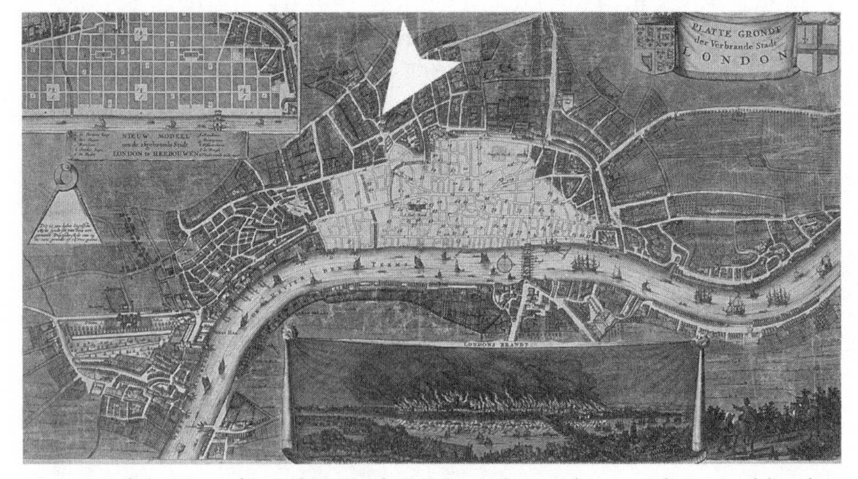


A map of the city of London made in 1666 shows the area destroyed by the Great Fire. Clerkenwell, William's neighbourhood, is marked with an arrow

dered by a flock of a thousand turkeys being shepherded from their birthplace in Norfolk to their place of death in the London markets, or by the 'ruggedness of the uneven streets' which Evelyn considers to have caused the deaths of 'so many of the fair sex and their offspring'.[5] Here the upper storeys of the old timber houses of the City still jut out and lean towards one another, enclosing in a semi-tunnel the streets along which Evelyn passes. These houses are 'the scurvyest Things in the World', according to a French visitor, their storeys 'low and widen'd one over another, all awry and in Appearance ready to fall'.[6]

Evelyn has been keeping notes for his famous diary since the age of eleven, and is also a versatile and enthusiastic scholar (Plate 28). His intellectual interests embrace both arts and sciences. He passes his time in writing papers for the Royal Society and in public works, such as serving as a commissioner of the sewers or on a committee for licensing hackney carriages.[7] Unlike his fellow diarist Pepys, he does not crave society's attention and is a quiet, sober Anglican who dislikes the louche atmosphere of the current court.

As his coach heads north out of the city, Evelyn's surroundings become more pleasant, almost rural. William Cavendish, now seventy-four years old, is once again resident at Newcastle House, his great London mansion, and is served both in London and Nottinghamshire by the remnants of his old household, reunited and revivified. In his youth, William rented a townhouse in the City, but by 1630 he had acquired a new, permanent London base for his annual visits to the capital. He chose a former nunnery in Clerkenwell, which was then a long-established but newly fashionable settlement adjacent to open meadows, with the springs of Sadler's Wells only a short walk away. In the years before the Civil War, the ambitious or newly prominent could not find space in the traditional 'millionaire's row' of the Strand, and indeed the noisome and noisy streets of the city and the river seething with boat traffic repelled them. Clerkenwell was becoming something of an aristocratic dormitory suburb.

As Evelyn approaches Clerkenwell Green, he enters an affluent neighbourhood, with the pastures and bowling greens of the city's northern margin not too far distant. Here are the gardens of the Charterhouse and the monastery of St John's, and near by the river Fleet and the open space of Hatton Garden. 'Codpiece Row', leading off Clerkenwell Green, bears the alternative name of 'Town's End'.[8] Now Evelyn passes the entrance to the church of St James, with its square tower rebuilt after a collapse in 1627; it was here that William's daughter Elizabeth was married in 1641.[9] William has as yet failed to pay his Poor Rates this year, and the parish wardens of St James are deterred from hounding him by his ducal status. Eventually they will give up asking for the required ten shillings and simply hope for 'what his Grace pleaseth'.[10] Beyond the church is Clerkenwell Close, surrounded by spacious and handsome houses. The fine brick residence on the west side of the close was once a temporary home of Oliver Cromwell.

On the east side of the close, the nunnery of St Mary's (now Newcastle House) was converted into a mansion after the Dissolution of the Monasteries and has perhaps inspired William's wife Margaret's risqué play *The Convent of Pleasure*.[11] Its cloisters and physical attachment to the church of St James were bound to appeal to William's residual fondness for the Gothic and romantic. He has built a gallery across the west end of the church's nave so that he can walk from his first-floor chambers straight into the church to hear a service. The house's great antiquity brings with it certain practical problems. London has a chronic shortage of burial space in its one hundred and thirty cramped churchyards, and the residents of neighbouring properties note that the 'skulls & bones of dead people' have been found in William's – formerly

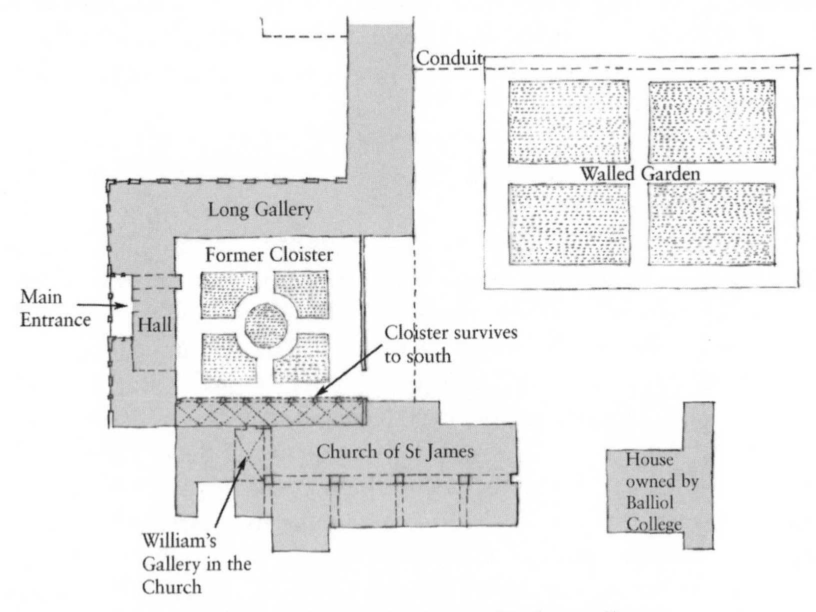


Plan of Newcastle House, Clerkenwell

the nuns' – garden.[12] The residents complain that 'ye rotting moisture coming from ye dead bodies has perished ye foundation of [their] houses'.[13]

It was only two years ago that William was elevated from marquis to duke. Londoners are intrigued by the new duke and duchess, and their behaviour during this particular stay in the city has caused much comment. William and his wife have every reason to be well disposed towards John Evelyn and his wife Mary, for it was Mary's mother who helped Margaret to prepare for her marriage to William in Paris in 1645. At the time, William had been so grateful that he promised her £1,000, but Evelyn notes somewhat sourly that 'now all was forgotten of that nature'.[14] Yet he has seen the Cavendishes several times in recent weeks, and on previous visits has been 'much pleasd, with the extraordinary fancifull habit, garb & discourse of the *Dutchesse*'.[15] Today, on 11th May, he has been invited to dine with the duke, whose fortunes have been transformed since his penniless exile in Antwerp, and Evelyn may even catch sight of England's most exotic duchess as well.

In 1660, the small Cavendish household in Antwerp rejoiced at the news that Charles II was to be restored to the throne, but William's return to England was less triumphant than he had hoped. He arrived too late to see the victorious entry of the king and his supporters into London, 'brandishing their swords and shouting, with unexpressable joy: The wayes straw'd with flowers, the bells ringing, the streetes hung with Tapissry, fountaines running with wine'.[16] After a dangerous crossing in a leaky ship, William passed his first night in England at Greenwich, where his supper nevertheless 'seem'd more savoury to him, than any meat he had hitherto tasted; and the noise of some scraping Fidlers, he thought the pleasantest harmony that ever he had heard'. 'Surely', he thought in bewildered joy, 'I have been sixteen years asleep, and am not thoroughly awake yet.'[17] When he reached London, one sight undreamt of was an immensely tall maypole (loved by William and forbidden by the Commonwealth) in the Strand outside Somerset House. As it was pulled vertical, 'little children did much rejoice, and ancient people did clap their hands saying, golden days began to appear'.[18]

With the returning Cavendishes came some '30 trunks & cases [. . .] containing only household stuff', but after years abroad William longed to see his houses and former possessions once again.[19] John Evelyn, who like William was forced to live on the continent during the Commonwealth, now looked forward to the return of 'the days of our fathers', when girls would care for 'cupboards of ancient useful plate, chests of damask for the table and store of fine Holland sheets fragrant of Rose or Lavender for the Bed'. Meanwhile, to complete this vision of old households reunited, 'youths would sing old Simon, Chevy Chase, and dance Brave Arthur, and draw a bow that made a proud Monsieur tremble at the whizz of a grey goose feather'.[20]

Yet William's golden days were a little slow in coming, and did not glitter as brightly as he might have hoped. His servants were scattered and demoralised, his houses almost derelict, and his son Henry, having moved to Welbeck so reluctantly, was dismayed at having to vacate the mansion once again. William and Margaret were initially forced to take inferior London lodgings in Holborn, as another family was occupying Newcastle House. Now that the military battles were over, the legal battles to reclaim their property were about to begin. There were pains as well as pleasures involved in returning home.

John Evelyn's coach draws up at the imposing entrance to Newcastle House itself. Unlike William's houses in Nottinghamshire and Derbyshire, the front of this mansion is brick-built.[21] It presents an intimidating front to the street, with its lower storey consisting of blank brick walls. Above this, classical columns fill the spaces between a row of high windows. A gateway flanked by decorative scrolls opens onto a small forecourt; it is overlooked by possible hidden watchers from the high first-floor windows of the main rooms. A second attic storey with dormers is hidden away behind the parapet roof. This modern roofline, combined with the Ionic columns on the front, cleverly gives this ancient house something of the contemporary appearance of an Italian palazzo. Evelyn, though, is a connoisseur of classical architecture of the newest, strictest kind. As he steps out of his coach and glances upwards, he probably finds the building a somewhat unsatisfactory compromise.

Evelyn steps into a hall as long and high as those of the Middle Ages, and indeed this part of the house was formerly the lodgings and hall of the prioress of the medieval nunnery of St Mary's. In the days of the nunnery, Evelyn would have entered via a screens passage at one end of the Hall, but the classicising of the house means that today he uses a

The entrance to Newcastle House

large door placed centrally. The former nunnery determines the whole layout of Newcastle House, for the refectory, to the north, has become the house's long gallery, and the square garden at the back was once entirely surrounded by the nuns' cloister; indeed, part of the cloister still remains. After William moved to Clerkenwell in 1630, 'John Plasterer', 'Thomas Tyler' and 'John Stayner' make an appearance in the records of the parish. Perhaps they were craftsmen newly come down from Nottinghamshire to work on improvements to William's new house, their surnames not yet familiar to the parish clerk.[22]

Evelyn has little time to linger in the shadowy hall, for William's usher shows him the way up the great staircase beyond in order to climb to the first-floor reception rooms. Evelyn catches his first glimpse of the aged but still hale figure of his host.

Contrary to the habit of his younger years, William is today almost certainly wearing a wig. The fashion was born in France, much earlier in the century, and the French king Louis XIV has his head shaved daily for the accommodation of the masterpieces made by his forty wig-makers.[23] Charles II brought the French craze for wigs with him on his return from exile, and all of fashionable London is now hiding its natural hair. Even Samuel Pepys, another diarist, has finally adopted the style, having changed his mind since the occasion four years ago when he 'did try two or three borders and periwiggs, meaning to wear one; and yet I have no stomach, but that the pains of keeping my hair clean is so great'.[24] Black is the most popular colour, in imitation of the king's own hair, which is 'shining black, not frizzled, but so naturally curling into great rings that it is a very comely ornament'.[25] Such is the great cost of hairpieces that wig-stealers have become a new danger on the London streets: the thieves employ a trained and cunning dog, or a small boy, to tweak a wig off the head. The thief himself then makes a noisy business of pretending to have witnessed the theft and of chasing the perpetrator out of sight, never to return.[26]

William's wig is restrained and rather sober in character: he does not approve of the most fanciful French fashions, and often makes fun of those who follow them. He shares these conservative views with John Evelyn, who is equally disparaging of the lavish Frenchified look. 'It was a fine silken thing which I spied walking the other day through Westminster Hall,' Evelyn scoffs in his book about the tyranny of fashion or 'mode', 'that had as much ribbon about him as would have plundered six shops and set up twenty country pedlars. All his body was dressed like a May-pole [. . .] and the colours were red, orange and blue.'[27] The basic form of the latest style for gentlemen is a long fitted waistcoat worn over knee breeches, though feathered hats, cravats and ribbons avoid any appearance of sobriety.

William now greets Evelyn with some cordiality, and has even unbent so far as to have come out onto the landing at the top of the stairs. On his last visit, a couple of weeks ago, Evelyn brought his wife to dinner at Newcastle House and was extremely flattered when William accompanied them not only down the stairs on their departure but right out into the court.[28] A less cordial host would have remained in the first-floor apartments. Evelyn now sinks into a low bow. An inferior may not keep his hat on in the presence of a duke, and as he removes his, Evelyn places one foot forward and sinks into his obeisance. A hundred years ago, he would have stepped backwards to bow, but the fashion has now changed, causing a writer on courtesy to warn that care must be taken to avoid bowing simultaneously, 'that the person of quality bowing civilly towards you, and offering to embrace you, may have a blow in the face with your head for his pains'.[29]

Evelyn and William have enjoyed free and frank exchanges with each other over the years, as indicated in the poem that William wrote for Evelyn on the occasion of Evelyn's own marriage – now long ago –

to the eleven-year-old Mary Browne. William outlined the benefits of marrying such a young girl: she must surely be a virgin, 'not spotted or yet sullied', and Evelyn can shape her into the mould he desires as she grows up. Not holding back from giving even the most intimate of advice, William recommends that Evelyn make his young wife 'a scabord for to fit thy sword', though if Evelyn's sword should prove 'too little or too big' when he first inserts it into Mary's 'scabord', he should be careful and gentle, just as when:

> Like a young Colt backt gently not by forse
> By skilful riding maks a ready horse.[30]

At his best, William's 'discourse is as free and unconcerned as his behaviour, pleasant, witty and instructive'.[31] Yet his manners in company are a little more stiff and formal than is normal in the new relaxed Restoration society. He is probably pleased when a guest does not immediately replace his hat on being given permission to do so but waits for a second urging from his host. Then, as a courtesy book suggests, the guest 'must do it with some reluctance, but not so as to be troublesome'.[32] Only when both parties belong to the same household may 'the inferiour [. . .] cover himself at the first request' after the salutation with politeness.[33] Margaret considers her husband's behaviour in society to be 'Courtly, Civil, easie and free, without Formality or Constraint', but despite his cordiality William's visitors are never allowed to forget that they are in the presence of a nobleman.[34] He detests the overelaborate French manners acquired by those who have travelled abroad, and indeed James Howell, in his *Instructions for Forreine Travell*, notes how those returning from the continent can be spotted at once by 'their *gate* and *strouting*, their *bending* in the *hammes*, and *shoulders*, and *looking upon their legs*, with *frisking* and *singing*'.[35] The poet Richard Flecknoe praises William for an informality that, strangely, has the effect of reinforcing his greatness. From those of whom he knows and approves, William does not expect hats to be doffed at a distance:

> He looks not (as some do) that you should d'off
> Your Hat, and make a reverence twelve-score off:
> Nor take Exceptions, if at every word
> You don't repeat your *Grace*, or else my *Lord*;
> But as they'd seem great men by *Pride*, so he,
> Is one indeed by noble curtesy:

And does appear a hundred times more great,
By leaving it, then they by keeping state.[36]

This apparently contradictory mixture of formality and informality, easy courtliness and yet grandeur worthy of respect is perhaps as close a description as an English writer can achieve of the stiff continental art of *cortesia* or courtly behaviour as it is still practised by the old-fashioned in England, an art which William learned in Italy over fifty years ago.[37]

On this intimate occasion, William does not lead his guest into 'ye great Dining Room' but into a smaller and more private parlour, a room whose name is taken from the French verb *parler* and which is a chamber for conversation.[38] Many of the rooms of the house look over the pleasant gardens to the east, and this view becomes the topic of debate.

As William and Evelyn look out, they see a cloister immediately below them enclosing a square garden laid out with lawn and paths. The arcaded walk surrounding it was formerly the nunnery cloister, its floor recently renewed with Flemish tiles. Unnoticed by anyone, a fragment of seventeenth-century bottle glass was trapped in the mortar during the job and will be recovered by archaeologists in three hundred years' time.[39]

Although the cloister garden is laid out just like the parterre at his own house at Sayes Court, John Evelyn probably has few genuine compliments for this garden. Pleasant though it is, it is also small and prim, on a single level, and lacks trees. Since 1652, Evelyn has been creating his own superlative garden at Sayes Court, and the writing of his book *Elysium Britannicum*, an encyclopaedic history of gardening, has occupied him for many years. His views have changed over time: initially he favoured French-style flower gardens, but now he is in favour of 'extensive' or rural gardening and the use of trees. In 1660, he even wrote a book called *The Manner of Ordering Fruit-Trees*. He anticipates in these writings the landscape gardens of the eighteenth century; in fact, it is Evelyn who introduces the word 'avenue' to the English language as a gardening term.

Evelyn's book *Sylva* (1664), again about trees, is of particular interest to William. (Evelyn himself admits that he 'has hardly the power to take off his Pen on the delightful subject of woods'.[40]) The book outlines some pioneering methods of cultivating trees, but is addressed to gentlemen rather than foresters. In it, Evelyn insists that major replanting must urgently take place in the wake of the depredations of the Civil War, and William cannot fail to agree. When, on his return to the

Midlands, he saw that his beloved park at Clipstone had been felled, he could not hide his feelings from his wife. Margaret considered that she had 'never perceived him sad or discontented for his own Losses and Misfortunes, yet when he beheld the ruines of that Park' she 'observed him troubled, though he did little express it'.[41]

At Newcastle House, though, schemes for the garden have taken second place in William's mind to plans for a magnificent *manège* yard, ambitious proposals that have never quite come to fruition. Beyond the cloister lies a larger garden, and William now outlines his proposals to Evelyn, a man who appreciates a fine horse. Unlike William, Evelyn has visited the birthplace of *manège* in Naples. There, in the riding house of the Spanish viceroy, he saw 'the noblest horses I had ever beheld, one of his sons riding the Menage with that address and dexterity as I had never seen anything approach it'.[42] Poignantly, his own *manège* horse was sent during the Civil War from the riding house to serve the king on the battlefield.[43]

Aspiring English horsemen have long been under the necessity of travelling to Naples in order to see the masters of their craft, or else to the Palace of the Louvre in Paris, where Monsieur de Pluvinel runs a similar school. Apart from the exclusive Royal Mews, there was no proper school of horsemanship in England before the Civil War, although the art did make a brief appearance on the syllabus of Sir Francis Kynaston's Museum Minervae in Bedford Street, Covent Garden, which opened in 1635. William therefore commissioned a proposal to be drawn up for a full-scale college of horsemanship here in Clerkenwell.[44] According to his plan, the posts and rails in the yard would be similar to those at de Pluvinel's academy. There were to be five individual vertical poles for training horses to turn in circles, equipment familiar from William's book on horsemanship. At one end of the yard an enormous stable with twenty-six stalls was proposed. At the other, an extensive residential building would be arranged in a series of independent suites round a courtyard like a college. It seems that the plan was for young horsemen to live and train in a collegiate atmosphere dedicated to horsemanship.

Yet William's proposed college was never built – perhaps the Civil War intervened – and it remains the pipe dream that he now expounds upon to Evelyn. In 1649, Sir Balthazar Gerbier succeeded in opening a similar academy, aimed at avoiding the necessity (as he put it) of sending 'young Gentlemen to any of the Forraigne Academies (where they shall learn no more qualities then now they may get at home, not altogether so many)'. Today, nearly twenty years later, *manège* is an art in decline. It will never regain the high place it held at court and society in the Cavalier years just before the Civil War.

It appears – perhaps to Evelyn's disappointment – that he and his host are going to dine alone. Both William and Evelyn are temperamentally inclined to talk about old times, and continue to do so over their meal. The room in which they take their dinner has been specially set up for the occasion, with table, chairs, sideboard and wine cooler standing by; the dining room dedicated solely to eating and not used for anything else will not evolve until the next century.[45] Evelyn waits for William to begin, for, as Antoine de Courtin remarks, a guest 'must not be the first to put your hand in the Dish, unless you be desir'd to help your Neighbour'; nor must you 'by any awkward gesture show any signs that you are hungry, nor fix your Eyes upon the meat, as if you would devour all'.[46] Napkin unfolded, William reaches for his cutlery. The use of a knife and fork is now quite normal: as the Marquis de Coulanges observes in the 1660s, 'Today everyone eats with a spoon and fork from his own plate, and a valet washes the cutlery from time to time at the buffet.'[47] A duke's dinner is served with much less of the towel twirling and bowing of William's masque in 1634, and the food on the table is likewise rather different.

Having lived so long abroad, William and the rest of the royal court have become accustomed to the continental fashion in food, especially the French fondness for sauces and stews, in addition to the traditional English roasts and puddings. Continental cookbooks such as *The French Cook* (1653) and *A Perfect School of Instruction for the Officers of the Mouth* (1682) are appearing in England in translation.[48] Courtiers dining with each other may well find the food served according to the 'French ease' or '*à la française*', which means that each guest serves him or herself from a table spread with dishes, with the host doing the carving. The servants' roles in the performance are by now much diminished, being restricted to bringing bread and clean plates.[49] After their residence abroad, the Cavendish family cookbook contains novelties such as a rich spiced sauce to accompany a boiled carp containing vinegar, half a pound of sweet butter, the blood of the fish, nutmeg, cloves and mace. 'When you dish it up,' the recipe concludes, 'strew a little ginger a bout ye brims of ye dish.'[50]

William certainly knows how to entertain according to the highest expectations of the king and his courtiers. In Antwerp, in 1658, he invited the exiled court to a stupendous entertainment at Rubens's house, with two hours of dancing and a banquet brought in on 'eight great chargers, each borne by two gentlemen of the court, wines and other drinks [. . .] being dispersed to all the Company', before dancing lasting another two hours. The guests were further amused by a song with lyrics written by William himself, sung by Margaret's Moorish pageboy 'dressed all in feathers'.[51]

Despite his ability to provide hospitality appropriate to court occasions, William is actually rather conservative in his tastes, and John Evelyn may well find the fashion for French-inspired 'kickshaws' (*quelque-choses*) or ragouts conspicuously absent from his dinner today. In one of her books, William's wife Margaret describes the foolishness of the fashionable 'Lady C.C.', a 'mode' lady, who sent back an old-fashioned 'chine of beef' to the kitchen because she considered that serving plain beef was 'not only an old but a country custom'. 'The truth is', Margaret pronounced decidedly, in a manner which says much about the tastes of the ageing Cavendish household, 'she showed herself a fool and behaved herself as mad.'[52]

Along with plain roast meat, there are vegetables on the table. It is only now, in the 1660s, that people begin to write down information about the varieties of, and dressings for, the vegetables that accompany the hearty meat dishes of the seventeenth century. Hannah Woolley, in the section of her book *The Compleat Servant-Maid* devoted to the cook maid, recommends the following menu for the month of May:

First Course

1. Boyl'd Chickens
2. Roasted Veal
3. Roasted Capons
4. Rabbets

Second Course

1. Artichoke Pye hot
2. Westphalia Bacon and Tarte
3. Sturgeon, Salmon, Lobsters
4. A dish of Asparagus
5. A Tansie [a bitter herb with yellow flowers][53]

The Earl of Northumberland owned silver dishes for 'salet' even in the 1620s, but now cruets for oil and vinegar or imported flasks of Italian glass are beginning to make regular appearances on polite tables.[54] John Evelyn loves vegetables and will even devote a whole book, *Acetaria*, to the subject of their preparation and dressing. He likes his 'sallats' to contain 'crude and fresh herbs [. . .] eaten with some acetous juice, oyl, salt, &c. to give them a grateful gust and vehicle'.[55] He gives very precise instructions: herbs must be washed and shaken in a cloth and cut with a silver rather than a steel knife; artichokes may be fried in fresh butter with parsley while small, but when larger must be 'bak'd in pies, with marrow, dates, and other rich ingredients'.[56] Garlic 'is not for ladies' palates nor those who court them'.[57] William, on his doctor's advice, eats raw vegetables only with circumspection. 'Sallads', Dr de Mayerne counsels him, 'cannot be without lemon or vinegar, eat not much, & no lettuce, they being hurtful to the Brayne.'[58]

The few servants who do remain in the room frequently bring clean glasses to the table. When William wishes to take a drink, he calls for a glass of wine. A waiter fills a glass (possibly one of the newfangled engraved variety, intended to imitate the qualities of rock crystal) at the sideboard and stands it upon a small salver to hand it to his master. William then drains it at a single draught (rather than sipping) and returns it to the servant's hands for rinsing and refilling. This, again, is an English practice, and a Frenchman notes that in his own country, 'if we be many in a company, we make no scruple to drink all out of a Glass, or a Tankard, which [the English] are not used to do: and if a Servant would offer to give them a Glass before it was washed every time they drink, they would be angry at it'.[59] On William's sideboard, the cistern and wine cooler are essential conveniences, and in newly built houses a special alcove is beginning to appear in the wall of a dining room to house them.[60] If his cistern and wine cooler are made of silver, they will be among a nobleman's most expensive purchases.[61] William's love of wine and drinking is frequently the subject of his poems:

> Give me the Canary the wholesome Sherry
> The Radical maligoe makes Us merry
> Sometimes the Claret, the Rhenish, the white
> To Heighten our wits, the Poet's Delight:
> The strong Greek wines with Sacrem Christey
> If drink of them much, will make your eyes misty.[62]

Here John Evelyn and his host are at odds. Evelyn has often complained about the English tendency, once the cloth is removed from the table, 'to drink excessively'. He notes that 'It is the afternoon's diversion; whether for the want of better to employ the time, or affection to the drink, I know not; but I have found some persons of quality, whom one could not safely visit after dinner without resolving to undergo this *drink-ordeal*.'[63] William perhaps makes use of Gervase Markham's cure to 'preserve a man from drunkenness', which is to take powdered betony and cabbage each morning,[64] but his servants have to deal with their master's inevitable hangovers:

> Thus we will drink, both day & all night
> And Quarrel some times, but never to fight
> When Ev'ry ones nod doth aches each head
> We'll have sum Porters to lead us to Bed.[65]

At Newcastle House, the dinner and other domestic arrangements appear to run like clockwork, yet this has not always been the case. The Cavendishes regained control of the house only as recently as 1662, and even then by a piece of legalistic thuggery characteristic of the returning Royalists exploiting their party's recapture of the upper hand. Even before the Civil War, William was in debt to the Copley family for unpaid loans.[66] In 1654, the trustees of William's estates had begged John Copley, with 'urgent importunity', to buy Newcastle House in order to settle the debts of William's dead son Charles, which he did.[67] After the Restoration, an Act of Parliament was passed restoring to William all the estates he had owned before May, 1642. William tried to reclaim Newcastle House under this act, but Copley, understandably, refused to release it. Only after a long legal struggle and a down payment of money did William regain his London home.

Even in William's absence in Nottinghamshire or elsewhere, Newcastle House is ably run these days by Mr Benoist. John Benoist was tutor to William's sons, and with the familiar loyalty and adaptability of the household servants who have accompanied William through his vicissitudes, he is now employed in administering accounts and sending bills up to be paid by the Welbeck treasury. The pedantic Mr Benoist accompanied William into exile before travelling back to England to try to raise money. He works hard at his figures and correspondence every morning until ten o'clock, when he goes out on business errands.[68] In London his tasks include buying books for Margaret, sending up 'silver buttons and loops', Dutch quills, boxes of lozenges and melons to Welbeck, paying an upholsterer and trying to resolve a dispute over the location of a leak in the conduit pipe that passes through William's and other neighbouring gardens.[69] Performing this last task, Mr Benoist will become enraged by the apothecary who lives next door to Newcastle House. The conduit is blocked beneath his garden, yet he refuses to allow Mr Benoist to dig to rectify the problem.[70] The pipes running beneath the streets of London are made of elm or lead, and frequent leaks and punctures mean that pressure is low and the supply only runs for two or three days a week. Fires are supposed to be doused only with water from carefully determined hydrant points. However, during last year's Great Fire, panicking householders dug up the pipes beneath the streets indiscriminately, causing all the pressure to drain away and the supply to fail.[71]

After the Restoration, William soon resumed his peripatetic life, travelling between Newcastle House, the court and his houses in the country. His arrival in London causes something of a stir throughout the city, one observer reporting that 'My Lord Duke of Newcastle entered this city the other day with a princely train, many of the nobility (his friends) meeting him out of town, and to-day gone to Court in great state and his good duchess.'[72]

Each time he changes residence, the upholstered chairs, writing desk, carpets and hangings of William's bedchamber and closet, in addition to a stable of his choicest horses, follow him from house to house in an immense logistical operation. He is ambivalent about the task of moving house. On the one hand, he complains about the 'many preparations for a London Journey' that 'to a Country man is more difficult then an East India voyage to some merchants', yet on the other, preparing to leave Welbeck for London, he shivers in anticipation of a trip to court: 'Trunks all packed up for London all could tell, Ready to take the Coach for heightened pleasure of Court & town.'[73]

While the master and mistress are absent, a skeleton staff of servants is left behind to look after the house, and they continue to be issued with their diet and annual wage. Only a weak, tentative heartbeat of life remains in houses left dark and quiet by the lord's absence. Sir John Hobart of Blickling Hall in Norfolk reduced his staff of twenty-seven to seven when he left the house for London; those remaining had the tasks of airing the rooms, 'looking to the gardens', caring for the furniture and on one occasion, making a swan pie to be dispatched to Sir John in London.[74] These servants sometimes find themselves under-occupied and quarrels can break out. Thomas Bamford, left in charge of nine servants at Welbeck 'since my Lord went' in 1656, complained that he had 'taken down the hangings in the best bed chamber 3 pieces, In the dining Chamber next it, 2 pieces, and the old bedchamber 5 pieces, brushed and laid up [. . .] as well as I can amongst such ugly and inanimate fellows as some of them be here'.[75] Of the one hundred and fifty suites of hangings that William had possessed before the Civil War, only ten or twelve were saved for his return.[76]

William travels between Welbeck and London by private coach. Since the Restoration, there have been some significant improvements in coach design that make the jouncing journey more comfortable, such as glass windows (in place of leather flaps) and sprung suspension.[77] William and Margaret possess a travelling coach as well as the striking model they use for visits to court; it is the sight of Margaret's black and silver vehicle for urban use that causes Samuel Pepys, an inveterate shopper, to acknowledge that his 'mind is mightily of late upon a coach'.[78] Sir Richard Powle of Shottesbrooke in Berkshire likewise possesses a best coach, a travelling coach and, indeed, an old coach 'past using', but then his prodigality might be explained by Andrew Marvell's opinion that he was incapable of riding on horseback because of venereal disease.[79] The secondary expenses of having a coach include parking fees in London (even in 1636, it was estimated that there were over six thousand coaches in the city[80]) and employing a postillion or boy to ride one of the front pair of what might be four or six horses. The postillion is a useful back-up in the event of an accident to, or the incapacity of, the coachman; William's postillion, Thomas Ramster, earns £2 and 10 shillings a year for his service.[81] In 1654, John Evelyn visited a friend whose household's hospitality to his coachman made him 'so exceedingly drunk that returning home we escaped incredible dangers'. On another occasion, the servants of his host at a house in Blackheath 'made our Coach-men so drunk that they both fell-off their boxes upon the heath, where we were fain to leave them'.[82]

When Margaret and William make the short journey from Clerkenwell to the Palace of Whitehall, they are attended by as many servants as possible. Samuel Pepys describes catching a glimpse of Margaret in her coach in the park:

> That which we and almost all went for was to see my Lady Newcastle; which we could not, she being followed and crowded upon by coaches all the way she went, that nobody could come near her; only, I could see she was in a large black coach, adorned with silver instead of gold, and so with the curtains and everything black and white, and herself in her cap.[83]

Her footmen in their velvet coats were much remarked upon, and as Pepys reminds us, 'the whole story of this lady is a romance and all she doth is romantic'.[84]

After eating and drinking, John Evelyn is finally judged worthy of the privilege he seeks. He is conducted through further first-floor rooms to Margaret's own suite and is allowed to sit 'discoursing with her Grace in her bed-chamber'.[85] It is still commonplace for a lady to welcome important male guests in her bedchamber, for it remains a multipurpose room, used for reception as well as rest. In fact, Evelyn has even been with the king into the bedchamber of the royal mistress, the Duchess of Portsmouth, in order to see her 'in her morning loose garment, her maides Combing her, newly out of her bed: his Majestie & the Gallants standing about her'.[86]

The lady now sitting opposite Evelyn is always unconventional in her appearance and manner (Plate 30). Evelyn shyly averts his eyes from her low-cut corsage and black-speckled face for fear of embarrassment. On his first visit to Newcastle House, some weeks previously, he found himself strangely attracted to Margaret's 'extraordinary fanciful habit',[87] and Margaret herself claims that she takes 'great delight in attiring, fine dressing, and fashions, especially fashions as I did invent myself'.[88] Samuel Pepys heard Margaret described by others many times before he saw her for himself, 'for all the town-talk is nowadays of her extravagance'. When he finally met her in person, he found her 'a very comely woman' dressed in a 'velvet cap, her hair about her ears, many black patches because of pimples about her mouth, naked-necked, without anything about it, and a black juste-au-corps [a close-fitting, knee-length coat]'.[89] Margaret is justly proud of her neck (which she sets off with a necklace of large pearls) and her bosoms. In order to make them appear plumper, she is accustomed to 'trim them up [. . .] by binding a gentle piece of Ribbon at the top of every one, and so appearing au Tour à la mode'.[90] Margaret is also an enthusiastic follower of the short-lived fashion in the 1660s for female cross-dressing and is sometimes to be found 'dressed in a vest' (or

Images of 'vertue' and 'vice' from the 1650s. 'Vice' sports a low-cut corsage, curls and black patches, all fashions favoured by Margaret Cavendish

waistcoat) and 'instead of courtesies, made legs and bows to the ground with her hand and head'.[91]

The 'black patches' on Margaret's cheeks are a current craze among fashionable ladies. Since 1650, notes one curious observer, ladies have 'entertained a vain custom of spotting their faces out of affectation of a mole, to set off their beauty, such as Venus had [. . .] some fill their visages with them, varied into all manner of shapes and figures'.[92] The more conventional, of course, are appalled by the habit, and one playwright describes ladies' faces:

> besmear'd and pierc'd
> With several sorts of patches
> As if some cats their skins had fled
> With scars, half moons, and notches.[93]

Like her husband, Margaret is unlikely to be wearing her own hair, for the fashion is for false curls wired to stand out from the head. 'A great lady', the playwright John Marston declaimed, 'should not wear her own hair; for that's as mean as a coat of her own spinning.'[94]

As well as preparing her striking toilette, Margaret has probably spent the morning writing in her closet; it was likely to have been a sudden inspiration for her work that kept her away from the dinner table. So fertile are her thoughts that her handwritten words on the page customarily 'seem rather as a ragged rout, than a well armed body, for the brain being quicker in creating, than the hand in writing'.[95] She even calls out to wake her waiting women in the middle of the night to take down urgent dictation of some new idea. During their residence in Antwerp, William's now-dead brother Charles used to rib Margaret for the hours she spent in the company of her thoughts and her imaginary fairies:

> Sir Charles into my chamber coming in,
> When I was writing of my 'Fairy Queen;'
> 'I pray' – said he – 'when Queen Mab you do see,
> Present my service to her Majesty.'[96]

The frontispiece to one of her books, *The World's Olio*, shows Margaret at work in her closet. Although she is alone, she is wearing a little crown on her head as befits the wife of the status-conscious William Cavendish.[97] Her closet is richly hung with patterned silk and a carpet covers her desk. On it are laid her paper, a tray holding her ink pot and quill, her manuscript in progress, a clock and a little bell to summon her waiting women. Margaret looks up in surprise, her deep concentration broken, while her fancies embodied as cherubs flutter about her head and attempt to crown her with laurel as the queen of poetry. One of the cherubs lifts the hangings, revealing not a wall but the wide strange spaces of Margaret's imagination. A poet who knew Margaret described her closet as a place of solitary literary endeavour rather than the more usual repository for luxuries and rarities:

> Is this a *Lady-Closet*? 't cannot be,
> For nothing here of *vanity* you see [. . .]
> Scarcely a *Glass*, or *Mirror* in't you find,
> Excepting *Books*, the *Mirrors* of the mind.[98]

John Evelyn is intrigued not only by Margaret's strange appearance but by her unusual, discursive, articulate manner, which confounds

Margaret is disturbed while writing in her closet

expectations of a great lady. On his last visit, he found her 'in a kind of Transport: suitable to her extravagant humor & dresse, which was very singular'.[99] Margaret and Evelyn's talk probably now turns to Margaret's enthusiasms, the subjects more proper for gentlemanly debate than for a duchess's pen: science and art, the laboratory and literature. Margaret, no less than her husband, is interested in natural philosophy and science, and London has become a new centre for scientific debate since the Restoration. 'A spirit of learning came in with the Restoration,' Bishop Burnet will write in his *History of his own Times*, and 'mathematics and the new philosophy were in great esteem'.[100] The king himself has a laboratory and observatory at the Palace of Whitehall, and Margaret is keen to visit the revivified Royal Society, of which John Evelyn himself is one of the founders.

Along with scientific topics, Margaret probably talks with Evelyn of the crowded playhouses of Restoration London, where both she and her husband have seen their own plays performed. Since 1660, when the playhouses reopened after the silent Commonwealth period, plays have sparkled with musical interludes and an arch, elegant, combative wit that was unknown before the Civil War. Both the king and his brother the Duke of York love plays and visit the theatres in person. Margaret and William's characters and their tribulations are often shown in household settings, providing numerous vignettes drawn from life. William and his wife are not the only aristocratic playwrights, as many of their peers also take up their pens. William, in particular, is aided in his writing by professional playwrights such as John Dryden and Thomas Shadwell. He even appointed Sir William Davenant, 'an eminent good poet, and loyal', to be Lieutenant-General of his Ordnance during the Civil War; their witty talk was more often of literature than guns.[101] Not everyone shared Margaret's high opinion of William's powers as a writer. Sir Philip Warwick described William's character as having 'too much of the razor in it: for he had a tincture of a Romantick spirit, and had the misfortune to have somewhat of the Poet in him'.[102] Both William and Margaret's works occasionally delight, but more often vex, the dedicated playgoer Samuel Pepys, who found William's play *The Humorous Lovers* 'the most ridiculous thing that ever was wrote'.[103]

As a poet and a lover of poetry, William hovers on the fringes of a group of writers who will become known to posterity as the Cavalier poets. Richard Lovelace, Andrew Marvell and John Suckling write about love and loyalty, taking a 'cavalier' approach to life in the sense of spontaneity, enthusiasm and informality, combining sensitivity and versatility with a love of beauty. 'To Amarantha, That She Would Dishevel Her Hair' is a title by Lovelace, while Marvell ponders on 'The Definition of Love'. The careless, stylish arrogance of these poets becomes all the more romantic if their losses and sufferings are considered. By the 1660s, many of their number have died on the battlefields of the Civil War or in continental exile. Suckling committed suicide by poison in Paris in 1641, while Lovelace was imprisoned for his support of the king.[104] On the other hand, the sweeping category of 'Cavalier' unfairly underestimates these poets' unique voices and committed, craftsmanlike approach.

Yet William, coming from a slightly older generation, is a little out of step with the Cavalier Poets. He prefers to continue emulating the Jacobean metaphysical poets of his youth and remains not quite original enough to have achieved a lasting independent reputation. He is something of a literary chameleon, lacking a distinctive voice of his own, although able to produce passable imitations of his poetic mentors, Ben Jonson and John Donne. It is striking that William does not take part in the contemporary fashion for emulating the classical precedents of the Roman authors, and his slightly low-brow taste for drama and farce may be the result of his contempt for, and lack of, formal education.[105]

Part of the reason for Jonson's and Donne's lasting reputation as great poets is that they indirectly question and challenge the contemporary source of authority: the court and its fashions. This raises a fascinating question for William Cavendish: if he, like them, cannot help constantly assessing and questioning the world and its values through his poetry, how could he ever have hoped to become a true court insider with the unshaken confidence of the Stuart kings? His poems reveal that he has too many frailties, passions and sympathies, as well as too finely honed a sense of the ridiculous, ever to have been a ruthless, cold-blooded careerist. His enthusiasm and infectious high spirits spill over from his admittedly sometimes plodding verses. In his poems – whether he is in a humorous mode, is criticising society or is suffering for love – he simply sounds like he's enjoying himself.

Women seem to bring out the best in William as a poet, and his most engaging efforts are all about, or dedicated to, his loves. He sometimes treats serious subjects lightly, as in his sweet and rueful poems written during his courtship of Margaret:

> Sweet Harte we are beggers, our Comforts tis seene
> That we are undunne, for the Kinge, and the Queene
> Which doth make us reioyce, with Royall braggs
> That now we doe footest, with Royall rags.[106]

But on other occasions, he produces touches of sincerity, such as when he writes a song to sing to her:

> So Bewtifull you are so fayre
> Transpayrent Ayre
> Doth sally, and doth stayne your skinne
> It is so thinne

The Gentlest blushe no where can hide
So soone its spide
And you each curled hayre those locks doth grace
Like pensild shadows for your lovely face.[107]

And then, in a minor key, he describes himself movingly as the ageing and decrepit lover in thrall to his mistress:

Like an old Soldier in Queene Venus warres
My wounds of love, turn'd all to mangl'd Scarrs
Loues broken speere, and bowed sworde doe meet
As offrings att your sacred Alters feete.[108]

These examples show that William is never afraid in his poems or intimate letters to appear weak, vulnerable, disappointed and human, and this shaft of light playing upon his personality makes him come alive. Although he has held high office and does truly fit the stereotype of a Cavalier, his poems bring him into closer focus than all of his contemporaries at the Stuart court. For all the detail that Anthony van Dyck captures in his paintings or that the State Papers preserve about William's contemporaries' lives, many of the other Cavaliers remain carefully composed and remote icons.

William's literary reputation in his lifetime – as an amusing but lightweight playwright – is intertwined with Restoration London's emphatically negative views on his wife. Margaret meets with a good deal of criticism, some of it surprisingly harsh for a duchess. Encountering Margaret face-to-face at last, Pepys finds 'The Duchesse hath been a good, comely woman; but her dress is so antic, and her deportment so ordinary, that I do not like her at all, nor did I hear her say anything that was worth hearing.'[109] John Evelyn's own wife does not share his good opinion of Margaret, summing her up in a vicious pen portrait:

I was surprised to find so much extravagancy and vanity in any person not confined within four walls. Her habit particular, fantastical, not unbecoming a good shape, which she may truly boast of. Her face discovers the facility of the sex, in being yet persuaded it deserves the esteem years forbid, by the infinite care she takes to place her curls and patches. Her mien surpasses the imagination of poets, or the descriptions of a romance heroine's greatness, her gracious bows, seasonable nods, courteous stretching out of her hands, twinkling of her eyes, and various gestures of approbation, show what may be expected from her discourse, which is as airy, empty, whimsical and rambling as her books, aiming at science, difficulties, high notions, terminating commonly in nonsense, oaths, and obscenity.[110]

Why does Margaret conjure up so much hostility in Restoration society? Perhaps part of the problem lies in her remarkable and advanced views on female equality. Men treat women, she writes, 'like Children, Fools, or Subjects, in flattering or threatening us, in alluring or forcing us to obey; and will not let us divide the World equally with them'.[111] Dorothy Osborne (letter-writer, 1627–95) commented that 'there are many soberer people in Bedlam'.[112] William considers sexism to be the true explanation of the venom that Margaret arouses. 'Here's the crime, a Lady wrote them,' William will rail, defending his wife and her books against her many critics, 'and to intrench so much upon the male prerogative, is not to be forgiven.'[113]

As the afternoon of conversation wears away, Margaret perhaps entertains her guest with the new drinks of coffee and chocolate. John Evelyn first saw '*coffé*' being drunk in Oxford in the 1630s by an exiled scholar from Constantinople who lived at Balliol College. The drink did not catch on until England's first coffee house opened in Oxford in 1650, but it is by now common at both public and private parties. Chocolate had also arrived in the 1650s, from Mexico via Spain, and is grated and whisked with eggs, milk, sugar, vanilla and spices into a rich cordial which 'restores lost strength [and] gives Appetite, wonderfully clearing the Spirits'.[114] Yet not everyone approves of the new stimulants: the writers of the anonymous *Women's Petition against Coffee* consider that it causes 'a very sensible Decay of that true Old English Vigour', and with a sideswipe at the current fashion for voluminous trousers, that 'Never did Men wear greater Breeches, or carry less in them of any mettle whatsoever.'[115]

After refreshment, talk now turns to another topic of pressing common interest. Evelyn and the Cavendishes are also united in their sense of subtle disappointment with the current court. William and Margaret's purpose in coming to London was to pay visits to the court of Charles II, William's former pupil, which is a very different place from that of his father. In contrast to Charles I's strict, well-ordered, hierarchical court, Evelyn writes that he can never 'forget the unexpressable luxury, & prophanenesse, gaming, & all dissolution' he found at Charles II's court, describing a typical scene of 'the King, sitting & toying with his Concubines Portsmouth, Cleaveland, & Mazarine: &c: A french boy singing love songs, in that glorious Gallery, whilst about 20 of the greate Courtiers & other dissolute persons were at Basset round a large table, a bank of at least 2000 in Gold before them'.[116]

Evelyn was not alone in being censorious of the court. When the courtiers removed themselves to Oxford to avoid the plague in London, the scholar Anthony à Wood found them 'neat and gay in their apparel' yet dirty and lazy in their sanitary arrangements, 'very nasty and beastly, leaving at their departure their excrements in every corner, in chimneys, studies, coal-houses, cellars. Rude, rough, whore-mongers; vain, empty, careless.'[117] Yet, at the same time, the university town was not without its own deviants: at All Souls College, a group of fellows was detected attempting to print an erotic book by Aretino on the University Press.[118]

Evelyn, like other 'Persons of Good Fashion and Good Appearance', encounters no difficulty in gaining access to the Palace of Whitehall to see the king dining in public several times a week, and in fact is a close and trusted associate of the monarch. For the great occasions of court life, elaborate and costly preparations are needed. The Earl of Bedford prepared for Charles II's coronation with the help of his mercer, silk-man (for gold, silver and silk lace), woollen-draper, tailor, milliner, haberdasher (for feathers), sempster, stocking-maker, shoemaker, periwig-maker, gown-maker, sword-cutler and belt-maker.[119] William's elevation to his dukedom two years ago was not an inexpensive business: he was expected to tip various members of the royal household to the tune of £340 in total, with payments to the Gentlemen Ushers of the Privy Chamber, the musicians and trumpets, the Yeomen Ushers, the Grooms and Pages of the Privy Chamber, the master cook, the drums, the staffs of the ewery, pantry, buttery and cellar, and many others, including the king's barber. Since William's son Henry moved up a rung of the peerage himself to become the new Earl of Newcastle at the same time as his father's promotion to a dukedom – and therefore had to make his own tips – the Cavendish family had to lay out more than £500 on the royal servants.[120]

When Margaret pays a reluctant visit to court, she is accompanied by the full panoply of attendants. She arrives in a train of three coaches: the first, drawn by two horses, is full of her gentlemen; she herself travels in the second, drawn by six horses; and the third, with four horses, contains her waiting gentlewomen. The latter are now far more numerous than in the Antwerp days and include Mistress Evans, Mistress Remington and Mistress Perkins, as well as Elizabeth Topp.

When Margaret descends from her coach, her train is carried by a 'young lady in white satin'. Margaret's rank and commanding personality take her straight to the top of the tree: 'Her first visit was to the King, who sent the Lord Chamberlain to conduct her to the Queen, where his Majesty came to her. This visit is thought extraordinary.'[121]

The public criticism of Margaret and William that swills around London is at odds with their powers of access to the king and queen. Yet the scurrilous rumours and slanders against them are somehow made acceptable by a hint that they reflect a carefully hidden royal opinion, and Margaret is even more outspoken than William on the supposed ingratitude of the Stuarts.

Despite the official language of flattery in the patent for William's dukedom, Charles II was bound by obligation rather than fondness in awarding the honour, or at least it was so perceived by William himself. When William retired from regular court life in favour of occasional attendance, Margaret recalled that he made a speech of protestation to Charles II: 'I am not ignorant, that many believe I am discontented; and 'tis probable they'l say, I retire through discontent.'[122] His failure to win one of the great court offices after the Restoration was obviously a sore point, for Margaret's writings include a further 'Oration against those that lay an Aspersion upon the Retirement of Noble men.'[123] Yet there was a good reason for Charles II's apparent ingratitude. On his return to England, he had to use the rewards and offices in his possession to bribe his enemies to give him their support, whereas he was able to take for granted the continued loyalty of his old friends like William. Clement Ellis, William's chaplain at Welbeck, was forced to make the best of William's retirement into the country: according to Ellis, Charles II's greatest possible gift to William was 'thus to bestow *YOUR-SELF* upon *YOUR-SELF* [. . .] then all the *Offices* and *Honours* which your *exemplary Loyalty* has merited'.[124] And even Charles II himself did not desist from the universal practice of belittling Margaret's appearance, if an anecdote by the Comte de Grammont is true. Grammont had encountered at court 'the devil of a phantom in masquerade, who would by all means persuade me that the queen had commanded me to dance with her [. . .] it is worth while to see her dress; for she must have at least sixty ells of gauze and silver tissue about her, not to mention a sort of pyramid upon her head, adorned with a hundred thousand baubles. "I bet," said [Charles II,] "that it is the Duchess of Newcastle."'[125]

John Evelyn remains captivated by Margaret's talk, her stories about her husband's life and her disparaging gossip about the court, 'till my Lord *Marquis* of *Dorchester* came in with other company, & then home'.[126] Evelyn leaves the way he came, descending through the gloomy house into the courtyard and thinking over the strange character he has left behind.

He has just taken leave of a living legend. As Margaret continues to receive the admiring compliments of the Marquis of Dorchester in her bedchamber at Newcastle House, she is at the height of her fame and is truly one of the seventeenth century's most remarkable women. She visits the Royal Society to see experiments performed, acknowledges the audience's applause from her box during performances of her plays and attracts a crowd of a hundred curious boys and girls to run along in the dust behind her carriage.[127] None of this is the behaviour expected of a duke's wife, but Margaret is never predictable.

# 9 – *A Conspiracy*

WELBECK ABBEY, 30TH OCTOBER–2ND NOVEMBER, 1670

In one of her books of philosophy, Margaret Cavendish dreams of flying through the skies of Nottinghamshire. One scene has her hovering magically over Welbeck Abbey and swooping down low in order to see the house and its inhabitants.[1] Among the figures moving through the courts and gardens is Margaret's husband, the now aged duke, still training his horses and practising his swordplay. Margaret grows 'troubled, that her dear Lord and Husband use[s] such a violent exercise [. . .] for fear of overheating himself'.[2]

The scene that Margaret imagines took place on many occasions throughout the 1660s or 1670s. Friday the 30th of October is such a day. It is late in the autumn of 1670, and late in the autumn of the life of the Duke of Newcastle. 'They say 'tis Cold at Welbeck,' writes William in one of his poems.[3] The emotional temperature of the household, formerly warm and affectionate towards its cherished lord, is in free fall alongside the plummeting temperature outside. William is now seventy-six, a great age, but his servants fear that he has embarked upon an inexorable decline that is hastened by the garrulous, querulous but protective figure of his second wife. Since their retirement from London life, Margaret and William have spent more and more time in the Midlands, becoming increasingly reclusive and eccentric in their mutual dependence. Back at Welbeck Abbey, the household factions and alliances shift once more in response to the return to residence of their old master and their new mistress. This day in October is the day that a wicked conspiracy against the duke and duchess begins to take shape.

While William is training his horses in the yard at Welbeck, a meeting is in progress. In his book-filled chamber, William's somewhat rebarbative steward, Andrew Clayton, is deep in conversation with John Booth and Francis Liddell, two of the so-called 'Northumberland men' in the household. The two outsiders are tenants of the northern estates that William inherited from his mother, and they regularly come to Welbeck for extended periods to transact their business. The three men in Clayton's chamber, seated around a carpeted table, create a candlelit scene of conspiracy familiar from so many paintings of dusky and rich seventeenth-century interiors.

This chamber is both Clayton's sleeping space and working office, and is dominated by both his books and his bed. An inventory of the bedding at Welbeck lists thirty-nine such personal chambers in the house, many with more than one occupant, plus other additional rooms containing beds.[4] A servant's wooden bed frame is typically furnished with a feather bed, a bolster, a quilt, three blankets, a rug and a counterpane; the quilt goes beneath rather than over the sleeper.[5] On one occasion, William's son Henry has a conversation with an upholsterer named Mr Putnam about the type of bedding he prefers. Henry recalls with pleasure how once on a visit 'he lay upon three quilts, and the undermost was a very thick one [. . .] the underquilt was made of canvas and the two other of finer stuff'. Mr Putnam 'told his grace we had sold many of them, and called them a set of quilts: and after his grace had lain on it, he sent for me the next day and told me he lay very easy and was very well pleased with it'.[6] Clayton's bed is furnished in the standard manner with two blankets and a counterpane on top of the feather bed, quilts and linen.

The books, the studded, lockable money chest, the reams of accounts and bags of money much in evidence around the room are the tools of Clayton's confidential and important business, and he is one of only three household servants paid the top rate of £25 a year in wages.[7] His tables and shelves are stacked with books containing 'many secrets of my Lord's interest'.[8] His job description is:

> to seale up any money as was not so received to London into one or more Bag or Bags and to rally the said Bags with the said moneys so sealed up into his Lordships treasury at Welbeck aforesaid called the Evidence House and to deliver the same to John Proctor who keeps the said money and the key of the same Evidence house for his Graces use.

His work takes him from his chamber to the Evidence House elsewhere in the abbey and out across the estates, collecting and accounting for money. This is a place of many comings and goings: the architectural writer Roger North recommends that in the bailiff or steward's room, 'the books of entrys may allwaies be open, and files of papers disposed, so as ready recourse is had to them'. Here, too, the bailiff should 'have his cash-chest; and is to receive and pay all, his books being ready to make entrys; and take his customers in and dispatch them', thus avoiding the need to send business visitors to the kitchen to consume expensive food and drink while waiting for their appointment.[9] Clayton's busy office therefore has two doors, both of which have today been carefully locked against the accidental incursions of his assistant, Joseph, whose room is adjacent.

The three men in conversation in Clayton's chamber today find themselves inflamed by a particular set of 'aggravating circumstances' that they talk over again and again, and indeed their complaints have been brewing for a period of some years. As William Gouge writes, when servants sit together, 'all their talke for the most part is of their masters and mistresses, whereby it commeth to passe that all the secrets of a house are soone known about the whole towne or city'.[10] After 1660, the Cavendish servants took their places once again for the protracted pattern of ceremony performed round their master, but they found him harder to please and less generous than before. The household has become a very different place from the bright days before the Civil War when it was full of builders, children and horses. While William has been engaged on his plays, love poems and architectural designs, his servants have become deeply divided. William's daughters have united against an incoming clique attached to Margaret: her unpopular but powerful personal servants brought back from Antwerp. Talk about plans to force these newcomers out of the household grows louder among Clayton and the old servants.

In addition, Margaret has never found it easy to relate to her stepson Henry. In her opinion, he had lacked dynamism during the financial and political difficulties of the 1640s, selfishly going home to England in search of a rich wife and abandoning his father to his penniless fate in Paris. Margaret now finds herself cast by William's children and loyal servants into the role of the wicked stepmother. Further factors combine to make her unpopular: she is fiercely intelligent and realises that corruption and poor management are rife in the household. Her outlandish appearance, unusual behaviour and socially inappropriate literary activities all reduce her status in the household's eyes. All this comes to a head at the end of October, 1670.

So great is the influence of the new duchess and her own servants that Clayton and his two colleagues are by now in real fear of losing their livelihoods as well as their (somewhat undeserved) reputations for honesty.[11] Earlier this very day, Clayton tells the others, he was called upon by William to act as a witness to yet another in a series of deeds enlarging Margaret's jointure. This has become a pattern in recent months and years, and the more land William makes over to Margaret for her maintenance after his death, the further William's children and his old retainers feel that their power base has been eroded.

There is also a more specific point to Clayton and his colleagues' grievances. A couple of years ago, Clayton had improperly promised that Liddell should pay a reduced rent on his lands at Ogle in Northumberland. Clayton received as a backhander a horse worth £80, a brood mare worth £20 and the promise of a fine colt. He also promised to persuade William Cavendish to pay back money lent by Liddell's family, and today Liddell is justly impatient that this has not happened. Now Clayton fears that he cannot keep his part of the bargain, for 'the Duchess did so narrowly of late inspect his Grace's affairs, as that he could make no alteration of the rental without being discovered; and he also found that she positively obstructed his Grace for paying of that £500 debt'. His inefficiency as an accountant combined with William's lack of interest in his own financial affairs has given Clayton an inflated sense of his own freedom to buy, sell and swindle with his master's money, and now he fears discovery.

Since her arrival in the household, Margaret has discovered many sharp practices among the servants, possessing, as she does, a much keener financial sense than her easy-going and generous husband. She certainly does not fit the mould of the seventeenth-century women against whom William Wentworth delivers a misogynistic warning in his *Advice to His Son*. Women should not get involved in estate management, Wentworth counsels, 'for flattering tenants will soon seduce a woman, who neither is like to have a true intelligence of the matter, nor so sound a judgement as the wiser sort of men have'.[12] Margaret, on the contrary, obviously took a certain precise pleasure in listing all of her husband's Civil War losses and expenses in the biography of him that she published three years ago, calculating that they came to exactly £941,303.[13] She also claims the skill of being able to run a grange or sheep farm 'indifferently well'.[14] In fact, her reputation as a keen, even harsh, estate manager has spread throughout the countryside. The Bishop of Lincoln describes a report running 'like wildfire' across Leicestershire 'that the Duchess of Newcastle was very severe in punishing those of the Forest in Nottinghamshire, taking away all the cattle that were not branded, as legally they ought to be'.[15]

Yet Clayton's financial concerns are only part of his problem. He also feels that the *esprit de corps* of the household community is slowly suffocating under the threat of unwelcome change, just as the parasitical mistletoe gradually strangles the thorn trees of the forest outside. Despite the opposition of its members, Margaret has certainly made her presence felt in the household. Her mental resilience is matched, in the opinion of the family doctor, by her body's unique physical strength: in prescribing a purging powder to empty the bowels, he considers that:

> One ounce is an ordinary dose for strong men. Weak folks, women & children must go less [. . .] and generally those which are easily moved either to vomit or purge, must have a lesser dose. My Lady-Marquess of Newcastell is one of those that is hardly moved to cast [. . .] her Ladyship must have a double dose at least & will not be moved to any purpose without two ounces, rather more.[16]

The household is well aware of Margaret's strength and power. Not only will his mistress make John Rolleston the secretary draw up new rentals, Clayton says, but she will also 'break up the family and go to Rant at London'. 'Her whole care and study', in Clayton's opinion, is 'nothing more then to enrich her self for a second husband, well knowing his Grace [can]not live Long', and her aim is 'To confound all retainers to the family'. For his own part, Clayton tells his colleagues Liddell and Booth that he is 'weary of his employment and would gladly be gone'. He is 'often involved in sharp and passionate quarrels between their Graces, and [. . .] he had ever underhand contradicted her Grace's designs, the which she more and more discovered and hated him perfectly for it'.

Yet Clayton fears that even if he decides to leave Welbeck, Margaret will not grant him 'a general Release', or the required permission to break his contract with the family. Such contracts or covenants usually cover matters such as duties, pay, conditions of employment and perks (the latter might include a cloak every two years, for example).[17] Clayton's contract, and the financial penalty attached to breaking it, is the 'very thing kept him in the family though by his stay he had lost a fortune of £4000 which he might have had with one Mrs Taylor a widow in Chesterfield who would very gladly have intermarried with him'.

Clayton could, of course, have risked a low-key and private marriage by special ecclesiastical licence for his Mrs Taylor, like others at Welbeck Abbey for whom the desire for matrimony was greater than their fear of losing their position. There are those on the staff who can provide a quick and quiet wedding for a price. A clerk or chaplain named Geoffrey Leadbeater who had 'for some months served' in William Cavendish's household is forced to beg for mercy after being sacked for performing 'a clandestine marriage of some of [his] Excellency's servants', a ceremony that would have been performed at night, secretly and without the permission of the parents of the bride and groom.[18] When Leadbeater found that his bishop was also instituting proceedings of excommunication against him, threatening his livelihood, he was forced to throw himself on William's charity.

In the chamber, Clayton now turns to his plans for the future. The other two men here will later recall his deadly serious statement that he has 'studied all ways in the world how to give her Grace a dead blow, and to divert his Graces affections from her'. The difficulty was that 'he could not find out any person living that would or durst tell his Grace such things as he had to say against her'.

Clayton's solution to the problem is simple: an anonymous letter to be addressed to her husband, outlining Margaret's true nature. The three of them should write such a 'Letter in an Unknown hand and without a Name', and plan the 'conveying of it to some posthouse, where it might undiscovered be brought to Welbeck'. 'Be questioned not', Clayton concludes, 'that it would produce such effects as that their Graces would part.'

Francis Liddell and John Booth digest Clayton's idea, and quickly see some merit in it. Liddell now turns to Booth, saying that Booth himself is 'the man fittest' to do the actual writing (Clayton's and Liddell's handwriting are already known to the duke) and reminding him of the potential advantages to them all. Booth is initially reluctant, but the arguments of the others win him over: 'these considerations wrought upon every of us and did very much promote the design'. The meeting breaks up, and the three men retire to their own chambers on 30th October with their plan – the sending of an anonymous letter – complete.

The next day, Saturday, is All Hallow's Eve. Francis Liddell rises very early in the morning and sets off through the house to return to Clayton's chamber. With a shudder heightened by his guilty conscience, he remembers that this is a day for commemorating the dead. Draughty Welbeck Abbey is full of the ghosts of the dispossessed monks, and the household are fond of frightening each other with tales of how

> Of old they say, dead bodies us'd to walk,
> And fright the living with their noise & talk.[19]

Yet Liddell reaches Clayton's chamber safely. After an hour's private conversation with Clayton, he leaves the room again in order to fetch John Booth, a somewhat junior partner in the conspiracy, and bring him to Clayton's chamber.

Opening Clayton's door, Booth discovers that 'Pen Ink & paper' have been provided for his work of writing the letter. Joseph, Mr Clayton's man, has been sent on a spurious errand to Chesterfield to have him 'out of the way', and the doors are locked once again. 'Now,' Liddell says to the other conspirators, and frames their plan in words that make it compatible with their belief in the fellowship of the household. He tells his colleagues of their good fortune that 'an opportunity [is] delivered into our hands to do our selves good and serve the family of Newcastle'.

Booth's fears of discovery, however, are not easily abated, and it is only after 'damned Reciprocal vows of secrecy with Joint and unanimous Consent, every of us contributing as much as in him lay' that the three set to their work.

They spend these hours plotting together without arousing suspicion, and part of the household's problem is the lack of work for and lack of supervision of the servants on William's part. As Henry Percy, Earl of Northumberland, considers, 'servants are never bold to deceive but where they find the master weak or careless [. . .] it is the master's fault, if an evil and dishonest servant serve him long'.[20] Servants who need instructing in further duties cannot always gain access to William's chambers. Even Clayton himself, William's intermediary, is often inaccessible to the lower servants. William Kitchin, a tenant and building contractor, complains that despite having gone to Welbeck for orders he found it impossible to speak even to Clayton, as he was 'that day [. . .] so busy with his Grace'.[21] Yet the dangers of idleness are recognised by the heads of households everywhere. Richard Hyrde, writing in 1526, fears that even manual work leaves the brain free to think dangerous thoughts. While busy with her handiwork, he says, a waiting maid's 'body may be busy in one place and the mind walking in another. While they sit sowing & spinning with their fingers [women] may cast and compass many peevish fantasies in their minds.'[22]

While Booth, Liddell and Clayton waste their employer's time in conspiracy, the other servants create a bustle of subdued activity throughout the house beyond Clayton's locked door. Despite the damage and losses of the Civil War, the abbey remains 'surrounded all with Wood, so close and full'.[23] To its inhabitants, it is a remote island lapped by the forest on all sides, and their community remains relatively self-contained. The accounts for the summers of 1667 and 1668, when William was away in London, were kept in detail to inform him of what was being done in his absence. They show the never-ending tasks of maintenance and improvement which form the backdrop against which the dramas between family and servants are played out. Even in London, William kept up a steady, if slow, trickle of orders by letter: he required, for example, a new gallery in his riding house and instructed Samuel Marsh the surveyor to design it, Richard Martin the craftsman to build it and Andrew Clayton to oversee the process.[24] The Welbeck accounts show that, meanwhile, William Lyantorke is employed to look after the brewhouse and vessels, Mr Hall is paid for carving work, William Walker the 'mat maker' is renewing floor coverings, and 'several labourers' are always kept on the books for odd jobs. Elizabeth Gibson makes 'the rooms and offices clean', Mrs Bunbury keeps house at Bolsover Castle, John Fentyman the locksmith makes repairs, while William Bramly sees to the plumbing.[25]

In the gardens outside Clayton's window, restoration works have long been in progress. Craftsmen are setting aright the little banqueting houses over the canal where they lean askew, cleaning them out 'handsomely', resetting their railings and mending the sides of the 'little river in the south Garden'. Humfrey Rowland receives payments for 'cleansing the pond', and a group of masons and brick-makers are hard at work repairing 'the terrace walk'. The little door in the south garden has been walled up, a work completed with some urgency because of William's fear that 'the fruit will all be stolen'.[26] Fruit trees grow against the garden walls and the base of the terrace walls, and the borders are set with pinks 'both in Gardens and Courts, or some other beautiful Flowers amongst the Pinks'. The walks are kept neat with mowing, rolling (John Evelyn recommends the use of a fragment of 'old columns of diminish'd Antiquities' from the Levant as a roller) and weeding, and 'the Terrace Walls to be kept as formerly with Honey suckles & sweet Briar'.[27] Throughout the summer, the grounds are kept constantly bright with fruit and flowers. William boasts of his garden's 'Swell'd Strawberries', 'ripe cherries', 'Sweet Gooseberry and woolly Peach', 'riper Plums', 'sweet woodbine', 'white and red roses', 'orange and lemon in my Porcelain Pot', 'Ripe Melons, without Art's hot glass', 'Golden apples', 'Katherine Pear', 'Prime-roses', 'Tulips', 'Lillies', 'Collombine', 'Daffadill', 'Cowslip', 'Dasey', 'the blushing Pinke, sweet Gilly-flower', 'Honny-suckles, French Mary-gold', 'Swell'd & clustered grapes', 'Nectarines' and 'Violets'.[28] But now, by October, Evelyn's book on gardening advises the seventeenth-century house-owner to sweep up 'all autumnal leaves fallen, lest the worms draw them into their holes and foul your garden'.[29]

What is the real nature of the relationship between William Cavendish as head of the household and his servants, apparently so industrious throughout the house and garden? William's occasional lapses from his responsibilities as head of a household have effects that reverberate far beyond the walls of Welbeck. The household is the basic unit of local government, and the head of a great household is also the king's servant through the offices of local government such as Lord Lieutenant of the county or Justice of the Peace. According to the Renaissance writer Baldassare Castiglione, possessing a magnificent household is one of the duties and qualities of a prince. A great man's beneficence in terms of the number in his household, their clothing, food and accommodation in its turn supports the king's power and the peaceful governance of the nation. If a household is well disciplined, then society as a whole will benefit.

William's own behaviour reflects something of this attitude. Tender and jovial with his wife and children, he can nevertheless exhibit a chilling courtesy towards inferiors. At the times when he is 'on duty' as the head of his household, his behaviour 'hath something in it of grandeur, that causes an awful respect towards him'.[30] Still, he finds it hard to reconcile his responsibility to maintain a magnificent coldness towards the members of his household with his naturally buoyant nature. The household is a place where order exists, yet favourites are allowed to break the rules. The master is placed on a pedestal of respect and deference, yet William often reveals his human side to those with whom he lives in the closest proximity.

According to the author of *Of Domesticall Duties* (1622), servants should be 'so full of courtesy as not a word shall be spoken by their masters to them, or by them to their masters, but the knee shall be bowed withall: they can stand houre after houre before their masters, and not once put on their hat: if they be walking after their masters, their master shall not turne sooner then their hat will be off, and that so oft as he turneth or speaketh to them'. A master should be firm with his household, and the servants' state of 'trembling feare is needful in regard of the small love that servants commonly beare to their masters'.[31]

William's wife Margaret recounts how her own parents tried to keep their children aloof from the household: they refused to allow 'any familiarity with the vulgar servants, or conversation: yet caused us to demean ourselves with a humble civility towards them, as they with a dutiful respect to us'.[32] She outlines the ever-present dangers to the children in a grand house, where without close supervision they will run wild 'into every dirty office, where the young master must learn to drink & play at cards with the kitchen-boy, & learn to kiss his mother's dirty maid for a mess of cream. The daughters are danced upon the knee of every clown and serving man, & hear them talk scurrilous to the maids.'[33]

Yet we see many such little vignettes of William talking, joking and swearing with his servants: referring to his Duchess as 'Peg' in front of Andrew Clayton, grumbling that he may be old but is not yet in his dotage, boasting that Captain Mazine knows him too well to ask a favour, while at the same time being quite unaware that the manipulative Sir Francis Topp is well able to secure his agreement to any proposal.[34]

Although it is quieter and gloomier now than it has ever been, Welbeck Abbey has never been an entirely rosy, cosy place. Nor is the household free from noise, stench, danger and hard labour. Many messy and dangerous events take place here: physicians order vomits or bleeding for their patients; flea-ridden paupers scramble for the rotten left-overs distributed at the gates; a mixture of pitch and frankincense is burnt to disinfect a chamber after a case of smallpox.

According to the literary scholar Wendy Wall, any seventeenth-century household has two contrasting characters. It is a place of chastisement and obedience, a tiny version of the Church and state. Yet, at the same time, it is a place of strange fantasies, where real people create their everyday lives far away from the eyes of officialdom. This centrality to people's lives explains why household scenes appear so often in stage plays written in the seventeenth century. Wall describes fantastical scenes of household life taken from these plays:

> . . . a prince trembles with uncontrollable passion at the sight of a milkmaid with her hands buried deep in milk; a householder hysterically sorts through a basket of soiled laundry to find traces of his sexual humiliation; a journeyman dreams of piping hot pancakes and live food marching through the London streets; a servant gleefully narrates the phantasmagoric tale of people butchered and eaten at the dinner table; a fieldworker panics that a lost needle might sodomize him.[35]

In the seventeenth century, violence, like charity, begins at home. In the Cavendish kitchens, urine, umbilical cords, skulls and breast milk are casually used as ingredients.[36] At Welbeck, a host of animals are disembowelled in the slaughterhouse or kitchen. In her book *The Compleat Servant-Maid*, the author Hannah Woolley recommends a brutal cure for a simple ague:

> Take two Running Cocks, pull them alive, then kill them. Cut them Cross of the Back, when they are almost cold take their Guts, and after you have made them clean, break them all to pieces.

The pieces are then to be pounded in a mortar and boiled in a distillation glass with milk, currants and herbs to make a soup. The language of the kitchens is bloody and violent: Woolley paraphrases the well-known 1508 *Book of Kerving* (or carving) to describe the appropriate vocabulary for an avian massacre such as that at Bolsover for William's masque of 1634. 'In cutting up small Birds it is proper to say thigh them,' she pronounces,

> as in thigh that Woodock, thigh that Pidgean: But as to other say, mince that Plover [. . .] Allay that Pheasant, untack that Curlew, unjoynt that Bittern, disfigure that Peacock, display that Crane, dismember that Hern, unbrace that Mallard, trust that Chicken, spoyl that Hen, sawce that Capon, lift that Swan, reer that Goose [. . .] unlace that Coney, break that Deer, leach that Brawn: For

Fish, chine that Salmon, string that Lamprey, splat that Pike, sawce that Plaice, and sawce that Tench, splay that Bream; side that Haddock, tusk that Barbel, culpon that Trout, transon that Eel, tranch that sturgeon, tame that Crab, barb that Lobster.[37]

The word 'carve' has the alternative meaning of 'to take at one's pleasure', so the kitchen maid carving or barbing her lobsters (roughly forty are consumed annually at Welbeck) does so with relish.

This carnage taking place out of sight but within scent of the Great Chamber and galleries is only one aspect of household life that is far removed from the image of unassailable grandeur presented by the facade of a seventeenth-century great house. At Welbeck Abbey, strangeness also lies in the lack of privacy, the sharing of beds between household members and strangers, the daily prayers and communal meals, the enforced celibacy, the passion for gaming, gambling and drinking, and the gory, smelly, strenuous and multifarious tasks required to win sustenance and warmth from the forested hills and wastes of north Nottinghamshire.[38]

Violence in the household does not belong only to the kitchen. An inquest will be held into a drunken quarrel between two officials at Welbeck who share a bed; the quarrel ended with one of them – Mr Slaughter – falling down the stairs and breaking his neck.[39] Seventeenth-century conduct books recommend that the master must beat his male servants and the mistress the female ones. These tasks are likely to be delegated by the socially superior to their male house steward or female housekeeper, but one Adam Eyre in 1647 noted in his diary how 'this morning I whipped Jane for her foolishness, as yesterday I had done for her slothfulness'.[40] According to Robert Cleaver's *Godlie Forme of Householde Government*, beatings should be administered by those of the same gender, because 'a man's nature scorneth and disdaineth to be beaten of a woman, and a maid's nature is corrupted with the stripes of a man'.[41]

Yet while William, as the master of the household, has the power physically to chastise his household, he must in his turn also undergo the painful and humiliating medical ministrations of his wife and servants: bleeding, vomits, purges and glisters (as enemas are known) made with ingredients such as 'Dung of white peacock', 'Livers of green frogs dried and pulverised' and boiled vipers ('usually given to Cause Sweat').[42] A method for curing an eye infection, for example, involves the nightmarish application of a louse to the eyeball. Pinning their patient down to a bed, the female servants will take several lice from their hair in order to 'put them alive into the Eye that is grieved and so close it up, and most assuredly the Lice will suck out the Web in the eye, and will cure it, and come forth without any hurt'. The warning that it will not hurt rings hollow.[43]

The hierarchies so carefully established by the heads of households are inevitably compromised and turned topsy-turvy on occasion. We have heard that the companion of William's youth, Sir Henry Wotton, considered a man's home to be 'the *Theatre* of his *Hospitality*, the *Seat* of *Selfe-fruition*, the *Comfortablest part* of his own *Life*, the *Noblest* of his Son's *Inheritance*, a kind of private *Princedom*', but the Cavendish household is all and none of these things. In his old age, there are few visitors to Welbeck and William's life is made uncomfortable by his children and servants. While he was once the happy prince of a blissful private kingdom, he is now considered by some of his subjects to be a lovesick old fool and by others a hated tyrant.

Andrew Clayton, as the mastermind behind the plot against the duchess, now dictates the first draft of the anonymous letter. 'The method propounded was this,' John Booth will later recollect, 'that we should first mind his Grace of that great Honour, and Esteem, the world had for him before the Late Rebellion; and that he went much Less in the Opinions of all, the cause whereof Right or wrong we were to cast upon her Grace.'[44] The composition of the letter, cynosure as well as scandal, has taken some time, and to avoid raising suspicion it is decided that Francis Liddell should go out for an hour to sit with old 'blind Mr Swinburn, and the rest' of the servants. Clayton and Booth can quite naturally spend the day together 'upon the accounts of our business, but it seemed not feasible that Liddell should be with us all a long; for though we pretended to tell money and paste accounts all day; nothing was done but in Order to this villainy'.

It is only at 'about 3 in the afternoon', with the hour for dinner in the Great Hall being well past, that Clayton and Booth are satisfied with their handiwork. At Clayton's urging, the letter contains a 'damned Scandal': the bold accusation that Margaret has committed adultery with the senior household officer Sir Francis Topp.

Topp is the English merchant whom the Cavendishes had encountered in Antwerp and who subsequently married Margaret's waiting woman Elizabeth. Topp, his wife Elizabeth and others from Antwerp such as 'Dutch Jane' make up the group of newcomers set on a collision course with Clayton's clique.

Factions within a household are one of the greatest dangers to its well-being, and all too often they form around a wife. In his *Advice to His Son* of 1609, the ninth Earl of Northumberland warns against exactly the kind of internecine warfare between different groups that now exists at Welbeck:

> Grip into your hands what power soever you will of government, yet will there be certain persons about your wife that you will never reduce – an usher, her tailor, and her women; for they will ever talk and ever be unreasonable; all which your officers will rather endeavour to please then your self [. . .] In a house thus governed, factions will be rife, as well amongst your own servants as amongst your friends and hers; for her friends will ever be the welcomest and best used, the train of women friends being ever the longest and most troublesome.[45]

Topp's responsibility is now to manage William's 'western affairs', the Cavendish lands owned in Somerset and the West Country. This occasions his use of a manor at Tomerton, as well as residence in his chilly chamber at Welbeck (where he has no fewer than six blankets).[46] Topp has an unenviable reputation among the 'old' Cavendish family: there are complaints on behalf of the 'poor Tenants of Botthamsall, who indeed have suffered much through ye crossness as I believe of Mr Top',[47] and William's daughter Jane frankly distrusts him. Two years ago, she reported to her sister on having met Mr Topp 'in his Coach in Hyde Park, I believe he could have wished I had not seen him there, he reports the thousand pound, my father was pleased to give me, is not yet due, truly I expect nothing, he can keep from me'.[48] Yet Topp's closeness to William gives him a certain amount of power in the household. As well as being associated with the unpopular duchess, his successful politicking gives him an unreliable aspect. He has a fawning character, being 'very ready willing and desirous to lend [you] all the service he can'.[49] He 'well knows his Grace's humour and when to time his motions', and others use him as an intercessor.[50]

Clayton's selection of Topp as his villain is further prompted by personal enmity. A few years ago, these two were close allies, banding together in a private and fraudulent 'design for lead to be shipped from Hull to London' against the interests of their employer. At the same time as William required lead for his building projects, Clayton and Topp sought the lowest-priced lead in Derbyshire for their own enterprise; as Topp wrote to Clayton, 'I know you can buy it as Cheap as any man.'[51] Maybe it was as this plan turned sour that the household became riven by the enmity between two of its key figures.

Clayton's choice of Topp for his calumny is understandable given the recent history of the family, but why the choice of the charge of adultery? The circumstances must exist for a credible case to be made, and Margaret's undoubted oddities of dress and personal expression leave her open to such a charge. Her publication three years ago of her laudatory biography of her husband has had a mixed effect on her public image. Some write fawning letters of praise, but it was reading *The Life of the thrice Noble, High and Puissant Prince William Cavendishe, Duke, Marquess and Earl of Newcastle, etc.* (the title sets the tone for the whole work) that caused Samuel Pepys to think her 'a mad, conceited, ridiculous woman, and he an asse to suffer [her] to write what she writes to him and of him'.[52]

Despite her serious intellectual commitment to her philosophy and writings, Margaret's having gone into print makes her vulnerable. The writer John Stainsby called her:

> The great atheistical Philosophraster,
> That avows no God, nor Devil, Lord nor Master

and addresses her as 'Shame of her sex, Welbeck's illustrous Whore'.[53] The complaints arise because of Margaret's inability to accept received authority. Even her doctor considers her difficult to treat, not because of 'ye nature of ye Disease [. . .] as for ye disposition of the Patient, who will not willingly submit to ye Counsel of her Physicians, be they never so good & so skilful', and considers that her unladylike 'occupation in writing of books [. . .] absolutely bad for health'.[54] Yet Margaret does have her supporters: when outsiders tell her to '*let writing Books alone, For surely Wiser Women ne'r writ one*', it is always her husband who urges her not to 'leave Writing, except when [he] would perswade [her] to spare so much time from [her] Study as to take the Air for [her] Health'.[55] Furthermore, in one published letter she tells a female correspondent that 'You writ in your last Letter, that I had given our Sex Courage and Confidence to Write, and to Divulge what they Writ in Print.'[56]

Yet, at the same time as creating a household where writing is an acceptable pastime for women, William's habit of casual dalliances has also created an atmosphere where aristocratic infidelity may be taken for granted. He continues to assert his rights over the persons of the female members of his household into extreme age. In the shaky hand of his final years, after Parkinson's disease has made inroads into the firmness of his grip, he still continues to write semi-pornographic doggerel about his conquests:

> Thy virgin mouth, with man should be fed,
> Thinkest that a kiss would Rob thy maiden head?
> Mistakest ye place, the faults are all in thee:
> And yet unJustly lays ye faults on me.[57]

He adds further bawdy musings on women in his private papers, recording, for example, the titillating story of the 'Good wife of our Parish' who

> once did Slide
> On Buttock, from Hay mow's top, Legs full wide,
> And light on pitch fork; Greater End went In
> The place you wet on.

As an unexpected result of her accident, the unfortunate goodwife came to prefer copulating with a pitchfork than with her husband.[58] William also enjoyed a joke about a 'wanton woman' –

> One asked if She were Well, & how she did.
> I answered Well, although she were Bed-rid[59]

– and is not above describing intercourse in the mixed geographical and nautical metaphors of a poor romantic novelist:

> Her breasts, two panting Hills In imitation
> Of billowed sail, move waves just In like fashion
> Mounts her main yard, & splits It in the skies
> In watery Clouds, twixt promontory thighs.[60]

The genre of seduction poems is well established, and some of William's sexual exploits are perhaps by now taking place in his imagination alone. Yet his complaints about the 'envious, malicious, foolish' maid who revealed her liaison with the duke ring true:

> Never was thing worse told for on my word
> You've angerd both your Lady, & your Lord.[61]

On this occasion, silence would have suited all parties better.

When even a duke's adultery arouses adverse comment, that a

duchess has committed it is a dreadfully serious accusation to be aired at the very heart of the household. What is worse, the cancer of rumour and scandal is even spreading into the next generation. William's relationship with his only surviving son Henry is now deteriorating dramatically, and Henry, too, is concerned about his father's growing reputation for chasing the maids.

Despite his pride in having a son to continue his dynasty, William and Henry seem often to be at odds. In her will, Henry's long-dead mother Elizabeth used a revealing turn of phrase that demonstrates her position as a supplicant to William in family matters. 'Now my Lord,' she wrote, 'for your Childer I am confident you Love them and so I hope you will ever do for your own sake,' a hint that William may one day change his views. She felt obliged to spell out the moral pressure on William to make her various loving bequests to her children: they are 'all I desire you to do for me', she says pitifully, and 'in law I know this will not stand good but it must be your goodness'.[62]

Now it seems that Elizabeth's unspoken fears for her family have come to pass. Her children are scattered and their father uncommunicative. Henry is living an expensive life in a rented Elizabethan mansion at Glentworth in Lincolnshire and now has six children of his own, five girls and a boy. He, too, fears Margaret's influence, and in particular William's increasingly clear desire to leave his wealth to her rather than to his grandchildren. 'I am very melancholy,' Henry writes, 'finding my Father more persuaded by his Wife than I could think it possible.'[63]

William, for his part, simply cannot understand Henry's concerns. When his servant John Hutton dared to speak to him on the matter, he wondered openly that Henry 'should trouble himself with nothing'.[64] 'You see, we are all honest folks here', William writes to his petulant son, '& have no unjust subtle designs, – for jealousies, doubts, fears & whispers are too womanish for me to trouble my self with [. . .] I am Confident you never had an Ill opinion either of my love to you & yours, – or that I was a fool.'[65] William, bluff and straight-talking as always, again demonstrates his failure to understand the subtlety of another person's point of view, and his relationship with his son flounders in bewilderment and frustration. It is only the very young who are free from the shadows of suspicion and mistrust. 'Sweet Harry' William calls his grandson, Henry's only son, and he boasts that although his own children dislike Margaret, 'Harry loves my wife better than any body, & she him I think.'[66] Young Harry, like William's own sons in their day, is preparing for an educational journey abroad.[67] Soon, a well-wisher will be hoping that he is learning elegant behaviour in France, for 'his improvements there is what is likely to give him advantage in his pretentions [of marriage] to any young person'.[68]

Henry and his wife Frances have, in fact, been begging for permission to return to live at Welbeck, the house to which they came so reluctantly in 1659. They have written William a strangely pensive and pleading letter that captures the brooding, anxious atmosphere in the household, putting their request into writing 'because we have not the boldness to speak it'.[69]

Their proposal is that 'they & their family may be admitted to live in the house with your Grace [. . .] protesting before almighty god that we have no other ends in it but your Graces safety & ye lengthening of ye life and ye continuance & increase of your Graces immortal honour'. Honour is of particular concern to Henry and his wife: they are anxious and embarrassed about the reports of William's philandering with the housemaids which continue to seep out of Welbeck and across the countryside. 'Servants are full of their own ends,' they say, '& especially some young women who being presumptuously and extravagantly ambitious do with their foolish thoughts fill town & country doing what they can to dishonour your Grace, which though it be not in their power to effect yet the very attempt of it must needs be to the great trouble of your Grace.'

With a magnificent air of self-sacrifice, Henry proposes a list of strictures on his family's movements and requirements that would minimise the inconvenience to his father if he were allowed to return home. He and his household would provide their own 'wine sugar all sort of Groceries soap and horsemeat'. Welbeck is no longer a hospitable open harbour for all comers and its Great Hall is dark and quiet compared to the old days. Henry proposes that 'our servants may have the same allowance of beef with your other servants & ourselves never at any time except strangers to the table to have above 4 dishes besides beef & one dish at supper'. Henry himself is no sybarite: he is in the unfortunate position of having been told by his doctors that, in order to prevent his convulsions, his 'meat should be seasoned with the Powder of frogs dried in an oven, & putten upon his meat as if it were nutmeg'.[70] In his petition, Henry further promises that 'no friends or acquaintances [. . .] shall trouble yr graces house at meals or night time or further than an afternoon visit'. He intends to keep another house near by in a state of preparedness so that if William is plagued by unwelcome visitors, 'we may go thither & entertain them that they may not trouble yr Graces but only come to see yr horses or in the afternoon'. Henry's own servants have obviously been a bone of contention in the past, for 'as for those servants about our persons [. . .] it shall be yr Graces pleasure put any away yr Grace dislikes & take any yr Grace is pleased to like'. It is extraordinary to read of the Earl of Ogle, now forty years old, promising his father that he will 'be obedient & observant' as he 'was formerly at 10 years of age & that none of us will offer in the least to meddle with any thing but to obey all your commands with all humility and affection'. As far as it is possible to deduce, this sad letter will have no effect on the old duke, and Henry's desired rapprochement with his father never quite comes about.

Henry's letter, while it opens up further murky vistas of dissatisfaction in the household, is quite separate from Andrew Clayton's conspiracy to have William divorce his wife, although Henry and Clayton are as one in their enmity towards her. By nightfall on Saturday, 31st October, 1671, Clayton's anonymous letter has been finished, transcribed by John Booth and judged by its creators to be 'fit for the post'.

Now, on Sunday, 1st November, the conspirators embark upon the risky process of getting it to the post office at Tuxford, which they consider to be far enough distant for members of the Cavendish household to visit it unrecognised. Booth's 'boy' takes the letter, riding a grey gelding belonging to Francis Liddell; he travels 'down the forest' and 'a back way' to avoid the houses of those who might recognise him. Clayton keeps the original of the letter and will retain it until 'that day that all the Northumberland men were called before their Graces in the Gallery'. Taking advantage of the resulting temporary lull in the activities of the Great Chamber, he pulls the draft out of his stocking and burns it in the fireplace there.

Meanwhile, Booth's boy successfully carries out his instructions: to come late to the postmaster's, to deliver the letter in haste, and then to lodge in an obscure inn at the end of the town, giving an account to no one either of his name or business. By the Monday evening he will be safely on his way back at Welbeck.

Monday, 2nd November, is a tense day for the conspirators, who expect their letter to arrive in the morning's post at 10 o'clock.[71] Monday morning brings with it *manège* practice, and all three of them should now take their places in the Riding House gallery, as usual, to watch William's horses 'a riding'. But Booth, the most reluctant conspirator, fears that in the circumstances he 'not be able to keep [his] countenance from being betrayed'.

The Riding House at Welbeck is by now even grander than it was when John Smithson designed it in the 1620s. The huge size of the building staggered the poet Richard Flecknoe:

> For the *Riding-House*, 'tis of so vast extent,
> It does some mighty *Temple* represent,
> Where seeing them ride, Admiring *Indians* wo'd
> Adore each *Horse* there as a *Semi-God*.[72]

William still trains his '18 or 20 manag'd horses' in person, much to the chagrin of his wife, who considers the exercise to be too strenuous. He is still searching for innovation in the stone-vaulted Great Stable and is trying out an unusual method to encourage his horses to feed with a good appetite: they are tied head to door and tail to manger 'from 7 to 11 to get them stomachs to their meat'.[73]

There have been both major and minor recent improvements to the 'Huge *Piazza*' surrounded by the Great Stable and Riding House.[74] Andrew Clayton has administered small payments, such as those 'for levelling the Ground before the Colt Stables to the Smithy door',[75] while an expensive new viewing gallery (like a box at the theatre) has been built in the Riding House itself. Accessible by a stair, it has a seven-light window for people to look down on the action below, just as they had always been able to in Smithson's more sophisticated design at Bolsover or as was possible in Rubens's former painting studio in Antwerp.

As the household servants look down from the balcony, William curses and swears at an unfortunate groom who has failed to tighten the girth of one of the horses to the cruel pitch necessary to stop the *manège* saddle from slipping down the horse's back. This is an old trick that an experienced horseman is well aware of: '*Horses* that are used to be *Girt Hard* [. . .] will so *Stretch* their *Bodies* and *Bellies Out*, with holding their *Breath*, that the *Grooms* have much ado to *Gird* them: And this is *Craftily* done of them, that they may have *Ease* after they are *Girded*, and then they let their Bodies *Fall* again.'[76]

Booth and Clayton agree that today they will skip the training session and absent themselves from the scene of the crime, taking horses and crunching across the crisp dead bracken and skeletal heads of the cow parsley in Sherwood Forest. They have the excuse that their work often causes them to ride out from Welbeck across the estates on business, and their absence will arouse little suspicion. Their destination today is Sookholme Manor, and they plan to spend the day there working on accounts with John Rolleston. Meanwhile, Liddell is left behind at Welbeck to observe the unfolding of events and to gather news.

Rolleston, William's faithful secretary for so many years, has finally married and moved out of the household to inhabit a manor house at Sookholme. His wife Elizabeth bore the maiden name of Barber, as did the wife of Captain Mazine, who now lives in the snug house he has built at Carburton, not far distant from Welbeck: these two Cavendish old-timers have married sisters.[77] Aged though Mazine now is, he remains honorary keeper of the royal stables and is often at court. His wife's family comes from Windsor and perhaps he met her there, now that Windsor Castle has become a frequent residence of the royal household.

Mazine and Rolleston are not the only members of the household whose thoughts have turned in recent years to bricks and mortar, stone and home. Clayton frequently inspects progress on the estate's various building projects just as John Smithson did in 1613. Rolleston and Mazine's houses at Carburton and Sookholme form part of a rash of new buildings across the Cavendish lands, for on his return to the Midlands William found his possessions sad and semi-derelict and his beloved forests felled for timber. Most of the old Cavaliers returning home from penurious exile settled down for a period of retrenchment, yet William seized the initiative, intending to make his houses even greater than before. He lost little time in calling in the builders, and a new hunting stand with jaunty battlements was soon under construction at his desecrated park in Clipstone.[78]

All across the Cavendish estates, the tenants are complaining about the poor condition of their houses and requesting money and workmen to put things right. Clayton is accustomed to receiving letters like that written a couple of months ago by Roger Hilton, the tenant of William's deceased brother's house at Wellingore in Lincolnshire. Hilton begged that Clayton 'will move his grace about the building of the stables & barns and barn house, at Wellingore [. . .] the repairs of the house [. . .] will be a very great charge'.[79]

Yet Welbeck Abbey and Bolsover Castle, William's favourite houses, have been his first priority. For some years, Clayton has been a frequent visitor to Bolsover, riding over once a fortnight to check on the progress of the works. In 1660, the castle was in a truly desolate state. During the Civil War, the Parliamentarians had ripped out doors and toppled battlements. Margaret remembered how both Welbeck and Bolsover were 'much out of repair, and this later half pull'd down; no furniture or any necessary Goods were left in them, but some few Hangings and Pictures'.[80] She imagined Bolsover Castle, the former pleasure palace of the Cavendishes, finding a voice to complain that:

> Within me hath a garrison been placed:
> Their guns and pistols all around me hung [. . .]
> My windows broke, the winds blow in, and make
> That I with cold like shivering agues shake.[81]

On William's return, repairs and vast improvements to the castle were quickly set in hand, lead ordered for the roofless gallery and the household mobilised for the works. At first, all went smoothly, and Clayton's reports to William were written in glowing terms:

> I was this day at Bolsover and find ye work goes on very well the stair into the Castle Court is the most noblest that ever I Saw The Bathing house and Arch betwixt the Old new Buildings and ye stone Walk is just finished The Gallery is ready for Lead, which I shall buy as soon as ye price falls to Ten pound per fother.[82]

The bathing house that Clayton mentions represents the height of luxurious sophistication. Not content with his outdoor fountain that could also be used as a plunge pool, William has commissioned a further elaboration to the castle's already elaborate plumbing system: a stone-built house in the lee of the high Stone Walk containing an indoor bath fed by a pipe.[83]

These tweaks to the gates and walls of the gardens were only the precursors to a much more splendid project to remodel the pre-war state apartments of the Terrace Range at Bolsover. Building projects boost the local economy and provide self-advancement for individuals. Back in 1613, at the building of the Little Castle, the Kitchen family, for example, were mere labourers, toiling for a few pence, but the Kitchens have taken advantage of the continuous Cavendish building projects to achieve positions of seniority. By the 1660s, they have become major building contractors, and one of them will even serve Henry Cavendish as a confidential household servant. How proud this William Kitchen must be, personal servant to a duke's son and a key figure in the country's most celebrated building projects. The Cavendishes' obsession for building gave him the opportunity to show his potential.

Day-to-day activities on site are overseen by the architect Samuel Marsh, who makes ranting complaints about the mendacious builders now engaged to carry out the work. The builder Joseph Jackson in particular receives the cut of Marsh's tongue for his men's wasting of building stone and their spoiling of various tools.[84]

Marsh comes from a family of quarrymen, but his flair for design has allowed him to rise up in the world to experience life in a variety of noblemen's houses across the Midlands. William will prove to be his best employer, and in due course Marsh is entered in the household's wage book, receiving payment as a regular household officer. He has found his niche in the household of the most lavish patron in the Midlands.

Marsh's designs for these new rooms at Bolsover in the 1660s are

The new state rooms of the Terrace Range at Bolsover, designed by Samuel Marsh and added under Andrew Clayton's supervision in the 1660s. William's achievement of arms surmounts the entrance

very different from the rooms built by the Smithsons before the Civil War. The architectural details are fashionably bold and dramatic, and the work includes a suite of the regular, rectangular state apartments leading one into another that provide the setting for Restoration court life. A grand dining room leads into a reception hall, then a withdrawing room, and then a state bedchamber with a dressing room and heated close-stool room located just off it. The bedchamber's occupant sleeps in the small and cosy dressing room before nipping through to the lofty (and draughty) bedchamber for the theatrical process of dressing before onlookers each morning. During their years of exile in France, Charles II and his courtiers experienced the formal rituals of Louis XIV's court, where the king allowed spectators to watch the ceremonies of dressing in the morning and going to bed in the evening; these rituals are now beginning to appear in English life. Seen empty of their cast of characters, these chains of baroque rooms appear sterile and almost indistinguishable; they only make sense when playing host to the courtly ceremonies of late-seventeenth-century life.

By Monday evening, Clayton and Booth are riding back along the short road from Sookeholme, and they find Liddell watching for them in the wood before the abbey gates. Now, 'with much joy', he tells them that he is certain that the letter has reached William's hands, 'for he said Mr Proctor took the Letters from the boy and brought them to his Grace'. John Proctor is the officer who runs the treasury at Welbeck and is responsible for issuing money from the Evidence House. The post that morning had contained the anonymous letter, along with four others: one from William's son Henry, one from Sir Francis Topp, one from Captain Mazine and a fourth from a French gentleman. Liddell described how Mr Proctor 'looking upon the Letters did tell his Grace, from whom every of them came; save one which he wondered whose it should be'. Liddell himself was shown the strange letter, and commented that he had never seen its handwriting before, although he secretly noticed and recognised the seal that he himself had put upon it. So far, so good.

After the conspirators have finished talking in the shadowy woods, they bring their horses into the court. Clayton and Booth, hungry, go to the King's Hall and call for a dish of meat for a private supper together. This quiet, low-key meal in the smaller King's Hall forms a contrast to the days when the Great Hall at Welbeck was daily full of the sound and smell of a large community eating supper together. In his written *Advice* to his former pupil Charles II, William stresses the benefits of eating communally and describes the favour and reputation that his uncle Gilbert Talbot used to earn by having his country neighbours to dine. They 'sat at my Lord's table next him', he addressed them as 'cousin', and 'my Lord had no business in the Country, but they did it for him'. For many years, William practised what he preached about communal dining in the Great Hall at Welbeck. Known as the 'common dining hall' by 1666, it was still being used for household meals, and according to its surviving menus William himself ate there on occasion. Yet, in the last few years, William's enthusiasm for entertaining has declined. One of the favours that his son Henry and his wife promise to perform if allowed to return to Welbeck is to help out 'when yr Grace is pleased to entertain any of your table yet if your Grace so pleases you need not dine with them at any time for we being at your table may entertain & receive any whomsoever your Grace would entertain without any occasion for them to take it ill'.[85] This growing reluctance to dine in public is not unusual among William's contemporaries. Roger North in the 1690s describes how, in the old days, a household's eating in the Great Hall indicated 'great dignity and plenty', but now 'the way of the world is chang'd, and the eating is devided, many servants wait, and take their repast after the master, who is served at a table in a room layd out for that porpose'. 'Therefore,' North finishes nostalgically, 'those wide halls are layd aside.'[86]

Before Clayton and Booth are halfway through their meal in the King's Hall, a servant comes in with instructions that Clayton must go up to see the duke. Now Clayton disappears up the stone stairs leading to the family lodgings, and Booth and Liddell are left alone. Clayton's departure leaves them tense with nerves and the fear of discovery, and they repair to Booth's chamber. Here they suffer the agony of being unable to talk freely because Alan Swinburn, another household officer, is present.

Only an hour later does Clayton return. Swinburn departs for bed, leaving the three free to confer once more. Clayton is quick to tell the others that William Cavendish had called him in to inform him of the receipt of the libel. The duke told Clayton quite openly that Margaret herself suspected that either Clayton or Gilbert Eagle or both of them had had a hand in it. Gilbert Eagle, a further member of the Eagle dynasty of household servants, has become a powerful figure in the household, considered to be worth courting by the tenants: on one occasion one of them requests a friend to give gifts (or bribes) to 'Mr Eagle & the Grooms, what ye shall think proper in this Case'.[87] William, much less willing than Margaret to suspect his long-standing servants, reassured Clayton that he did not share his wife's suspicions and gave his own view that it was an old enemy, the parson of Mansfield. Yet this was followed by a serious blow for the conspirators: William had 'further added the Author was both a fool and a Knave to think he should be directed by Libels'.

Clayton has further details of his conversation with the duke to pass on to his eager listeners. In order to 'colour his ignorance', Clayton had asked whether the letter was written in verse, and 'his Grace answered no; it was a serious thing in prose and did seem to court him much at the beginning but had abused Peg (as he pleased to call her Grace) abominably'. The letter, then, appears to have failed to make the desired impact. Yet there is nothing further that the conspirators can do but to 'be secret and to wait the event'.[88] So ends another day at Welbeck.

Now time begins to pass more quickly. For the next few days, the household is in turmoil as the hunt for the culprits begins. Mistress Evans is sent to Tuxford secretly in Margaret's carriage to try to find out who posted the letter, but returns without success. Normality gradually returns, and the conspirators are thankful to remain undetected. Despite their high hopes, nothing at all seems to have changed in the close relationship between William and his wife.

With the passage of time, the strain of keeping their secret starts to tell on the conspirators and the cracks in their partnership begin to widen. John Booth is the weakest link. Half-demented by guilt and his financial problems, he finally flees from Welbeck. Six months later, he meets with Clayton once again in order to tell his former colleague that he is resolved to confess his guilt and to cast himself upon 'their Graces' mercy. Clayton now realises that he is doomed and his countenance falls, though he mutters, as Booth will recollect, that 'he prayed God that I did not accuse some that were innocent'.

'Thus we did wickedly conspire against her Grace,' concludes Booth in his confession to a Justice of the Peace made in July, 1671, 'and God hath brought it to light that we may receive shame and punishment.'

Francis Liddell also shamefacedly signs a confession to his guilt, in the grim-faced presence of his former household colleagues Edward Ogle, John Proctor and Gilbert Eagle.

His plot in ruins about him and betrayed by his colleagues, Andrew Clayton is heading for ruin. He is charged with financial crimes as well as libel. Despite his apparent industry in keeping the accounts, the household finances have always been in a parlous state, and servants sometimes have to beg for their wages. Poor Christopher Matlock and his 'aged wife', for example, having 'in these distracted times spent the greatest part of their poor estate' were owed £17 and 10 shillings in wages for their service at Welbeck. It remained unforthcoming, despite Matlock's pleas to William that 'your honour would be pleased to take your promises into consideration, & give order that he may have his salaries paid him'.[89]

Clayton comes to discover that because of Margaret's suspicions a 'special caution' has been given that his accounts should neither be signed nor a discharge given, but only a simple receipt written for money he pays into the treasury. For months he has lived under fear that Margaret will demand a 'grand accompt' at some time to suit herself, which will 'certainly ruin him' as he cannot account for all the money he has had in his possession over the years.[90]

Particular problems arose when Clayton was left in charge during William and Margaret's absences in London. He found himself deep in trouble when there was not enough money in the treasury to meet household outgoings. Despite his having used his own cash to keep the household solvent, Clayton discovers that his actions are open to misinterpretation. His trial, when it begins, generates a huge amount of paperwork about the workings of the household and its failings: how accounts are kept, how rents are bagged up and stored in the treasury by John Proctor.

Preparing documents in his defence, Clayton describes how, when William and Margaret went to London, he was left

> behind at Welbeck to look after the said Employments and wages of returning money to London and to pay of the said Bills and charges of buildings and to any other fitting payments for his Grace and his Lady for the board wages of his servants and others who had then diet in his Grace's family when he was in the Country and otherwise thereupon his Grace upon his going to London appointed your orator to take the money or part of the money then remaining in the said Evidence house.[91]

Now Clayton falls ill while temporarily away from Welbeck, and on his recovery finds he lacks the documents he needs to support his case. His servant returns to the abbey in search for the necessary papers, but with appropriate symbolism finds the door to Clayton's chamber – once locked by the conspirators to keep out the rest of the household – locked against him. Clayton complains that

> the passage of [my] chamber [was] locked up in which Chamber [I] had divers of apparell and some other things and diverse receipts and acquittances the payment of a considerable part of the disbursements aforesaid (though for the greatest part thereof were receipts were over given) and divers other writings.[92]

These special pleas, however, cannot disguise Clayton's guilt.

Despite the setback of Clayton's spectacular fall from grace, the old servants still hope eventually to triumph and to drive the newcomers out of the household. Only a few years later, their opportunity finally arrives.

# 10 – *A Second Deathbed*

WELBECK ABBEY, 25TH DECEMBER, 1676

It is Christmas Day, 1676, and at Welbeck Abbey a lonely old man lies dying.

Having suffered from Parkinson's disease for many months, William can no longer perform his accustomed role of lover. 'Cupid, I've served thee this many a year,' he writes in his final days, and even now he is still addicted to women.[1] 'Oh Gods,' he begs only months before his death, 'release me from loves damned thrall,' and pours scorn on himself as an aged lover:

> Wth a dry Palm, and Crows feet in his eyes
> Stoops in his back, and nothing by his thighs
> Increasing Belly, & decreasing Member
> And no wit left, but past sins to remember.[2]

The last days of a duke are a troubling time for his family and household. Everyone wonders who will be favoured with inheritance, and access to the sickroom is jealously monitored in case of last-minute alterations to the will. In future years, lengthy depositions will be made about the final sickness of William's son, Henry, in the hope of proving he was out of his mind when he made his final, divisive will. Not so with William: he has been prepared for several months, and there is little left on his conscience besides his last great building project. This is one of the few things he regrets on his deathbed.

William's thoughts have been turning towards death for several years. In 1671, he was given royal permission to prepare himself a 'tomb among the kings' in Westminster Abbey.[3] Only two years later, the 'Garter King of Arms', three heralds and a procession of peers and peeresses accompanied his wife Margaret's corpse to the new Cavendish vault there.[4] She lies beneath Grinling Gibbons' monument (with its dedication to William, the 'Loyall Duke') in the north aisle. William's instinct about her in those heady Parisian days was sound: the monument confirms that Margaret has been a faithful and loving wife, staying 'with her Lord all the time of his banishment & miseries & when he came home never parted from him in all his solitary retirements'.

One result of Margaret's death was the fall from power of her servants within the household. A relation wrote triumphantly to Henry's wife Frances that it must be 'much to yr satisfaction, that lady Topp & her daughter, is gone from Welbeck, I hope never to return thither any more, I hope your ladyship my honoured Lord & all yours will still be more firmly fixed in my Lord Duke's favour & affection'.[5] Yet the results were not quite as clear-cut as Frances's correspondent hoped. Devastated by the death of his beloved 'Peg', William did indeed find himself forced upon the society of his old servants and children, but sought relief from his melancholy by throwing himself into his last and greatest building project.

Only two years ago, he embarked upon the great mansion that would prove to be his last work. During his lifetime, the Cavendish estates as a whole have provided materials and labour for projects at Welbeck Abbey, Slingsby Castle in Yorkshire and Bolsover Castle, and now a final house, Nottingham Castle, is under construction. The county is amazed that a man so old has so much energy. Robert Thoroton, Nottinghamshire's great historian, marvelled that the 'Duke, who this present year 1674, though he be above eighty years of age, hath a great number of men at work pulling down and clearing the Foundations of the old Tower that he may build, at least, part of a New Castle there', making the old connection between William's title as Duke of Newcastle and his obsession with building.[6] The remains of the medieval keep of Nottingham Castle were cleared away in preparation for the grandest and most baroque of the aged duke's houses. Its massive columns and Italianate palazzo outline are in fact an attempt to perfect the house William had built at Bolsover in the 1630s. His unfinished project is one of the few matters that can still interest him, as his will, written only two months before today, demonstrates. This spells out how William's recalcitrant son Henry must complete the house according to the 'forme and modell thereof by me layd and

William's last great mansion: Nottingham Castle. Over the east entrance is the statue of William on horseback that rioters destroyed

designed'.[7] William has tied up much of Henry's money in the hands of trustees, so that it may only be spent on the building work. Work to date has only risen as high as the first storey, but Henry is legally obliged to see the project through. The finished house will dominate the city's skyline throughout the coming centuries.

Welbeck Abbey, where William now lies, is considerably different to the house in which his father had died in 1617. Oddly enough, it has never quite been completed. William's father's grand remodelling petered out, as did his own attempt to refashion the range incorporating the Great Hall, and the main improvements in his lifetime have been limited to the stables, the fabulous Riding House of course, and to the walks and balustrades in the water gardens. Most of William's efforts have been concentrated elsewhere, chiefly on his castles at Bolsover and now Nottingham, projects dedicated to his own father. He even purchased the site of Nottingham Castle because of his father's fondness for the romantic ruin it had been. William bought it when it came onto the market as it was 'a seat which had pleased his Father very much' and 'he would not leave it since it was offer'd to be sold'.[8]

The closed doors, the gathering of the family and the low voices of the servants must be familiar to the very few who remember Sir Charles's death in 1617. In a mortal sickness, the great state bed proves less convenient than a simple pallet. In his own last days, William's son

Henry will lie 'upon a pallet bed which stood with ye head thereof to ye wall, by ye coming in of ye door' and bid visitors 'stand forward or further into ye Room that he might see' them.[9] Now is the time for William's final words to his children.

His last admonitions to his son delivered, life drains out of William's body at some point during the course of Christmas Day. The servants are standing by to take his corpse down to London, for, unlike the burial of his father, mother and first wife in Bolsover Church, William's status means that his funeral is a national event. As is commonly the case, a wax effigy of his dead body will be displayed to mourners for several days in the Great Chamber of Newcastle House. Then William's effigy and body will be brought down the black-draped stairs and through the hall, before being carried in a torch-lit procession out of Clerkenwell Close to make its last journey towards Westminster. The way lies through a city much changed since William's early days at court. Like 'a *Phoenix* in her ashes', London has recovered from the fire, and the West End is now becoming the fashionable place to live.[10] The new Leicester Square forms only part of a huge swathe of speculative houses that have sprung up between Clerkenwell and Westminster. The route taken by William's corpse is circuitous, by the way of 'ye feilds & by Leinster Garden Wall & by Tart Hall, which will be ye privatest'.[11] Since the death of William's father Sir Charles, a daytime funeral with a great procession of mourners as a show of political strength has been replaced by a nocturnal procession of closed coaches, a more individual and private response to death.[12] William's final destination is a place next to Margaret in the vault at Westminster Abbey.

London's response to William's death is quietly respectful rather than wildly grief-stricken. He has, in a sense, lived too long and become almost an embarrassment to the court of Charles II with his harping on about the king's father and his pre-war notions of courtesy and honour. William doubtless died still aggrieved that his loyalty throughout the Civil War was not – to his mind – sufficiently rewarded, but then his reputation never fully recovered from the blow he dealt it by running away after the battle of Marston Moor.

To his possible chagrin had he known it, William's role in the great affairs of the court and nation will come to be overshadowed by the memory of his achievements in other areas of life. His book on riding really was revolutionary, although at the time of his death this is not fully recognised. Still, even today, in 1676, William has already ensured

William and Margaret's monument, designed by Grinling Gibbons, in the north transept of Westminster Abbey

his immortality, because his great houses will continue to impress and amaze visitors for centuries. Through them, and his poetry, he has provided the means for future generations to imagine the whole lost world of the courtly Cavaliers.

The year following William's death, the decease will be reported of 'Captain Mazine, the old great horseman', whose honorary place in the royal household is given to another of William's old servants, Mr Eagle (whose father had also served in the Cavendish household).[13] William's secretary John Rolleston lives until the age of eighty-four in his manor house near Welbeck; after his death his wife decides that his tomb should say first and foremost that he had been 'well belov'd by ye High & mighty Wm late Duke of Newcastle & his noble family'.[14] Mr Benoist continues to administer the affairs of William's son, Henry, his former pupil, and becomes tutor to Henry's own son, Harry. Mr Kitchen the builder rubs his hands at the thought of the lucrative contracts that Henry may be encouraged to place with him. Henry's daughters wonder if their father will let them marry the men of their choice and which of them will become his greatest heiress. The circling for position has begun once again and allegiances shift once more, for the household's life will continue under its new master.

# Afterword: William Cavendish's Legacy

William Cavendish's greatest legacy was his array of great seventeenth-century houses. His household was one of the very last of the extensive, medievally inspired organisations that were once the country's primary social units, yet within it many new and recognisable domestic practices began to take shape.

In William's lifetime, we find table forks, napkins laid on the lap, flushing toilets, glass wine bottles, underpants and even the umbrella making their first appearances in England. Meals were becoming recognisable, with the main course followed by the dessert. You could buy a recognisable printed book, though you had to visit the printer and bookbinder separately. Houses like the Little Castle were just beginning to have something in common with our own, with separate living and dining rooms, bedrooms and studies, while the Great Hall of medieval houses had begun its sorry descent down to the level of the meagre entrance passage that forms the 'hall' of the modern home. Men were starting to leave the formerly high-status household jobs such as gentleman usher or steward in order to go out to work in business or the professions, and women were beginning to take over the household roles of housekeeping and cooking that they would retain for at least three centuries. Yet, at the same time, other women were beginning to publish their written work, the handshake was replacing the doffing of the hat and the English were flirting with republicanism.

In order to see the rooms in which these momentous changes happened, it's possible to visit many of the houses mentioned in this book. Bolsover Castle is the most accessible, and the Little Castle in particular remains remarkably redolent of the seventeenth century. A large ingredient of its attraction is the emptiness of its rooms: no Victorian clutter or unsightly electric lights here mean the effect is austere but authentic. From the high Stone Walk you can see the Fountain Garden now planted with seventeenth-century varieties, but William's great Terrace Range lies roofless since its lead was plundered for improvements to Welbeck in the eighteenth century. The Little Castle was not regularly used after William's death until the nineteenth century, when it became the home of the snobbish Reverend Gray, vicar of Bolsover, and his wife. They found the Cavendishes' castle deliciously romantic, revelling in its 'most dismal desolation, wainscots torn down, windows rattling in every pane, doors off their hinges', while the pictures on the walls were 'shot through with arrows'.[1] This odd couple refurnished it in a ludicrously baronial style that appealed to the writers of the many spurious Victorian historical romances that were set here; examples include *The Romaunt of Bolsover Castle* (1845) and *Bolsover Castle: A Tale from Protestant History of the Sixteenth Century* (1846). After the death of the Grays, the castle was opened to visitors by the Duke of Portland, until 1945, when he placed it in the care of the Ministry of Public Buildings and Works. This body's successor, English Heritage, still welcomes visitors to the site today.

In 1996, I became English Heritage's Assistant Inspector of Ancient Monuments and Historic Buildings, and it was my job to help research a great re-presentation project being undertaken there. During this project we made new red taffeta hangings for the Marble closet, repainted the Pillar Parlour in black, walnut and gold as indicated on Smithson's drawings, scripted an audio tour narrated by Andrew Clayton, made a film showing William and Margaret dancing together in a darkened closet and staged a wonderful event where riders demonstrated the manoeuvres of the *manège* amid the dust of the Riding House. In between times I was transcribing documents in the British Library, Nottingham University Library, Lambeth Palace Library, Sheffield City Archives, Lincoln Record Office, the Bodleian Library and a number of other places, tracking down William's letters in his crazy and increasingly familiar handwriting and visiting the other buildings connected to his life.

Welbeck Abbey is far less readily accessible, but then very little survives that William Cavendish would have recognised. After his death, his name and at least part of his wealth travelled through three generations of the female line: through his granddaughter Margaret to the

Holles family, and then through her only child Henrietta, who married Edward Harley, second Earl of Oxford. The redoubtable Henrietta Cavendish-Holles-Harley also had a single child, another Margaret, who married William Bentinck, second Duke of Portland, with the result that her descendants took – and retain – the name of Cavendish-Bentinck. The abbey, remodelled in the eighteenth, nineteenth and twentieth centuries, is deeply intriguing to architectural historians, but as a military college and private residence access to the public is not possible.

In Northumberland, William's castles at Bothal and Ogle are also private residences, but William's brother Sir Charles's house, Slingsby Castle in Yorkshire, lies in ruins. Also ruinous are the houses in Lincolnshire rented by William's brother and son, Glentworth and Wellingore. Very few fragments remain of the Palace of Richmond, though the area yields rich pickings for archaeologists. The King's Manor in York still remains intact, and if you visit the battlefield of Marston Moor you can see the copse where the bodies of four thousand of William's Whitecoats remain buried in one of the country's largest mass graves. In Antwerp, Rubens's house, apparently so intact, was actually almost completely rebuilt during the Second World War.

Newcastle House in London ended up in the hands of William's granddaughter Elizabeth, Duchess of Albemarle, who became famous as the second supposedly 'mad' duchess to live there.[2] During her widowhood after her first husband's death, she refused to marry anyone but the Emperor of China. Her second husband, the Earl of Montagu, won her hand by impersonating him. After her death in 1734, Newcastle House fell on hard times, becoming used as a cabinet-maker's workshop before being demolished by one James Carr for the sale of its materials.[3] In the sale he retained one lot for his own use, and it is therefore speculated that Newcastle House was the source of the fine early-eighteenth-century panelling which still survives in Carr's own house at 12 Albemarle Street, Clerkenwell.[4] By 1893, Newcastle House had been replaced by a row of houses still called 'Newcastle Row', and part of the cloister of the nunnery still exists in the corner of a dank London park.

In due course Nottingham Castle, the last great house of the Cavendishes, became something of a white elephant. William's grandson died only four years after William's own death in 1676, so the line of Dukes of Newcastle for whom William had built this 'new castle' petered out after only two generations. After the subsequent spat among a number of claimants to William's legacy, the castle ended up in the possession of Thomas Pelham, a relation by marriage of one of William's granddaughters. Pelham complained, 'seeing the Bare shell of y$^{e}$ House can be of little or no value, but rather an expence', but his architect, the playwright John Vanbrugh, with his eye for the dramatic, persuaded him to choose 'this Castle for [his] Northern Seat'.[5] Improvements made the draughty house tolerably comfortable, but it was to be burnt down by rioters in 1831. Then the equestrian statue of William Cavendish was pulled down, and by some strange chance his carved foot ended up on the floor of a junk shop in Victorian London.[6] Rebuilt by the local architect Thomas Chambers Hine, the castle is now the city's art gallery.

The lasting reputation of William's fellow Cavaliers rose again with the nineteenth-century Romantic movement. G. M. Trevelyan's rose-tinted description of Charles I's courtiers, using St John's College in Oxford as their Civil War headquarters, stands out as an evocation of their attraction: 'They strolled through the garden, as the hopeless evenings fell, listening, at the end of all, while the siege guns broke the silence with ominous iteration. Behind the cannon on those low hills to northward were ranked the inexorable men who came to lay their hands on all this beauty, hoping to change it to strength and sterner virtue.'[7] The authors of the spoof history textbook *1066 and All That* expressed the same idea in a different way:

> Charles I was a Cavalier King and therefore had a small pointed beard, long flowing curls, a large, flat, flowing hat and *gay attire*. The Roundheads, on the other hand, were clean-shaven and wore tall, conical hats, white ties and *sombre garments*. Under these circumstances a Civil War was inevitable.[8]

William Cavendish has a well-deserved place among the 'wrong but romantic' Cavaliers, but his reputation has been fiercely contested. On the one hand, those like Horace Walpole condemn William and Margaret's social and literary pretension. 'What a picture of foolish nobility was this stately poetic couple,' he writes, 'retired to their own little domain, and intoxicating one another with circumstantial flattery on what was of consequence to no mortal but themselves!'[9] Yet William's apologists, won over by Margaret's hagiographical biography, take him at his wife's estimation: brave, generous and loyal. Geoffrey Trease, better known as a children's writer, took this view in

*Portrait of a Cavalier* in 1979, which lovingly portrayed all of William's blithe charm, spirit and optimism.

According to the censorious Lucy Hutchinson, William never found a comfortable place for himself in London and should have remained in the Midlands: it was 'a foolish ambition of glorious slavery' that 'carried him to Court, where he ran himselfe much in to debt'.[10] In 2003, I, too, felt the lure of London and became Chief Curator of Historic Royal Palaces, the independent charity that looks after the unoccupied royal palaces of the Tower of London, Hampton Court Palace, the state apartments at Kensington Palace, the Banqueting House at Whitehall and Kew Palace in Kew Gardens.

Here in London, the palaces are magnificent, the documentary sources are rich and the royal dramatis personae melodramatic. Yet I left behind me in Derbyshire and Nottinghamshire my fondest memories of William, the eccentric, erratic, maddening and ridiculous – yet 'Loyall' and lovable – Duke of Newcastle.

# Acknowledgements

I would like to thank the people who helped me along the way with this book and the D.Phil. thesis upon which it is based. First and foremost are Maurice Howard, a super supervisor, and Mark Girouard, who, through his book *Robert Smythson and the Elizabethan Country House*, first introduced me to Bolsover Castle. The following people all helped with either encouragement or information or both: Malcolm Airs, Charles Avery, Catherine Barne, Susan Bracken, Steven Brindle, Karen Britland, Anne Brookes, Clare Browne, John Burditt, James Campbell, Rosa Schiano di Cola, Marie-Louise Coolahan, Rosalys Coope, Nicholas Cooper, Tarnya Cooper, Ben Cowell, Gillian Darley, Carl Depauw, David Durant, Trevor Foulds, Alan Gardner, Robert Harding, Paula Henderson, Adrian Henstock, Robert Howard, David Howarth, Liz James, Nigel Llewellyn, Arthur McGregor, David Mitchell, Sir Oliver Millar, Richard Morris, Christopher Norton, Lawrence Stewart Owens, Michael Partington, Timothy Raylor, the late Annabel Ricketts, Christopher Ridgeway, Martin Ripley, Harry Rowland, Barney Sloane, John Thorneycroft, Rutger Tijs, Malcolm Underwood, Anthony Wells-Cole, Adam White, Amanda White, David Withey, Adrian Woodhouse, Rosemary and the late Patrick Wormald, and Sir Marcus Worsley.

I'm particularly grateful to my former colleagues from English Heritage's Bolsover Castle project: Tom Addyman, Mark Askey, Glyn Coppack, Judith Dobie, Tony Fleming, Nick Hill, Helen Hughes, Richard Lea, Stephen Paine, Richard Sheppard and Mike Sutherill. For access to Cavendish buildings, I'm indebted to Derek Adlam and Keith Crosland at Welbeck Abbey, and especially Derek for all sorts of help;

to Dawn Beer and Charles Sample at Bothal Castle; Mr and Mrs Boanas at Ogle Castle; Tony and Joy Shaw Browne at Cavendish Lodge, Clipstone, and of course, my most sincere thanks go to John Coulson, Christine Paulson, Sarah Chapman and all the girls both now and formerly at Bolsover Castle.

To my friends the curators of the exhibition 'Royalist Refugees' in Antwerp in 2006 I give special thanks: Ben van Beneden, Ursula Härting, Karen Hearn, Lynn Hulse, James Knowles, Simon Stock and Nora de Poorter.

Peter Furtado has kindly allowed me to reproduce material from my article 'Reining Cavaliers' in *History Today*, Vol. 54 (9), September, 2004, pp. 9–15. Dorothy Johnson gave me kind permission to quote from the Portland collection in the Department of Special Collections and Manuscripts at the University of Nottingham, where I've felt very welcome. Thanks, too, to the Society of Antiquaries and the British Academy for their financial support of earlier parts of this research, especially those leading to my article on William's architectural patronage in the *Transactions of the Ancient Monuments Society*'s 2006 volume.

For advice and encouragement about book-writing, I am grateful to the late Giles Worsley, Michael Jones, Simon Jenkins and Zoe Pagnamenta. Felicity Bryan is electricity in human form. Julian Loose is an evil genius as an editor, always cruel, always right and always funny. The very kind people who read and improved various drafts for me were: David Adshead, Mark Askey, Ian Bahrami, Ben van Beneden, Gillian Blake, John Cloake, John Coulson, Heather Ewing, Esther Godfrey, Karen Hearn, Paula Henderson, Nick Hill, Katherine Ibbett, Ann Plackett, Lindsay Sagnette, Julie Sanders, David Swinscoe, Elaine Walker, Jenni Waugh and Henry Volans. Of course, the mistakes are mine, not theirs, and like Margaret Cavendish in her preface to her biography of William Cavendish, I hope that whatsoever 'shall be found amiss, will be favourably pardoned by the candid readers, to whom I wish all manner of happiness'.

My final thanks go with love to Peter, Enid and Tom Worsley.

This book is dedicated to Mark Hines, with thanks for our ten happy years together.

PICTURE CREDITS

## *Plate Sections*

1: © The Palace of Westminster. 2, 9, 13, 14, 15, 17, 19, 20, 29: © English Heritage. 3, 4, 6, 7, 8, 25, 30: Private Collection. 5: Paula Henderson. 10: Lucy Worsley. 11, 16: Chris Puddephatt. 12, 18, 21, 22: The Royal Collection © 2007 Her Majesty Queen Elizabeth II. 23, 26: Stad Antwerpen © Foto: Collectiebeleid. 24: Museo del Prado, Madrid. 27: Stad Antwerpen © Foto: Stefan Dewickere. 28: National Portrait Gallery, London

## *Illustrations in the Text*

1, 9, 13–15, 19, 20, 26, 33, 35, 42: Mark Hines. 2: From an engraving in Francis Sandford, 'The Solemn interment of George Duke of Albemarle' (1670), plate 3, *His Grace's Watermen 12*. British Library shelfmark Tab.1315.b. 3: Royal Institute of British Architects Library, Drawings Collection, The Smythson Collection, III/1(1). 4: From Randle Holme, *An Academie or Store of Armory & Blazon* (Book III, Chapter 9, plate 3), apparently published in 1688. British Library shelfmark CUP25.c.8. 5, 22: The Trustees of the Chatsworth Settlement. 6: From V. Scamozzi, *Les Cinq Ordres d'architecture de Vincent Scamozzi* (Paris, 1685), facing p. 137: Historic Royal Palaces. 8: RIBA Drawings Collection. The second is from The Smythson Collection, III/13. 10: Engraving by Lucas Vorstermans after Abraham van Diepenbeeck, in William Cavendish, *Méthode Nouvelle et Invention Extraordinaire de dresser les Chevaux* (Antwerp, 1657–8) Plate 8. 11: RIBA Drawings Collection, The Smythson Collection, III/1(3). 12: Pepys Library, Magdalene College, Cambridge. 16: By courtesy of Sir Reresby Sitwell. 17: RIBA Drawings Collection, The Smythson Collection, III/1(11). 18: An engraving, by Thod. van Kesel after Abraham van Diepenbeeck, in William Cavendish (1657–8), Plate 35. 21: Georg Phillip Harsdörffer, *Vollstandiges und von newem vermehrtes Trincir-Buch* (Nuremberg, 1665), British Library shelfmark BL 1037c18. 23: 'The Sucklington Faction or Roaring Boyes' (1641), British Library shelfmark 669f4(26). 24: The Duke of Northumberland/Syon House. 25, 36: Ashmolean Museum, Oxford. 27: Illustration from Sir John Harrington, *The Metamorphosis of Ajax* (1596), British Library shelfmark C21A5. 28: © The British Museum, Wenceslaus Hollar's print of *Richmond* (1638), no. 1058 in Pennington's index of Hollar's works. 29: The Fitzwilliam Museum, Cambridge. 30: Illustrated in John Cruso, *Militarie Instructions for the CAVALL'RIE* (1632), British Library shelfmark 717.m.18. 31: © The British Museum, no. 547 in Pennington's index of Hollar's works. 32: From *The Bloody Prince, or a Declaration of the most cruel practices of Prince Rupert and the rest of the Cavaliers* (1643), British Library Thomason Tracts E99.14. 34: 'A DOGS ELEGY OR RUPERT'S TEARS', (London, 27th

July, 1644), British Library shelfmark E.3(17). 37: Prints by J. Harrewijn, courtesy of the *Rubenshuis* museum. 38: Erasmus de Bie, *View of the Meir (Gezicht op de Meir)*. Collection: Musée d'Ixelles, Brussels. Photography: Mixed Media, Brussels. 39: From Margaret Cavendish, *CCXI Sociable Letters* (London, 1664), frontispiece. 40: Nottingham University Hallward Library, Department of Special Collections and Manuscripts, Pw V/25, f.140r. 41: A print by Marcus Willemsz Doornick (1666), The Guildhall Library, Corporation of London. 43: From the 'Crowle Pennant', the collector's edition of Thomas Pennant's *Some Account of London, Westminster and Southwark* (London, 1790), Vol. 7, Plate 291 © The British Museum. 44: From Francis Hawkins (trans.), *Youths Behaviour* (London, 1654), British Library shelfmark 8405aaa10. 45: Frontispiece from Margaret Cavendish, *The World's Olio* (London, 1671). 46: From Avray H. Tipping, *English Homes*, Vol. 3, No. 1, Late Tudor (1922). 47: Image by John Clee, reproduced in Charles Deering, *Nottinghamia vetus et nova, or an Historical Account of the Ancient and Present State of the town of Nottingham* (Nottingham, 1751), facing p. 170, British Library shelfmark 984.e.7. 48: The Dean and Chapter of Westminster Abbey. Chapter openers: British Library, shelfmark CUP25.c.8. British Library illustrations all © the British Library Board. All rights reserved.

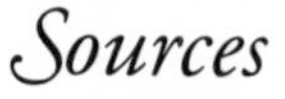

# Sources

## PRIMARY SOURCES

The main body of the Cavendish family papers descended through three generations of the female line in the eighteenth century.[1] Welbeck Abbey remains in the Cavendish-Bentinck family, although the dukedom is extinct. The family's documentary archive was given to the nation in several batches over the course of the twentieth century. Many volumes of political and personal papers were given to the British Museum and are now to be found as additional manuscripts in the British Library. Of particular relevance are volumes 70499 and 70500, which were partially transcribed in the Historical Manuscripts Commission's *13th Report on the Manuscripts of his Grace the Duke of Portland preserved at Welbeck Abbey*, Appendix II. They contain letters and estate papers from William's lifetime. However, a far greater body of estate papers was given in several batches to the Nottinghamshire Records Office, now known as the Nottinghamshire Archives, while further personal and literary papers were given to the University of Nottingham.

Letters to, from or about William Cavendish survive in other archives, including the following: Balliol College, Oxford; the Bodleian Library, Oxford (abbreviated in Notes to 'Bod.'); the British Library (abbreviated to BL); the British Museum, Print Room; Castle Howard, Yorkshire; Chatsworth House, Derbyshire; the College of Arms; the Derbyshire Record Office; Finsbury Library Local Studies Collection, the London Borough of Islington; the Guildhall Library, London; Hovingham Hall, Yorkshire; Lambeth Palace Library; Lincoln City Library; the Lincolnshire Archives; the London Metropolitan Record Centre; the Museum of London Archaeology Service; the National Archives (abbreviated to TNA); the Northumberland Record Office; the Nottinghamshire Archives (abbreviated to NA); a private collection; Renishaw Hall, Derbyshire; the RIBA Drawings Collection; the Sheffield City Archives (abbreviated to SCA); the Staffordshire Record Office; St John's

College Archives, Cambridge; University of Nottingham, Hallward Library, Department of Manuscripts and Special Collections (abbreviated to UN); Warwickshire Record Office.

## *Early and Modern Editions of Contemporary Printed Material*


Anon., *A true Relation of HIS MAJESTIES Motion from* Wales *to* Lichfield *in* Staffor*dshire [. . .] in pursuit of His Majesties Horse to* Welbeck-*House* (London, 20th August, 1645).

– *Letters and Poems in Honour of the Incomparable Princess, Margaret, Dutchess of Newcastle* (London, 1674).

– *A Collection of Letters and Poems: Written by several Persons of Honour and Learning [. . .] to the Late Duke and Dutchess of Newcastle* (London, 1678).

– *Mémoires de la Vie du Comte de Grammont* (Cologne, 1713), Ed. A. Hamilton (Philadelphia, 1888).

– *A Collection of Ordinances and Regulations for the Government of the Royal Household* (London, 1790).

– *The Character of an Oxford-Incendiary* (London, 26th April, 1645).

Aubrey, John, *Aubrey's Brief Lives*, Ed. Dick Oliver Lawson (Bungay, Suffolk, 1972).

Baker, Thomas, *History of the College of St John the Evangelist, Cambridge* (written some time before 1717, published Cambridge, 1869).

Bentinck, William, sixth Duke of Portland, *Men, Women and Things* (London, 1937).

Birch, Thomas (Ed.), *The Court and Times of James I, illustrated by authentic and confidential letters, from various public and private collections* (London, 1848).

Boorde, Andrew, *The Breviary of Healthe* (n.p., 1552).

Bromley, Sir George, *A Collection of Original Royal Letters* (London, 1787).

Burke, Sir Bernard, *A Visitation of the Seats and Arms of the Noblemen and Gentlemen of Great Britain and Ireland*, second series (London, 1855).

Burton, Robert, *The Anatomy of Melancholy* (Oxford, 1621), Ed. Holbrook Jackson (London and New York, 1972).

Cavendish, Margaret, Duchess of Newcastle, *Poems, and Fancies* (London, 1653).

– *Philosophicall Fancies* (London, 1653).

– *The World's Olio* (London, 1655, 1671).

– *The Philosophical and Physical Opinions* (London, 1655, 1663).

– *Natures pictures drawn by Fancies pencil to the life* (London, 1656).

– *Playes written by . . . the Lady Marchioness of Newcastle* (London, 1662).

– *Orations of Divers Sorts* (London, 1662).

– *CCXI Sociable Letters* (London, 1664).

– *Philosophical Letters: or, Modest Reflections . . .* (London, 1664).
– *Observations upon Experimental Philosophy . . . The Description of a New Blazing World* (London, 1666).
– *The Life of the thrice Noble, High and Puissant Prince William Cavendishe, Duke, Marquess and Earl of Newcastle, etc.* (London, 1667, 1675).
– *Grounds of Natural Philosophy* (London, 1668).
– *Plays, never before printed* (London, 1668).
– *Letters and Poems in Honour of the incomparable Princess, Margaret, Duchess of Newcastle* (London, 1676).
– *A True Relation of the Birth, Breeding and Life, of Margaret Cavendish, Duchess of Newcastle written by herself*, Ed. Sir Edgerton Brydges (Lees Priory Press, 1814).
– *Letters written by Charles Lamb's 'Princely Woman,' Margaret Lucas to her future husband, William Cavendish, Marquis, afterwards Duke of Newcastle, 1645*, Ed. R. W. Goulding (Roxburghe Club, 1909).
– *The Phanseys of William Cavendish, Marquis of Newcastle, addressed to Margaret Lucas and her Letters in reply*, Ed. Douglas Grant (London, 1956).
– *The Convent of Pleasure and Other Plays*, Ed. Anne Shaver (Baltimore and London, 1999).
Cavendish, William, Duke of Newcastle, *A Declaration made by the Earl of New-Castle [. . .] For his Resolution of Marching into YORKSHIRE* (York, 1642).
– *A Declaration and Summons sent by the Earl of Newcastle to the town of Manchester to lay down their arms* (London, 1643).
– *A Proclamation* (York, 1643).
– *The Country Captaine, and The Varietie, Two Comedies, Written by a Person of Honor* (London, 1649).
– *Méthode et Invention nouvelle de dresser les Chevaux* (Anvers, 1657–8).
– *A New Method, and Extraordinary Invention, to Dress Horses* (London, 1667).
– *The Humorous Lovers, A Comedy* (London, 1677).
– with Thomas Shadwell, *The Triumphant Widow, or the Medley of humours* (London, 1677).
– *A Pleasante & Merrye Humor off A Roge*, Ed. Francis Needham, Welbeck Miscellany No. 1 (Bungay, 1933).
– *A Collection of Poems by Several Hands*, Ed. Francis Needham, Welbeck Miscellany No. 2 (Bungay, 1934).
– *The Phanseys of William Cavendish, Marquis of Newcastle, addressed to Margaret Lucas, and her Letters in reply*, Ed. Douglas Grant (London, 1956).

– *Ideology and Politics on the Eve of Restoration: Newcastle's Advise to Charles II*, edited and introduced by Thomas P. Slaughter (Philadelphia, 1984).
– *A Declaration made by the Earl of Newcastle, with notes on the Civil War in Yorkshire*, Ed. S. Reid (London, 1987).
– *Dramatic Works, by William Cavendish*, Ed. Lynn Hulse, The Malone Society Reprints, Vol. 158 (Oxford, 1996).
Chamberlain, John, *The Letters of John Chamberlain*, Memoirs of the American Philosophical Society, Vol. 12.1 (Philadelphia, 1939).
Chamberlayne, Edward, *Anglie Notitia, or, The Present State of England* (London, fourth edn, 1670).
Chester, J. L., *The Marriage, Baptismal and Burial Registers of the . . . Abbey . . . of Westminster* (London, 1876).
Christie, Manson and Woods, Ltd, *Catalogue of Valuable Printed Books from the Titchfield Library at Welbeck Abbey* (London, 17th March, 1954).
Cleland, James, *The Institution of a Young Noble Man* (n.d., reissued in 1611 and 1612), Ed. Max Molyneux (New York, 1948).
Collins, Arthur, *Historical Collections of the Noble Families of Cavendishe, Holles, Vere, Harley and Ogle* (London, 1752).
Cooper, William Durrant (Ed.), *Savile Correspondence*, The Camden Society (London, 1858).
de Courtin, Antoine, *Rules of Civility* (London, 1678).
Cruso, John, *Militarie Instructions for the CAVALL'RIE* (1632), facsimile edition, Ed. Peter Young (Kineton, 1972).
van der Doort, Abraham, *Catalogue of the Collections of Charles I*, Ed. Oliver Millar, The Walpole Society, Vol. 37 (Glasgow, 1958–60).
Dugdale, Thomas, *England & Wales Delineated* (London, 1586).
Ellis, Clement, *A SERMON Preached on the 19th of May 1661 . . . Before His EXCELLENCY WILLIAM Ld MARQVIS of NEWCSTLE. at his House of WELBECK* (Oxford, 1661).
Ellis, Rev. W., *The Registers of Bothal with Hebburn, in the county of Northumberland* (Sunderland, 1901).
Evelyn, John, *A Character of England* (London, 1659).
– *Fumifugium, or the Inconvenience of the Aer and Smoak of London Dissipated* (London, 1661).
– *Acetaria* (London, 1699).
– *The Miscellaneous Writings of John Evelyn*, Ed. William Upcott (London, 1825).
– *The Diary of John Evelyn*, Ed. E. S. de Beer (Oxford, 1955).
Flecknoe, Richard, *Heroick Portraits* (London, 1660).
– *A Farrago of Several Pieces, being a supplement to his poems, characters, heroick portraits, etc.* (London, 1666).

– *Euterpe Revived* (London, 1675).
Fuller, Thomas, *The Worthies of England* (London, 1662).
Gaihard, Jean, *The Compleat Gentleman* (London, 1678).
Gedde, Walter, *Sundry Draughts Principally Serving for Glaziers and not Impertinent for Plasterers and Gardiners* (London, 1615–16).
Goltzius, Hendrik, *The Illustrated Bartsch, Netherlandish Artists, Hendrik Goltzius*, Ed. Walter L. Strauss (New York, 1982).
Gouge, William, *Of Domesticall Duties* (London, 1622).
Gray, John Hamilton, *Autobiography of a Scots County Gentleman* (n.d., privately printed).
Green, Mary A. E. (Ed.), *Letters of Queen Henrietta Maria* (London, 1857).
– (Ed.) *Calendar for the Proceedings of the Committee for Compounding, 1643–1660*, Part 3, 1647–June 1650 (London, 1891).
Grimston, Harbottle, *A Christian New-Year's Gift* (Cambridge, 1644).
Grose, Francis, *The Antiquities of England and Wales* (London, 1785–7).
Grose, Francis and Thomas Astle, *The Antiquarian Repertory* (London, 1807–9).
Guillemeau, Jacques, *Child-birth, or the happy deliverie of women* (London, 1612).
Halliwell, J. O. (Ed.), *A Collection of Letters Illustrative of the Progress of Science in England, from the reign of Queen Elizabeth to that of Charles the Second* (London, 1841).
Harrison, William, *The Description of England* (1587), Ed. Georges Edelen (Washington DC, 1968).
Hawkins, Francis (trans.), *Youths Behaviour* (London, 1654).
Hawkins, Henry, *Partheneia Sacra* (Rouen, 1633).
Hovenden, R. (Ed.), *The Register of the Christenings, Mariages and Burialles in the Parishe of St James Clarkenwell*, Harleian Society (London, 1885).
Howell, James, *Instructions for Forreine Travell* (London, 1642).
Hunter, Joseph, *Hallamshire, The History and topography of the parish of Sheffield*, Ed. Alfred Gatty, second edn (London, 1875).
Hutchinson, Lucy, *Memoirs of the Life of Colonel Hutchinson*, Ed. C. H. Firth (London, 1885); Ed. James Sutherland (Oxford, 1973).
Hyde, Edward, Earl of Clarendon, *The History of the Rebellion and Civil Wars in England*, Ed. W. D. Macray (Oxford, 1888).
Jonson, Ben, *Vnderwoods* (London, 1640).
– *Works*, Eds C. H. Herford and P. Simpson (Oxford, 1925–52).
King, Rev. R. J., *Warsop Parish Registers* (Mansfield, 1884).
Knoop, D. and G. P. Jones (Eds), 'The Bolsover Building Account, 1612–13,' *Arts Quatuor Coronatorum*, Vol. 36, Part 1 (London, 1936).
Knowler, William, *The Earl of Strafforde's Letters and Despatches* (London, 1739).

Langbaine, Gerard, *An Account of the English Dramatick Poets* (Oxford, 1691).
– *et al.*, *The Lives And Characters Of The English Dramatick Poets* (London, 1699).
Laud, Archbishop, *The Works of Laud*, Eds J. Blisse and W. Scott (Oxford, 1847–60).
Lindley, David (Ed.), *Court Masques, Jacobean and Caroline Court Entertainments, 1605–1640* (Oxford, 1995).
Markham, Francis, *The Booke of Honour* (London, 1625).
Markham, Gervase, *The English Hous-Wife* (London, 1664 edn).
Masére, Francis, *Select Tracts relating to the Civil Wars in England* (London, 1815).
Morrison, Fynes, *An Itinerary* (London, 1617).
Nichols, John, *Illustrations of the Manners and Expences of Antient Times in England in the Fifteenth Sixteenth and Seventeenth Centuries* (London, 1797).
– *The Progresses, Processions and Magnificent Festivities of King James the First* (London, 1828).
Nicholson, John, *Catalogue of the Printed Books in the Library of his Grace the Duke of Portland, at Welbeck Abbey, and in London* (London, 1893).
Noel, Nath., *Bibliotheca Nobilissimi Principis* JOHANNIS *Ducis de* Novo-Castro (London, 17th March, 1719).
Noorthouck, John, *A New History of London* (London, 1773).
North, Roger, *Of building, Roger North's writings on architecture*, Eds Howard Colvin and John Newman (Oxford, 1981).
Osborne, Dorothy, *Letters of Dorothy Osborne to William Temple*, Ed. G. C. Moore Smith (Oxford, 1928).
Overburie, Sir Thomas, *New and Choise Characters* (London, 1615).
Palladio, Andrea, *I Quattro Libri dell'Architettura* (Venice, 1570).
Partridge, John, *Good Huswives Closet* (London, 1584).
Peacham, Sir Henry, *The Compleat Gentleman* (London, 1622), Ed. G. S. Gordon (Oxford, 1906).
Pegge, Samuel, *Sketch of the History of Bolsover and Peak Castles*, Vol. 32 of *Bibliotheca Topographica Brittannica* (London, 1785).
Pepys, Samuel, *The Diary of Samuel Pepys*, Eds R. Latham and W. Matthews (London, 1970–6).
Percy, Henry, ninth Earl of Northumberland, *Advice to his Son* (1609), Ed. G. B. Harrison (London, 1930).
de Pluvinel, Antoine, *L'instruction du Roy en l'exercise de monter a cheval* (Paris, 1627).
Puttick and Simpson, Messrs, *Catalogue of Books from the Library of a*

*Noble Duke*, William Arthur Cavendish-Bentinck, sixth Duke of Portland (1857–1943) (10–11th August, 1885).
Roesslin, Eucharius, *Birth of Man-Kinde*, tr. Thomas Raynalde (London, 1604).
Rubens, Peter Paul, *Palazzi di Genova* (Antwerp, 1622), Ed. Heinz Schomann (Dortmund, 1982).
Rushworth, John, *Historical Collections* (London, Part 2, 1680; Part 3, 1691).
Rye, William Brenchley, *England as seen by foreigners* (London, 1865).
Sabbatini, Nicolà, *Pratica di fabricar scene e machine* (Ravenna, 1638).
Sanderson, Sir William, *A Compleat History of the life and raigne of King Charles fron his cradle to his grave* (London, 1658).
Sarpi, Paolo, *Lettere di Fra Paolo Sarpi*, Ed. F.-L. Polidori (Firenze, 1863).
Shute, John, *The Firste and Chiefe Groundes of Architecture* (1563), Ed. Lawrence Weaver (London, 1912).
Skinner, Thomas, *The Life of General Monk: Late Duke of Albemarle* (London, 1723).
Strafford, Thomas, *The Earl of Strafforde's Letters and Dispatches*, Ed. William Bowyer (London, 1739).
Strong, Arthur Sandford, *A catalogue of letters and other historical documents exhibited in the library at Welbeck* (London, 1903).
Stuart, Arbella, *The Letters of Lady Arbella Stuart*, Ed. Sarah Jane Steen (Oxford, 1994).
Symonds, Richard, *Diary of the Marches of the Royal Army*, Camden Society (London, 1859).
Thompson, Edward Maunde (Ed.), *Correspondence of the Family of Hatton*, Vol. 1 (Camden Society, 1878).
Thoroton, Robert, *The antiquities of Nottinghamshire, extracted out of records, original evidences, Leiger Books, other Manuscripts, and Authentick Authorities* (London, 1677).
Vaughan, R. (Ed.), *The Protectorate of Cromwell* (London, 1838).
Vernon, John, *The Young Horseman* (London, 1644).
Waldstein, Baron, *The Diary of Baron Waldstein*, Ed. G. W. Groos (London, 1981).
Walpole, Horace, *Anecdotes of Painting in England, with some Account of the principal Artists* (Strawberry Hill, 1762).
— 'Horace Walpole's Journals of Visits to Country Seats, &c.', Ed. Paget Toynbee, *The Walpole Society*, Vol. 16 (n.p., 1927–8).
Warburton, Eliot, *Memoirs and Correspondence of Prince Rupert and the Cavaliers* (London, 1849).
Warwick, Sir Philip, *Memoires of the Reigne of Charles I* (London, 1701).
Webster, W. F. (Ed.), *Nottinghamshire Heath Tax Returns 1664: 1674*, Thoroton Society Record Series, Vol. 37 (1988).

Wentworth, Sir William, *Advice to his son* (1604), in J. P. Cooper (Ed.), *Wentworth Papers 1597–1628*, Royal Historical Society Camden, Fourth Series, Vol. 12 (1973).

Whetstone, George, *A critical edition of George Whetstone's 1582 An Heptameron of Civill Discourses*, Ed. Diana Shlanka (New York and London, 1987).

White, Kennet, *Memoirs of the family of Cavendish* (London, 1708).

Woolley, Hannah, *The Compleat Servant-Maid, or, The Young Maidens Tutor* (London, 1677).

— *The Queen-like Closet* (1684).

Wotton, Henry, *The Elements of Architecture; collected by Henry Wotton, Knight, from the best authors and examples* (London, 1624; Farnborough, 1969).

Wright, Thomas, *The Passions of the Minde* (London, 1601).

## SECONDARY MATERIAL

Akkerman, Nadine and Marguérite Corporaal, 'Mad Science Beyond Flattery: The Correspondence of Margaret Cavendish and Constantijn Huygens', *Early Modern Literary Studies,* Special Issue 14 (May, 2004).

Anderson, Christy, 'Learning to Read Architecture in the English Renaissance', in *Albion's Classicism*, Ed. Lucy Gent (New Haven and London, 1995).

Airs, Malcolm, *The Making of the English Country House, 1500–1640* (London, 1975).

— 'The Designing of Five East Anglian Country Houses, 1505–1637', *Architectural History*, Vol. 21 (1978).

— *The Buildings of Britain: Tudor and Jacobean* (London, 1982).

— *The Tudor and Jacobean Country House: A Building History* (Stroud, 1995).

Anon., *English Heritage Battlefield Report: Marston Moor, 1644* (1995).

Anzilotti, Gloria Italiano, *An English Prince: Newcastle's Machiavellian Political Guide to Charles II* (Pisa, 1988).

Ashley, Maurice, *The English Civil War* (London, 1974).

Avery, Charles and Katherine Watson, 'Medici and Stuart: A Grand Ducal Gift of "Giovanni Bologna" Bronzes for Henry Prince of Wales (1612)', *The Burlington Magazine*, Vol. 115 (August, 1973).

Bailey, Thomas, *Annals of Nottinghamshire, A New and Popular History of the County of Nottingham* (London, 1853).

Barley, M., 'John Mazine and Manor Farm, Carburton', *The Transactions of the Thoroton Society of Nottinghamshire*, Vol. 92 (1988).

Barratt, John, *The Battle for York, Marston Moor, 1644* (Stroud, Gloucestershire, 2002).

Batho, Gordon (Ed.), *A Calendar of Shrewsbury and Talbot Papers at the College of Arms* (London, 1971).
— 'Gilbert Talbot, 7th Earl of Shrewsbury', *Journal of the Derbyshire Archaeological and Natural History Society*, Vol. 43 (1973).
Belcher, J. and M. E. Macartney, *Later Renaissance Architecture in England* (London, 1901).
Bibby, R., *Bothal Observed, a Survey of a Northumbrian Castle, Village and Church* (Newcastle upon Tyne, 1973).
Bickley, Francis, *The Cavendish Family* (London, 1911).
Bill, E. G. W. (Ed.), *A Calendar of Shrewsbury and Talbot Papers in the Lambeth Palace Library* (London, 1966).
Birch, Thomas, *The History of the Royal Society of London for Improving of Natural Knowledge, from its first rise* (London, 1756; New York and London, 1968).
Blyth, Derek, *Flemish Cities Explored* (London, 1990).
Bowles, John, *John Evelyn and His World* (London, 1981).
Boynton, Lindsay, 'William and Richard Gomm', *The Burlington Magazine*, Vol. 72 (June, 1980).
Bradbury, D. J., *Welbeck Abbey* (Mansfield, 1986).
— *Welbeck and the 5th Duke of Portland* (Mansfield, 1989).
Broadhead, Ivan E., *Yorkshire Battlefields* (London, 1989).
Brodhurst, Francis, 'Sir William Cavendish', *Journal of the Derbyshire Archaeological and Natural History Society*, Vol. 29 (1907).
Brown, Cedric, 'Courtesies of Place and Arts of Diplomacy in Ben Jonson's Last Two Entertainments for Royalty', *The Seventeenth Century*, Vol. 9, No. 2 (1994).
Brown, Peter, *In Praise of Hot Liquors* (York, 1995).
Bryson, Anna, *From Courtesy to Civility, Changing Codes of Conduct in Early Modern England* (Oxford, 1998).
Burke, John, *A Visitation of the Seats and Arms of the Noblemen and Gentlemen of Great Britain* (London, 1852).
Cerasano, S. P. and M. Wynne-Davies (Eds), *Renaissance Drama by Women: Texts and Documents* (London, 1996).
— (Eds), *Readings in Renaissance Women's Drama* (London, 1998).
Chaney, Edward, *The Grand Tour and the Great Rebellion* (Geneva, 1985).
Cliffe, J. T., *The World of the Country House in Seventeenth-Century England* (New Haven and London, 1999).
Cloake, John, *Palaces and Parks of Richmond and Kew* (Chichester, 1995).
Colvin, Howard (Ed.), *The History of the King's Works*, Vol. 2, 1066–1485 (London, 1963).
— (Ed.), *The History of the King's Works*, Vol. 3, 1485–1660 (London, 1975).

– *A Biographical Dictionary of British Architects, 1600–1840* (third edn, New Haven and London, 1995).
Condren, Conal, 'Casuistry to Newcastle: The Prince in the World of the Book', in Nigel Phillipson and Quentin Skinner (Eds), *Political Discourse in Early Modern Britain* (Cambridge, 1993).
Coope, Rosalys, 'The "Long Gallery": its origin, development, use and decoration', *Architectural History*, Vol. 29 (1986).
Corson, Richard, *Fashions in Hair* (London, 1980).
Cressy, David, *Birth, Marriage and Death* (Oxford, 1997).
Cromwell, T. K., *A history and description of the Parish of Clerkenwell* (London, 1828).
Crook, David, 'Clipstone Park and "Peel"', *Transactions of the Thoroton Society of Nottinghamshire*, Vol. 80 (1976).
Cunnington, C. Willett and Cunnington, Phillis, *The History of Underclothes* (London, 1951).
Cunnington, Phillis, *Costume of Household Servants* (London, 1974).
Cust, Richard, *The Forced Loan and English Politics, 1626–1628* (Oxford, 1987).
Cutts, J. P., 'When were the Senses in such order plac'd?' *Comparative Drama*, Vol. 4 (1970).
Deering, Charles, *Nottinghamia vetus et nova, or an Historical Account of the Ancient and Present state of the town of Nottingham* (Nottingham, 1751).
Depauw, Carl, *Rubens House, Antwerp* (Antwerp, 2000).
*Dictionary of National Biography* (Oxford, 2004).
Downman, Edward Andrews, *A History of Bolsover: its town, castle, Bethlehem etc.* (Derby, 1895).
Drage, Christopher, 'Nottingham Castle, a Place Full Royal', *Transactions of the Thoroton Society of Nottinghamshire*, Vol. 93 (1989).
Durant, David N., *Bess of Hardwick: A Portrait of an Elizabethan Dynast* (London, 1977, 1999).
Durant, David N. and Philip Riden (Eds), 'The Building of Hardwick Hall', *Derbyshire Record Society*, Vol. 4 (1980).
Edwards, Edward, *The Life of Sir W. Ralegh* (London, 1868).
Eiche, Sabine, 'Prince Henry's Richmond, the Project by Costantino de' Servi', *Apollo* (November, 1998).
Emberton, Wilfred, *The English Civil War Day by Day* (Stroud, 1995).
Erickson, Amy, *Women and Property in Sixteenth Century England* (London, 1993).
Esdaile, Katharine A., *English Church Monuments, 1510–1840* (London, 1946).
Evett, David, *Literature and the Visual Arts in Tudor England* (Athens, GA, and London, 1990).

Ezell, M. J. M., '"To Be Your Daughter in Your Pen": the Social Functions of Literature in the Writings of Lady Elizabeth Brackley and Lady Jane Cavendish', *Huntington Library Quarterly*, Vol. 51 (1988).
Falkus, Christopher, *The Life and Times of Charles II* (London, 1972).
Faulkner, Patrick, *Bolsover Castle* (Department of the Environment Official Guidebook, 1972).
Firth, C. H., 'Cavendish, William, Duke of Newcastle, 1592–1676', in *The Dictionary of National Biography*, Ed. Leslie Stephen, Vol. 9 (London, 1887).
Foulds, Trevor, '"This Greate House, So Lately Begun, and All of Freestone": William Cavendish's Italianate *Palazzo* Called Nottingham Castle', *Transactions of the Thoroton Society of Nottinghamshire*, Vol. 106 (2002).
Fowler, Alastair, *The Country House Poem* (Edinburgh, 1994).
Fraser, Antonia, *King Charles II* (London, 1979).
Fraser, H. and R. Hughes, *Historic Houses of Barbados* (Barbados, 1982).
Friedmann, Alice, *House and Household in Elizabethan England: Wollaton Hall and the Willoughby Family* (Chicago, 1989).
– 'Did England Have a Renaissance?' in *Cultural Differentiation and Cultural Identity in the Visual Arts*, Studies in the History of Art, No. 27, Eds Susan J. Barnes and Walter S. Melion (Hanover and London, 1989).
Fumerton, Patricia, *Cultural Aesthetics, Renaissance Literature and the Practice of Social Ornament* (Chicago and London, 1991).
Garrard, James, *A catalogue of the gold and silver plate, the property of His Grace the Duke of Portland* (Chiswick, 1893).
Gent, Lucy (Ed.), *Albion's Classicism, the Visual Arts in Britain, 1550–1660* (New Haven and London, 1995).
Girouard, Mark, 'The Smythson Collection of the RIBA', *Architectural History*, Vol. 5 (1962).
– *Robert Smythson and the Architecture of the Elizabethan Era* (London, 1966).
– 'Elizabethan Chatsworth', *Country Life* (22nd November, 1973), Vol. 154, pp. 1668–73.
– *Life in the English Country House* (New Haven and London, 1978).
– *Robert Smythson and the Elizabethan Country House* (New Haven and London, 1983, revised edn).
– 'Early Drawings of Bolsover Castle', *Architectural History*, Vol. 27 (1984).
Girouard, Mark and David N. Durant, *Hardwick Hall* (The National Trust, 1996).
Gittings, Clare, *Death, Burial and the Individual in Early Modern England* (London and Sydney, 1984).
Glanville, Philippa and Hilary Young (Eds), *Elegant Eating* (London, 2002).
Glover, S., *History of the County of Derby* (Derby, 1829).

Godfrey, Eleanor S., *The Development of English Glassmaking, 1560–1640* (Oxford, 1975).
Gordon, D. J., 'Poet and Architect: The Intellectual Setting of the Quarrel between Ben Jonson and Inigo Jones', *Journal of the Warburg and Courtauld Institutes*, Vol. 12 (1949).
Goulding, R. W., 'The Welbeck Abbey Miniatures belonging to His Grace the Duke of Portland, K.G. A catalogue raisonné', *The Walpole Society*, Vol. 4 (London, 1916).
— 'Henrietta, Countess of Oxford', *Transactions of the Thoroton Society of Nottinghamshire*, Vol. 27 (1923).
— *Margaret (Lucas) Duchess of Newcastle* (Lincoln, 1925).
— (rev. Adams), *Catalogue of the Pictures of the Duke of Portland* (London, 1936).
Grant, Douglas, *Margaret the First. A Biography of Margaret Cavendish, Duchess of Newcastle* (London, 1957).
Gray, John Hamilton, *Bolsover Castle* (Chesterfield, 1868, 1883, 1894).
de Groot, Jerome, *Royalist Identities* (Basingstoke, 2004).
Harding, G. R. and H. W., *Catalogue of the Ornamental Furniture, Works of Art and Porcelain at Welbeck Abbey* (London, 1897).
Harris, John, Stephen Orgel and Roy Strong, *The King's Arcadia: An Exhibition to Mark the Tercentenary of Inigo Jones* (London, 1973).
Harris, John and Gordon Higgott, *Inigo Jones, Complete Architectural Drawings* (London, 1980).
Harrison, Molly, *The Kitchen in History* (Reading, 1972).
Hart, Vaughan, *Art and Magic in the Court of the Stuarts* (London, 1994).
Hassall, W. O., 'The conventual buildings of St Mary Clerkenwell', *Transactions of the London and Middlesex Archaeological Society*, Old Series Vol. 14 (1940).
Hearn, Karen (Ed.), *Dynasties, Painting in Tudor and Jacobean England, 1530–1630* (London, 1995).
Henderson, Paula, 'A Shared Passion: The Cecils and Their Gardens', in Pauline Croft (Ed.), *Patronage, Culture and Power, The Early Cecils, 1558–1612* (London and New Haven, 2002).
— *The Tudor House and Garden* (London and New Haven, 2005).
Herrup, Cynthia, *A House in Gross Disorder: Sex, Law and the 2nd Earl of Castlehaven* (New York and Oxford, 1999).
Hill, C. P., *Who's Who in Stuart England* (London, 1988).
Hine, Thomas Chambers, *Nottingham, its Castle. A Military Fortress, a Royal Palace, A Ducal Mansion, Blackened Ruin, A Museum and Gallery of Art* (London, 1876).
Hole, Christina, *The English Housewife in the Seventeenth Century* (London, 1953).

Hope, Annette, *Londoners' Larder* (Edinburgh, 2005).
Hopkins, Lisa, 'Play houses: Drama at Bolsover and Welbeck', *Early Theatre*, Vol. 2 (1999).
Howard, Maurice, *The Early Tudor Country House: Architecture and Politics, 1490–1550* (London, 1987).
Howarth, David, *Lord Arundel and His Circle* (New Haven and London, 1985).
Hughes, Paul, 'Some Civil Engineering Notes from 1699', *Local Historian*, Vol. 26 (May, 1996).
Hulse, Lynn, 'Apollo's Whirligig: William Cavendish and his Music Collection', *The Seventeenth Century*, Vol. 9 (1994).
— '*The King's Entertainment* by the Duke of Newcastle', *Viator*, Vol. 26 (1995).
— 'The Duke of Newcastle and the English Viol', *Chelys, Journal of the Viola da Gamba Society*, Vol. 29 (2001).
Hunt, Tristram, *The English Civil War at First Hand* (London, 2002).
Hunter, Joseph, *Hallamshire. The History and Topography of the Parish of Sheffield*, Ed. A. Gatty (London, 1869).
Huvenne, P., *The Rubens House, Antwerpen* (Antwerp, 1990, 1997).
Jones, E. Alfred, *Catalogue of the Plate Belonging to the Duke of Portland . . . at Welbeck Abbey* (London, 1935).
Jones, Kathleen, *A Glorious Flame, the Life of Margaret Cavendish, Duchess of Newcastle, 1623–1673* (London, 1988).
Keen, Maurice, *Chivalry* (New Haven and London, 1984).
Kelliher, Hilton, 'Donne, Jonson, Richard Andrews and the Newcastle Manuscript', *English Manuscript Studies 1100–1700*, Eds Peter Beal and Jeremy Griffiths, Vol. 4 (London, 1993).
Kermode, Frank, 'The Banquet of Sense', *Shakespeare, Spenser, Donne: Renaissance Essays* (London, 1971).
Kettle, Pamela, *Oldcotes, the Last Mansion Built by Bess of Hardwick* (Cardiff, 2000).
Kirke, Henry, 'An Aristocratic Sqabble', *Journal of the Derbyshire Archaeological and Natural History Society*, Vol. 33 (1911).
Lees-Milne, James, *The Age of Inigo Jones* (London, 1953).
Letts, Malcolm, *As the Foreigner Saw Us* (London, 1935).
Lewalski, Barbara, *Writing Women in Jacobean England* (London, 1993).
Lindsay, Philip, *Hampton Court, A History* (London, 1948).
Lister, J. L. and W. Brown, 'Seventeenth Century Builders' Contracts', *Yorkshire Archaeological Journal*, Vol. 16 (1902).
Litten, Julian, *The English Way of Death* (London, 1991).
Llewellyn, Nigel, *The Art of Death, Visual Culture in the English Death Ritual, c.1500–c.1800* (London, 1991).

Lobel, M. and W. Johns, *The British Atlas of Historic Towns* (Oxford, 1989).
Longueville, T., *The First Duke and Duchess of Newcastle upon Tyne* (London, 1910).
MacCaffrey, Wallace T., 'Talbot and Stanhope: An Episode in Elizabethan Politics', *Bulletin of the Institute of Historical Research*, Vol. 33 (1960).
Macfarlane, Alan, *The Origins of English Individualism, The Family, Property and Social Transition* (Oxford, 1978).
Manpower Services Commission, 'Survey of Park and Garden at Hardwick', unpublished report for the National Trust (1986).
Marquiss, Richard, *The Nature of Nottinghamshire* (Buckingham, 1968).
McCoy, Richard C., *The Rites of Knighthood, The Literature and Politics of Elizabethan Chivalry* (Berkeley and London, 1989).
McGrath, Elizabeth, 'The Painted Decoration of Rubens' House', *Journal of the Warburg and Courtauld Institutes*, Vol. 41 (1978).
Mercer, Eric, 'The Houses of the Gentry', *Past and Present*, Vol. 5 (1954).
Merritt, F. (Ed.), *The Political World of Thomas Wentworth, Earl of Strafford, 1621–1641* (Cambridge, 1996).
Mertes, Kate, *The English Noble Household, 1250–1600, Good Governance and Politic Rule* (Oxford, 1988).
Miller, John, *Charles II* (London, 1991).
Mitchell, David, 'Banquet Napkins: Their Design, Ownership and Use, 1550–1650', CIETA, Bulletin 81 (2004).
Montégut, Emile, *Le Maréchal Davout – Le Duc et la Duchesse de Newcastle* (Paris, 1882).
Morrah, Patrick, *Prince Rupert of the Rhine* (London, 1976).
Mowl, Tim, *Tudor and Jacobean Style* (London, 1993).
— and Brian Earnshaw, *Architecture without Kings, the Rise of Puritan Classicism under Cromwell* (Manchester, 1995).
Muller, J. M., 'Rubens' Museum of Antique Sculpture: An Introduction', *Art Bulletin*, Vol. 59, No. 4 (1977).
Mullinger, J. B., *History of St John's College, Cambridge* (London, 1901).
Murray, Charles Fairfax, *Catalogue of the Pictures of His Grace the Duke of Portland, at Welbeck Abbey, and in London* (London, 1894).
Newman, Peter, *The Battle of Marston Moor* (Chichester, 1981).
Nicoll, Allardyce, *Stuart Masques* (New York, 1968).
Noorthouck, John, *A New History of London, including Westminster and Southwark* (London, 1773).
Olney, R. J., 'The Portland Papers', *Archives*, Vol. 19 (1989).
Orlin, Lena Cowan, *Private Matters and Public Culture in Post-Reformation England* (Ithaca and London, 1994).
Oswald, Arthur, 'A Sight-Seeing Tour in 1676', *Country Life*, Vol. 106 (1949).

Parkes, Joan, *Travel in England in the Seventeenth Century* (Oxford, 1925).
Parry, Graham, *The Golden Age Restor'd, the Culture of the Stuart Court, 1603–42* (Manchester, 1981).
— 'Cavendish Memorials', *The Seventeenth Century*, Vol. 9, No. 2 (1994).
Paston-Williams, Sara, *The Art of Dining* (The National Trust, 1993).
Peacock, John, 'Inigo Jones' Stage Architecture and Its Sources', *Art Bulletin*, Vol. 64, No. 2 (1982).
Pennant, Thomas, *Some Account of London, Westminster and Southwark* (London, fifth edn, 1813).
Peterson, Richard S., 'The Iconography of Jonson's *Pleasure Reconciled to Virtue*', *Journal of Medieval and Renaissance Studies*, Vol. 5 (1975)
Pevsner, Nikolaus, 'The Architecture of Mannerism', in H. Spencer (Ed.), *Readings in Art History*, Vol. 2 (1969).
Picard, Liza, *Restoration London* (London, 1997).
Pinks, William J., *The History of Clerkenwell*, Ed. Edward J. Wood (London, 1865).
Platt, Colin, *The Great Rebuildings of Tudor and Stuart England* (London, 1994).
Plumb, J. H. and H. Weldon, *Royal Heritage* (London, 1977).
Pope-Hennessy, John, 'Some Bronze Statuettes by Francesco Fanelli', *Burlington Magazine*, Vol. 95 (1953).
Porter, Roy, *London, A Social History* (London, 1994).
Porter, Stephen, *Destruction in the English Civil Wars* (Stroud, 1994).
Praz, Mario, *An Illustrated History of Interior Decoration* (London, 1964).
Raber, Karen L., '"Reasonable Creatures", William Cavendish and the Art of Dressage', in *Renaissance Culture and the Everyday*, Eds Patricia Fumerton and Simon Hunt (Penn, 1999).
Raylor, Timothy, '"Pleasure Reconciled to Virtue": William Cavendish, Ben Jonson and the Decorative Scheme of Bolsover Castle', *Renaissance Quarterly*, Vol. 52 (1999).
Raylor, Timothy and Jackson Bryce, 'A Manuscript Poem on the Royal Progress of 1634', *The Seventeenth Century*, Vol. 9, No. 2 (autumn, 1994).
Richards, Judith, '"His Nowe Majestie" and the English Monarchy', *Past and Present*, No. 113 (November, 1986).
Richardson, John, *The Annals of London* (Berkeley, 2000).
Rogers, Joseph, *The Scenery of Sherwood Forest* (London, 1908).
Round, J. H., 'The Origins of the Cavendishes', *Family Origins and Other Studies* (London, 1930).
Rowe, Nick, 'My Best Patron: William Cavendish and Jonson's Caroline Drama', *The Seventeenth Century*, Vol. 9, No. 2 (autumn, 1994).
Russell, Conrad, *The Causes of the English Civil War* (Oxford, 1987–8).

– 'The First Army Plot of 1641', *Transactions of the Royal Historical Society*, Series 5, Vol. 38 (1988).
– *The Fall of the British Monarchies, 1637–42* (Oxford, 1991).
Rye, W., *England as Seen by Foreigners* (London, 1865).
Sambrook, Pamela, *Country House Brewing in England, 1500–1900* (London, 1996).
Schittich, Christian and Gerald Staib, *Glass Construction Manual* (Basel, Switzerland, 1999).
Scott, Eva, *The Travels of the King, Charles II in Germany and Flanders, 1654–1660* (London, 1907).
Sealy, Lucy, *The Champions of the Crown* (London, 1911).
Seddon, P. R., 'The Nottinghamshire Elections for the Short Parliament of 1640', *Transactions of the Thoroton Society of Nottinghamshire*, Vol. 80 (1976).
– 'Major General Edward Whalley and the Government of Nottinghamshire, 1655–56', *Transactions of the Thoroton Society of Nottinghamshire*, Vol. 103 (1999).
Sharpe, Kevin, *The Personal Rule of Charles I* (New Haven and London, 1992).
Sharpe, Kevin and Peter Lake (Eds), *Culture and Politics in Early Stuart England* (Basingstoke and London, 1994).
Sheppard, Richard, 'Sutton Scarsdale Hall', unpublished report for English Heritage (1997).
Sherland, W. J., *The Birds of Sherwood Forest* (London, 1869).
Smith, Logan Pearsall, *The Life and Letters of Henry Wotton* (Oxford, 1907).
Smith, R. S., 'Glass-making at Wollaton in the Early Seventeenth Century', *Transactions of the Thoroton Society of Nottinghamshire*, Vol. LXVI (1962).
Smuts, R. Malcolm, *Court Culture and the Origins of a Royalist Tradition in Early Stuart England* (Philadelphia, 1987).
Stainton, L. and C. White (Eds), *Drawing in England from Hilliard to Hogarth* (British Museum, 1987).
Starkey, David (Ed.), *The English Court: From the Wars of the Roses to the Civil War* (London and New York, 1987).
Starr, N. C., '*The Concealed Fansyes,* A Play by Lady Jane Cavendish and Lady Elizabeth Brackley', *Proceedings of the Modern Languages Association,* Vol. 46 (1931).
Stone, Lawrence, *The Crisis of the Aristocracy* (Oxford, 1965).
– *The Family, Sex and Marriage in England, 1500–1800* (London, 1977).
Stoye, John, *English Travellers Abroad 1604–1667* (revised edn, London and New Haven, 1989).

Strickland, Agnes, *Lives of the Queens of England* (London, 1867).
Strong, Roy, *The Renaissance Garden in England* (London, 1979, 1998).
— *Henry, Prince of Wales and England's Lost Renaissance* (London, 1986).
Summerson, John, *Architecture in Britain, 1530–1830* (London, 1953; ninth edn, London and New Haven, 1993).
Swinscoe, David and Martine, *Swinscoe, Blore and the Bassetts* (Leek, Staffordshire, 1998).
Thompson, A. H., *The Premonstratensian Abbey of Welbeck* (London, 1938).
Thomson, Gladys Scott, *Life in a Noble Household, 1641–1700* (London, 1937 and 1965).
Thurley, Simon, *The Royal Palaces of Tudor England, Architecture and Court Life, 1460–1547* (New Haven and London, 1993).
— *Hampton Court* (London and New Haven, 2003).
Tijs, Rutger J., *P. P. Rubens en J. Jordaens, Barok in Eigen Huis* (Antwerp, 1983).
— *Renaissance en Barokarchitecture in België* (Tielt, Lanuso, 1999).
Toynbee, M. R., 'Views of Richmond Palace in the Reign of Charles I', *The Antiquaries Journal*, Vol. XXVIII (July–October 1948).
Trease, Geoffrey, *Nottingham, A Biography* (London, 1970).
— *A Portrait of a Cavalier* (London, 1979).
Turberville, Arthur Stanley, *A History of Welbeck Abbey and its Owners, 1539–1879* (London, 1938).
Walker, Elaine, 'The Duke of Newcastle and the Spanish Horse', *Andalusian: Dedicated to the Spanish and Portuguese Horse*, Issue 2 (2003).
Wall, Wendy, *Staging Domesticity* (Cambridge, 2002).
Wedgwood, C. V., *Thomas Wentworth, First Earl of Strafford, 1593–1641, A Revaluation* (London, 1961).
Wells-Cole, Anthony, 'Who was Walter Gedde?', *Furniture History*, Vol. 24 (1990).
— *Art and Decoration in Elizabethan and Jacobean England* (London and New Haven, 1997).
Whitaker, Katie, *Mad Madge: The Extraordinary Life of Margaret, Duchess of Newcastle, the First Woman to Live by Her Pen* (London, 2003).
Wilkinson, Catherine, 'The New Professionalism in the Renaissance', in *The Architect: Chapters in the History of the Profession*, Ed. Spiro Kostof (New York, 1977).
Wilson, Derek, *All the King's Women: Love, Sex and Politics in the Life of Charles II* (London, 2003).
Woodhouse, Adrian, 'Nottingham Castle', *Country Life* (27th July, 2000) pp. 70–5.
Woodward, Donald, *Men at Work. Labourers and Building Craftsmen in the Towns of Northern England, 1470–1750* (Cambridge, 1995).

Worden, Blair, *Stuart England* (Oxford, 1986).
Worsley, Giles, 'Schooling Movements', *Country Life* (4th October, 1990), Vol. 184, pp. 158–60.
— *The British Stable* (New Haven and London, 2004).
Worsley, Lucy, *Hardwick Old Hall* (English Heritage, 1998).
— 'A Set of Seventeenth Century Caesars from Bolsover Castle', *Collections Review*, English Heritage, Vol. 2 (1999).
— *Bolsover Castle* (English Heritage, 2000).
— 'Building a Family: William Cavendish, First Duke of Newcastle, and the Construction of Bolsover and Nottingham Castles', *The Seventeenth Century*, Vol. 19, No. 2 (autumn, 2004).
— 'A Bawdy Fountain at Bolsover Castle in the "Artisan Mannerist" Style', *Renaissance Studies*, Vol. 19, No. 1 (February, 2005).
— 'The Architectural Patronage of William Cavendish, First Duke of Newcastle', *Transactions of the Ancient Monuments Society*, Vol. 50 (2006).
Yeatman, J. P., 'Bassano's Church Notes. A Forgotten Fact of Derbyshire History', *Journal of the Derbyshire Archaeological and Natural History Society*, Vol. 16 (1894).
Young, Alan, *Tudor and Jacobean Tournaments* (London, 1987).

### *Unpublished Theses*

Anderson, Christy, 'Inigo Jones' Library and the Language of Architectural Classicism in England, 1580–1640', D.Phil. thesis, Massachusetts Institute of Technology (1993).
Dias, Jill, 'Politics and Administration in Nottinghamshire and Derbyshire 1590–1640', D.Phil. thesis, University of Oxford (1973).
Walker, Elaine, '"To Amaze People with Pleasure and Delight": An Analysis of the Horsemanship Manuals of William Cavendish, First Duke of Newcastle (1593–1676)', Ph.D. thesis, University of Birmingham (2005).
Wilks, T. V., 'The Court Culture of Prince Henry and His Circle 1603–1633', D.Phil, thesis, Oxford University (1987).

# Notes

## CHAPTER 1: A DEATHBED

1. This impression of the bedchamber is extrapolated from similar scenes of deathbeds such as that attributed to David des Granges, 'The Saltonstall Family' (*c.*1637), Tate Britain, London.
2. Such a shoehorn, dated 1594, was displayed at the Harley Gallery at Welbeck in 2005.
3. The physical descriptions of William and his father are based on the effigies on Sir Charles's tomb in Bolsover Church.
4. Margaret Cavendish, *The Life of the Thrice Noble, High and Puissant Prince William Cavendishe, Duke, Marquess and Earl of Newcastle, etc.* (London, 1667), pp. 150, 151.
5. University of Nottingham, Hallward Library, Department of Special Collections and Manuscripts, Pw V/26, f. 15r.
6. Bod. Clarendon MS 39, f. 155, R.W. (i.e. Mr Watson) to William Edgeman, Breda (22nd April, 1650); *CSPD, 1657–8*, Ed. M. A. E. Green (London, 1884), p. 300, Thomas Ross to Secretary Nicholas (24th February, 1658).
7. BL Thomason Tracts, E279 (6) (26th April, 1645).
8. Arthur Collins, *Historical Collections of the Noble Families of Cavendishe, Holles, Vere, Harley and Ogle* (London, 1752), p. 21.
9. Margaret Cavendish (1667), p. 142.
10. William Cavendish, *A New Method, and Extraordinary Invention, to Dress Horses* (London, 1667), p. 41.
11. Henry Wotton, *The Elements of Architecture* (London, 1624; Farnborough, 1969), p. 82.
12. HMC *Salisbury MSS*, Vol. 19 (1964), pp. 129–30.
13. John Evelyn, *The Diary of John Evelyn*, Ed. E. S. de Beer (Oxford, 1955), Vol. 3, p. 127.

14 The documents do not place Katherine and her younger son in the house on the day but their presence seems likely.
15 Francis Markham, *The Booke of Honour* (London, 1625), p. 48.
16 John Aubrey, *Aubrey's Brief Lives*, Ed. Oliver Lawson Dick (Bungay, Suffolk, 1972), pp. 216–17.
17 *Youths Behaviour*, tr. Francis Hawkins (London, 1654), p. 5. Anna Bryson, *From Courtesy to Civility, Changing Codes of Conduct in Early Modern England* (Oxford, 1998), led me to this and other books on courtesy.
18 Antoine de Courtin, *Rules of Civility* (London, 1671), p. 24.
19 Thomas Wright, *The Passions of the Minde* (London, 1601), p. 54.
20 UN Pw V/25, f. 141r.
21 UN Pw V/24, f. 40.
22 NA DDP.114.56 (1613); NA DDP.119.9 (1606); UN Pw V/25, f. 32, 'To the memory of his most faithful Servant and Cosen Mr Henry Ogle'; Bod. Rawlinson POET 16, 'On my good and true friend Mr Henry Ogle'.
23 NA DD4P.42.31 will (3rd August, 1632).
24 NA DDP.50.72; NA DD4P.52.140.
25 UN Pw 1/385.
26 NA DD3P.14.19 (1601).
27 It's not clear if he is already part of the household in 1617, but in 1619 he was knighted alongside William's younger brother Charles by James I during a royal visit to Welbeck. John Nichols, *The Progresses, Processions and Magnificent Festivities of King James the First* (London, 1828), Vol. 3, p. 560.
28 BL MS Add 70499, f. 252.
29 J. T. Cliffe, *The World of the Country House in Seventeenth-Century England* (New Haven and London, 1999), p. 132.
30 Cliffe (1999), p. 140.
31 BL Add MS 32454, ff. 46v–48r.
32 Sir William Wentworth, *Advice to his son* (1604), in J. P. Cooper (Ed.), *Wentworth Papers 1597–1628,* Royal Historical Society, Camden, Fourth Series, Vol. 12 (1973), p. 16.
33 UN Pw 1/432 (8th May, 1669).
34 UN Pw 1/621 (23rd December, 1671); UN Pw 1/315.
35 UN Pw V/25, f. 141v.
36 'A note of Seuerall Instruments and Setts of bookes Remaining in diuers roomes of the house, taken the 9th of Nouember. 1636', quoted in Lynn Hulse, 'The Duke of Newcastle and the English Viol', *Chelys, Journal of the Viola da Gamba Society*, Vol. 29 (2001).
37 UN Pw 1/331 (undated document, pre-1634).

38 NA DDP.8.107 (14th January, 1617); marriage of 'Mr Henry Lukin and Katherine Jessopp Decemb. 22' (1618), register of Worksop Priory.
39 Henry Thoroton, *The Antiquities of Nottinghamshire*, additions by J. Throsby (1790–7), Vol. 3, p. 371; Rev. R. J. King, *Warsop Parish Registers* (Mansfield, 1884), p. 7.
40 NA DDP.15.50 (4th October, 1615); NA DD2P.28.379 (1629).
41 There is no evidence that John is present, but it seems likely.
42 Lynn Hulse, 'Apollo's Whirligig: William Cavendish and his Music Collection', *The Seventeenth Century*, Vol. 9 (1994), pp. 213–46, quoting Lambeth Palace Library, MS 3203, f. 574.
43 Quoted in Hulse (1994), p. 216.
44 *Ibid.*
45 'A note of Seuerall Instruments and Setts of bookes Remaining in diuers roomes of the house, taken the 9th of Nouember. 1636', quoted in Hulse (2001).
46 UN Pw V/25, f. 15v.
47 UN Pw V/90, f. 60.
48 NA DD4P.42.31, will (3rd August, 1632) and probate (5th August, 1636).
49 Quoted in Phillis Cunnington, *Costume of Household Servants* (London, 1974), p. 23.
50 UN Pw 1/672.
51 Quoted in Cliffe (1999), p. 150.
52 This is the figure given for the income of the Cavendish estates just before the start of the Civil War by Margaret Cavendish (1667), p. 98.
53 Quoted in Alice Friedman, *House and Household in Elizabethan England* (Chicago, 1989), p. 44.
54 *Ibid.*, p. 42.
55 Sir Thomas Overburie, *New and Choise Characters* (London, 1615), pp. D3–D4.
56 Cliffe (1999), p. 86.
57 NA DD6P.1.19.10 (27th March, 1617).
58 Julian Litten, *The English Way of Death* (London, 1991), p. 13.
59 Cliffe (1999), p. 84.
60 Lambeth Palace Library, Talbot Papers MS 694, f. 90, Charles Cavendish to Henry Butler (16th February, 1610).
61 *Ibid.*, MS 702, f. 47.
62 Collins (1752), p. 21.
63 *Calendar of the Manuscripts of the Marquis of Salisbury at Hatfield House*, Vol. 9, London (1902), p. 229.
64 Lambeth Palace Library, Talbot Papers, MS 709, f. 33, from Welbeck (8th December, 1599).

65 Margaret Cavendish (1667), p. 4.
66 *Ibid.*, p. 134.
67 Poem by Ben Jonson engraved on Sir Charles's monument in Bolsover Church. Sir Charles's actual death will take place in April, 1617.
68 Graham Parry, 'Cavendish Memorials', *The Seventeenth Century*, Vol. 9, No. 2 (autumn, 1994), p. 278.

CHAPTER 2: A BUILDING SITE

1 Sir Charles and William cannot be placed for certain at the building site on 12th June, 1613, though it is likely that they would have paid visits throughout the summer to see progress. The fact that on this day the accounts show that John Smithson received a special gift of three shillings on top of his expenses suggests that such a progress visit took place today.
2 The household at Welbeck arises at six, more than an hour later than the menial labourers. I have assumed that John Smithson, although no longer living in the household, still rises at six, has breakfasted and made his ten-mile journey from Kirkby-in-Ashfield to Bolsover.
3 BL Harleian 4955, f. 201r, Ben Jonson, 'The King and Queene's entertainement at Boulsover in July 1634'.
4 Sir Bernard Burke, *A Visitation of the Seats and Arms of the Noblemen and Gentlemen of Great Britain and Ireland*, second series (London, 1855), Vol. I, p. 167.
5 On 4th October, 1615, John Smithson is granted the lease on Lunnes Farm, Kirkby-in-Ashfield (NA DDP 15/50), a property already in his tenure. He has presumably been living there since the start of work at Bolsover.
6 BL Harleian MS 4955, f. 199v.
7 Malcolm Airs, *The Tudor and Jacobean Country House, A Building History* (Stroud, 1995), p. 73.
8 *Ibid.*, p. 46.
9 John Smithson's drawings are in the Royal Institute of British Architects Drawings Collection and are reproduced in Mark Girouard, 'The Smythson Collection of the RIBA', *Architectural History*, Vol. 5 (1962).
10 Airs (1995), p. 171.
11 *Ibid.*
12 My reason for assuming this is that the quarry masons are the first to be listed in the accounts.
13 The Stone Centre and the stone-yard tours run by the National Trust at Hardwick Hall provide useful details about a mason's work.
14 Airs (1995), p. 113.
15 *Ibid.*, p. 47.

16 *Ibid.*, p. 154.
17 *Ibid.*, p. 180.
18 *Ibid.*, p. 188.
19 *Ibid.*, p. 51.
20 Anthony Wells-Cole, 'Who was Walter Gedde?' *Furniture History*, Vol. 24 (1990), pp. 183–6.
21 Airs (1995), p. 93.
22 NA DD.6P.1.25.3, 'A Booke of the Buyldinge Charges At Boulsover the yeare of oure Lorde God : 1613 : Begininge the : 2 : of November : 1612 :', reproduced as D. Knoop and G. P. Jones (Eds), 'The Bolsover Building Account, 1612–13', *Arts Quatuor Coronatorum*, Vol. 36, part 1 (London, 1936).
23 Airs (1995), p. 187.
24 NA DDP.65.32; DDP.65.34.
25 Knoop and Jones (1936), p. 15.
26 *Ibid.* I'm grateful to Mark Askey for the information about the location of the limekiln.
27 Donald Woodward, *Men at Work. Labourers and Building Craftsmen in the Towns of Northern England, 1470–1750* (Cambridge, 1995), p. 237.
28 *Ibid.*, p. 241.
29 Knoop and Jones (1936), p. 49.
30 Woodward (1995), p. 209.
31 *Ibid.*, p. 216.
32 Airs (1995), p. 193.
33 Knoop and Jones (1936), p. 23.
34 John Bold, *John Webb* (Oxford, 1989), p. 168.
35 Airs (1995), p. 114.
36 *Ibid.*, p. 120.
37 Knoop and Jones (1936), p. 32.
38 NA DD.2P.24.73 (second fortnight in May, 1667).
39 There is no evidence for this, but Christopher Wren had a 'closet' in the site compound during the building of Hampton Court, and it seems likely that Smithson had one too.
40 Airs (1995), p. 3.
41 Walter Gedde, *Sundry Draughts Principally Serving for Glaziers and not Impertinent for Plasterers and Gardiners* (London, 1615–16).
42 Eleanor S. Godfrey, *The Development of English Glassmaking, 1560–1640* (Oxford, 1975), p. 207.
43 Airs (1995), p. 127; R. S. Smith, 'Glass-making at Wollaton in the Early seventeenth Century', *Transactions of the Thoroton Society of Nottinghamshire,* Vol. LXVI (1962), pp. 24–34.

44 Smith (1962), p. 25.
45 Christian Schittich and Gerald Staib, *Glass Construction Manual* (Basel, Switzerland, 1999), p. 10.
46 The top floor of the Little Castle is completed with brick instead of masonry.
47 NA DD3P.14.19.
48 NA DD6P.1.25.3, Period 2 (24th December, 1612 to 23rd January, 1613). The accountant records that this brickman was given 2s. 6d. 'by master per me' rather than by the accountant on his own initiative, as is usually the case, so possibly Mr Lukin, Sir Charles ('master') and the brickman were all present for a site meeting.
49 There is a 'brick house' and a 'tyle kiln' at Welbeck, where brick is much more dominant in the construction than at Bolsover, by 1652. NA DD6P.1.18.22.
50 Airs (1995), pp. 115–7.
51 RIBA Drawings Collection, The Smythson Collection, III/1 (3); III/1 (11–14).
52 Written in the margin of Horace Walpole's edition of Collins (1752), BL pressmark 1322.ff.8.
53 Quoted in David Durant, *Bess of Hardwick* (London, 1977 and 1999), p. 30.
54 Durant (1999), p. 32.
55 UN Pw 1/315.
56 Margaret Cavendish (London, 1667), p. 3.
57 Quoted in Durant (1999), p. 142.
58 *Ibid.*, pp. 77–8.
59 Chatsworth House, Hardwick MS 8, Household accounts (1600).
60 Anthony Wells-Cole, *Art and Decoration in Elizabethan and Jacobean England* (New Haven and London (1997), p. 266.
61 H. Fraser and R. Hughes, *Historic Houses of Barbados* (Barbados, 1982) p. 16.
62 Airs (1995), p. 31.
63 James Cleland, *The Institution of a Young Noble Man* (n.d., reissued in 1611 and 1612), Ed. Max Molyneux (New York, 1948), pp. 91–2.
64 Wotton (1624), pp. 11–12.
65 HMC, *Salisbury MSS* (London, 1964), Vol. 19, p. 129 (3rd May, 1607).
66 *Ibid.*, pp. 129–30.
67 John Harris, Stephen Orgel and Roy Strong, *The King's Arcadia. Inigo Jones and the Stuart Court* (London, 1973), p. 43; Sabine Eiche, 'Prince Henry's Richmond: The Project by Costantino de' Servi', *Apollo* (November, 1998), pp. 10–14.
68 HMC, *Salisbury MSS*, Vol. 19, pp. 129–30.

69 Thomas Fuller, *The Worthies of England* (1662), p. 280, quoted in Girouard (1978), p. 108.
70 Ben Jonson, *Oberon, the faery Prince* (1611), quoted in John Harris, Stephen Orgel and Roy Strong, *The King's Arcadia: Inigo Jones and the Stuart Court* (London, 1973), p. 48.
71 Margaret Cavendish (1667), p. 142.
72 Lambeth Palace Library, MS 709, f. 33, Thomas Coke to [the Countess of Shrewsbury] from Welbeck (8th December, 1599).
73 Margaret Cavendish (1667), p. 141.
74 *Ibid.*; BL Harleian MS 6988, f. 111v.
75 Aubrey (1972), p. 218.
76 BL Harleian MS 4955, f. 82v, verses by Dr Andrews.
77 BL Add MS 70499, f. 220.
78 BL Stowe MS 172, f. 224v, Sir Henry Wotton to an unnamed lord, Amiens (28th March, 1612).
79 Bod. Clarendon MS 109, p. 70.
80 Thomas Birch (Ed.), *The Court and Times of James I, illustrated by authentic and confidential letters* (London, 1848), Vol. 1, p. 163.
81 Bod. Ashmole MS 1729, f. 220v, Wotton to the Earl of Salisbury, Luniburge (probably 9th May, 1612) (damaged).
82 BL Stowe MS 172, f. 224, Wotton to Sir Thomas Edmondes (28th March, 1612), quoted in Smith (1907), Vol. 2, p. 1.
83 HMC, *10th Report, Appendix 1, on the Manuscripts of G. Wingfield Digby, Esq., of Sherborne* (London, 1885), p. 582, Dudley Carleton to John Digby (11th May, 1612).
84 *C. S. P. Venetian* (London, 1905), Vol. 12, p. 363.
85 Bod. Ashmole MS 1729, f. 221 (9th May, 1612).
86 Margaret Cavendish (1667), p. 148.
87 *C. S. P. Venetian* (London, 1905), Vol. 12, p. 374.
88 Smith (1907), quoting Fabrizio Mei, from Cologne (14th July, 1612) to the government of Lucca.
89 Margaret Cavendish (1667), p. 4.
90 See Christie, Manson and Woods Ltd., *Catalogue of Valuable Printed Books from the Titchfield Library at Welbeck Abbey Sold by Order of His Grace the Duke of Portland, K.G.* (London, 17th March, 1954), lot 176.
91 Cleland (1612), pp. 91–2.
92 Wotton (1625), p. 53.
93 *Ibid.*, p. 51.
94 I am grateful to Mark Askey for pointing this out.
95 Airs (1995), p. 7.
96 RIBA Drawings Collection, The Smythson Collection, III/7 (1).
97 Wotton (1624), p. 98.

98 David Evett, *Literature and the Visual Arts in Tudor England* (Athens, Georgia and London, 1990), p. 137.
99 Christy Anderson, 'Learning to Read Architecture in the English Renaissance', in Lucy Gent (Ed.), *Albion's Classicism, The Visual Arts in Britain, 1550–1660* (New Haven and London, 1995), pp. 263, 269.
100 TNA SP.29.246.145, Mr Thomas Povey to Williamson (25th September, 1668). It's not clear whether Povey was visiting Welbeck Abbey or Bolsover Castle.

CHAPTER 3: IN A CLOSET

1 BL Add MS 70499, f. 199.
2 The Mansfield carrier was named 'ffleteger' in 1656, UN Pw 1/242.
3 W. J. Sherland, *The Birds of Sherwood Forest* (London, 1869), pp. 13, 145.
4 Robert Thoroton, quoted in Richard Marquiss, *The Nature of Nottinghamshire* (Buckingham, 1968), p. 25.
5 Joseph Rogers, *The Scenery of Sherwood Forest* (London, 1908), p. 295.
6 William Cavendish (1667), p. 94.
7 The earliest mention of John Mazine is in 1632, when he is described as 'Of Welbeck, gent', NA DD2P.28.126. I have taken the liberty of imagining him in the household seven years earlier.
8 Margaret Cavendish (1667), p. 67.
9 William Cavendish (1667), p. 182.
10 Margaret Cavendish (1667), p. 151.
11 I'm particularly grateful to Elaine Walker for her help with this passage.
12 UN Pw V/25, f. 141v.
13 Quoted in Friedman (1989), p. 48.
14 Description of the door based upon the surviving seventeenth-century doors at Bolsover Castle.
15 UN Pw V/25, f. 141v.
16 Quoted in Friedman (1989), p. 48.
17 NA burials, 1637, transcript of the registers of the parish of Norton Cuckney.
18 Andrew Boorde, *The Breviary of Healthe* (n.p., 1552), f. xliir.
19 UN Pw V/25, f. 143r, 'Of Buttlers'.
20 Pamela Sambrook, *Country House Brewing in England* (London, 1996), p. 48.
21 UN Pw V/25, f. 141r.
22 Molly Harrison, *The Kitchen in History* (1972), p. 28.
23 UN Pw V/25, f. 68.
24 *Ibid.*
25 E. Alfred Jones, *Catalogue of Plate Belonging to the Duke of Portland . . . at Welbeck Abbey* (London, 1935), p. 84.

26 Northumberland Record Office, MS ZAN M15/A 23bi, pp. 65–6.
27 Sir Thomas Overburie, *New and Choise Characters* (London, 1615), 'A Foote-man'.
28 De Courtin (1678), p. 20.
29 Elizabeth is shown as a tiny woman in her portrait by William Larkin: the chair beside her appears to be enormous, and she is much smaller than the other ladies of the Howard family in Larkin's series. Elizabeth was a member of the Howard family by her first marriage. See J. Jacob and J. Simon, *The Suffolk Collection, Catalogue of Paintings* (London, 1974).
30 R. W. Goulding, *Catalogue of the Pictures Belonging to His Grace the Duke of Portland*, revised by C. K. Adams (Cambridge, 1936), No. 364.
31 NA DD6P.1.19.18, Lady Katherine's will.
32 One of these was exhibited at the Harley Gallery in 2005.
33 This survives in a private collection.
34 Durant (1999), p. 4.
35 Cliffe (1999), p. 192.
36 Notes from David Swinscoe, historian of Blore, Staffordshire.
37 *Ibid.*
38 Henry Howard dies in September, 1616, and is buried on 11th October. James Howard, Elizabeth's first son, is buried 24th December, 1616 (Blore Parish Register).
39 Girouard (1978), p. 56.
40 Parry (1994), p. 285.
41 RIBA Drawings Collection, The Smythson Collection, II/13, design for a closet or business room.
42 John Aubrey, *Aubrey's Brief Lives*, Ed. Dick Oliver Lawson (Bungay, Suffolk, 1972), pp. 216–17.
43 Hulse (2001).
44 Girouard (1978), p. 135.
45 Colin Platt, *The Great Rebuildings of Tudor and Stuart England* (London, 1994), p. 98.
46 BL Add MS 70499, f. 196.
47 UN Pw V/25, f. 17.
48 Edward Chamberlayne, *Anglie Notitia, or, The Present State of England* (London, fourth edn, 1670), p. 475.
49 *Ibid.*, pp. 478–9.
50 Friedman (1989), p. 47.
51 NA DD6P.1.19.26.
52 Friedman (1989), p. 47; UN Pw 1/672.
53 We don't know the details of how Elizabeth's bedchamber is furnished in 1625, as its first inventory dates from after her death. In 1662, 'the

Ould Lady of Newcastle Chambr' contains a feather bed, bolster, quilt and rug, UN Pw 1.595.

54 Girouard (1978), p. 94.
55 C. Willett and Phillis Cunnington, *The History of Underclothes* (London, 1951), p. 36.
56 Hannah Woolley, *The Compleat Servant-Maid* (London, 1677), p. 72.
57 UN Pw 1/24, f. 25r.
58 De Courtin (1678), p. 45.
59 UN Pw 1/30–31 (1666).
60 UN Pw V/90, f. 4v.
61 Jacques Guillemeau, *Child-birth, or the happy deliverie of women* (London, 1612).
62 Tim Mowl, *Tudor and Jacobean Style* (London, 1993), pp. 184–5.
63 John Bowles, *John Evelyn and his World* (1981), p. 84; UN Pw V/90, f. 116v.
64 UN Pw 1/395 (1654).
65 Worden (1986), p. 243.
66 UN Pw V/25, f. 83v.
67 BL Harleian 4955, f. 48r.
68 Eucharius Roesslin, *Birth of Man-Kinde*, tr. Thomas Raynalde (London, 1604), pp. 154, 153.
69 Guillemeau (1612), p. 99.
70 BL Harleian 4955, ff. 49v–50r; Guillemeau (1612); James Knowles, pers. commun.
71 David Cressy, *Birth, Marriage and Death* (Oxford, 1997), p. 86.
72 *Ibid.*
73 BL Harleian 4955, ff. 48r–48v.
74 Guillemeau (1612), p. 99.
75 BL Add MSS 70499, f. 93, 'Whitehall this 21 of Aprill' (1620?).
76 UN Pw V/25, ff. 21r–22v.
77 NA DD.P6.1.19.26.

CHAPTER 4: A MASQUE

1 It is not completely certain where William Cavendish slept on the night of the 29th, but it seems more than likely that he is already at Bolsover preparing to receive his royal guests. If this is correct, he will be using the tiny but luxurious bedroom prepared by his father in the Little Castle.
2 UN Pw V/26, f. 90v, 'Day-breake'.
3 The hangings must have covered the areas left undecorated.
4 Margaret Cavendish (1667), p. 151.
5 Sara Paston-Williams, *The Art of Dining* (The National Trust, 1993), p. 157.

6 BL Harleian MS 4955, f. 82: 'When Bolser Castle I doe name,/ Mee thinkes Newcastle is the same:/ Bolser a Castle is, and newe;/ which shewes Newcastle is your dewe', by Richard Andrews.
7 UN Pw 1/25, ff. 64–5.
8 Nick Rowe, 'My Best Patron: William Cavendish and Jonson's Caroline Drama', *The Seventeenth Century*, Vol. 9, No. 2 (autumn, 1994).
9 Ian Donaldson, 'Jonson, Benjamin (1572–1637)', *Oxford Dictionary of National Biography* (Oxford, 2004).
10 *Ibid.*
11 BL Add MS 4955, f. 203.
12 *Ibid.*, quoted in Hilton Kelliher, 'Donne, Jonson, Richard Andrews and The Newcastle Manuscript', in Peter Beal and Jeremy Griffiths (Eds), *English Manuscipt Studies*, Vol. 4 (1993), p. 134.
13 BL Harleian 4955; Richard Flecknoe, *A Farrago of Several Pieces* (London, 1666).
14 BL Add MS 70499, f. 202 (13th/23rd June, 1636); f. 212 (16th October, 1636); f. 214 (26th October, 1636).
15 Ben Jonson, *The New Inn*, I.1.29, quoted by Nick Rowe, 'My Best Patron: William Cavendish and Jonson's Caroline Dramas', *The Seventeenth Century*, Vol. IX, No. 2 (autumn, 1994), p. 205.
16 UN Pw V/26, f. 162.
17 William Cavendish's preface to Margaret Cavendish, *Philosophical and Physical Opinions* (London, 1655, 1663).
18 BL Add MS 70499, f. 184 (25th August, 1635).
19 BL Harleian 4955, f. 202v.
20 *Ibid.*, f. 203.
21 *Ibid.*
22 John Rushworth, *Historical Collections, Part 2* (London, 1680), Vol. 1, p. 283.
23 William Knowler (Ed.), *The Earl of Strafforde's Letters and Dispatches* (London, 1739), pp. 101–2, the Earl of Newcastle to the Lord Deputy, Welbeck (5th August, 1633).
24 Rushworth (1680), p. 283.
25 Fynes Morrison, *An Itinerary*, London (1617), Part 3, Book 3, p. 150.
26 Knoop and Jones (1936), p. 53.
27 UN Pw 1/672; Paston-Williams (1993), pp. 156–7.
28 BL Add MS 70500, f. 6; NA DD.4P.63.40.
29 UN Pw V/24, f. 38.
30 Gervase Markham, *The English Hous-Wife* (London, 1664 edn), p. 186.
31 *Ibid.*, p. 187.
32 William Harrison, *The Description of England* (1587), Ed. Georges Edelen (Washington DC, 1968), p. 133.

33 NA DDP.106.1.

34 In 1636, John Yeates, another 'cooke att Welbeck', is buried in the parish church of Norton Cuckney, and in 1663, a Phillip Yates 'From Welbeck' is also buried there (Transcript of the Registers of the Parish of Norton Cuckney, NA). William Yates's farm was in the village of Thorpe, near Blore, in Staffordshire, so he presumably followed Elizabeth Bassett to Welbeck on her marriage in order to serve her as a cook and returned to his birthplace for his retirement.

35 UN Pw V/26, f. 162.

36 Hulse (2001).

37 NA DD2P.24.73, f. 102 (NB this evidence dates from the 1660s).

38 Although it dates from much later, we do know that the household's bedding inventory accords feather beds, bolsters and blankets to the kitchen boys and scullery maid (UN Pw 1/595), and NA DD2P.24.73, f. 115, refers to Goodwife Lemon (NB this evidence dates from the 1660s).

39 Overburie (1615), 'A French Cooke'.

40 Knoop and Jones (1936), pp. 25–7; Harrison (1972), p. 23.

41 RIBA Drawings Collection, The Smythson Collection, III/I 14; the drawing is included among others for Bolsover Castle.

42 Harrison (1972), p. 22.

43 Knoop and Jones (1936), pp. 31–3.

44 NA DDP.50/37; Rev. Hamilton Gray, *Bolsover Castle* (Chesterfield, 1894), p. 38.

45 It will be rediscovered during the remaking of the road running up from Shuttlewood in the early twentieth century.

46 This description of the Cistern House is based on investigation and analysis by Richard Sheppard, Trent and Peak Archaeological Unit.

47 David N. Durant and Philip Riden (Eds), 'The Building of Hardwick Hall', *Derbyshire Record Society*, Vol. 4 (1980), p. xx, quoting Chatsworth Archives, Hardwick MS 6, f. 25v.

48 UN Pw 1/5.

49 UN Pw 1/672.

50 *Ibid.*

51 NA DD6P.1.27.2 (February, 1630); UN Pw V/25, f. 68v.

52 Gilbert, Earl of Shrewsbury to John Harpur (30th March, 1603), quoted in Joseph Hunter, *Hallamshire. The History and Topography of the Parish of Sheffield*, Ed. A. Gatty (London, 1869), p. 93.

53 Warwickshire Record Office, CR 136.B.2453, a list of fowl served at William's entertainment for Charles I (1634).

54 Harrison (1972), p. 32.

55 UN Pw 1/671.2; UN Pw 1/672.

56 Harrison (1972), p. 31.

57 UN Pw V/25, f. 68v.
58 Cliffe (1999), p. 151.
59 Knoop and Jones (1936), p. 44.
60 UN Pw 1/669.
61 Philip Lindsay, *Hampton Court, A History* (London, 1948), p. 92.
62 Paula Henderson, 'A Shared Passion: The Cecils and their Gardens', in Pauline Croft (Ed.), *Patronage, Culture and Power, The Early Cecils, 1558–1612* (London and New Haven, 2002), p. 99.
63 John Chamberlain, quoted in Airs (1995), p. 6.
64 Lucy Worsley, 'A bawdy fountain at Bolsover Castle in the "artisan mannerist" style', *Renaissance Studies*, Vol. 19, No. 1 (February, 2005).
65 NA DD.6P.58.75a (albeit much later) includes wages for 'women for weeding the Camomil walke [. . .] 6 dayes'; 'the Terrass Walls to be kept as formerly with Honey suckles & sweet Briar and Jessamin', UN Pw 2/651 (10th October, 1704).
66 Cliffe (1999), p. 160.
67 RIBA Drawings Collection, The Smythson Collection, III/1 (11).
68 When English Heritage restored the fountain to working order in 2000, the technical difficulties were almost insuperable. It was the engineers' opinion that the fountain must never have played satisfactorily.
69 This stage direction only appears in the printed edition of the text: Ben Jonson, *Works*, Vol. 3 (London, 1641), 'The Under-wood', p. 283.
70 Allardyce Nicoll, *Stuart Masques* (New York, 1968), p. 38.
71 *Ibid.*, p. 67.
72 Agnes Strickland, *Lives of the Queens of England* (London, 1867), p. 385.
73 In recent years, much building work has been in progress at Bolsover, including the construction of a vast range of state apartments extending southwest from the Little Castle along the bluff. The rate of progress of the works (under John Smithson's supervision) is hard to untangle, but there are reasons to believe that the new gallery and state bedchamber there are not yet complete. Girouard (1983), p. 266.
74 Dr Rosalys Coope discovered that a set of printed engravings (by Pieter Jode [1570–1634] after paintings by Marten de Vos [1532–1603]) provided William's painters in the ante-room at Bolsover with their ideas and figures for these scenes. She was kind enough to lend me her notes.
75 This interpretation of events comes from Tim Raylor: '"Pleasure Reconciled to Virtue": William Cavendish, Ben Jonson, and the Decorative Scheme of Bolsover Castle', *Renaissance Quarterly*, Vol. 52 (1999), pp. 402–39.
76 Lucy Worsley, 'Building a Family: William Cavendish, First Duke of Newcastle, and the Construction of Bolsover and Nottingham Castles', *The Seventeenth Century*, Vol. 19, No. 2 (autumn, 2004), pp. 233–59.

77 Quoted in Airs (1995), p. 6.
78 T. Slaughter (Ed.), *Ideology and Politics on the Eve of Restoration: Newcastle's Advice to Charles II* (Philadelphia, 1984), p. 64.
79 Overburie (1615), p. E3.
80 Margaret Cavendish (1667), pp. 149–50.
81 Bod. MS Rawlinson POET. 16, 'a songe'.
82 Sir Philip Warwick, *Memoires of the Reigne of Charles I* (London, 1701), p. 236; Edward Hyde, Earl of Clarendon, *The History of the Rebellion and Civil Wars in England*, Ed. W. D. Macray (Oxford, 1988), Vol. III, p. 383.
83 UN Pw 1/74.
84 UN Pw V/25, f. 140r.
85 UN Pw V/26, f. 114. Cecily Manners (born Tufton) married Francis, sixth Earl of Rutland some time after 1608, had two children and died a widow in 1653. Leslie Stephen (Ed.), *The Dictionary of National Biography* (Oxford, 1885–90), Vol. 12, p. 934.
86 The stage directions for Jonson's masque fail to describe exactly where the feast took place, but it would be normal for the Great Chamber to be used.
87 Harrison (1587 and 1968), p. 197.
88 Margaret Cavendish (1667), p. 105.
89 Lambeth Palace Library, Shrewsbury Papers, MS 694, f. 63.
90 Philippa Glanville and Hilary Young (Eds), *Elegant Eating* (2002), p. 52.
91 UN Pw V/26, f. 162.
92 Glanville and Young (2002), p. 52.
93 Markham (1664 edn), p. 99.
94 BL Add MS 70500, ff. 110r–111v, 'A particular of the Goods at Boielsouer Castle' (*c.*1676).
95 Information from Dr Rosalys Coope.
96 BL Add MS 70500, ff. 110r–111v.
97 RIBA Drawings Collection, The Smythson Collection, III/1 (2), design for marble room, Bolsover Castle.
98 Raylor (1999), p. 423.
99 Hulse (1994), p. 39, note 6.
100 BL Harleian 4955, f. 199r.
101 BL Add MS 70500, f. 110r.
102 Harrison (1972), p. 65.
103 Glanville and Young (2002), p. 54.
104 UN Pw 1/367.
105 Harrison (1972), p. 57.
106 Glanville and Young (2002), p. 82.
107 Markham (1664 edn), p. 98; David Mitchell, 'Banquet Napkins: Their Design, Ownership and Use, 1550–1650', CIETA, Bulletin 81 (2004), p. 49.

108 UN Pw V/90, ff. 83v, 84r, 85v.
109 John Partridge, *Good Huswives Closet* (London, 1584), 'To make Paste of Sugar, whereof a man may make all manner of fruites and other fine thinges with their forme, as platters, dishes, glasses, cuppers, and such like things [. . .] and when you have done, you may eate them vp', 'Cap. 13'.
110 See Patricia Fumerton, *Cultural Aesthetics, Renaissance Literature and the Practice of Social Ornament* (Chicago and London, 1991).
111 BL Harleian 4955, f. 199v.
112 *Ibid.*
113 *Ibid.*
114 The fact that these dancers carry props is hinted at by their characters' names, and compare Inigo Jones's sketches for similar ante-masque characters in other entertainments.
115 Information from Maurice Howard.
116 Simon Thurley, *Hampton Court* (London and New Haven, 2003), p. 107.
117 Nicoll (1968), p. 208.
118 BL Harleian 4955, f. 200v.
119 *Ibid.*, f. 201r.
120 *Ibid.*
121 *Ibid.*, f. 202r.
122 *Ibid.*, f. 201v.
123 Shakespeare, *The Tempest*, Act Four, Scene One.
124 George Whetstone, *A critical edition of George Whetstone's 1582 An Heptameron of Civill Discourses*, Ed. Diana Shlanka (New York and London, 1987), p. 76.
125 William Knowler (Ed.), *The Earl of Strafforde's Letters and Dispatches* (London, 1739), p. 274, Wentworth to William Cavendish, Dublin (19th July, 1634).
126 D. J. Gordon, 'Poet and Architect: The Intellectual Setting of the Quarrel between Ben Jonson and Inigo Jones', *Journal of the Warburg and Courtauld Institutes*, Vol. 12 (1949), pp. 152–78.
127 Lucy Hutchinson, *Memoirs of the Life of Colonel Hutchinson*, Ed. James Sutherland (Oxford, 1973), p. 46.
128 Harbottle Grimston, *A Christian New-Year's Gift* (Cambridge, 1644), BL Thomason Tracts, E 1210(1), pp. 103, 105.
129 Clarendon (1888), Vol. 1, Book I, Chapter 167, pp. 104–5.

## CHAPTER 5: A ROYAL PALACE

1 William can be placed at Richmond in July, 1638, but the exact date on the relevant letter is illegible (Sheffield City Archives, Wentworth

Woodhouse Muniments, Strafford Papers, 18/96). The events of the day described – the riding lesson, the dinner, the boat trip – are all known to have taken place at Richmond but cannot be linked to this specific day. The programme of the day is therefore speculative but likely.

2 John Cloake, *Palaces and Parks of Richmond and Kew* (Chichester, 1995), Vol. 1, p. 189.

3 Margaret Cavendish (1667), pp. 79–80.

4 Strickland (1867), p. 390.

5 William Cavendish (1667), p. 7.

6 Margaret Cavendish (1667), p. 79.

7 BL Harleian MS 6988, f. 101.

8 BL Add MS 70499, ff. 198, 200.

9 *Ibid.*, f. 198.

10 Sheffield City Archives, Wentworth Woodhouse Muniments, Strafford Papers, 18/30.

11 Landesbibliothek Kassel, MS Hass. 68, f. 79v, quoted in Giles Worsley, *The British Stable* (New Haven and London, 2004), p. 61.

12 *CSPD 1638–9*, Eds J. Bruce and W. D. Hamilton (London, 1871), p. 460 (14th February, 1638/9); Moses Glover's map (1635), Duke of Northumberland, Syon House, shows the complex making up 'That Auntient & sometime Flourishing Shene; Formerly Hon.erd In Repute, now onely in Ruins [. . .] Now it is onely a Stable for ye Kings Greate Horse; And dwelling of Certayne officers thereunto Apperteyneing.'

13 BL Harleian 7623, f. 12v.

14 Roger North, *Of Building*, Eds Howard Colvin and John Newman (Oxford, 1981), pp. 95–6.

15 William Cavendish (1667), p. 125.

16 Quoted in Giles Worsley (2004), p. 44.

17 *Ibid.*

18 BL Harleian 7623, f. 19r.

19 *Ibid.*

20 *CSPD 1627–8*, Ed. John Bruce (London, 1858), p. 160.

21 BL Harleian 7623, f. 19r.

22 Jerome de Groot, *Royalist Identities* (Basingstoke, 2004).

23 James Alan Rennie, *In the Steps of the Cavaliers* (London, 1954), p. 14.

24 William Cavendish (London, 1667), pp. 7, 9.

25 John Nichols, *The Progresses, Processions and Magnificent Festivities of King James the First* (London, 1828), Vol. 4, p. 969.

26 *Ibid.*, Vol. 3, p. 215.

27 BL Thomason Tracts, E 783, Sir Balthazar Gerbier, 'The Interpreter of

the Academie for Forrain Langvages, and all Noble Sciences, and Excercises'.

28 Cliffe (1999), p. 157.

29 Nikolaus Pevsner and Bridget Cherry, *Buildings of England, London 2: South* (1983), p. 462.

30 See Moses Glover's map (1635), Duke of Northumberland, Syon House.

31 *Ibid.*

32 Manuscript at the College of Arms, quoted in Francis Grose and Thomas Astle, *The Antiquarian Repertory* (London, 1807–9), Vol. 2, pp. 313–17, and G. Kipling (Ed.), *The Receyt of the Ladie Kateryne*, Early English Text Society (Oxford, 1990), pp. 71–3.

33 Grose and Astle (1807-9), Vol. 2, pp. 313–17.

34 BL Harleian 7623, f. 15.

35 *Ibid.*

36 *Ibid.*, f. 15v.

37 *Ibid.*

38 *Ibid.*

39 BL Harleian MS 6988, f. 112r.

40 BL Harleian 7623, f. 17v.

41 *Ibid.*, f. 17r.

42 *Ibid.*, f. 10v.

43 *Ibid.*

44 *CSPD 1638–9*, Eds John Bruce and W. D. Hamilton (London, 1871), p. 2 (2nd September, 1638).

45 BL Harleian 7623, f. 18v.

46 *CSPD 1640–41*, Ed. W. D. Hamilton (London, 1882), p. 333 (n.d. 1640).

47 BL Harleian MS 6988, f. 101.

48 UN Pw V/25, f. 7r.

49 BL Harleian MS 7623, f. 14.

50 *Ibid.*, f. 17v.

51 *Ibid.*, f. 14v.

52 *Ibid.*

53 *Clarendon State Papers* (Oxford, Clarendon Printing House, 1773), Vol. 2, pp. 7–8, Mr Secretary Windebank to the Earl of Newcastle (19th March, 1637).

54 *Ibid.*, Newcastle to Windebank, 'Welbeck' (21st March, 1637).

55 For example, Christopher Falkus, *The Life and Times of Charles II* (London, 1972), p. 18.

56 TNA SO 1/3, f. 8v, quoted in Sharpe (1992), p. 243.

57 *CSPD 1639*, Ed. W. D. Hamilton (London, 1873), pp. 508–9, Bishop Duppa (18th September, 1639).

58 John Evelyn, *The Diary of John Evelyn*, Ed. E. S. de Beer (Oxford, 1955), Vol. 4, p. 410 (6th February, 1685).
59 Derek Wilson, *All the King's Women* (London, 2003) p. 2.
60 Sheffield City Archives, Wentworth Woodhouse Muniments, Strafford Papers, 18/57.
61 *Ibid.*, 18/76.
62 Hutchinson (1973), p. 61.
63 Grose and Astle (1807–9), Vol. 2, pp. 313–17; TNA E 317 Surrey 46, reproduced in W. H. Hart (Ed.), *The Parliamentary Surveys of Richmond . . . 1649* (1871, copy at Richmond Local Studies Library), p. 3.
64 *HMC Report of the Manuscripts of the Earl of Denbigh*, part V (London, 1911), p. 8.
65 C. P. Hill, *Who's Who in Stuart England* (London, 1988), pp. 94–5.
66 *CSPD 1639–40*, Ed. W. D. Hamilton (London, 1877), p. 459 (14th February, 1640).
67 Hart (n.d.), p. 4.
68 Grose and Astle (1807–9), Vol. 2, pp. 313–17; Hart (n.d.), p. 4.
69 Antonia Fraser, *King Charles II* (1979), p. 13.
70 George Conn, papal agent at the court of Henrietta Maria, to Francesco Barberini (17th September, 1638), quoted in Edward Chaney, *The Grand Tour and the Great Rebellion* (Geneva, 1985), p. 309.
71 BL Harleian 7623, f. 9.
72 *CSPD 1638–9*, Eds John Bruce and W. D. Hamilton (London, 1871), p. 182 (20th December, 1638).
73 BL Harleian MS 6988, f. 112r.
74 Evelyn, *Diary*, Vol. 4, p. 410 (6th February, 1685).
75 Hart (n.d.), p. 4.
76 Margaret Cavendish (1667), p. 151.
77 Quoted in Cunnington (1951), p. 39.
78 *Ibid.*, pp. 40–3.
79 *Ibid.*, pp. 42–3, 32.
80 *CSPD 1638–39*, Eds John Bruce and W. D. Hamilton (London, 1871), p. 485 (19th February, 1639).
81 BL Add MSS 70499, f. 252, Edward Kyrton to the Earl of Newcastle (20th August, 1641).
82 *CSPD 1639–40*, Ed. W.D. Hamilton (London, 1877), p. 154 (10th December, 1639).
83 Quoted in Richard Corson, *Fashions in Hair* (London, 1980), pp. 209, 213.
84 Sheffield City Archives, Wentworth Woodhouse Muniments, Strafford Papers, 18/96.
85 Fraser (1979), p. 12.

86 BL Harleian MS 6988, f. 95.
87 For example, see *CSPD, 1638–9*, Ed. John Bruce (London, 1871), p. 179.
88 BL Harleian 7623, f. 16.
89 *Ibid.*
90 *CSPD 1639/40*, Ed. W. D. Hamilton (London, 1877), p. 378; BL MS 70499, f. 242, The Earl of Pembroke and Montgomery to the Earl of Newcastle (29th September, 1639).
91 *CSPD, 1640–41*, Ed. W. D. Hamilton (London, 1882), p. 486; *CSPD 1639–40*, Ed. W. D. Hamilton (London, 1877), p. 179 (19th December, 1639).
92 BL Add MS 70499, f. 237.
93 Margaret Cavendish (1667), p. 7; *CSPD, 1641–3*, Ed. W. D. Hamilton (London, 1877), Vol. 1, p. 62 (29th July, 1641), Thomas Wiseman to Sir John Pennington.
94 Airs (1995), p. ix.
95 Hart (n.d.), p. 4.
96 John Timbs and Alexander Gunn, *Abbeys, Castles and Ancient Halls of England and Wales* (London and New York, n.d.), p. 137.
97 Peter Eisenberg's notes on England (1614), quoted in W. Rye, *England as Seen by Foreigners* (London, 1865), p. 172.
98 Cloake (1995), pp. 194–5.
99 'Orders and regulations for the government of the Queen's Household, made May 1, 1627, and signed by their Majesties', in *A Collection of Ordinances and Regulations for the Government of the Royal Household* (London, 1790), p. 340.
100 Grose and Astle (1807–9), pp. 313–17.
101 BL Harleian 7623, f. 9.
102 Sharpe (1992), p. 218.
103 Judith Richards, '"His Nowe Majestie" and the English Monarchy', *Past and Present*, No. 113 (November, 1986), p. 81.
104 BL Harleian 7623, f. 17.
105 *Ibid.*
106 *Ibid.*, f. 4r.
107 UN Pw V/25, f. 68v.
108 *CSPD 1637–8*, Ed. John Bruce (London, 1869), p. 361 'The Earl of Newcastle is made groom of the stole to the Prince, and his sole gentleman of the bedchamber' (12th April, 1638).
109 Quoted in Cloake (1995), p. 142.
110 There is no evidence to connect the scene to this particular day, but a print of Wenceslaus Hollar's view of Richmond Palace shows the princes and their governor making an outing to the river bank. Although the figure in the print is not named as William Cavendish, my reasons for the

identification are as follows: Hollar's original drawing of Richmond Palace shows a different group of figures on the bank (M. R. Toynbee, 'Views of Richmond Palace in the Reign of Charles I', *The Antiquaries Journal*, Vol. XXVIII [July–Oct., 1948], pp. 163–5). The print was issued in 1638, the year that William was appointed governor to the prince, and the party shown clearly includes the two little princes, wearing hats, while their attendants are bareheaded. The dominant attendant is likely to have been William, as the date of the engraving connects it with the setting up of the prince's household and William's appointment as its head.

111 Cloake (1995), p. 185.
112 *Ibid.*, p. 188.
113 Eiche (1998), p. 12.
114 *Ibid.*, pp. 13–14.
115 Cloake (1995), p. 180.
116 *Ibid.*, p. 181.
117 Richmond Palace, *c.*1630, by an unknown artist. Fitzwilliam Museum.
118 The colours can only be seen in painted versions of the engraving, cf. Toynbee (1948), p. 165.
119 Fraser (1979), p. 19.
120 *CSPD 1639*, Ed. W. D. Hamilton (London, 1873), pp. 508–9 (18th September, 1639).
121 *CSPD 1640-41*, Ed. W. D. Hamilton (London, 1882), p. 6 (2nd September, 1640).
122 *Ibid.*, pp. 11, 32, 33, (4th September, 1640, 9th September, 1640).
123 *CSPD, 1641–3*, Ed. W. D. Hamilton (London, 1877), Vol. 1, pp. 8, 18.
124 Margaret Cavendish (1667), p. 9; *CSPD, 1641–3*, Ed. W. D. Hamilton (London, 1877), Vol. 1, p. 24.

## CHAPTER 6: A BATTLE

1 Bod. Clarendon State Papers, 181, an original endorsed by Clarendon 'Sir Hugh Cholmley's Memorials'.
2 John Barratt, *The Battle for York, Marston Moor, 1644* (Stroud, Gloucestershire, 2002), p. 71.
3 Clarendon (1888), Vol. 3, pp. 382-3.
4 *HMC Portland*, Appendix, Part 1 (London, 1891), Vol. 1, p. 701.
5 Ian Roy, 'Rupert, Prince and Count Palatine of the Rhine and Duke of Cumberland (1619–1682)', *Dictionary of National Biography* (Oxford, 2004).
6 Clarendon (1888), Vol. 3, pp. 382–3.
7 Warwick (1701), p. 236.
8 John Morrill, 'Cromwell, Oliver (1599–1658)', *Oxford Dictionary of National Biography* (Oxford, 2004).

9 BL Harleian MS 6988, f. 173, Charles I to William (Oxford, 5th April, 1643).
10 *Ibid.*, f. 145, Henrietta to William (Newark, 18th June, 1643).
11 BL Harleian MS 7003, f. 25, Henrietta Maria to William (Oxford, 15th March, 1643).
12 BL Harleian MS 7359, f. 7r.
13 NA DD.P6.1.19.26.
14 As visible in York Public Library, 'A Draught of His Majesties Manner house at York', Jacob Richards (*c.*1685).
15 *RCHM 78, Hastings* (London, 1930), Vol. 2, p. 128, Per(cy) Tomkins to Mrs. (Sarah) Fretchville (5th May, 1644).
16 Tristram Hunt, *The English Civil War at First Hand* (London, 2002), p. 126.
17 Margaret Cavendish (1667), p. 121.
18 *Ibid.*, p. 140.
19 Eliot Warburton, *Memoirs and Correspondence of Prince Rupert and the Cavaliers* (London, 1849), Vol. 2, p. 446, quoting notes to Prince Rupert's diary.
20 Anon., *The Pythouse Papers*, p. 19, quoted by Longueville (1910), pp. 137–8.
21 Warwick (1701), p. 243.
22 Margaret Cavendish (1667), p. 47.
23 Barratt (2002), p. 70.
24 Steve Murdoch and Tim Wales, 'King, James, Lord Eythin (1589–1652)', *Oxford Dictionary of National Biography* (Oxford, 2004).
25 Sir Hugh Cholmley, 'Memorials Touching the Battle of York', quoted in Anon., *English Heritage Battlefield Report: Marston Moor, 1644* (1995), p. 19.
26 Roy (2004), p. 5.
27 Reproduced in Emberton (1995), p. 116; Roy (2004).
28 Roy (2004), p. 5.
29 Bowles (1981), p. 101.
30 BL Thomason Tracts, E.3/17, *A DOGS ELEGY, OR RUPERT'S TEARS* (London, 1644).
31 Warburton (1849), Vol. II, p. 438.
32 Barratt (2002), p. 80.
33 Sir Hugh Cholmley, 'Memorials Touching the Battle of York', quoted in *English Heritage Battlefield Report* (1995), p. 19. The timing of the various conversations between Prince Rupert and William varies in the various accounts of the battle. I have taken the liberty of including a variety of sources rather than relying on any particular one.

34 Sir Henry Slingsby, quoted in *English Heritage Battlefield Report* (1995), p. 18.
35 *English Heritage Battlefield Report* (1995), p. 1.
36 Simeon Ashe, quoted in *English Heritage Battlefield Report* (1995), p. 11.
37 Quoted in *English Heritage Battlefield Report* (1995), p. 4.
38 Sir Henry Slingsby, quoted in *English Heritage Battlefield Report* (1995), p. 18.
39 Quoted in *English Heritage Battlefield Report* (1995), p. 4.
40 Simeon Ashe, quoted in *English Heritage Battlefield Report* (1995), p. 11.
41 Barratt (2002), p. 84.
42 Ivan E. Broadhead, *Yorkshire Battlefields* (London, 1989), p. 165.
43 Peter Newman, *The Battle of Marston Moor* (Chichester, 1981), pp. 76–7.
44 Barratt (2002), p. 100.
45 'A More Exact Relation of the late Battell neere York' by Scoutmaster-General Lionel Watson, serving in the Earl of Manchester's army, quoted in *English Heritage Battlefield Report* (1995), p. 15.
46 Mrs Thornton, quoted in Newman (1981), p. 63.
47 Lionel Watson, quoted in *English Heritage Battlefield Report* (1995), p. 15.
48 Rupert's diary, quoted in Barratt (2002), p. 97.
49 Quoted in Barratt (2002), p. 149.
50 Barratt (2002), pp. 84–5.
51 This exchange is taken from Bod. Clarendon MS 1805. It is worth noting that this was written some years after the battle.
52 Sir Hugh Cholmley, quoted in *English Heritage Battlefield Report* (1995), p. 19.
53 Bod. Clarendon MS 1805.
54 Sir Hugh Cholmley, quoted in *English Heritage Battlefield Report* (1995), p. 19.
55 Bod. Clarendon MS 23, f. 230r, notes on events in the north (n.d.) in Clarendon's own hand.
56 Barratt (2002), p. 105.
57 Arthur Trevor, a Royalist, quoted in *English Heritage Battlefield Report* (1995), p. 5; Sir Hugh Cholmley, quoted in *English Heritage Battlefield Report* (1995), p. 19.
58 Sir Hugh Cholmley, quoted in *English Heritage Battlefield Report* (1995), p. 19.
59 Margaret Cavendish (1667), p. 47.
60 Lionel Watson, quoted in *English Heritage Battlefield Report* (1995), p. 6.

61 Simeon Ashe, quoted in *English Heritage Battlefield Report* (1995), p. 11.
62 *Ibid.*
63 Margaret Cavendish (1667), p. 48.
64 www.earlofmanchesters.co.uk/MarstonMoor.html (consulted 15th May, 2005).
65 Captain William Stewart, quoted in *English Heritage Battlefield Report* (1995), p. 6.
66 Barratt (2002), p. 131.
67 Lionel Watson, quoted in *English Heritage Battlefield Report* (1995), p. 16.
68 Margaret Cavendish (1667), p. 48.
69 Captain John Vernon (a Parliamentarian cavalry officer), *The Young Horseman* (1644), BL Thomason Tracts E.48(8), p. 43.
70 Sir Hugh Cholmley, quoted in *English Heritage Battlefield Report* (1995), p. 19.
71 Arthur Trevor, royalist messenger, quoted in Hunt (2002), p. 129.
72 Sir Hugh Cholmley, quoted in *English Heritage Battlefield Report* (1995), p. 19.
73 Margaret Cavendish (1667), p. 48.
74 Lionel Watson, quoted in *English Heritage Battlefield Report* (1995), p. 7.
75 Quoted in John Morrill, 'Cromwell, Oliver (1599–1658)', *Oxford Dictionary of National Biography* (Oxford, 2004), p. 6.
76 Simeon Ashe, quoted in *English Heritage Battlefield Report* (1995), p. 12.
77 Margaret Cavendish (1667), p. 49.
78 W.H., a captain in the army of the Eastern Association, quoted in Barratt (2002), p. 109.
79 Margaret Cavendish (1667), p. 49.
80 William Lilley, quoted in Barratt (2002), p. 136.
81 Lieutenant-Colonel James Somerville, a Scot, quoted in *English Heritage Battlefield Report* (1995), p. 7.
82 Sir Hugh Cholmley, quoted in *English Heritage Battlefield Report* (1995), p. 19.
83 Margaret Cavendish (1667), p. 50.
84 Lionel Watson, quoted in Hunt (2002), p. 130.
85 Sir Henry Slingsby, quoted in Barratt (2002), p. 141.
86 Newman (1981), p. 127.
87 'The father and son think it very opportune to renew the treaty with my Lord of Newcastle; and thereupon Sir John writes that letter, which was after (at the battle of York) taken in my Lord's cabinet and cost both the Hothams their heads.' Quoted by Longueville (1910), p. 97.

88 Margaret Cavendish (1667), p. 50.
89 Warburton (1849), Vol. 2, p. 468.
90 Clarendon (1888), Vol. viii, p. 82.
91 BL Add MS 70499, f. 258.
92 BL Thomason Tracts, E 279(2), 'The Character of an Oxford-Incendiary' (London, 26th April, 1645), p. 7.
93 *CSPD, 1644*, Ed. W. D. Hamilton (London, 1888), p. 379 (25th July, 1644).
94 Quoted in Geoffrey Trease, *A Portrait of a Cavalier* (London, 1979), p. 143.

CHAPTER 7: A HOUSEHOLD DIVIDED

1 William Cavendish (1667), p. (b)2 v.
2 Elaine Walker, '"To Amaze People with Pleasure and Delight": An Analysis of the Horsemanship Manuals of William Cavendish, First Duke of Newcastle (1593–1676)', University of Birmingham Ph.D. (2005).
3 William Cavendish (1667), p. 50.
4 *Ibid.*, p. (b)2; Margaret Cavendish (1667), p. 67.
5 BL Add MS 70499, f. 196.
6 Elizabeth McGrath, 'The Painted Decoration of Rubens's House', *Journal of the Warburg and Courtauld Institutes*, Vol. 41 (1978), pp. 245–77. As has often been pointed out, the restorers of Rubens's house in the 1940s, working from the Harrewijn plates, mistakenly thought that the heavy decoration on the 'Italian' part of the building was sculpted in relief rather than painted with a three-dimensional effect.
7 Rutger J. Tijs, *P. P. Rubens en J. Jordaens, Barok in Eigen Huis* (Antwerp, 1983).
8 Rubens shows the summer house and such a garden in his painting *The Walk in the Garden.* Alte Pinakothek, Munich, published in Tijs (1983), p. 130.
9 William Cavendish (1667), p. (b)2 v.
10 William Cavendish, *La Méthode et Invention nouvelle de dresser les Chevaux* (Anvers, 1657–8). The first edition is printed 1658, but on some copies the date has been changed to 1657 in an early hand. Quotations are taken from the English edition of 1667.
11 William Cavendish (1667), p. bv.
12 *Ibid.*, p. (c)2v.
13 Margaret Cavendish (1667), p. 65.
14 *Ibid.*, p. 66.
15 Quoted by Trease (1979), p. 157.
16 Margaret Cavendish (1667), p. 73.

17 *Ibid.*, p. 75.
18 Miniature in a private collection.
19 Rubens's house had almost fallen apart by the beginning of the twentieth century. This description is taken from its appearance today, which is the result of an extensive restoration process undertaken in the 1940s. The restorers had little, if any, evidence for the interior of each room, but their recreation is in a typical style for seventeenth-century Antwerp.
20 Bowles (1981), p. 23.
21 Margaret Cavendish, *A True Relation of the Birth, Breeding and Life of Margaret Cavendish*, Ed. Sir Egerton Brydges (Lee Priory edn, Kent, 1814), p. 28.
22 Margaret Cavendish (1667), p. 64.
23 Goulding (1909), p. 16.
24 *Ibid.*, p. 18.
25 BL Add MS 70499, ff. 259–98.
26 BL Add MS 32497, f. 110r.
27 *Ibid.*, f. 50.
28 BL Add MS 70499, f. 347, Bruges (20th August, 1657).
29 Bowles (1981), p. 27; quoted in Derek Blyth, *Flemish Cities Explored* (London, 1990), p. 147.
30 *Ibid.*, p. 152.
31 Quoted by C. H. Firth (Ed.) in *The Life of William Cavendish* (London, 1886), p. 357.
32 UN Pw V/25, f. 141v.
33 *CSPD, 1652–3*, Ed. M. A. E. Green (London, 1878), p. 467.
34 UN Pw 1/670.
35 Margaret Cavendish (1667), p. 53.
36 UN Pw 1/79.
37 UN Pw V/90, f. 14r.
38 UN Pw 1/78, f. 2.
39 *CSPD, 1657–8*, Ed. M. A. E. Green (London, 1884), p. 300, Thomas Ross to Secretary Nicholas (24th February, 1658).
40 Bod. Clarendon State Papers, No. 285, R. W. (i.e. Mr Watson) to William Edgeman at Madrid (Breda, 22nd April, 1650).
41 UN Pw 1/537.
42 UN Pw V/90, ff. 17, 112.
43 *Ibid.*, f. 20r (24th May, 1648).
44 BL Add MS 70499, f. 355 (15th November, 1659).
45 *Ibid.*, f. 351.
46 *Ibid.*, f. 355v.
47 *Ibid.*.
48 *Ibid.*, f. 356.

49 Poem by William Cavendish. UN Pw 1/26, f. 131.
50 Portrait after the school of van Dyck, Goulding (1936), No. 404.
51 BL Add MS 70500, f. 13, Henry Cavendish, 'a brief account how I came to bee eight thousand pounds in Debt'.
52 UN Pw V/90, f. 20v.
53 UN Pw 1/292/6c.
54 Colonel Van Peire and then Colonel Beeton; Bolsover Castle was under the charge of Colonel Muschamp; Margaret Cavendish (1667), pp. 87, 88.
55 UN Pw 1/367.
56 The ditch is mentioned in the eighteenth century, NA DD.5P.6.1.2 (3rd April, 1747).
57 Adam Littleton, 'A Sermon at the Funeral of the Right Honourable the Lady Jane Eldest Daughter to his Grace William Duke of Newcastle' (London, 1669), p. 46.
58 Although Elizabeth married in 1641 (aged about fourteen), her collaboration with her sister Jane on poems and plays suggests that she still spent part of her time at Welbeck.
59 'Short Memorial', in Masére, *Select Tracts relating to the Civil Wars in England* (1815), p. 431, quoted in Longueville (1910), p. 105.
60 Margaret Cavendish (1667), p. 105.
61 *CSPD, 1644*, Ed. W. D. Hamilton (London, 1888), pp. 404–5 (6th August, 1644).
62 Bod. Rawlinson MS POET16, 'Poems, Songs and a Pastorall (and a play) by the rt. hon. the lady Jane Cavendish and lady Elizabeth Brackley' (*c.*1670); Lady Jane Cavendish and Lady Elizabeth Brackley, 'The Concealed Fancies', in S. P. Cerasano and M. Wynne-Davies (Eds), *Renaissance Drama by Women: Texts and Documents* (London, 1996), pp. 132–54; Jane Cavendish and Elizabeth Brackley, *The Concealed Fancies* (1996 edition), p. 145.
63 *Ibid.*, p. 143.
64 BL Harleian, 911, 'R. Symonds. Diary of the Marches of the Royal Army, Apr–Aug. 1645', f. 153v.
65 UN Pw 1/5.
66 Littleton (1669), p. 47.
67 E.g. NA Norton Cuckney Parish Registers (30th June, 1644).
68 Littleton (1669), p. 45.
69 Bod. Rawlinson MS POET 16, 'The Speakeing Glass'.
70 *Ibid.*, 'On my Worthy friend Mr Richard Pypes'.
71 Littleton (1669), p. 46.
72 Bod. Rawlinson MS POET 16, 'Lifes Weather Glass'.
73 *Ibid.*, 'Loves Conflict'.

74 *Ibid.*, 'Thankes letter'.
75 *Ibid.*, f. 3.
76 UN Pw 1/367.
77 Littleton (1669), p. 48.
78 Quoted in N. C. Starr, '*The Concealed Fansyes,* A Play by Lady Jane Cavendish and Lady Elizabeth Brackley', *Proceedings of the Modern Languages Association,* 46 (1931), p. 804.
79 Margaret Cavendish (1667), p. 91.
80 Cunnington (1974), p. 8.
81 Overburie (1615), 'A Chamber-Mayde'.
82 Hannah Woolley, *The Compleat Servant-Maid* (London, 1677), pp. 61–2.
83 *Ibid.*, p. 61.
84 Jane Cavendish and Elizabeth Brackley, *The Concealed Fancies* (1996 edn), p. 148.
85 Bod. MS Rawlinson POET 16, 'On a Chamber-mayde'.
86 Margaret Cavendish, *Nature's Pictures by Fancy's Pencil*, London (1656).
87 Bod. MS Rawlinson POET 16, 'The Carecter'.
88 UN Pw V/25, f. 140r.
89 Woolley (1677), pp. 165–6.
90 North (1981), p. 94.
91 Liza Picard, *Restoration London* (London, 1997), p. 134.
92 Harrison (1972), p. 68.
93 Hannah Woolley, *The Queene-like Closet* (London, 1670), p. 125.
94 UN Pw V/25, f. 140r, 'of a washer', 'of a startcher' and 'of a waytinge Gentlewoeman'.
95 Margaret Cavendish, *A True Relation* (1814), p. 5.
96 Woolley (1677), p. 156.
97 UN Pw V/24, f. 12.
98 This, at least, was the case in a bedding inventory that dates from 1662. UN Pw 1/595.
99 Cliffe (1999), p. 104.
100 UN Pw 1/670.
101 UN Pw V/24, f. 19r.
102 Jane Cavendish and Elizabeth Brackley, *The Concealed Fancies* (1996 edn), p. 134.
103 Alison Findlay, '"She Gave You the Civility of the House", Household Performance in *The Concealed Fancies*', in S. P. Cerasano and Marion Wynne-Davies (Eds), *Readings in Renaissance Women's Drama* (London, 1998), p. 264.
104 Anon., *A true Relation of HIS MAJESTIES Motion from Wales to Lichfield in Staffordshire . . . Also, the Marches of the Scots . . . in pursuit of His Majesties Horse to Welbeck-House* (London, 20th August,

1645), BL Thomason Tracts E 279(1), No. 9, p. 6; Clarendon (1888), Vol. 4, pp. 88–9; HMC Report 55, *Report on Manuscripts in Various Collections*, Vol. 7 (London, 1914); 'Manuscripts of H. C. Staunton esq.', p. 374; Symonds (1859), p. 227.

105 *CSPD, 1645–47*, Ed. W. D. Hamilton (London, 1891), p. 227 (13th November, 1645).

106 UN Pw 1/79.

107 *Ibid.*

108 UN Pw 1/86 (27th March, 1656).

109 Hannah Woolley, *The Gentlewomans Companion; or, a Guide to the Female Sex* (London, 1682), p. 52.

110 UN Pw 1/118.

111 UN Pw 1/ 84.

112 Thurley (2004), p. 225.

113 Bowles (1981), p. 94.

## CHAPTER 8: A BEDCHAMBER CONVERSATION

1 John Evelyn (1955), Vol. 3, p. 482 (11th May, 1667).

2 John Evelyn, *Fumifugium, or the Inconvenience of the Aer and Smoak of London Dissipated* (1661), in *The Miscellaneous Writings of John Evelyn*, Ed. William Upcott (London, 1825), p. 210.

3 *Ibid.*, p. 220.

4 John Richardson, *The Annals of London* (Berkeley, 2000), p. 144.

5 Quoted in Picard (1997), p. 7.

6 Malcolm Letts, *As the Foreigner Saw Us* (London, 1935), p. 37.

7 Douglas D. C. Chambers, 'Evelyn, John (1620–1706)', *Oxford Dictionary of National Biography* (Oxford, 2004).

8 John Ogilby's map of London, 1677.

9 R. Hovenden (Ed.), *The Register of the Christenings, Mariages and Burialles in the Parishe of St James Clarkenwell*, Harleian Society (London, 1885) (the original manuscript is lost from the London Metropolitan Archives).

10 Clerkenwell Poor Rate Books, Finsbury and Islington Local Studies Library.

11 Margaret Cavendish, *The Convent of Pleasure and Other Plays*, Ed. Anne Shaver (Baltimore and London, 1999).

12 Balliol College Archives, MS B.21.20, p. 1 (*c*.1659).

13 *Ibid.*, MS B.21.18 (*c*.1659).

14 John Evelyn (1955), Vol. 3, p. 481 (24th April, 1667).

15 *Ibid.*, p. 478 (18th April, 1667).

16 *Ibid.*, p. 246 (29th May, 1660).

17 Margaret Cavendish (1667), p. 85.

18 *The Citie's Loyalty Displayed*, quoted in Picard (1997), p. 8.
19 Nadine Akkerman and Marguérite Corporaal, 'Mad Science Beyond Flattery: The Correspondence of Margaret Cavendish and Constantijn Huygens', *Early Modern Literary Studies*, Special Issue 14 (May, 2004), 2.1-21, letter 9.
20 Bowles (1981), p. 81.
21 John Noorthouck, *A New History of London* (London, 1773), p. 751.
22 London Metropolitan Records Centre MS P76.JS.1.001, Parish Registers of St James, Clerkenwell. John, son of John Plasterer and Alice his wife, was baptised on 27th December, 1630; *ibid.*, Mary, daughter of Thomas Tyler and Mary his wife, was baptised on 31st December, 1630; *ibid.*, Fayth, daughter of John Stayner and Cislye his wife, was baptised on 16th February, 1631.
23 Corson (1980), p. 215.
24 Samuel Pepys, Vol. iv (1971), p. 130 (9th May, 1663).
25 Quoted in Worden (1986), p. 176.
26 Corson (1980), p. 224.
27 Quoted in Worden (1986), p. 181.
28 Evelyn (1955), Vol. 3, p. 481 (27th April, 1667).
29 De Courtin (1678), p. 120.
30 BL Add MS 32497, ff. 145v–146r. I am grateful to Gillian Darley for drawing this poem to my attention.
31 Margaret Cavendish (1667), p. 150.
32 Courtin (1678), p. 22.
33 *Youths Behaviour*, tr. Francis Hawkins (London, 1654), p. 11.
34 Margaret Cavendish (1667), p. 150.
35 James Howell, *Instructions for Forreine Travell* (London, 1642), p. 182.
36 Richard Flecknoe, *A Farrago of Several Pieces being a supplement to his poems, characters, heroick portraits, etc.* (London, 1666), 'On Welbeck', p. 12. In his dedication to Margaret, Flecknoe stated that the poems were written 'under your *Graces* Roof at *Welbeck*'.
37 Howarth (1985), p. 36.
38 The rooms in Newcastle House include 'ye Hall the Stairs, ye great Dining Rome & ye BedChamber', BL Add MS 37998, f. 241 (undated, probably late 1676 or early 1677).
39 Barney Sloane *et al.*, *St Mary's, Clerkenwell*, publication draft 1, Museum of London Archaeology Service (April, 1997), 'Buildings 5 and 6: The North Range and Cloister Walk'.
40 Bowles (1981), p. 121.
41 Margaret Cavendish (1667), p. 92.
42 Bowles (1981), p. 51.
43 Worsley (2004), p. 69.

44 The plan today remains in the archives of Balliol College (MS B.21.24), owners of the property neighbouring Newcastle House. As William Cavendish is one of the few people in the country interested enough in horsemanship to build such a scheme, it seems possible that the idea was his and that he sent the plan to his neighbours for comment.
45 Glanville and Young (2002), p. 20.
46 De Courtin (1678), p. 123.
47 Glanville and Young (2002), p. 54.
48 Annette Hope, *Londoners' Larder* (Edinburgh, 2005), p. 87.
49 Glanville and Young (2002), p. 48.
50 UN Pw V/90, f. 91v.
51 *CSPD, 1657–8*, Ed. Mary A. E. Green (London, 1884), p. 311, Sir Charles Cotterell to Nicholas (1st March, 1658).
52 Margaret Cavendish, *CCXI Sociable Letters* (London, 1664), p. 67.
53 Woolley (1677), p. 147.
54 Glanville and Young (2002), p. 60.
55 John Evelyn, *Acetaria* (London, 1699), in *The Miscellaneous Writings of John Evelyn*, Ed. William Upcott (London, 1825), p. 734.
56 *Ibid.*, p. 735.
57 *Ibid.*, pp. 763, 742.
58 UN Pw V/90, f. 16v.
59 Jean Gaihard, *The Compleat Gentleman* (London, 1678), Book 2, p. 66.
60 Glanville and Young (2002), p. 79.
61 *Ibid.*, p. 96.
62 UN Pw V/25, f. 95 (19th November, 1675).
63 John Evelyn, *A Character of England* (1659), in *The Miscellaneous Writings of John Evelyn*, Ed. William Upcott (London, 1825), p. 158.
64 Gervase Markham, *The English Housewife* (London, 1615), quoted in Sambrook (1996), p. 147.
65 UN Pw V/25, f. 98.
66 £1,200 owed to 'Mr Cropley' is listed in a 'Schedule of such Principall debts of the Earle of Newcastle's' contracted prior to 1642. NA DD4P.35.14.
67 HMC, *7th Report, The House of Lords Calendar* (London, 1879), Part 1, Appendix, p. 135, petition of John Cropley of Clerkenwell (16th November, 1660).
68 UN Pw 1/20 (30th June, 1673).
69 UN Pw 1/592/2; Pw 1/16.
70. UN Pw 1/16.
71 Picard (1997), p. 7.
72 *Hastings MSS* (1930), Vol. 2, p. 152, J. J(acques) to Theophilus, seventh Earl of Huntington (9th May, 1665).

73 Sheffield City Archives, WWM Str. P. 12/267; UN Pw V/26, f. 28r.
74 Cliffe (1999), p. 94.
75 UN Pw 1/4.
76 Margaret Cavendish (1667), p. 105.
77 Cliffe (1999), p. 123.
78 Pepys, Vol. viii (1974), p. 187 (26th April, 1667).
79 Cliffe (1999), p. 123.
80 *Ibid.*, p. 126.
81 UN Pw V/670 (1661).
82 Cliffe (1999), p. 130.
83 Pepys, Vol. viii (1974), p. 196 (1st May, 1667).
84 *Ibid.*, p. 163 (26th April, 1667).
85 Evelyn (1955), Vol. 3, p. 482 (11th May, 1667).
86 Evelyn (1955), Vol. 4, p. 343 (4th October, 1683).
87 Evelyn (1955), Vol. 3, p. 478 (18th April, 1667).
88 Margaret Cavendish, *A True Relation* (1814), pp. 5, 31.
89 Pepys, Vol. viii (1974), p. 186 (26th April, 1667).
90 Constantijn Huygens to Utricia Swann (5/15 Sept. 1653), quoted in Akkerman and Corporaal (2004).
91 Edward Maunde Thompson (Ed.), *Correspondence of the Family of Hatton*, Vol. 1 (Camden Society, 1878), p. 47, Sir Christopher Lyttelton to Christopher Lord Hatton (7th August, 1665).
92 Bulwer, *The Artificial Changeling* (1650), quoted in Corson (1980), p. 227.
93 *Wit Restored* (1658), quoted in Corson (1980), p. 227.
94 John Marston, *Mountebank's Masque* (n.d.), quoted in Corson (1980), pp. 226–7.
95 Margaret Cavendish, 'A true Relation of my Birth, Breeding and Life', in *Nature's Pictures* (London, 1656), p. 384.
96 Margaret Cavendish, 'An Epilogue to The Pastime of the Queen of Fairies', in *Poems and Fancies*, reproduced in E. Jenkins (Ed.), *A Cavalier and His Lady* (London, 1872), p. 87.
97 Margaret Cavendish, *The World's Olio* (London, 1676), frontispiece.
98 Flecknoe (1666), 'On the Dutchess of Newcastle's Closet', p. 13.
99 Evelyn (1955), Vol. 3, p. 481 (27th April, 1667).
100 Quoted in Worden (1986), p. 191.
101 Warwick (1701), p. 236.
102 *Ibid.*, p. 235.
103 Pepys, Vol. viii (1974), p. 163 (11th April, 1667).
104 George Parfitt, *English Poetry of the Seventeenth Century* (London and New York, 1995), pp. 26–38.
105 I'm grateful to James Knowles for his help with this section.

106 BL Add MS 32497, f. 54r.
107 *Ibid.*, f. 33r.
108 *Ibid.*, f.11.
109 Pepys, Vol. viii (1974), p. 243 (30th May, 1667).
110 Mrs Evelyn's letter to Dr Bohun, quoted in Austin Dobson's edition of Evelyn's *Diary* (1906), Vol. 2, p. 271.
111 *Ibid.*, '*The Preface*'.
112 Dorothy Osborne, *Letters of Dorothy Osborne*, Ed. G. C. Moore Smith (Oxford, 1928), p. 41.
113 William's 'epistle to justifie the Lady Newcastle', in Margaret Cavendish (1655).
114 Broadsheet of *c.*1710, quoted in Peter Brown, *In Praise of Hot Liquors* (York, 1995), p. 32.
115 Quoted in Hope (2005), p. 74.
116 Evelyn (1955), Vol. 4, p. 413 (6th February, 1685).
117 Quoted in Worden (1986), p. 178.
118 *Ibid.*
119 Thomson (1937 and 1965), pp. 86–7.
120 UN Pw 1/ 329, 330.
121 HMC, *12th Report* (London, 1890), appendix vii, p. 47, newsletter (23rd April, 1667).
122 Margaret Cavendish (1667), p. 89.
123 Margaret Cavendish (1662), p. 66.
124 Ellis (1661), 'Dedicatory Epistle'.
125 Anon., *Mémoires de la Vie du Comte de Grammont, contenant particulièrement l'Histoire Amoureuse de la Cour d'Angleterre sous la Règne du Roi Charles II* (Cologne, 1713), quotation from A. Hamilton (Ed.), *Memoirs of Count Grammont* (Philadephia, 1888), pp. 153–4.
126 Evelyn (1955), Vol. 3, p. 482 (11th May, 1665).
127 Pepys, Vol. viii (1974), p. 243 (30th May, 1667); p. 163 (11th April, 1667); p. 209 (10th May, 1667).

CHAPTER 9: A CONSPIRACY

1 Margaret Cavendish, *Observations upon Experimental Philosophy . . . the Description of a New Blazing World* (London, 1666), p. 109.
2 *Ibid.*, p. 110.
3 UN Pw V/25, f. 151v.
4 UN Pw 1/595 (1662).
5 For example the 'upper nursery', *ibid.*
6 UN Pw 1/296.6.g (1691).
7 UN Pw 1/670.
8 UN Pw 1/432 (8th May, 1669).

9 North (1981), p. 139.
10 William Gouge, *Of Domesticall Duties* (London, 1622), p. 629.
11 UN Pw 1/315, f. 2.
12 William Wentworth (1604, 1973), p. 21.
13 Margaret Cavendish (1667), p. 102.
14 Margaret Cavendish, *Sociable Letters* (London, 1664), p. bv.
15 *CSPD 1671*, Ed. F. H. Blackburne Daniell (1895 and 1968), p. 426, William Fuller, Bishop of Lincoln, from Stamford, to Joseph Williamson (12th August, 1671).
16 UN Pw V/90, f. 7v.
17 Cliffe (1999), p. 90.
18 UN Pw 1/171.
19 UN Pw V/26, f. 117r.
20 Henry Percy, ninth Earl of Northumberland, *Advice to his Son* (1609), Ed. G. B. Harrison (London, 1930), p. 77.
21 UN Pw 1/168.
22 Quoted in Wendy Wall, *Staging Domesticity* (Cambridge, 2002), p. 13.
23 Margaret Cavendish (1666), p. 109.
24 Strong (1903), III D I, p. 56.
25 NA DD.2P.24.73.
26 Strong (1903), III D I, p. 56.
27 Bowles (1981), p. 114; UN Pw 2/651.
28 UN Pw V/26, f. 127.
29 Bowles (1981), p. 123.
30 Margaret Cavendish (1667), p. 150.
31 Gouge (1622), pp. 602, 616.
32 Margaret Cavendish, *A True Relation* (1814).
33 Margaret Cavendish, *The World's Olio*, London (1671), p. 79.
34 UN Pw 1/315; Pw 1/79; Pw 1/165.
35 Wall (2002), p. 5, and the following passage also owes much to Wall's work.
36 *Ibid.*, p. 16.
37 Woolley (1677), p. 30; and again Wall (2002).
38 Wall (2002), p. 7.
39 NA DDP/65/70.
40 Adam Eyre, *Diary of Adam Eyre* (9th October, 1647), quoted in Christina Hole, *The English Housewife* (London, 1953), p. 126.
41 Robert Cleaver, *Godlie Forme of Householde Government* (1598 and 1612), quoted in Cliffe (1999), p. 97.
42 UN Pw V/90, ff. 23v, 52r.
43 Wall (2002), p. 14.
44 UN Pw 1/315, f. 4.

45 Percy (1609, 1930), pp. 99–100.
46 UN Pw 1/389; Pw 1/392; Pw 1/595.
47 UN Pw 1/510.
48 UN Pw 1/90.
49 UN Pw 1/166.
50 UN Pw 1/165.
51 UN Pw 1/503 (8th February, 1662).
52 Pepys, Vol. ix (1976), p. 123 (18th March, 1668).
53 Bod. Ashmole 36, f. 187, No. 185.
54 UN Pw V/90, ff. 25; 115.
55 Margaret Cavendish (1664), p. b.
56 *Ibid.*, p. 225.
57 UN Pw V/25, f. 125.
58 *Ibid.*, f. 140r.
59 *Ibid.*, f. 144v.
60 UN Pw V/26, f. 63v.
61 *Ibid.*, f. 125v.
62 NA DD.P6.1.19.26.
63 Strong (1903), p. 63.
64 BL Add MS 70500, f. 33.
65 *Ibid.*, f. 37.
66 *Ibid.*, f. 53.
67 BL Add MS 70499, f. 133.
68 UN Pw 1/35.
69 UN Pw 1/74.
70 UN Pw V/90, f. 22v.
71 UN Pw 1/315, f. 5.
72 Flecknoe (1666), pp. 10–11.
73 Arthur Oswald, 'A Sight-Seeing Tour in 1676', *Country Life*, Vol. 106 (1949), p. 529.
74 Flecknoe (1666), p. 10.
75 NA DD.2P.24.73.
76 William Cavendish (1667), p. 114.
77 Nottinghamshire Archives, PRNW, John Rolleston of Sulkholme or Sokeholme (1681), 'Nottinghamshire Marriages Index up to 1699', in *Nottinghamshire Family History Society*, Vol. 84 (1992), p. 214.
78 NA DD4P.70.43, endorsed 'Charges of a Stand in Clipstone parke'.
79 UN Pw 1/456 (6th August, 1670).
80 Margaret Cavendish (1667), p. 91.
81 Margaret Cavendish, 'A Dialogue between a Bountiful Knight and a Castle Ruined in War', *Poems and Fancies* (1653), reproduced in Alastair Fowler, *The Country House Poem* (Edinburgh, 1994), pp. 315–6.

82 UN Pw 1/669 (n.d., *c.*1665).
83 Richard Sheppard, 'Some Recent Archaeological Investigations at Bolsover Castle', unpublished report for English Heritage (April, 2005).
84 UN Pw 1/624c (18th December, 1667).
85 UN Pw 1/74.
86 North, *Of Building* (1981), p. 126.
87 UN Pw 1/461 (n.d., *c.*1669).
88 UN Pw 1/315, f. 5.
89 UN Pw 1/179.
90 UN Pw 1/315, f. 3.
91 NA DD2P.24.73, f. 7.
92 *Ibid.*, f. 24.

CHAPTER 10: A SECOND DEATHBED

1 UN Pw V/25, f. 86 (2nd October, 1675).
2 *Ibid.*, f. 123 (15th July, 1676); f. 137.
3 In *Letters and Poems in Honour of the Incomparable Princess, Margaret, Dutchess of Newcastle* (London, 1674), pp. 107–8, John Dolben, Bishop of Rochester and Dean of Westminster, to William (2nd July, 1671).
4 BL Add MS 12514, f. 282/290.
5 BL Add MS 70500, f. 50.
6 Robert Thoroton, *The antiquities of Nottinghamshire, extracted out of records, original evidences, Leiger Books, other Manuscripts, and Authentick Authorities* (1677), p. 490.
7 TNA Prob.11/353 (formerly PCC Hale, quire 22); a copy exists at NA DD 6P/1/19/30.
8 Margaret Cavendish (1667), p. 91.
9 UN Pw 1/298.6.c.
10 John Dryden, quoted in Roy Porter, *London, a Social History* (London, 1994), p. 93.
11 BL Add MS 37998, f. 241, Henry Cavendish to John Mazine (n.d.).
12 Clare Gittings, *Death, Burial and the Individual in Early Modern England* (London and Sydney, 1984), p. 189.
13 William Durant Cooper (Ed.), *Savile Correspondence*, Camden Society (1858), p. 63.
14 UN Pw 1/593, a copy of the inscription on a tablet in Warsop church.

AFTERWORD

1 Reverend Hamilton Gray, *Autobiography of a Scotch Country Gentleman*, privately printed with Mrs. Gray's *Memoirs and Memorials* (n.d., but after 1866).
2 Thomas Skinner, *The Life of General Monk: Late Duke of Albemarle*

(London, 1723), p. 412; Thomas Pennant, *Some Account of London* (London, 1790, fifth edn, 1813), p. 149.

3 Details in the Minute Book of St James's Church Vestry Meetings, Finsbury Library.

4 Information from David Withey, Finsbury Library Local Studies Collection.

5 BL Add MS 33054, f. 70v; G. Webb, *J. Vanbrugh, the Works* (London, 1928), Vol. 4, p. 105; Kerry Downes, *Sir John Vanbrugh* (London, 1987), pp. 377–8.

6 Thomas Chambers Hine, *Nottingham, Its Castle. A Military Fortress, A Royal Palace, A Ducal Mansion, Blackened Ruin, A Museum and Gallery of Art* (London, 1876), p. 20.

7 G. M. Trevelyan, quoted in J. H. Plumb and Huw Wheldon, *Royal Heritage* (London, 1977), p. 116.

8 Walter Carruthers Sellar and Robert Julian Yeatman, *1066 and All That* (London, 1930), pp. 63–4.

9 Horace Walpole, *A Catalogue of the Royal and Noble Authors of England* ('new edition', Edinburgh, 1796), p. 183.

10 Hutchinson (1973), p. 61.

SOURCES

1 R. J. Olney, 'The Portland Papers', *Archives*, Vol. 19 (1989), pp. 78–87.

# *Index*

Illustrations are shown in *italics*